Pay up and play the game

Pay up and play the game

Professional Sport in Britain
1875–1914

WRAY VAMPLEW

Reader in Economic History
Flinders University of South Australia

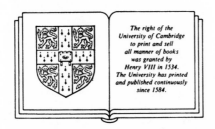

The right of the
University of Cambridge
to print and sell
all manner of books
was granted by
Henry VIII in 1534.
The University has printed
and published continuously
since 1584.

CAMBRIDGE UNIVERSITY PRESS

Cambridge
New York   New Rochelle
Melbourne   Sydney

PUBLISHED BY THE PRESS SYNDICATE OF THE UNIVERSITY OF CAMBRIDGE
The Pitt Building, Trumpington Street, Cambridge, United Kingdom

CAMBRIDGE UNIVERSITY PRESS
The Edinburgh Building, Cambridge CB2 2RU, UK
40 West 20th Street, New York NY 10011–4211, USA
477 Williamstown Road, Port Melbourne, VIC 3207, Australia
Ruiz de Alarcón 13, 28014 Madrid, Spain
Dock House, The Waterfront, Cape Town 8001, South Africa

http://www.cambridge.org

First published 1988
First paperback edition 2004

A catalogue record for this book is available from the British Library

Library of Congress cataloguing in publication data

Vamplew, Wray.
Pay up and play the game.
Bibliography.
Includes index.
1. Professional sports – Great Britain – History – 19th
century. 2. Professional sports – Economic aspects –
Great Britain. 3. Professional sports – Great Britain –
History – 20th century. I. Title.
GV6O5.V36 1988   796′.0941   88-4355

ISBN 0 521 35597 4 hardback
ISBN 0 521 89230 9 paperback

To Janice
who puts sport in its proper perspective
but who still appreciates how
important it is to me

Contents

List of tables

Preface

This book emerges out of a traumatic personal experience some two and a half decades ago when I was called before the selectors and informed that I would no longer be considered for the university rugby team, which, of course, played the union version of the game. What was my heinous crime? I had not questioned the parentage of the referee, nor had I committed gross indecency in the depth of the scrum. All I had done was play a few games of rugby league, but this was enough to have me deemed a professional and hence ineligible to participate in union matches. To me this seemed harsh justice as I was never good enough to get paid, officially or otherwise: all that I ever found in my boots were sweaty socks. What, I wondered, was so special about professional sportsmen that simply to play alongside them, even second-rate ones, was sufficient to contaminate my amateurism? My interest in the professional was further roused a few years later when I realised that the enigmatic, spectacled batsman who ran me out in a school cricket match was making a living doing the same thing at test level!

The actual stimulus to write this book arose more recently, after I had emigrated to Australia, where I became more aware of some of the special features of a career in modern professional sport. First, there are the restrictions placed by political and sports authorities on the mobility and earning capacity of professional sportsmen. The possible arbitrary nature of these was highlighted by a test series in which England (minus men who had played in South Africa plus a South African) lost to Australia (plus a South African) in a country which had banned the entry of West Indians who had played in South Africa, but which simultaneously conducted record trade with the land of apartheid, while the television commentary was given by a South African, living in Australia, but who had once captained the English team! Second, I witnessed the development of an interesting master–servant relationship in which the Australian Cricket Board virtually allowed Dennis Lillee, a superb player but a poor sportsman, to get away with kicking an opponent, throwing tantrums and an aluminium bat, and betting against his own side. Finally, there is the issue of the relatively early retirement of professional sportsmen: increasingly I found players, far less grey-haired than myself, being described as veterans in the twilight of their careers.

As an economic historian I became interested in tracing whether or not these restrictions, power relationships and retirement problems had always existed. What follows is the result of my investigations into the history of the professional sportsman and his necessary antecedent, the commercialisation of sport. This book looks at the British case and a later work will contrast the situation in Britain with the Australian experience. Part one provides two overviews. One gives a historical appreciation of the commercialisation of sport in the light of modern criticisms of such market-oriented activity. The other concentrates on what economic historians can offer to sports history, a relationship to which, hopefully, this book has made a contribution. Part two traces the influence of economic variables such as incomes and working hours on the development of popular sport and pays particular attention to the late nineteenth and early twentieth centuries when sport, especially spectator sport, was revolutionised in character, structure and organisation. Victorian entrepreneurs have often been castigated by economic historians for the slow development of new industries in this period, yet these same historians have paid scant attention to commercialised sport, which was one of the economic success stories of those years. The rest of the book focuses upon this key period. Part three considers whether gate-money sports companies operated as conventional businesses or whether they gave priority to winning over the pursuit of profit. This has obvious implications for their market behaviour and thus for any assessment of entrepreneurial performance. An attempt is also made, though on a necessarily restricted scale, to discover who was financing the sports industry. Part four first details the struggle to establish professionalism in British sport and then looks at professional sport as an occupation, paying particular attention to earnings, career prospects, unionism, and the restrictions imposed on the operation of markets for professional sportsmen. Finally, an examination of some social problems reveals the long association which commercialised sport has had with gambling, player misconduct and spectator violence.

For those reviewers who judge an author by what he sets out to do, let me say that the objective of this work was to produce a quantified economic, and slightly social, history of commercialised sport by the application of comprehensible economic theory to hard, empirical data.

Where possible, and sometimes where not, I have tried to generalise. The book is not comprehensive – data shortages and space limitations preclude even an attempt to be all-embracing – and in the main has been restricted to an analysis of four major sports, football north and south of the Scottish border, county cricket, horse-racing and rugby league. Nor are these sports covered to the depth they deserve. I have not attempted to write their definitive history but have concentrated on those aspects of most interest to me as an economic historian. Even as economic history it is intended only as a beginning, as the first steps of a marathon enterprise. Many questions remain unanswered; many issues are still to be discussed. Hopefully this book will serve as a launching pad for the economic history of sport. Nothing would please me more than that all my chapters be rendered obsolete within the next decade, for it would signal that substantial research had been undertaken in the subject.

For that other school of reviewers who prefer to consider the book which they would have written, let me point out that this study is not about such professional sportsmen as huntsmen, yachting crews, gillies and gamekeepers. Neither is it about why people play or watch sport. Whether it is to get away from the spouse, to attain social esteem or peer group acceptance, or one of a myriad other motivations, I have taken it as given that many people wish to participate, vicariously or actively, in sport of some kind. Nor am I devoting half a volume to defining what I mean by sport. Admittedly the famous *Badminton Library* monographs on sport included dancing, and the *Sport and Sportsmen* series has a volume on commercial shipbuilding! Nevertheless I would argue that, except on the fringes, sport is generally recognisable and that any attempt à la Huizinga or Caillois to further classify or delineate along the lines of combat/conquest, skill/chance, etc. runs the risk, as does even the amateur/professional dichotomy, of confusing the goalposts with the bedposts.

Acknowledgements

First, and undoubtedly foremost, I must thank my family for their sacrifices and toleration during the maturation of this manuscript. Indeed my children, Ailsa and Peter, have grown up with the book. Both of them can now thrash me at table tennis, though I remain invincible at darts, the only sport in which I can still dream of representative honours. To my wife, Janice, who once missed the solitary sunny day of an English summer because she was working with me in a cellar at Old Trafford, I can only promise that next time we will visit the Highlands . . . and not for the caber-tossing.

Second, I would like to acknowledge those organisations who granted me access to their records: Ayr Racecourse Committee, Derbyshire C. C. C., Essex C. C. C., the Football Association, the Football League, Heart of Midlothian F. C., Kent C. C. C., Lancashire C. C. C., Leicestershire C. C. C., the Professional Footballers' Association, the Rugby League, the Scottish Football Association, Sheffield Wednesday F. C., Warwickshire C. C. C., York Racing Committee and Yorkshire C. C. C. Without their liberality there would have been no book. Perhaps I can be less generous to the Scottish Football League, whom I suspect must be a profit-oriented enterprise as they kept the stamps which I had enclosed in the hope of a reply. I am also most grateful to the many people who rendered research assistance to the project: Robyn Day, Rosemary Giles, Di Kitch, Chris Paino, Leonie M. Randall, Ralph Simeone, Catherine Uhlmann (who also rescued my notes from the ravages of a bushfire), Janice Vamplew and Peter Vamplew. Their rates of pay in no way reflected the level of my gratitude. Others, too numerous to detail, assisted in a voluntary capacity by suggesting sources, commenting on draft chapters, and generally giving encouragement: everything that is wrong with this book is probably their fault. Special mention must be made of Chuck Korr, whose morale-boosting friendship has been a serendipitic aspect of my research in sports history. Financial assistance, without which this book would have had an even longer gestation period, came from the Australian Research Grants Scheme, the Carnegie Fund, Edinburgh University and Flinders University. I would also thank my colleagues and students at both the latter institutions for encouraging me to research and teach sports history at a time when it had not gained the degree of academic acceptance which it now enjoys. Not least I appreciate the RSI-defying work of Marie Baker and Barb Triffett. Finally, I would also like to acknowledge one reviewer who, although he thought that my history of horse-racing was a load of rubbish (he expressed it more politely and subtly), somewhat masochistically looked forward to my next sports history book: well, Mr Longrigg, here it is.

A guide to prices, 1870–1914

Price indices, 1870–1914 (1984 = 1,000)

Year	Index A	Index B	Year	Index A	Index B	Year	Index A	Index B
1870	44	44	1885	35	35	1900	34	36
1871	46	46	1886	32	33	1901	32	34
1872	50	51	1887	31	32	1902	32	34
1873	51	50	1888	32	33	1903	32	34
1874	47	48	1889	33	33	1904	32	33
1875	44	46	1890	33	34	1905	33	34
1876	44	46	1891	33	34	1906	35	37
1877	43	44	1892	31	32	1907	37	38
1878	40	40	1893	31	32	1908	33	34
1879	38	39	1894	29	29	1909	34	36
1880	40	40	1895	28	29	1910	36	38
1881	39	39	1896	28	29	1911	37	40
1882	39	40	1897	28	29	1912	39	41
1883	38	40	1898	29	31	1913	39	42
1884	35	38	1899	31	33	1914	39	42

Sources: B. R. Mitchell and P. Deane, Abstract of British Historical Statistics, Cambridge, 1962; B. R. Mitchell and H. G. Jones, Second Abstract of British Historical Statistics, Cambridge, 1971; O. E. C. D., Historical Statistics, 1960–1981, Paris, 1983; O. E. C. D., Economic Surveys: United Kingdom, Paris, 1986.

The above table is offered as assistance to those readers who would like to convert the prices, costs, turnover, earnings and investment figures cited in the volume into modern equivalents. Index A is based on the Sauerbeck–Statist price indices and Index B on the Rousseaux price indices. Both have deficiencies and no claim is made for their absolute accuracy, though they indicate adequately price trends in the period. They were converted to a base of 1984 = 1,000 by the use of indices cited in the sources. Despite problems involved in chain-indexing the series, the indices provide a useful guide to the present value of late Victorian and Edwardian incomes and expenditure. For those readers who prefer a rule of thumb, if they multiply 1870s data by 20–5, 1880s by 25–30, 1890s by 30–5, 1900s by 30 and 1910–14 by 25 they will obtain a reasonable mid 1980s figure.

Part I

An overview

When it comes to exploiting a game as a huge spectacular and commercial organisation then one feels that a dishonour is done to the very name of sport.

> G. B. Pollock-Hodsell, 'Then and now: association football',
> *Badminton Magazine*, XXXVII, 1913, p. 508

If the spirit of cricket is to be maintained, the business aspect must soon be put under some restraint, or our national sport will degenerate into the professionalism of modern football.

> H. Gordon, 'The past cricket season', *Badminton Magazine*, XV,
> 1903, p. 413

It is far better that England, which has always been the recognised champion of pure amateurism, should be last in every contest than we should descend to the commercialisation of our amateur sport.

> *The Economist*, 30 August 1913

The leading tendency in modern pastime is to develop its spectacular aspect, mainly, if not entirely, from commercial motives.

> *Spectator*, 2 July 1898

Chapter 1

Is money the root of all evil?
A historical appreciation of
commercialisation in sports

Everyone knows that British soccer fans are hooligans. Those in doubt need only consider an incident after a Scottish Cup Final played, almost inevitably, between the Glasgow duo of Rangers and Celtic. These clubs are soccer's representatives in the religious bigotry which permeates Scotland, Celtic being a Catholic-based side and Rangers a hard-line Protestant team who between 1914 and 1984 have selected only two Catholic players, one non-practising and the other by mistake.[1] With both religious and local supremacy at stake the fans of these clubs have a large emotional attachment to their teams and any threat to their football can have serious consequences. At full time in the game the scores were level and the spectators eagerly anticipated extra time as had been falsely advertised in the press. When it became apparent that the match was not going to continue, angry fans began to invade the pitch. Eventually some six thousand of them were fighting each other, assaulting the police, pulling down barricades and goalposts, setting fire to the payboxes, and attacking the firemen who came to deal with the blaze. One hundred and eighteen people finished up in hospital and only by a miracle was no one killed.[2] A typical day in the life of a modern football hooligan? Possibly – but this particular event took place in 1909, over three-quarters of a century ago!

This is no isolated example of a so-called modern sports problem occurring historically. There are many such instances but they are not part of the folklore which has developed around sport. Intellectual snobbery has meant that for too long *trained* historians have been reluctant to involve themselves in sports history, with the result that myth and ignorance have been pervasive. One of the most significant of the myths is that sometime in the past there was a 'golden age' of gentlemanly amateurism in sport. The period is not always specified, but the usual implication, at least for Britain, is that it was the late Victorian era. At this time, it is alleged, participants played the game, umpires' decisions were accepted, crowds did not riot, drugs were not taken, and the few professionals who did exist knew their place and were respectful to their employers.[3] Modern sport, with its emphasis on money, is seen as having changed all this.[4] Franchise shifts by greedy owners and strikes by greedy players have demonstrated that loyalty to the club or to the fan is a meaningless concept. Moreover, sport is unlike a production line on which everyone can earn a bonus: ultimately there can only be one winner in sport. So as rewards to the successful have risen, increasingly the end has come to justify the means; hence the development of violence in the form of the professional foul, the use of drugs to improve performance, and the resort to sharp practice to ensure victory. The virus of violence has also spread to the terraces, particularly at soccer matches. Commercial-ised sport attracts large crowds but too often partisanship takes pre-cedence over sports appreciation, and both vicarious winning *and* losing generate thuggery amongst rival supporters. So inflamed have crowds become that in order to curb their excesses many modern sports grounds bear more resemblance to the Berlin Wall than to athletic arenas.

It may be true that these occurrences are a direct consequence of the growing amount of money in sport, but what many people forget – or perhaps were never aware of – is that sport became commercialised a long time ago. Although there had been isolated examples before, it was in the late nineteenth century that gate-money sport developed on any scale. Rising incomes and increased leisure time for the urban working class created a market which sports entrepreneurs responded to. Sport became an industry and economics became of prime importance: sports clubs adopted company status with limited liability; shareholders replaced members and directors took over from committeemen; heavy investment was made in gate-money sports facilities and sports events became organised on a regular basis so as to cover such overhead costs.

By the 1900s a paying crowd of over 20,000 could be expected at an important county cricket match; race crowds of 10,000 to 15,000 were not unusual, double this could be anticipated at leading meetings, and perhaps 70,000 to 80,000 at a major Bank Holiday event; first-division soccer games in England generally attracted around 15,000 spectators, cup ties substantially more and, north of the border, Scotland versus England football internationals never had less than a crowd of 100,000 fans from 1906 to 1914.[5] Substantial capital expenditure was undertaken to accommodate these crowds: Newbury racecourse, opened in 1906, had a share capital of £80,000 and one estimate put the aggregate investment of leading soccer clubs at around £2 million.[6] Returns from these investments were limited by Football Association and Jockey Club legislation to 5% and 10% respectively, not that high but still above government bond level.[7] There were, however, large rewards for some sporting entrepreneurs. In the 1890s the owner of a reputable stallion could be obtaining over £1,000 a year in stud fees, and during his 22-year stud career an outstanding animal, such as *St Simon*, probably returned well over £200,000.[8] Some professional players also did well out of the game. In 1904 the benefit match and subscription lists for George Hirst, a star cricketer, produced over £3,700; lesser talented but loyal players could expect a late career bonus in the order of £800.[9] All this was dwarfed by the rewards to a top jockey such as Fred Archer, champion rider for 13 consecutive seasons, who obtained at least £8,000 per annum through retainers, presents and riding fees.[10]

Not only was sport commercialised many decades ago, but it also faced problems and criticism then because of its involvement with money. Franchise shifts were a case in point. Despite some opposition from fans Arsenal F. C. changed its ground from Plumstead to Highbury in order to attract larger crowds.[11] More generally, some clubs, usually from less densely populated areas, were sacrificed by League colleagues in an effort to raise overall attendances for their sports cartels.[12] What soccer enthusiast today can recall Ardwick, Bootle, Burton Swifts, Darwen and Northwich, all foundation members of the English Football League second division? In Scotland, Vale of Leven, Renton and Dumbarton, all at one time Scottish Cup winners or League champions, were voted out of the Scottish League partly because their virtually village populations could not produce enough revenue at the gate. Furthermore, the accepted rules of the game were tampered with in the interests of Mammon, and traditional sports found their character changed simply to get more people through the turnstiles. In horse-racing long-distance, staying events gave way to sprints, two-year-old and handicap racing, all of which had a sufficient degree of unpredictability about the result to attract working-class punters; and in rugby the split between the professionals and the Rugby Union produced two distinct versions of the game, with differences in the number of players, methods of scoring, and style of play. Professional sportsmen, too, were sometimes more concerned with pay than play. Flashpoint combinations at the club level can be found in soccer, rugby and cricket, and in 1909 the Professional Footballers' Association threatened a national strike for the abolition of wage control in soccer, a move which only crumbled when their employers' association, the Football League, used the reserve army of amateur players as a bargaining weapon.[13]

The growing financial importance attached to winning also resulted in problems. Some participants were so determined to win that they adopted either more skilful tactics or more dubious practices in order to ensure victory; others had to follow suit simply in order to compete effectively. On the legitimate side this included the employment of professionals and on the illicit, such items as drugs, foul play and corruption. Admittedly drugs were for animals rather than athletes, but still the American invasion of the British turf in the late nineteenth century led to chemistry making a mockery of the formbook till the development of the saliva test in 1910.[14] Deliberate foul play by soccer professionals in an attempt to prevent their opponents from scoring, eventually had to be combated by the introduction of the penalty kick.[15] Corruption, too, raised its head, particularly in sports connected with gambling: it is no coincidence that one meaning of 'jockey' is to cheat or deceive. Several soccer players were suspended for attempting to fix matches and the 'test match' system of promotion and relegation in English League football was abandoned partly because the results of some games were thought to have been prearranged.[16]

Crowd disorder, too, was a feature of some commercialised sports. Almost inevitably the bringing-together of sports fanatics in large numbers produced crowd problems. One soccer historian has concluded that 'riots, unruly behaviour, violence, assault and vandalism appear to have been a well-established, but not necessarily dominant pattern of crowd behaviour at football matches at least from the 1870s'[17] and in horse-racing violence was never far away, especially when backers felt that they had not had a fair run for their money.[18] Eventually, in order to protect their incomes and property, sports entrepreneurs took action to curb the worst of the excesses, but nevertheless crowd problems remained a feature of commercialised sport in the early twentieth century.[19]

There is thus an observable pattern of the emergence of commercialisation injecting more money into sport, which in turn intensified the importance of winning and stimulated corruption, sharp practice and the like. However, this is not to say that sport would have been problem-free had it not been engulfed by the wave of commercialisation. One way to assess this is to adopt a counterfactual approach and consider some alternative scenarios to widespread commercialised sport. It is clear that both the most realistic alternatives, precommercialised sport and contemporary amateur sport, were not without their 'evils'.

Corruption occurred in precommercialised sport because, in the absence of sponsorship or entrepreneurship, many sports were dependent upon patronage from upper-class gamblers. This was particularly true of cricket matches and race meetings, which were often, if not mainly, organised for the purposes of wagering. However, where there is gambling there is a possibility of cheating. Consider, for example, William Lambert, a star cricketing mercenary, who was banned from Lords for his patently obvious attempts to throw the match between England and a Nottingham XXII in 1817;[20] or the fact that, in the horseflesh version of mutton dressed as lamb, the 1844 Derby, the classic race for three-year-old horses, was won by a heavily disguised five-year-old.[21] Other precommercialised sports suffered from a surfeit of violence. In mob football there were no referees, and customs rather than rules governed play; with village often arraigned against village and with up to a thousand participants there was plenty of opportunity to settle old scores. Moreover, there was a whole host of sports in which the intention was to injure an opponent: cudgelling, where the blood had to run an inch before victory could be claimed; cut-legs and kick-shins, in which whips and boots respectively were utilised till one participant conceded; and prizefighting, with its unlimited number of rounds during which the loser was battered into exhaustion. Violence was not just against people: brutal animal sports, such as cock-fighting and bull- and badger-baiting, were regular features of the rural sporting calendar.

If we move forward to the era in which professional sport became widespread, it is apparent that amateur sport was far from being pristine pure. Many amateurs were so only in name. In Scotland the soccer players of Celtic held a successful strike for higher wages in 1890, three years before professionalism was officially recognised by the Scottish football authorities.[22] The home of shamateurism, however, was English cricket: liberal 'expenses' and 'jobs' as assistant to the secretary allowed many amateurs to take home more money than most professionals; indeed W. G. Grace, the shamateur *par excellence*, demanded, and got, £1,500 to tour Australia in 1873/74 as an amateur when the professionals received only £170, and 18 years later he obtained £3,000 plus expenses for a similar venture.[23] Corruption, too, was not unknown in amateur circles: in 1894 the Scottish Amateur Athletics Association set up an Athletic Abuses Commission, whose investigation of betting and race-fixing led to the suspension of several leading performers.[24]

Money, however, was not the root of all that was evil in amateur sport; other 'immoral activity' stemmed from the desire to win, which was strong even without the incentive of monetary reward. Fame, at local or national level, could be spur enough. Grace was certainly no 'sportsman' and was frequently guilty of sharp practice and intimidation,[25] and there is no doubt that the Treorchy–Aberdare rugby union match of 1905 was fixed to allow the away team to win the Glamorgan championship.[26]

More generally, rules had to be changed in many amateur sports simply because some participants found ways around the existing regulations.[27] And such was the narrow patriotism engendered by representational sport at the London Olympics of 1908 that the supposedly neutral British officials used their megaphones to urge on the home team. Others were alleged to have deliberately broken the winning tape in order to force a rerun when a British 400-metre runner was being beaten by his American opponent.[28] Needless to say, this was the last Olympics at which the host nation supplied all the officials. Nor was violence by both crowds and players a stranger to amateur sport. The Cambridge cricket team was actually manhandled by the spectators after their captain ordered his bowler to send three deliveries to the boundary so as to avoid having to enforce the follow-on – this at the University match of 1896, one of the middle- and upper-class social events of the year.[29] Moreover, intentional rough play seems to have been endemic in English public-school football as athletic masters sought to turn boys into men.[30] It might also be considered socially offensive that many amateurs attempted to exclude working men from their sports by decree. The definition of amateur varied between sports but most had social connotations which reached their extreme in the Amateur Rowing Association's debarring from amateur status anyone 'who is or has been by trade or employment for wages a mechanic, artisan, or labourer, or engaged in any menial duty'.[31]

Impartial observers might also criticise amateur sport for some of the values inculcated into its followers.[32] Although they might be acceptable, indeed even desirable, at the micro-level of the individual sport, at the macro-level of society they could be positively dangerous. Manliness is fine but, unless controlled, it can result in brutality on the field and arrestable offences off it. Courage is to be applauded but there is a fine line between courage and foolhardiness, as young British officers found to their cost in the First World War. Products of the English public-school system, they led their men over the top as though it was a charge of rugby forwards, but instead of hard-tackling full backs they ran into machine-gun fire. *Esprit de corps* can be fun but it can also result in confrontation riots between groups of rival fans and, at a wider level, it may breed xenophobia: 'my team right or wrong' may help community solidarity but 'my country right or wrong' can have disastrous consequences. Moreover, although the unquestioning acceptance of a captain's authority may be necessary for a football defence, 'I was only obeying orders' has proved a less than adequate defence in other circumstances.

So far it has been argued that, although sport may have a poor public image, abuses associated with sport are not a uniquely modern phenomenon; nor, historically, were they confined to commercialised sport. It can indeed be suggested that the modern economy's association with sport has brought some advances. The sports consumer has certainly gained through the application of technology. For example, the forces of darkness have been overcome by improvements in floodlighting. In the 1890s the limits to music-hall illumination meant that only sports events such as boxing, which were confined to a small area, could be adequately lit. Too many football matches had to be abandoned because it got dark, but all attempts to play night games under lights were failures whether judged by players, spectators or technologists.[33] Modern floodlighting, however, has enabled sports events to be fitted into time slots for the convenience of the paying spectator. The elements, too, have been combated, with drainage, and heating and building developments, allowing matches to be played on grounds which would otherwise have been unfit, and enabling spectators to attend sheltered from the worst of the weather. For those who cannot or will not turn out to watch, even in the best climatic conditions, communications technology can now bring sport to their fireside.

The other major group which has gained has been the sports labourers. Sport was certainly not fun for such people as Johnny Briggs, a Lancashire cricketer who had turned his arm over for 14 years but who had his application for a benefit match rejected as 'premature'. Shortly afterwards he had an epileptic seizure on the field and was committed to Cheadle asylum.[34] Nor can Peter McWilliam have been happy that there was no insurance scheme operated by the Scottish Football Association, for his career was ended when he broke his leg playing for his country.[35] Fred Archer gained economic rewards but at what cost? For most of his racing life his daily diet during the season was warm castor oil, a strip of dry toast and half a glass of champagne. Eventually the effort of getting his weight down left him open to illness and while in a feverish state he shot himself.[36] The life of the nineteenth-century sports professional was one of constant insecurity through fear of injury in an industry with a high accident rate, through fear of his annual contract not being renewed, and through fear that someone more able would come along to take his place. Much of this still holds today, but then, depending upon his sport, he also faced artificial restrictions on his earnings capacity, his occupational mobility, and even on his leisure time.[37] The maximum wage imposed by soccer's legislators in 1901 halved the earnings of some star players; and part-timers in both soccer and rugby league found that their employers had firm views on what constituted a respectable occupation outside the game. It was not easy for a player to improve his lot by switching allegiances: in cricket, if he wished to change his employer he had to stand out of the game for two years, and in soccer he could not change at all if his existing employer objected; once he had signed for a club he was tied for life and his only choice, if dissatisfied, was to quit the game. Rugby league professionals also found their leisure circumscribed by a 'working clause' by which they were only eligible to play on Saturday afternoons if they could demonstrate that they had worked full time during the preceding week. This reached ludicrous extremes when Broughton Rangers, cup winners in 1902, were fined because their players had not worked on the morning of the final.[38] Professional sportsmen were the last of the bonded men and they must be grateful that those days have gone and they are no longer denied the basic conditions of employment enjoyed by the rest of the population.

Gate-money sport is a marketed product and, like all other goods offered for sale, it is subject to fluctuations and trends in demand. Sports entrepreneurs, either at club or sport level, do not possess a monopoly in the leisure market. Historically, changes in taste, induced or exogenous, have altered the structure and character of British sport: brutal animal sports have been outlawed because of changed attitudes towards cruelty; prizefighting, professional athletics and cycle-racing have all declined as spectator sports because corruption prevented results from reflecting ability; and participation in sports such as ice- and roller-skating has been influenced by boom-and-bust fashionability. Today the media has changed the once unglamorous image of darts and snooker, and the traditional spectator sports of soccer and county cricket are holding inquests to discover why they are less popular than they were. Ultimately consumers pay their money and make their choice. If they do not like aspects of what they see in modern commercialised sport then they can withdraw their support and spend their money elsewhere. Nevertheless the fact that commercialised sport, with all its attendant ethical problems, exists on the scale that it does, suggests that, except in a few declining sports, insufficient customers have become disenchanted enough to force changes upon sport in general. Despite their after-match grumbles, *most* sports consumers seem to be satisfied with *most* of what they see. Money may be the root of much that is evil in modern sport, but, as in the past, sports consumers appear to be willing to continue to spend that money.

Chapter 2

Comments on the state of play: economic historians and sports history

The late Bill Shankly, doyen of football managers, once dismissed the implicitly critical statement that 'soccer was a matter of life and death to some people' by commenting that in fact 'it was much more serious than that'.[1] So it is with sport in general: it can be fun, but it can also have significant political, social and economic consequences. So it is with sports history: studying it can be as much fun as playing sport, but it can also be just as serious. Unfortunately, historians have been slow to appreciate this. One *aficionado* in the early twentieth century lamented that 'it is a surprising circumstance that the national idiosyncrasy of which many of us are proudest – our love for sport – has hitherto signally failed to arouse the enthusiasm of . . . the historian'.[2] Little has changed a century later when it could be commented that 'one thing that mattered to most working men in late Victorian England was how they spent the time when they were not at work. It is a history still largely to be written.'[3] Economic historians in particular have failed to take up their pens.

Sport has become big business: vast amounts are invested in the creation of the sports product and its economic spin-offs; sports superstars earn high incomes, as much from off-field as on-field activities; and sports consumers by the million pay at the gate to watch them play, and even more are secondhand spectators via the printed and electronic media. However, as was pointed out in the previous chapter, this has been no sudden economic miracle: sport became an industry perhaps a century ago. Sports professionalism goes back even further: eighteenth-century England saw many athletic young men being given employment as estate workers on account of their cricketing prowess, and diminutive grooms frequently found themselves riding as jockeys to satisfy the high-stake gambling of their masters.[4]

Yet, despite this long association of sport and money, economic historians have been reluctant to involve themselves in sports history. An edition of the *Journal of Sport History* in 1983 surveyed the previous decade's significant contributions to sports history. In all, for Britain, Europe and the United States, some 500 items were mentioned, of which only 16 had overt economic orientation and of these only one was by an economic historian and only two by economists.[5] Looking at it from the other end of the pitch, of the 1,300+ items on British economic history published in 1982, and cited in the *Economic History Review*'s bibliographic survey, only six had anything to do with sport.[6] It is perhaps symptomatic of the attitude of economic historians to sport, and indeed to other leisure activities, that until recently the developing leisure industries were virtually ignored in the debate on the standard of British entrepreneurship in the late nineteenth century.[7]

As with other historians, intellectual snobbery is partially responsible: sport was, as one commentator has aptly put it, deposited in the trunk labelled 'not wanted on the serious voyage through life' and as such was deemed unworthy of academic study.[8] This left the field to untrained historians, and their nostalgic, often self-indulgent, approach of celebratory, anecdotal works which ignored wider historical implications served only to reinforce the view that sports history was inferior history. However, resistance to the descent from the ivory tower has weakened and sports history has gained from the general move towards history from below – ironically a traditional feature of economic history – yet economic historians have still been unwilling to venture along the path cleared by their social history colleagues. Although two decades ago Professor Arthur Cole, one-time president of the Economic History Association, argued that economic historians should 'give attention to the periods when men could refrain from work as well as those when the work was in progress', there has been little response to his plea.[9] People at work – excluding professional sportsmen – and the results of their activities have remained the virtually exclusive focus of economic history.

One reason for sport receiving such negligible attention is that economic historians too frequently fasten themselves in the straitjacket of economic theory and are unwilling to research new areas until a change in economic theory, or the emergence of a new branch of it, provides them with a lead. The economic theory pertaining to sport is still in its infancy and hypotheses have not yet achieved the respectability of becoming laws – the material on maximisation of crowd attendances is a good example of this[10] – and economic historians have not rushed in where high-flying economists have refused to tread.

Perhaps the economists resent the popularity of the sportsman: they may have read – at least the literate ones in a trade increasingly catering to the numerate may have – of the boy at Marlborough who, when asked to write an essay on whether the most useful citizen was the professional cricketer or the political economist, chose the former on the grounds that he gave pleasure whereas the latter 'few understood and was dull'.[11] More reasonably, the lag of economists and economic historians behind sociologists and social historians in taking up sports studies may be attributable to the latter being prepared to believe that sport can be a microcosm of wider society, in that gender roles, class structures and racial attitudes can all be reflected in a nation's sports, whereas the former are unwilling to accept a similar implication for the economy. Indeed some of the economics of sport do appear unusual. The ideal market position of a conventional business would be monopoly, but this is less desirable in sport, for what economic use is it to be heavyweight champion of the world but to have no challengers? In almost every sport competitors combine to produce a saleable commodity – what Walter Neale called the 'product-joint' as opposed to the joint products of many business enterprises.[12] There is also a strong school of thought which argues that many sports clubs do not obey the economic rules of the game because they are utility-maximisers rather than profit-maximisers, in that they are willing to sacrifice profits for the sake of winning games and championships.[13] Other economic peculiarities which come to mind include the unproductive input–output relationship of much game-bird preservation and the amalgam of investment and consumption which figures in the decision to become a racehorse owner or a football club director.[14]

Economic historians should involve themselves in sports history if only to remove some of the economic misconceptions perpetrated by those who know no better. Sports history should be no exception to the tenet that a major function of any history is to prevent the abuse and misuse of history. Setting the sports record straight, and thus preventing myths from becoming conventional wisdom, is a prime duty of all historians. The previous chapter has demonstrated the considerable amount of dross in the so-called 'golden age' of gentlemanly amateurism, in which it now appears that participants did not always play the game. Similarly it has been shown that, despite the phrase, 'It's not cricket', emphasising the moral values of that noble game, the sport actually has a long history of cheating and sharp practice.[15] Perhaps there are few economic myths to be dispelled, simply because economic aspects have rarely been considered in the past, but the recent move into sports history by historians of all creeds may produce a new mythology because of their misunderstanding of economics.[16] Yet the economic history of sport can be more than a corrective tool. It is, especially if taken in the wider context of leisure, a subject worthy of serious study in itself. First, sport is now a major industry, part of the corporate world, and as such its development ought to be traced in the same way as should that of any other important industry. Moreover, even in an age where privatisation has become the catchword, sections of the sports industry are probably amongst the most regulated industries worldwide because of the income which gambling yields to governments. Second, even those economic historians who do not accept that sport reflects the economy must acknowledge that the economy affects sport. Indeed, as will be shown in succeeding chapters, much of the development in British sport in the eighteenth and nineteenth centuries can be attributed to four economic variables: the structure of the economy, the volume of non-working time, income levels, and the supply of energy. Third, the perceived weakness of current economic theory relating to sport can be taken as an intellectual challenge: economic historians can use their ideas and historical empiricism to make a significant contribution to the formulation of the economic theory of sport. This would be particularly relevant to such issues as the development of a theory of profit-taking rather than profit-maximisation and the refinement of the economic theory of voluntary organisations.

Nevertheless, even in the application of conventional economic theory, economic historians can bring a fresh approach to sports history simply by offering a differentiated product. By virtue of their training they should ask different questions from those posed by historians from other schools of thought. Forgetting the diagrams and equations, though to the initiated these can help in interpretation, even the very basic application of some economic concepts to the markets for sport and sportsmen could assist in developing a new view of sports history.

If we start with the supply side of the sports market, an examination of land, labour and capital – the vital factors of production – entrepreneurs who bring the factors together, and technology – the way in which they are put together – raises some interesting issues. Land, of course, is intrinsic to all sport. Chronologically there has been a move from mob football traversing miles between villages, and cricket matches without boundaries, to games on limited and defined areas; in the late nineteenth century land values were pushed up in England as golfers sought to purchase social exclusivity and Scottish landlords pocketed extra bawbees from the rentals for shooting and fishing rights; and these days rising urban land values are increasingly forcing sports groups to seek government assistance and, in the private sector, have encouraged the intensive use of land via squash courts, indoor cricket pitches, and multi-purpose sports complexes. Labour is not merely the sports persons, but covers all those involved in the production of the sports commodity. A major development here has been the gradual undermining of the traditional volunteerism at club and association level. As far as capital, or more precisely investment funds, is concerned, it is apparent that relatively little outlay was required for early sport, except perhaps for racehorse owners' commitments to thoroughbred stock. Over time, however, not only have more facilities been required, they have also become more expensive.

The financing of these outlays is intimately associated with entrepreneurship, which can, of course, be public or private enterprise. Initially most was private, often by publicans hoping to sell alcohol to spectators and participants. Later, other entrepreneurs sought to make profits directly from sport by organising events and charging spectators for the privilege of viewing them. But what of football club directors and their ilk? Whether they were seeking profits, directly or indirectly, or looking for psychic income as superfans is a current major topic of investigation.[17] Other businessmen sought to assist their firms by sponsoring works sports teams which they hoped would create company loyalty and reduce labour turnover; sport thus was seen as having a utilitarian aspect in promoting human capital formation. Increasingly, however, decisions on the allocation of sports resources are being made at local and national level. However, it should be noted that such intervention in the sports market, though it may be greater than before, is not new; in the nineteenth century the British government subsidised horse-racing and rifle clubs for military purposes.[18]

Technology has two major components, one involving organisation and the other more conventional technical aspects. Hence the development of leagues to provide regular, organised competition comes within the ambit of technology as does the use of new constructional techniques to provide stadiums within which the events actually take place. Technical change can be used to render sports organisation more economically efficient, as with drainage and covered stands to combat the weather, transport improvements to widen and deepen spectator catchment areas, or starting gates to reduce the chaos at the beginning of horse races. It can also create new sports. History abounds with examples: bicycling, car-racing, ice-hockey, trampolining and, more recently, hang-gliding and wind-surfing. Indeed probably no sport has remained unscathed by technological change.

Individual demand for sport has some basic parameters set by price, income, taste and time. Income and wealth often influence the type of sports activity undertaken and at the higher levels act as a means of rendering certain sports exclusive to particular social groups. Although costs would have to change drastically for twelve-metre yacht-racing to become the province of the masses, other activities can be more price-sensitive. Cheaper access to skiing, for example, has broadened its support base, but, more generally, price discrimination at sports events – extra for the grandstand – is a method of maximising revenues by supplying different markets at different prices. Tastes can be changed with the introduction of new sports products or, as some sports administrators will be well aware, by dissatisfaction with the existing commodity. These facets of demand apply to all products, but, unlike most other goods, sport also has a temporal aspect in that it is generally consumed at particular points in time. Thus the time available for sports consumption is not just a matter of the volume of 'free time', but where those non-working hours are located in the work–leisure calendar. In aggregate terms, life expectancy is also a determinant of the demand for sport. This leads to a consideration of the widening of demand from the individual to the aggregate population. Numbers, density, and the age and sex structure, can all have an influence: a sparsely populated area will generate less demand than a concentrated market; an older population will be less physically active than a younger one; and some sports tend to be more or less favoured by different sexes.

There is an economic history to be written on the contribution of sport to the economy: on the employment generated by the demand for caddies, gamekeepers and greenkeepers, huntsmen, yachting crews, laundry-women, money-checkers and a host of other labourers, skilled and unskilled, casual and permanent; and on the multiplier effects of investment in football, golf, tennis, cricket and myriad other sports clubs which produce complementary investment by specialist-equipment manufacturers, outfitters and printers. Then there is the symbiotic relationship which has developed between sport and the media. The press provides free publicity but attracts the purchases of those who wish to read about yesterday's match or next week's team; for others, of a gambling persuasion, it throws open the stable doors. Transport, too, has gained from sport. Although no railway or bus company was ever dependent upon sports clubs, their demand for facilities helped spread overhead costs, as did the northern jaunts of armed gentry and salmon-stalking Americans. Indeed, Gleneagles, Turnberry, Cruden Bay and the like were all railway-sponsored golfing centres, with hotels attached. Perhaps a cost–benefit approach could be adopted and these positive contributions assessed against such matters as the crop damage often attributed to hunts and the loss of agricultural land to predatory golfers.

Turning to the demand for professional sportspersons, it should be noted that it is essentially a derived demand, dependent upon what is happening in the market for commercialised sport. Nevertheless the basic determinants of demand – price, income and taste – need to be examined. Prices offered for a sportsperson's services vary between sports and between players, and they are offered in a variety of forms, including fees, retainers, presents, appearance money and testimonials. A major issue is whether star performers, particularly in team sports, have been allowed their full economic rents, that is the amounts above normal wages attributable to the scarcity value of their particular skills. The payments to club professionals are limited by the wages fund, that part of the club's revenue set aside for such labour expenditure as wages, signing-on fees, or transfer payments to other clubs. Historically these funds have not been a function solely of gate-receipts but also of public appeals and philanthropic patrons. To some extent taste may be associated with economic discrimination, as in the virtual absence of professional sportswomen in the nineteenth century and the preference of many English county cricket clubs for amateur players despite their being no cheaper than professionals. On the supply side, the ethnic, class and geographical background of recruits to the sporting profession should be examined in order to assess the effective transfer earning of a career in sport, that is the amount sufficient to keep the sportsman playing his game. What is becoming apparent is that sport had a low opportunity cost for most professionals as the bulk of careers were very short; hence the problem of retirement at an age when non-sportspersons are in mid-career was generally applicable only to the successful professionals.

The interaction of supply and demand in the market place has not always been allowed to operate freely: matches were often more competitive than markets. Many leagues can be viewed as cartels, with a central controlling body setting the economic rules, operating quality control via promotion and relegation and other restrictions on entry, and, as mentioned in the previous chapter, circumscribing the economic freedom of sports labourers in an effort to maintain equality of competition. Some sports authorities also interfered with the rights of capital by limiting the dividends which clubs could pay to their shareholders.

So far this chapter has proceeded as though economic history is an entity, but there is a wide spectrum varying from institutional history to the application of sophisticated statistical techniques. Practitioners of different branches of the discipline will approach sports history in different ways, though there should be the common thread of asking economic questions in a temporal setting. The histories of clubs, associations and other sporting bodies could be written as business histories. Labour history, too, has a virtually untapped source in sport as, barring ghost autobiographies, very little has been written on sport as a career. Two major items could be put on the agenda: sports biographies *en masse* so that generalisations can be attempted; and unionism in sport to ascertain whether or not sportsmen were influenced by labour relations developments in wider society. In general, economic historians can bring a fresh quantitative sense to sports history: Clapham's famous dictum that economic historians should ask 'how large, how long, how often, how representative' must not be cast aside as they venture into new fields.[19] To distances run, heights jumped and times recorded, should be added data on costs, revenues, earnings, career lengths, attrition rates and the like. Here, perhaps, the econometricians can come into their own in analysing such issues as influences on crowd attendances or determining the revenue or consumption functions of sports clubs. A major caveat should be made: whatever methodology is adopted it would be poor history if economic theory was applied uncritically.

It is not being suggested that an economic history perspective is necessarily the best way to study sports history. Far better would be an interdisciplinary approach, particularly when it is borne in mind that the assumptions of economists are often the research topics of other social scientists. However, most economic historians, including this author, are prisoners of their training and few feel confident enough to tackle 'total' sports history; presumably this can be left to French sports historians! Nevertheless, should economic historians concentrate on the economic aspects of sport they must not imply that social, political or legal factors are less important: the Football League is a commercial cartel, but it may also be part of the class struggle.

Economic historians can, of course, assist sports historians of a different complexion by providing answers to such questions as: How many people were employed in the sports industry? What was the turnover and output of the industry? How much was invested in particular sectors? What was the typical rate of return? As many social historians have demonstrated, sport is more than just a commodity in the market place. Nevertheless, if social historians are to have an adequate quantitative foundation for their hypotheses on such matters as social control, then the economic aspects of commercialised sport are not only worthy of, but require, serious study: which brings us back to the Shankly riposte.

Part II

The development of professional gate-money sport

The future chronicler of the Victorian era, when noticing social changes, will find himself compelled to devote much of his space to the enormous increase of sport and athletic games. Sixty years ago boxing was dying, as duelling had perished shortly before, by a discreditable death. Golf was only known in Scotland, and like curling, the other favourite game of Scotchmen, showed no sign of sallying forth to conquer other lands. Cricket was just entering a more scientific stage, but no one could have predicted the ascendancy it has since gained. The University Boat Race was not yet in its infancy, and ten years afterwards, instead of the serried thousands who now repair to the banks of the Thames to see it rowed, a few hundreds of University men galloped abreast of the competitors, and it was esteemed amusing if they succeeded in driving into the water the thin fringe of lookers-on who occupied the banks. Football had not migrated from the boys' playground. In certain old towns by ancient custom at Eastertide balls were unscientifically kicked along the streets to the danger of windows and disgust of quiet people. As for football attaining its present development, such a thought had entered no one's head.

Quarterly Review, CLXXXVIII, 1898, p. 419

Chapter 3

Popular recreation before the Industrial Revolution[1]

I

Work in pre-industrialised Britain was more intermittent than it is today: for most workers there was no such thing as a regular working week or even a regular working day. A major reason for this lay in agriculture's dominance of economic activity. Work effort on the land would be greatest at planting and harvesting and less intense during other times of the arable year. Hedging, ditching, dung-spreading and threshing provided some winter and springtime employment but nowhere near the level obtaining from May to September. Similarly, in pastoral agriculture there would be peaks of activity associated with sheep-shearing and the autumnal slaughter of livestock. Agrarian pursuits were also subject to seasonal and irregular climatic influences: certainly in winter, frost, snow, heavy rain and fewer daylight hours reduced the amount of outdoor work which could be done.

Other economic activities were also subject to seasonal and irregular fluctuations. All trades, of course, suffered from the problem of demand – both its limited absolute level and its vicissitudes – but additionally there were specific supply-side constraints. Processes utilising agricultural products would, within the limits set by the ability to hold stocks, fluctuate with both the aggregate and the seasonal supply of those inputs. The winter climate also enforced idleness on many trades, particularly where overland or seaborne transportation of goods was required. Hence building, quarrying, coal-mining, fishing, seafaring, repairing roads and shipbuilding, among others, reduced their level of activity as the weather worsened. Even wars were affected: the logistics of feeding and transporting the labour-intensive armed services were beyond the technology of the times, and soldiers and sailors were frequently stood down in autumn. The prevailing technology also meant that textile processes, too, were seasonally affected: the drying of woven cloth on tenters required dry weather, bleaching needed strong sunlight, and fabric-printing called for frost-free days. Available drainage techniques also effectively restricted some mining to the drier months of the year. Other trades, however, found their lean times elsewhere in the year. Summer droughts, for example, could interfere seriously with milling, iron-making, washing and cleansing operations, and, of course, with riverborne commerce.[2]

Although much economic activity was seasonal, the extent of idleness among the work force should not be exaggerated. Labour was less specific than it was to become and, within the constraints set by skill requirements, many workers switched from one occupation to another as the demand for their services fluctuated. Certainly in agriculture the economic rigours of winter underemployment could be partially ameliorated by work in cottage crafts, whereas at harvest time such domestic weaving or nailmaking would be set aside as everyone concentrated upon getting in the crop, not only to ensure the community's survival but also to reap the annual financial bonus which harvest earnings provided. Nevertheless, particularly in winter, work irregularities might coincide rather than counterbalance, and it remains true that there was a large reservoir of underemployed labour whose free time was forced upon them rather than chosen voluntarily.[3]

Others had little choice as to when they had to work. Some jobs had to be undertaken at specific times, often dictated by nature rather than by man.[4] Fishermen and other seafarers were dependent upon the tides; securing the harvest required labour from dawn till dusk; and sheep and cattle had to be safeguarded at lambing and calving time. This task orientation of time generally led to uneven working hours, though not always; it was necessary, for instance, to milk cows fairly regularly.

Although the structure of the economy partly determined the seasonal nature of productive activity, it has been argued that the long periods of less intensive work at other times was a function of the population's physical capacity to work. Low and unpredictable food supplies combined with debilitating disease to make energy a scarce resource and to necessitate long stretches of rest and recuperation after prolonged bouts of hard work. Leisure preference was involuntary in that idleness was essential to health.[5] Statistically the argument is unsubstantiated. It hinges on a calculation of calorie intake which was based on Gregory King's estimate of grain consumption in 1695. Higher estimates were rejected and other sources of nutrition ignored. The historical scenario, however, does lend support to the thesis. In the fifteenth, sixteenth and early seventeenth centuries roughly one harvest in four was so deficient as to threaten the bulk of the population with starvation or serious under-nourishment.[6] Additionally, demographic studies have revealed high mortality rates consequent upon endemic and epidemic disease.[7]

Much of the argument so far has ignored the possibility that both irregular hours and the amount of work done could be a matter of choice. Task-work labourers, independent craftsmen, and workers in the putting-out system could, within the requirements of a week's or a fortnight's output, shorten or lengthen their working day. Frequently this meant periods of idleness followed by bouts of intense labour.[8] At other times rises in real wage rates could lead to a reduction in the amount of labour supplied by those workers who possessed a preference for leisure.[9]

One path-breaking study of miners in the fifteenth and sixteenth centuries has postulated backward-sloping individual labour supply curves conditioned either by status or the price of consumables.[10] Landless miners, initially the minority, geared their work effort to obtaining a predetermined level of consumption and hence produced less when the market price of their output increased. Miners who were also peasant farmers similarly controlled their work intensity in the mines in order to satisfy an income expectation sufficient to cover rent and a stable consumption pattern consistent with their position in the village hierarchy. Such was the importance of status that they chose to earn and expend less than the professional miners (from whom they wished to be distinguished), who, although landless, were not poor and did not conform to the consumption conventions of village society.

It has been speculated that such socially constrained consumption levels were common amongst peasants engaged in other labouring work.[11] However, such status-determined consumption could have become less relevant to the economy as a whole once population pressure resulted in an increasing number of landless labourers. Moreover, it is feasible that this group could revise their income expectations upwards. This occurred among the Mendip miners, who, although working towards a fixed real income in the short run, actually raised their expenditure levels in the longer run.[12] Thus the level of income expectation and the self-imposed limit to productivity was not immutable.

One possible reason for the undermining of leisure preference was the increasing range of consumer goods becoming available. Although meat can be substituted for cheaper foodstuffs, where the basic consumables are edibles there is a physiological limit set to consumption. Moreover, with a limited variety of other consumer goods the marginal utility gained from spending decreases rapidly. Even the delights of the tavern can pall. However, there is less chance of satiation if the range of goods offered for sale can be broadened. Once this occurs, income expectations may be revised upwards.

It has been argued that such a broadening of supply occurred in early modern England and that, from the mid sixteenth century, rural industries developed in many scattered parts of the nation, producing stockings, pins, starch, soap, lace, knives and other cheap consumer goods for the domestic market.[13] The earnings of the workers involved generated domestic purchasing power, the expenditure of which was reinforced by the growing proportion of the population not tied by social constraints on their consumption. Entrepreneurs responded and offered both more goods and a wider choice, which in turn could have caused a revision of income expectations, though perhaps at the family rather than the individual level. By 1700 consumption above subsistence level was well established.[14] For a significant, though regionally concentrated, proportion of the population the consumption of goods had eaten into their consumption of leisure.[15]

Nevertheless, the greatest inroads were yet to be made and it can be asserted that for the bulk of the population, or at least for those who had some choice in their supply of labour, a rise in real wage rates generally saw the price effect of more expensive leisure (in terms of the opportunity cost of foregone earnings) outweighed by the income effect (in that more leisure could be afforded). Leisure, of course, was the most readily available consumer good. Most people thus had abundant leisure time.[16]

II

Of course not all non-working hours would have been spent in freely chosen leisure activities. As with modern suburbia's lawn-cutting and in-law visiting, pre-industrial man would be faced with social obligations which he could not ignore, and it was not only God's wrath that might be brought down on the village parishioner who failed to attend church. Additionally, depending upon their earnings and the degree of non-monetisation in their local economy, the populace would have had to devote some of their nominally free time to tasks such as making their own clothes, repairing their dwellings, and possibly cultivating a garden for foodstuffs. Nevertheless, sporting and other recreational activities were pursued, many of which mirrored aspects of the society and economy in which they occurred.[17]

Clearly much recreation reflected the rural environment. Most wakes, fairs and parish feasts came at times of slack in the agrarian work calendar, with a particular concentration in the lull between spring sowing and the summer harvest and also in the post-harvest break.[18] Moreover, in this latter period harvest labourers would have money to spend on celebration, as would those farm servants whose terms of hiring ended at Michaelmas. The widespread use of animals in recreation also stemmed from an agrarian society. No doubt horse-racing originated from rival owners debating the respective merits of their mounts; cock-fighting, throwing at cocks, and possibly even bull-baiting were a way of disposing of surplus male stock; badger-baiting was an 'entertaining' method of pest control; and aristocratic hunting, hawking, fowling and fishing, and its emulation by the lower ranks of society, was simply making use of what existed naturally. Over time, however, some animals, such as racehorses, hunters and cocks, began to be bred more for the sport and less for the farm. Another final rustic link was the extensive use of land, a luxury of a nation with a population density of only 43 to the square kilometre in 1750 and considerably less in earlier years.[19] Football matches, often with one village ranged against another, could traverse many acres of countryside; horse-racing, too, could cover several kilo-metres of common, heath and wasteland; cricket had no boundaries with all hits having to be run out; and, of course, blood sports were rarely fixed in locale.

England, however, was not totally rural. Indeed London had an esti-mated population of some 400,000 in 1650 and over half a million at the end of the seventeenth century, by which time it was the largest city in western Europe.[20] Certainly the size of the metropolis influenced its rec-reational activities in that it was there that commercialisation, exhi-bitionism and professionalism in sports, and in other activities, began to develop.[21] This was because the concentration of population allowed for audiences large enough to encourage entrepreneurial outlays. Elsewhere there was little chance of commercialised sport emerging on any scale: the density of population was too low to provide a viable market. Although one in ten Englishmen lived in the capital, the majority of urban dwellers outside London lived in towns of between 650 and 900 persons and, of course, three-quarters of the population still lived in villages and ham-lets.[22]

Many recreational pursuits were closely allied with gambling. Some of this was the petty betting of the masses backing their prowess, or that of their animals, at alehouse games and sports, but mainly it was associated with the wealthier members of the population. Generally it was the aristocracy and gentry who owned the racehorses and high-class fighting cocks and who patronised the pugilists, wrestlers, athletes and cricket teams, and, although when their champions challenged others they were performing a paternalistic duty in providing entertainment for the community's holiday, their main interest was in the wager accompanying the challenge.[23] Heavy gambling was a status symbol as it was a means of conspicuous consumption at a time when both investment opportunities and the supply of consumer goods were limited.

Although some sports cut across class lines, and the gentry enjoyed several leisure pursuits of the masses, concern for rank and status made it essential that the lower echelons were not free to participate in the recreations of the elite.[24] In most cases expense alone would be a sufficient deterrent: no peasant or farm labourer could afford to play royal tennis and few had sufficient resources even to feed a pig let alone own a racehorse or hunter. Where cost did not work, then the law could be applied, in particular the Game Laws. These originated in an Act of 1670 which restricted the taking of game to lords of manors or to those with an annual income from landed property of at least £100 per annum.[25] Although possibly primarily designed to protect property, they were also intended, in the words of a contemporary, 'to prevent persons of inferior rank, from squandering that time, which their station in life requires to be more profitably employed'.[26] In practice, like many laws, they could not be totally enforced, but generally they served to make lower-rank emulation of higher-rank bloodsports a covert rather than a public event.

Alcohol was an important rural product and many adult recreational activities involved its use. One reason was that the alehouse was one of the few fixed places for recreation and the publican was one of the few people to provide organised entertainment.[27] He would supply the bull or the badger for baiting, provide the pit for the cockfight, hire the itinerant entertainers, or pay the musicians who played while his customers danced. He might charge a fee to those who set their dogs on the bull, but mainly he expected to make his money by selling drink. Even when additional attractions were not provided the alehouse faced little competition either as a social centre or as a meeting place. Daylight, fine-weather recreation may have made use of the market place, public thoroughfares, the common fields, or even the churchyard, but come dusk or rain there were few alternatives to the tavern. Even the Church made use of drinking in its 'church ales', at which the congregation would drink together to celebrate their saint's day or the completion of a communal task, such as the mowing of the churchyard, or perhaps to solicit funds for religious or charitable purposes.[28] The secular equivalent were the 'bid ales', at which a brew would be sold to raise money for a needy neighbour.[29] Alcohol was also used to lubricate working hours: farmers frequently supplied their labourers with beer, and a wage assessment of 1725 allowed two half-hours each working day for drinking.[30]

Alcohol also had its narcotic aspect in a society in which life was hard, painful and frequently short. Merrie England should not be sentimental-ised. Disease constantly threatened man, his crops and his animals. The bulk of the population was dependent upon the local harvest and, although by the mid seventeenth century England was avoiding the extremes of subsistence crises, both undernourishment and near-starvation remained ever-present menaces. Early death meant that family support was often transient; life chances for the masses were determined by landlords and substantial householders; opportunities for social mobility were negligible; and underemployment was the norm. Con-sequently between a quarter and a half of the populace lived and died in poverty.[31] In the face of dearth, death, or economic disaster, the average man was powerless: no wonder many turned to the social and psychologi-cal comfort of drink.

The violence of much recreation may also have owed something to the harshness of existence in pre-industrialised Britain. Violent entertainment reached its extreme in public hangings and witch-burning, but featured also in many sports. Doubtless where virulent disease and early death were commonplace the chance of injury in sport would be considered a minor matter. Football, often with unlimited numbers, resembled a riot (and often became one), with local custom rather than laid-down rules governing the players' behaviour. Descriptions of many matches lead to a suspicion that the ball was merely incidental to the game and that kicking the opposition was just as useful a tactic. Settling old scores perhaps took precedence over making new ones. Clearly limbs, and occasionally lives, were at risk.[32] In many sports the ultimate objective was to physically injure an opponent. At least in pugilism and wrestling the combatants were unarmed, but in cudgelling, single stick and backsword, sticks and clubs were used to crack open an opponent's head, break his nose, or knock out his teeth. Then there was cut-legs, in which contestants lashed each other's legs with whips, and kick-shins, where heavy-booted men literally kicked each other's shins until one cried enough.[33] These sports were for the common people. Violence in sport at the other end of the social scale had been associated with military usefulness: tournaments and sword play had been ways of developing courage and martial arts. However, as success in warfare became more dependent upon tactics and organisation and less upon prowess in personal combat, it became harder to find members of the gentry and nobility who were willing to chance injury for the sake of recreation.[34]

Violence was not done just to men. When human life was cheap, scant regard would be paid to the treatment of animals. By modern standards there was much cruelty in the various forms of baiting, in dog and cock fights, in throwing cudgels and broomsticks at tethered cocks, and in thrashing fat hens with a flail.[35] Some of these brutal sports appealed to both high- and low-born, but blood sports were more rank-oriented. Participation costs and the Game Laws restricted the hunting of deer and hares and the shooting or hawking of birds to the wealthier members of landed society. These sports still had martial utility in that military manoeuvres could be rehearsed and the skill of riding practised.

The preceding discussion lends support to the hypothesis of an energy-scarce society. It can be hazarded that leisure in such a society would tend to be passive rather than active, would utilise time rather than energy and, if organised, would be infrequent rather than regular. This seems to be the case, though in the current state of knowledge it is impossible to be dogmatic on the issue. Certainly it would seem that active, organised physical recreation was an infrequent affair, generally taking place only annually or at major holidays. This concentration of formal recreation – as opposed to informal gossiping and drinking – at particular times of the year may have reflected the fact that in at least one of these periods – that following the harvest – food, and hence energy, would have been relatively plentiful. Whether at other times alcohol may have provided nutrition is a matter for conjecture.[36] What is clearer is that, apart from some mob football matches and perhaps dancing, physically strenuous leisure pursuits were minority activities. In general people watched rather than played. Much participation was probably vicarious, with villagers cheering on their champions and owners testing the merits of their animals in baiting and fighting. Most sports were individual rather than group-oriented, and even for these individuals endurance of pain was often more important than physical stamina.

A poorly fed population had to be onlookers rather than players. However, at this time their poverty meant that generally they were not paying spectators. Any sports event which required capital outlay was dependent upon patronage. Some would come from publicans – petty capitalists seeking to sell more ale to those attracted to their cockpit or skittle alley. Paternalistic landowners might also see the provision of sports, particularly at holiday times, as part of their social obligations to the communities which they headed. Yet other patronage, as suggested above, would stem from the gambling activities of the aristocracy and gentry.

III

Recreation was not merely fun and games. A consideration of the economic and, especially, the social aspects of pre-industrialised leisure makes it apparent that such activities were not simply ephemeral: they had deep significance for both society and members of that society.

Leisure had its economic aspects, though not so much in direct commercialisation for there were few people who made their living out of leisure. The petty entrepreneur in charge of the cock-throwing or bull-baiting might make some money out of the particular event but he could not earn a living from such infrequent attractions. Itinerant entertainers – quack doctors, musicians and travelling players – might fare better, but possibly the real professionals in the recreation sector were the publicans and the whores.[37]

There was, however, some intermingling of economic and recreational activity. At markets, and particularly at fairs, the major objectives of buying and selling goods, or of hiring labour, were often accompanied by entertainment ranging from informal gossiping to organised dancing and animal sports.[38] The 'bid ales' and 'church ales' could be enjoyable ways of providing poor relief. Poaching could combine profit with pleasure: it brought meat and money but also sport. Defying the Game Laws, with their threat of imprisonment or death, must have given a thrill for, despite the risk, some poachers retained the antlers of the deer they killed.[39] In many occupations there was no strict demarcation between work and leisure, and time at work could be passed pleasurably in singing, story-telling, or just talking, for there was no clank of heavy machinery to hinder these activities. In an economy with much underemployment annual productivity would not have been adversely affected by such recreation within the work situation: indeed, by enabling work to be done to a rhythm, singing could have improved the daily productivity of work gangs doing simple tasks.

Recreation also served social–psychological purposes. Certainly it was a counterbalance to the harshness of life and labour. At some times simply not working might suffice; at others, such as the parish feast, the mass of the population could, for a while, forget the real world and its laws, conventions and worries. There would be relief from care and, if the harvest had been good, possibly from budget constraint too. For a while some individual sportsmen would be in charge of their own destinies. For others, drinking and dancing would loosen inhibitions and for some, particularly servants, most of whom were single, the holiday provided a scarce opportunity for sexual encounters. Clearly, sexual licence prevailed at many fairs, as documented by contemporary critics or, in the realms of harder evidence, as revealed in the bastard births some nine months later.[40]

Some fairs gave the people a chance to be irreverent to authority. For a day or so roles could be reversed, conventional proprieties could be challenged and the customary deference to rank neglected. Instead of doffing caps or stepping aside, soot, mud, cabbages or dead cats and dogs might be thrown at respectable passers-by.[41] Unpopular figures of authority might be burned in effigy, and traditionally in some districts Game Laws and other property rights might be disregarded on a particular day of the year.[42] All this was more or less tolerated by those in authority, possibly because they wished to be popular, perhaps because the incidents caused embarrassment rather than physical harm, or maybe because a plebeian mob was not a group to challenge. The most likely explanation, however, is that of social control of a bread-and-circuses variety. Festivities allowed the populace to let off steam and go back to work content. They could not hope for fundamental social change so both they and the gentry accepted a ritual which temporarily gave them a sense of power. Occasionally things would get out of hand, usually it would seem at football matches, where the numbers would give the mob power,[43] but generally, so long as the irreverence was ritualised, it served to cement the social order rather than disrupt it. And, of course, genteel patronage of horse-racing, cock-fighting, pugilism and cricket, and the provision of feasts on royal wedding days, election days and the like, served to remind the community who was at its head.

Recreation was important to the community. The state of communications made life parochial with a very limited geographical range of social contact.[44] It was thus important for the community to be bound together. In themselves parish wakes and feasts contributed to group solidarity in that everyone could participate and there was open-house hospitality. Group identity could also be strengthened by football, and later, cricket matches against other villages, or when support was given to the local wrestling champion as he fought an outsider. Although the closeness of the community may have contributed to the lack of opportunity for social mobility, it did mean that individual status was determined by local happenings and so performances at sports and other recreations could bring public esteem and enhanced social status.

IV

Whether religion had ever held sway over recreation is difficult to ascertain. The medieval Church had provided entertainment for the masses in its Mystery Plays and possibly in its services, but the prevalence of other recreational pursuits suggests that this did not satisfy the populace. It is clear, as argued above, that religious holy days fitted into the agricultural year and occurred when the labour force could be spared from the land.[45] Even in the Middle Ages complaints were being made about the perversion of holy days into holidays and, increasingly, observance of saints' days owed more to secular attractions than to religious piety.[46] Further disregard for Christian proprieties came with the secular consecration of the 'Saint Monday' holiday by those who could choose their working hours, though when this first developed is not known.[47] Any changes in the respective social and religious components of family observance of births, deaths and marriages can only be speculated upon.

Prior to the Industrial Revolution there was one sustained attempt to change popular leisure activities when religion, in the form of Puritanism, challenged recreation.[48] Even after the Reformation the Established Church calendar was punctuated with saints' days on which work should have given way to worship. To the disgust of the Puritans many of the populace preferred secular entertainment to preaching or prayer. Concern over such misuse of holy days was not new, but the Puritans went beyond merely railing at those who participated in licentious, violent, or drunken recreational activities: their political influence enabled them to promote legislation which directly affected the people's leisure. The old Church festivals smacked too much of Popery and were forsaken in favour of a concentration of religious devotion upon the Sunday. The fourth commandment was then reinforced by a series of statute laws which prohibited a host of activities on the Sabbath. The Puritans were not satisfied solely with strict Sabbatarianism: even on other days recreation was to be tightly controlled. Drinking, gambling and the sports associated with it, profanity and prostitution were obvious targets for prohibitive legislation; brutal sports were outlawed as a double evil providing pleasure for the spectators as well as pain to the animals; even dancing was frowned upon because as a result of it 'many maidens have been unmaidened'.[49] Indeed many Puritans felt that any leisure which did not contribute to a person's religious development was heinous. To them the exercise of religion was exercise enough. Rest helped revive the body for the hard work which glorified God; anything else was idleness and hence sinful.

In practice much continued as before. Enforcing the legislation nationally proved impossible because Puritanism had failed to gain whole-hearted public support for its recreational policies. The majority of the people saw nothing being offered to replace what the Puritans were trying to take from them. Attempts to use force to impose Puritan ideals on the community only demonstrated that the populace had not been won over. Many public opinion leaders – parsons, farmers and country gentlemen – continued to accept or even patronise the traditional leisure activities, and the agricultural economy still had room for the old festivals and celebrations. This is not to say that nothing changed. Where there was an efficient local administration and sufficient local support many public recreations were put down, though what people did in private was less easy to police. The extent to which Puritanism succeeded in its campaign against popular recreation is conjectural, though the available evidence suggests that, although battles were won, the war was not.[50] The old sports and customs proved remarkably resilient. Despite a century of Puritan pressure the post-Restoration era saw them flourishing almost as strongly as ever.

Although the pressure group power of Puritanism waned it did not lose all of its influence. Many of those concerned with public order had some sympathy with Puritan principles of social conduct when expressed in a less extreme form. Certainly Sabbatarianism experienced a ratchet effect: indeed not only were the laws on Sunday activities not repealed, but further restrictive legislation was actually enacted. Puritan-type attitudes to Sunday recreation, animal cruelty, and intemperance, were adopted by other religions, both Established and, especially, Non-conformist. Most important of all, many of the Puritan ideas on social behaviour suited the needs of industrial capitalism, which was to emerge as an economic force in the eighteenth century. In terms of the requirements of the economy Puritanism had been before its time: the pre-industrialised economic system could accommodate traditional recreational activities. An industrialised economy, however, made different demands and, if the nation was to industrialise, leisure patterns and practices had to be changed.

Chapter 4

Sporting activities and economic change, 1750–1830[1]

Beginning in the mid eighteenth century the British economy underwent a structural transformation as industry came more into prominence. In turn industrialisation had an impact on popular recreation as it called for new work patterns. Admittedly, hard and sustained effort had been demanded by agriculture at harvest time, but in industry, particularly factory industry, the pressure was less seasonal and more unrelenting. What was required in industry was regular hours and, above all, long hours. Unit overhead costs could only be reduced if the growing volume of machinery and other capital equipment was intensively employed, particularly as in some industries the initial physical productivity gains of the new methods of production over the old were not significantly large.[2] Even in industries which were relatively unmechanised economies could be obtained by task specialisation and labour synchronisation. Admittedly, with work being collected at long intervals, there was enough slack in the domestic system to tolerate members of the production chain working different hours, but, where the work force was more concentrated, embryo assembly lines could often be operated and, for such a cooperating or integrated labour force, productivity was much higher when they worked the same hours.[3]

It was no easy task to persuade a labour force to accept the new work discipline.[4] Indeed initially it was difficult enough to get workers into the factories at all. Not only was working from dawn to dusk, six days a week, virtually throughout the year, alien to traditional work patterns but, for many, industrial employment would involve geographical as well as occupational mobility. Estrangement from familiar surroundings, both at home and at work, meant that few had the courage to leap into the brave new world of industrialisation. Hence, initially at least, employers could not be too selective over whom they hired and, despite their high turnover rates, pauper apprentices and migratory labour had to be resorted to simply to get the numbers required. Since many factories already resembled workhouses in appearance and in the use of overseers, such employment of paupers merely confirmed the worst fears of factory-averse labourers.

In such situations of labour scarcity the effectiveness of fines, dismissals, or even the physical chastisement of children and apprentices, as disciplinary measures was weakened. Not until industry was established were employers in a position to utilise these measures to good effect. By then, too, continued rural overpopulation had reduced the opportunity for industrial workers to leave and return to the land. Moreover, although there were many instances of trade combinations, and others of collective bargaining by riot, there was not, even well into the Industrial Revolution, a unified working class capable of rendering effective opposition to the changed working conditions.[5] So once the aggregate urban labour supply situation changed in favour of the employers there was little option but to accept the new work discipline.

But this lay in the future and, even when successful, disciplinary methods served only to obtain a minimum performance level: they did not change the labour force's attitude to work. A longer-term solution lay with the increased earnings obtainable for working longer hours. The majority of workers were already consumers in a money economy and the habit of earning and spending cash was an established one. Certainly the cash stimulus appeared to work at harvest time for agricultural labourers when long hours of unremitting toil would be put in, but this lasted only a few weeks and, to the labouring poor, could make all the difference between basic subsistence and a slightly more comfortable living. Whether it would work all the year round was less clear, especially as many contemporaries maintained, as had their sixteenth- and seventeenth-century predecessors, that increased pay inevitably produced less work.[6] Yet, as suggested earlier, the supply-of-labour problem was perhaps really a supply-of-goods problem. Unless the workers' consumption horizons could be stretched, the labour force would exhibit a preference for leisure at an output level below that desired by their industrial employers: there was no point in working harder if there was nothing to spend the extra money on. An increased range of consumer goods was vital as a demonstration of the better material life which hard work could bring. Although individual employers could not force their workers to consume more than a limited quantity of the goods they themselves manufactured, the truck shop, though primarily a device to save on working capital, could be used to instil the consumption habit in the work force. Outside the factory gates, a widening range of retail outlets and developments in the distributive system contributed to the 'shop window' effect and, in turn, were stimulated by the consumer demand which this engendered.

Increasingly, in industry at least, leisure preference become offset and outweighed by the work–consumption ethic, which, although it was not necessarily adopted by each individual worker, was nevertheless sufficient in its aggregate impact to increase the supply of labour offered.[7] There may have been time lags in which the short-run response to increased wage rates was increased leisure, but, once the wage rises proved not to be transient, consumption patterns were adjusted accordingly. That opportunities for higher incomes and increased spending were being taken in the later eighteenth century is evidenced by the spread down the social scale of the consumption of tobacco, tea, sugar and other commodities previously considered luxury imports, and the vast increase in the consumption of the products of the Industrial Revolution itself, with cheap cotton goods, cast-iron utensils, commercially produced soap and many other products all finding their major market at home.[8] Once workers accepted that they wanted higher consumption standards, then not only would wage incentives be more effective, but the way was open for the use of fines and dismissals as a disciplinary threat to that standard. Many workers, however, had been convinced that time was now indeed money and that leisure was, in opportunity cost terms, no longer a free good. The implication is that increasingly there would be less free time available to factory workers in industrialising Britain.

II

The acceptance by the work force that leisure cost them money enabled working hours to be extended, but inevitably the trade-off between less leisure and more income was not absolute. Even for those workers with low leisure preference, Sundays were generally free from labour and, despite increasing pressure, numerous holidays were still recognised. Some leisure activities can, of course, be regarded as consumption and their finance may have induced a need to work. However, two major recreational items, gambling and drinking, had the seeds of work ethic destruction in-built, for successful gambling can obviate the necessity to work and heavy drinking can render effective work impossible. Hence what their workers did in their free time was of concern to many industrial and commercial employers and they thus supported the general middle-class move to soften manners and to impose its own morality on a society in which the 'aristocracy and working class were united in their drunkenness, profaneness, sexual indulgence, gambling, and love of cruel sports'.[9]

The traditional way of life was to be discredited and the importance of work upgraded: the idle rich and the idle poor were both to be condemned. Respectability was to be the aim of all society. Hence a campaign was mounted against popular customs, sports, holidays, fairs, drink, idleness, bad language and uncleanliness.

As just suggested, the attempt to change the workers' attitudes to leisure was not solely by the employers. Political economists lent their support, using the example of the Irish peasantry to illustrate the dangers of idle and improvident conduct.[10] Evangelicals, within and without the Established Church, argued that traditional recreations led to moral and spiritual disorder and that they had to be put down as a first step towards civilising the masses and making them more receptive to religious instruction.[11] Virtually all religions, from High Anglican to Primitive Methodist, believed that worldly pleasure was spiritually corrosive: drink rotted the moral fibre as well as the liver; along with gambling it led directly to crime; sexual indulgence, whether casual or commercial, had always been castigated; and, naturally, Sunday recreation continued to be condemned. Traditional sports were associated with all these evils and hence were inherently sinful. Individual preachers pushed the message home to their congregations and occasionally carried it to the unconverted. Collective action came from campaigning pressure groups, designed to inculcate Christian values into the public via tracts and periodicals but also determined to confront those who refused to listen: for example, in its first two years of existence, Wilberforce's Society for the Suppression of Vice (1801) promoted 623 successful prosecutions for breaking the Sabbath Laws.[12] To this end Humanitarian Christians formed the R. S. P. C. A. (1824), the Teetotal Movement (1829), and the Lord's Day Observance Society (1831).[13] Other attacks on traditional recreations came from those who feared that mob football, excessive drinking, role reversals, bonfire celebrations and the abuse rather than the use of fairs could lead to property damage and public disorder, perhaps as a prelude to social instability.[14] The Revolution across the Channel and the agitation at home after the Napoleonic Wars gave point to these anxieties, though the fact that municipal by-laws rather than statute laws were the legal weapons employed against football and the abuse of alcohol suggests that what was feared was local riot rather than national insurrection.[15]

If adults were too set in their ways to change it was possible that the next generation might be more amenable to manipulation. Thus the religious bodies used children's education as a means to instil respectability into the population; many of the middle class believed that the lessening of ignorance would reduce crime; others saw it as a means of cementing social stability by promoting a due sense of obedience in working-class children; and employers felt that schooling could mould their future labour force into shape.[16] The employers were not primarily concerned with literacy. For them the benefits of educating their potential workers were that schools would reconcile the children to punctuality, discipline, confinement and regular hours, while a suitable curriculum would drive home the message of the Devil finding work for idle hands, factory or otherwise.[17]

III

Economic change was not confined to the industrial sector: agriculture, too, underwent a transformation. If there had been a pre-industrial energy shortage, then more energy must have become available for the population to have been capable of the extra effort demanded by industrialisation. Increased earnings from working harder and longer enabled individuals to purchase more energy, either directly as extra food or indirectly by the substitution of goods made by others, or services performed by others, for tasks previously undertaken by themselves. However, for the community as a whole to have more energy either more food had to be produced or more imported. Improvements in both husbandry techniques and in agrarian organisation meant that domestic agriculture generally coped with the rising demand. More land was brought into cultivation; yields were increased; fodder crops filled the hungry gap and reduced the autumnal slaughter of farm animals; legumes replenished the fertility of the soil as did the increased volume of manure from the growing number of livestock; selective breeding and lessened animal disease improved the quality and quantity of meat available to the consumer; enclosure allowed experimentation, facilitated the consolidation of farms with ensuing economies of scale, cut down on indiscriminate livestock breeding and reduced the spread of contagious animal diseases; and the development of mixed farming, particularly on the lighter lands, enabled arable and pastoral farming to advance symbiotically.[18] It is clear from contemporary guesstimates, and from production figures for industries which utilised agrarian raw materials, that agricultural output increased significantly in the eighteenth century, but the deficiencies of both demographic and agricultural statistics make it impossible to prove that the populace generally was better fed as the period progressed.[19] Imports of foodstuffs, particularly corn, supplemented domestic production, but the issue of per capita food consumption must at present remain a quantitative mystery. Recent work using data on height by age as a proxy for nutrition and health supports the general picture of improved nutrition in that the modal heights of recruits aged 22–7 into the Chatham Division of the Royal Marines rose from 66.1 inches in 1755–65 to 67.2 inches in 1818–27.[20] However, other data on the mean heights of thirteen-year-olds show a downward trend from the late 1780s until about 1812, after which there was a rapid increase.[21] What is fairly certain is that over the eighteenth century people ate more regularly and the spectre of famine diminished. Despite cases of severe shortages, and even starvation in some localities, recurrent and widespread food crises, at least for the English, were pretty much events of the past.[22]

By contributing to a healthier and more energetic population, agricultural change promoted the possibility of an altered work–leisure relationship, particularly in those sectors of the economy where regular intensive labour was required. Moreover, even though climate and the calendar remained the major determinants of agrarian work patterns, the changes also influenced working habits on the land. Although rural population expansion lessened the incentive to mechanise, there was still substantial investment in agriculture via enclosure, consolidation, road-building, fencing, drainage, and the construction of farm buildings. One estimate is that fixed capital formation in agriculture rose from £2.2m per annum in the period 1761–70 to £4.1m per annum in 1801–10, and that working capital rose from £138m in 1760 to £185m in 1800.[23] A consequence of this was that, although perhaps less profit-maximising than industrialists – because of land's value as a social or political asset – landowners and larger farmers became more concerned with farm productivity and the efficient use of resources. Their position as employers was strengthened by the oversupply of farm labour due to population expansion and to the undermining of small-scale owner-occupiers by the costs of enclosure.[24] This enabled them to demand an increase in hours, if not daily then certainly annually.

Agricultural change could also have had an influence on the nature of rural recreation. Under the growing influence of the market economy custom was giving way to an emphasis on private property rights. Not only were the customary economic practices of gleaning and fuel-gathering becoming less tolerated, but also the traditional 'right' to sport in a field at certain times of the year.[25] The loss of common rights consequent upon enclosure further reduced the open space available for recreation, particularly football. Finally, fodder crops and other improvements gave man some control over his environment and lessened the rationale for the maypole and other fertility rites, which originally had been central to many rural holidays.[26]

IV

Thus, in both the agricultural and, particularly, the industrial sectors, there were strong economic influences acting to change traditional sports. Moreover, workers were generally unorganised and unable to resist their employers' demands, especially as population growth pushed bargaining power in favour of capital. These economic forces were supplemented by the efforts of evangelical reformers who believed that brutal sports led directly to moral and spiritual disorders and by those who feared that mob football could easily turn into the riot which it resembled, with consequent damage to persons, property and social stability.

Before considering the impact of these forces arraigned against traditional recreation, two points have to be made. First, it should be emphasised that most studies of pre-industrialised leisure have concentrated on documented activities to the relative exclusion of routine, informal recreation, such as family celebrations of births and marriages, digging in the garden, or even relaxing by doing nothing, which were 'in terms of the hours involved, more prominent than the large public celebrations and sporting events'.[27] Short of spiritualist oral history, such neglect is perhaps inevitable. Unfortunately it does mean that all that can be assessed is the success, or otherwise, of the movement against specified, organised leisure activities such as blood sports or mob football; very little can be said as to whether or not the volume and character of all types of recreation were altered. Second, despite claims that leisure, including sport, was becoming more commercialised in the eighteenth century, the bulk of organised entertainment for the lower ranks of society still tended to be irregular and frequently on a one-off basis.[28]

If we now turn to the attack on traditional popular recreations it is clear that holidays would be under fire, for not only did they mean absence from work, but they also often resulted in boisterous, drunken and licentious behaviour. Here the reformers hit their target. Certainly those workers whose employers took a lead from the Bank of England found their labour-free days cut dramatically. In 1761 this institution closed its doors for 47 holidays. Progressively these were reduced to 44 in 1808, 18 in 1830 and only 4 in 1834.[29] A similar erosion occurred in the Cornish mines, where by 1842 miners could take off only Good Friday and Christmas Day.[30] Holidays were also reduced to between five and twelve days per year in most textile mills by the early nineteenth century, though in many cases even these had to be compensated for by working overtime.[31] When the reduction in holidays is considered along with the extension of the working week it is apparent that free time for the industrial worker had significantly decreased. One estimate puts the increase in annual work done at over a third, rising from around 3,000 hours a year in the mid eighteenth century to over 4,000 by the early nineteenth.[32]

Whether traditional sports suffered to the same extent is less clear. It has been argued that during the Industrial Revolution such sports were seriously undermined, but the chronological impact of the anti-recreational forces is not easy to determine.[33] An effort to assess the decline by around 1830, the classical end of the Industrial Revolution, was made by surveying contemporary literature.[34] Selective reportage and the metropolitan bias of some of the source material ruled out any attempt to be systematic, comprehensive or quantitative. What can be suggested is that, despite a long period of attrition, many traditional sports were still being played in the 1820s, though to what extent is conjectural. Football, never as fashionable among the gentry as cricket or horse-racing, had faded though occasional games were chronicled, and some of the more violent sports, such as cudgelling, rarely merit a mention except in connection with rural fairs. Violence, however, had not totally disappeared from the sporting scene as pugilism and wrestling remained well to the fore, the former centred on London, and the latter, despite some entrepreneurial activity by publicans in the metropolis, regionally concentrated in Cornwall and Devon, and in Cumberland and Westmorland. Animal sports also continued, with horse-racing, thanks to upper-class support, the most popular. Cock-fighting, too, was common, perhaps because of its links with race meetings, but dogfights, ratting and baiting were on the decline, though they featured in several metropolitan dens and were prominent in some other localities. Other sports documented included cricket, though now less associated with local holidays; pedestrianism, usually endurance feats for large wagers; and rustic sports such as climbing greasy poles, catching a soaped pig, running for smocks, and jumping in sacks.

One possible reason for the survival of some sports was that it was not until after the Reform Act of 1832 that the middle classes were able to use their numbers at national level to change the legal status of certain traditional recreations. Most attempts before then to outlaw cruel animal sports failed to obtain sufficient parliamentary support. At local-government level more could be done, depending, of course, upon the class and political composition of the municipal authorities. Generally the reformative pressure groups were established too late to have any significant influence before 1830 and their victories over adherents of cruel sports, drinking and Sabbath-breaking lay in the future. However, even if laws and by-laws were enacted there remained the problem of enforcement. In the 1820s bull-baiting was already illegal and prizefight spectators and participants could be prosecuted either as members of a riotous assembly or for breaching the peace, but such activities continued, partly because many members of the gentry still lent their patronage or tacit approval to such character-building, courage-forming recreation, and magistrates, perhaps covert sympathisers themselves, were reluctant to prosecute where local notables were involved.[35]

In any case the illegality – or the brutality – of many sports did not matter to many of the populace, for the reformers had failed to capture their hearts and minds. To them, along with poaching and smuggling, bull-baiting and pugilism were accepted illegal practices. One reason for this was that working-class education had not fulfilled the expectations of its middle-class promoters. For a start it was not compulsory and indeed there may have been little opportunity for some to obtain schooling. The controversy regarding the volume of education provided in the period 1790–1830 is not yet over, but, even if it is correct that there was no decline, it is also true that most children received relatively little formal education. The actual influence of schooling has not been investigated fully, but it is not clear that it necessarily served the needs of the employers. Certainly their direct provision of educational facilities would have given industrial proprietors control over the curriculum, but initially the supply of elementary education was left mainly to the Charity and Sunday Schools; possibly there were calls of a higher priority on the industrialist's limited capital or perhaps employers were reluctant to incur the costs of general training (as opposed to work-specific training) when they could not guarantee that the pupils would remain in their employment.[36] Nevertheless the attitudinal approach of bible-based education coincided with the disciplinary aims of the employers. However, many workers were well aware that an attempt at social control was being made and thus, when they could afford it, they preferred to pay to send their children to schools of their own choosing where literacy – of more economic relevance to them – would be the prime educational objective.[37] Moreover, it is a moot point whether children internalised the concepts of hard work and self-discipline or merely complied with the wishes of the instructor for the sake of a quiet school life. Additionally, hours in school were short and there were many other influences on the children, not all of which reinforced the lessons of the classroom.

Perhaps the major reason for the survival of traditional recreations lay with the state of economic development. It is becoming apparent that the Industrial Revolution was a more drawn-out process than used to be believed.[38] Britain in 1830 had not been transformed into a fully industrialised urban nation and could still accommodate some of the old activities. Little confidence can be placed in any industrial employment statistics for the early nineteenth century because of definitional and data problems.[39] Nevertheless, it can be confidently asserted that factory employees remained a distinct minority of the occupied population until the middle of the nineteenth century. Even in 1851 there were more domestic servants than textile factory workers.[40] Definitional problems also plague measures of urbanisation but it can be reckoned that, despite the mushroom growth of some cities, England, as a whole, maintained a majority of its population as non-urban inhabitants until mid century.[41] Capital formation may give an indication of the need for work discipline. Certainly there was a substantial increase in investment: one estimate has fixed capital formation rising from an annual average of £6.6m in the years 1761–70 to £28.3m in the period 1821–30.[42] Yet £14.3m of this latter figure was in transport, dwellings and public buildings/works, which would not necessitate extensive use of labour to render them productive. Nor would all the £10m in industrial and commercial fixed capital formation result in factory discipline embracing the industrial labour force. Both London, the largest manufacturing district in Britain at the beginning of the nineteenth century, and the Birmingham area had their industry dominated by workshop technology and the putting-out system (now urban rather than rural), which enabled self-employed craftsmen and piece-work domestic workers still to choose their own hours of labour, including the continued celebration of Saint Monday.[43] Even by the mid nineteenth century the factory system had not been widely established in these areas: indeed for Britain as a whole it has been estimated that 5½ million of the 7¼ million industrial workers were employed in non-mechanised industry.[44]

Despite agrarian development, traditional recreation had even more potential for survival in agricultural areas than in industrial ones. After all it was to these areas that the activities were traditional. Agrarian change had been a first step on the road to industrialisation for, without an increase in agricultural productivity, workers could not have been released for factory labour. However, before 1830 mechanisation was not a major contributor to this development and hence longer holidays – at an appropriate time in the agrarian calendar – could be accommodated.[45] Rural fairs, although increasingly pleasure-oriented, had not degenerated into the tumultuous assemblies decried by urban reformers, and still retained a marketing aspect, both for labour and goods.[46] Economic attitudes on the land had hardened, but there were still sufficient landowners who practised old-fashioned paternalism, which included a toleration of popular recreations, even the rougher varieties.[47]

Commercialised sport, in the sense that people paid to watch others play, existed in the eighteenth century. Notably in London, entrance fees were charged to watch prizefights and cricket matches and, more generally around the country, to enter the grandstands at race meetings.[48] Yet such events were spasmodic rather than regular, except in that the local race meeting might be an annual occurrence. Even in London, with its vast potential market, investment designed to provide more regular sports entertainment proved disastrous: both Figg's amphitheatre and Broughton's boxing emporium were short-lived and the proprietor of the Artillery cricket ground went bankrupt.[49]

Although transport deficiencies severely limited spectator catchment areas, the increased urbanisation of the late eighteenth and early nineteenth centuries provided sports entrepreneurs with more concentrated markets. Nevertheless, petty pub-sponsored activities aside, the survey of sport around 1830 revealed no instances of sports events catering for the working-class spectator being held on a regular basis. Generally race meetings remained associated with local holidays; prizefights, under increasing attack from the magistracy, were arranged only occasionally; and quality cricket matches, particularly in the provinces, were still infrequent affairs. It is significant that even in London, with a dense population within easy travelling distance, attempts to develop enclosed gate-money racecourses in 1826, and again in 1837, failed to attract sufficient paying customers.[50]

The basic reason for this lack of regular commercialised sport was insufficient working-class spending power. There has been considerable debate over working-class earnings during the Industrial Revolution, particularly regarding the period 1790–1840, though the very fact that there has been such controversy might suggest that any overall gains were marginal: one can argue about the existence of fairies at the bottom of the garden, but the presence of giants can hardly be a matter for discussion.[51] Recent research has suggested that *industrial* workers made real-income gains from about 1820.[52] However, the structural shift of employment within the economy by 1830 was insufficient to allow most working men to afford more than an occasional outing. Regular sports spectatorship required further economic development and a larger aggregate increase in discretionary spending power. Not until the economic benefits of industrialisation were passed onto the mass of the population could a significantly large and regular paying clientele be relied upon.

Chapter 5

The precursors of commercialised sport, 1830–75

I

In the quarter century from 1830 the sports scenario began to change significantly. On the one hand, a shift in the locus of political power led to the national outlawing of brutal animal sports and a clampdown by many local authorities on football, pugilism and other traditional and violent sports. On the other hand, the spread of the railways and a rise in working-class spending power pointed the way to future developments.

The increased political strength of the middle-class reformers enabled them to influence legislation against traditional recreations. The Highways Act of 1835 illegalised street football; a series of Acts outlawing brutal sports culminated in the abolition of public cock-fighting in 1849; and four years later betting shops were also placed beyond the legal pale. At a narrower geographical level, municipal authorities increasingly legislated to control those popular recreations which were deemed unsuitable to a modern urban environment, its property and its commerce. Over time the threshold of what would be tolerated was progressively raised, and what was accepted was more closely supervised and regulated.[1]

Nevertheless making laws was one thing; enforcing them quite another. Neither parliamentarians nor aldermen bore the brunt of implementation. That task lay with local control agents – the police – who in many areas were a relatively new institution. Their intervention into working-class leisure was clearly resented by men and women who felt humiliated by the 'move-on' system which hit at the traditional freedom of assembly in the streets.[2] In practice different policies were adopted, depending upon the nature of the illegal activity. In the case of cock-fighting, illegal drinking, gambling and prostitution – what might be termed regular irregularities – constant surveillance drove them underground or out into the countryside, the presumption being that once they became clandestine the number of adherents would decline. Alternatively, according to the disposition of the current chief constable, they were allowed to exist in particular areas out of sight – and hence out of mind – of the more respectable inhabitants, with ritual arrests being made from time to time. Much firmer action was taken regarding the annual events involving substantial numbers of potentially drunk and violent participants, for by their nature mob football, bonfire celebrations and the baser aspects of traditional fairs and wakes could hardly be pushed out of sight. In some cases suppression was the rule, though until the futility of resistance was accepted such a clampdown often generated more violence than it was intended to put down. Some fairs, bonfires and wakes, however, persisted through the century, but not in their traditional form, as this would have involved too much loss of face by both the local authorities and the police. Instead such activities were tamed and transformed under the influence of middle-class patronage and entrepreneurial initiative, and with the police, increasingly confident in their ability to cope with festive crowds, controlling those aspects deemed illegal.[3]

In the shorter run the reforming pressure groups also had some victories, in particular successful prosecutions which they brought against those involved in cruel sports, some strengthening of the Sunday Observance laws, and the number of working-class teetotallers who signed the pledge. Nevertheless they won only battles not the war. Class prejudice cost the R. S. P. C. A. working-class sympathy, for, although its inspectors prosecuted the working man who abused animals, the society refused to condemn the hunting, shooting and fishing of its upper-class patrons.[4] Although the half-guinea subscription must have deterred some potential members, the Lord's Day Observance Society did receive some working-class support, but this faded once it became certain that the Sabbath would be kept free from labour: the bulk of the labouring population was concerned only with clause one of the first commandment![5] Although it had genuine conversions to its credit, basically the teetotal movement was preaching to the already converted and did little to lessen the role of alcohol in working-class life.[6] Indeed in the new industrial cities drink provided an escape from the monotony and regimentation of work and from the squalor of the urban environment. One major change was that alcohol was increasingly taken out of the workplace and drinking began to be concentrated into the evenings and weekends, but here the prime mover was the employer and not the teetotal campaigners.[7]

The association of these reform groups with organised religion possibly weakened their chances of taming the masses, whose ties with the Established Church were certainly nominal only.[8] Methodism, however, proved more attractive to many of the working class, particularly as it began not just to condemn and oppose traditional leisure activities, but to offer something to replace them. Its adherents had always enjoyed revival meetings, hymn-singing and other religious fare, but in mid-Victorian Britain they also participated in seaside trips, processions and parades, bands and choirs, and annual teas. The teetotal movement, too, offered similar activities and, like Methodism, often aimed them at children or the family as a whole.[9] 'Rational recreation' was emerging as a counterattraction to rougher, less respectable activities; previously, reformers had sought to prohibit certain activities and had offered nothing to replace them, save apparently hard work. Such developments also occurred in rural areas, where the gentry, of changed character but still a powerful influence, no longer patronised animal and violent sports but now supported benefit clubs and friendly societies, sponsoring their annual outings, dinners and club days.[10] Other members of the middle class pushed 'rational recreation' of an improving kind in the form of libraries, museums and educational societies. However, these were undermined by charges, which rendered so-called public institutions exceedingly private, by regulations, which deterred the working man, and by overt and offensive patronisation.[11]

Counterattractions of a different kind were offered by publicans, who, like bookmakers and prostitutes, had a vested economic interest in the survival of some traditional working-class recreations. In fact the unrivalled range of functions offered by the public house cemented its place at the centre of the working man's leisure. Progressively publicans had replaced the now civilised gentry as patrons of prizefights, cockfights and the like. Furthermore the pub simultaneously served as a meeting place, a club, a library, a place of entertainment, a shop and a bookmaker's office.[12] Despite their illegality, bookmaking and prostitution continued to flourish under the stimulus of a ready demand, perhaps because betting and sex, like alcohol, met psychological needs as much as economic wants.[13]

Nevertheless, some working men aspired to respectability. The literature stresses the development of an artisan subculture associated with trade unionism and radical politics which emphasised sobriety, order, education, self-respect and self-improvement and hence set its face firmly against the old popular culture.[14] Unionists in Derby, for example, attempted to stop the annual football game.[15] Although such working men were in the minority, the fact that they, perhaps the most articulate and politically conscious of the working class, were not favourably disposed towards the traditional recreational activities must have hindered effective resistance to the challenge being made on them.

Generally, however, refinement did not replace roughness. The new moral standards failed to permeate deep into the working class. As one historian, writing of London but with general applicability, put it: 'the great majority of workers were not Christian, provident, chaste or temperate'.[16] 'Rational recreation' had no appeal to them. What had, as the next chapter suggests, was commercialised leisure, partly of course because, at least initially, it did not necessarily seek to undermine the unholy trinity of sex, alcohol and gambling.

II

Although the railways granted a temporary reprieve to some of the oppressed sports, in particular prizefighting, by allowing participants and spectators to travel to isolated areas away from magisterial interference, in the longer run they revolutionised sport by widening the catchment area for spectators and by enabling participants to compete nationally.[17]

Prior to 1875 cricket and horse-racing in particular benefited. When William Clarke promoted his original All-England XI in 1846, the first team of wandering professional sportsmen, his peripatetic players often had problems reaching their destinations. During the next two decades, however, Clarke's team and its imitators found that railway expansion greatly eased their travel difficulties as they played cricket for profit the length and breadth of England.[18] The railways also made a major contribution to the development of horse-racing by enabling horses to race outside the traditional circuits without undue cost or waste of time. From the mid 1850s they encouraged a structural shift in the organisation of racing, so that, eventually, instead of half a dozen regional circuits in which horses had been walked to meetings, there emerged a national schedule of major meetings and a fluctuating set of lesser events, extremely local in character and seldom having a permanent date in the *Racing Calendar*. A major boost was given to two-year-old racing – the numbers almost quadrupled between 1837 and 1869 – as these immature horses could not have withstood the strain of long-distance walking. The ease of travel also enabled leading jockeys to ride at more meetings, the best officials to act nationwide, and owners to select their training quarters without regard to the proximity of a racecourse. The provision of special race trains also encouraged followers of the turf to attend race meetings other than the ones in their immediate vicinity.[19]

By the 1850s more people could afford such railway excursions. Although there is debate over the course of real wages during the Industrial Revolution, even the most pessimistic of historians accept that they rose after the mid 1840s.[20] There was certainly an improvement in the 1860s, perhaps an increase of 10% in average real wages over the previous decade.[21] But was there still the time for recreational activities? It has been argued that factory work intensified in the 1830s and 1840s and that by that time the factory worker had internalised the time–thrift ethic and accepted long and unremitting hours of labour.[22] Even if this is true – and it may be coloured by an overemphasis on the northern textile industries – the majority of workers nationwide in 1851 were not subject to factory discipline: despite an exodus from the land, agriculture remained the largest single employment sector; outwork survived in several manufacturing industries; and there were still significant numbers of self-employed craftsmen who controlled their own working hours.[23] Over the next two decades, however, there was a narrowing of these two work experiences. On the one hand farmers, fearful of the effects of Corn Law repeal, adopted more capital-intensive methods and became more productivity-conscious; outwork began to degenerate into the long hours of sweated trades; and steam power intruded into the workshops on a subletting basis and necessitated a loss of time independence.[24] On the other hand new work patterns began to emerge in factory industry as the greater application of steam, with its vast potential for raising productivity, allowed work intensity to increase but within the context of shorter hours: workers simultaneously gained reduced hours *and* higher wages.[25]

Employers modified their view that leisure should be reduced to a minimum. They began to realise that long hours were not necessarily productive in themselves as workers could get too tired to perform effectively. There was also an acceptance that leisure, of a suitable kind, might in fact be beneficial for productivity, for leisure time was when the labour force rejuvenated itself, when the supply of human fodder for the industrial system was kept in working order. Initially, reductions in working hours possibly came from philanthropic employers but were taken up by others when the economic benefits were appreciated.[26] Other employers, unenlightened by moral idealism or economic argument, were eventually forced to reduce hours by government legislation.[27] After 1850 trade union pressure, too, at least for skilled and semi-skilled workers, became as important as parliamentary legislation.[28]

Two major developments occurred. One was the granting of an annual week's holiday, though it was unpaid and suited the employer as it gave him time to have boilers scraped and furnaces overhauled.[29] Eventually this led to the seaside holiday replacing the day trip for the working-class excursionist. Of more significance for commercialised sport was the coming of the Saturday half-day. Early finishing on a Saturday was a recognised way of reducing hours from the 1840s, was statutory in textile mills from 1850 and, although not universal, was common in many trades by the late 1860s.[30] For those workers who had shifted from workshop and unmechanised industry into steampowered factories, this actually involved an increase in hours as, in effect, Saint Monday was exchanged for Saturday afternoon.[31] A time period was being created into which commercialised sport could be slotted. Admittedly, factory workers had not been averse to taking a day off to attend local race meetings, but this was no basis on which to develop regular gate-money events.[32]

If there was both money and substantial free time available, why did commercialised sport catering to the working class not emerge in this period? In a way it did. Large crowds at cricket matches, professional athletic challenges, rowing regattas and race meetings have all been documented and, even if such events did not charge entry fees, sports spectatorship could involve spending on several complementary activities, such as travel, betting and refreshments.[33] Higher real earnings meant that more workers could finance such spending more often. Many publicans also opened their own grounds for gambling sports such as footraces, knur and spell, and feats of strength and endurance, though it is not clear whether they charged admission or simply relied on liquor sales.[34] Certainly there does not appear to have been any team sports or large crowds involved.

Entrepreneurs elsewhere in the leisure sector also responded to the rise in working-class spending power. By the 1840s itinerant entertainers were opening up provincial markets for public lectures and magic-lantern entertainment and, on a larger scale, travelling shows and menageries. The public house 'free and easy' was also being transformed via the singing saloon and concert room into an incipient music hall. Then, during the next two decades, railway companies regularised excursion promotion and took it out of the hands of friendly societies and petty entrepreneurs, and the music hall emerged as a highly capitalised enterprise, both in London and in the provinces, with the entertainment itself being the marketed commodity rather than food and liquor.[35]

Nevertheless, circumstances were not totally propitious for the development of large-scale, regularly organised, gate-money sport. Rising incomes, sufficient leisure time, and improved transport had stimulated the emergence of new race meetings – 62 in the 1850s and 99 in the following decade, mostly commercial speculations designed to extract money from the racegoer via the stands, booths or facilities of the town. However, the failure rate among these enterprises could not have been encouraging to anyone considering investment in a gate-money course: of those founded in the 1850s only 20 lasted for at least five years and only

16 for ten years; and of those begun in the 1860s the respective survival figures were 50 and 24.[36] A reason for this could have been that the increase in real wages was either inequitably distributed or that the increase among the lower paid was still insufficient to create much discretionary purchasing power. Support is lent to this argument by the composition of railway excursionists. If the experience of Birmingham trippers is any guide, then, although there had been a widening downwards in their social range on local, cheap trips in the 1850s, most working-class excursionists before the 1870s were artisans.[37]

The establishment of commercialised sport as a feature of popular leisure had to wait until its potential market was both widened and deepened by the rapid rise of real wages in the 1870s and 1880s. By then, partly due to parliamentary legislation in the late 1860s and to trade union pressure in the early 1870s, there had been a lessening of regional and occupational discrepancies in the recognition of Saturday afternoon as time off work and a nationwide time slot had been created in which that market could be tapped.[38]

Chapter 6

The rise of professional
gate-money sport, 1875–1914

I

The standard of living in the years 1875–1914 has not received the attention given by historians to the Industrial Revolution period. There is, however, substantial agreement that real wages generally rose till about the turn of the century but then declined, interrupting a long upward trend which, on the basis of the most quoted estimate, had seen a rise of some 60% from 1870 to the 1890s.[1] The extent of the decline should not be exaggerated as the average real wage between 1900 and 1913 still remained above that for the 1890s as a whole.[2]

Nevertheless some caveats must be made. First, there are problems in the construction of the indices: recorded wage rates may not accurately reflect actual earnings and the budget weightings, especially those for rent, are imperfect.[3] Second, it is clear that there were significant regional variations which are hidden in national figures.[4] Finally, the experiences of different occupations varied according to the levels of cyclical and technological unemployment.[5] Having said this, it must be emphasised that, unlike in the Industrial Revolution debate, there is no controversy that real wages generally increased in the last three decades of the nineteenth century.

Increased spending power made it possible for the working class to purchase more energy. In turn this encouraged two middle-class groups to attempt to persuade workers, or their children, to participate actively in sport. Beginning in the 1860s, and accelerating in the 1870s with the expansion of a national school system, muscular Christians – young ministers and teachers often themselves products of public-school athleticism – sought to evangelise through the medium of sport.[6] Sport gave them a point of contact for conversion, but, more than that, sport was character-forming as it taught self-discipline and team spirit and it offered a counterattraction to gambling, drink and crime. Hence they initiated or helped form football and cricket teams, especially in the urban–industrial areas of the North and the Midlands. In Birmingham in the 1870s and early 1880s almost 21% of cricket clubs and 25% of soccer clubs had religious affiliations and, of the 112 football and 227 cricket teams in Liverpool in 1885, 25 and 36 respectively had such connections.[7] Secondly, some industrial employers and business proprietors saw sport as having a utilitarian function in promoting human capital formation. Thus they sponsored or assisted in the formation of works teams as a means of reducing labour turnover by creating loyalty to the firm and perhaps also to increase productivity by keeping their workers fit.[8] The chronology of this involvement is difficult to determine. Pilkingtons, the glassmakers, was running a cricket team in the 1860s, but most nine-teenth-century works teams appear to be a product of the last two and a half decades.[9]

Nevertheless, despite the vast increase in the supply of energy in the late nineteenth century, brought about particularly through imports of cheap meat and grain, it does not seem that the majority of working men were stimulated to active sports participation.[10] Studies of both Birmingham and Liverpool have outlined the growth in the provision of sports facilities, and of parks and open spaces in which games could be played. They have also shown the development of league and cup competitions in a variety of sports.[11] Yet, despite a total population in 1891 of 518,000, Liverpool had only 224 cricket teams in 1890 and 212 soccer clubs in 1892, and Birmingham possessed only 214 cricket clubs in 1880 despite its population a year later being 401,000.[12] Even allowing for female non-involvement and several teams to a club, the figures still suggest that playing sport, at least at an organised level, was very much a minority activity. Quantitative data at a national level are not easy to find, but Football Association estimates of between 300,000 and 500,000 amateur soccer players in England around 1910, when the total male population aged between 15 and 39 totalled some $7\frac{1}{4}$ million in 1911, is hardly indicative of a substantial commitment to sports participation.[13]

Possibly the muscular Christians, the industrial employers and the local authorities had not anticipated that so many of the working class would not be interested in playing games.[14] However, they did not mind watching others play and, as entrepreneurs were quick to realise, they were even willing to pay for the privilege. Commercialised spectator sport for the mass market became one of the economic success stories of late Victorian Britain. Large crowds at sports fixtures, of course, were nothing new, but, as is shown later in this chapter, now they were being attracted regularly.

II

Changes in economic variables played a major role in this development. Foremost was the substantial increase in working-class spending power. There are, of course, difficulties in generalising about *the* working class: at any time the skilled artisan could probably afford a wider range of recreational activities than the unskilled labourer or factory hand. Indeed, before the 1880s, most of the rise in spending power was attributable to money wages moving ahead of prices and was thus probably restricted to those groups with the strongest bargaining power, but from the 1880s falling prices, especially for food, brought greater prosperity to the working class as a whole.[15] It is not being argued that every working man, let alone his family, could afford to attend sports events; clearly, contemporary social surveys repudiate such a notion.[16] However, many budget studies which show how much is left for recreation and other spending after meeting necessary expenditure are deficient in that they are reluctant to accept that *all* spending is optional. Humans are perverse creatures, often finding greater satisfaction in activities other than meeting basic physiological needs. We will never know how many soccer fans nutritionally could not 'afford' to be at the game.

Increased life expectancy both deepened and widened the potential market for spectator sport. By 1901 the total population of Britain was over 45 million and the death rate had fallen to under 17 per 1,000. The trend towards smaller families may also have increased discretionary spending power.[17] Moreover, between 1871 and 1901 the proportion of the population living in urban areas had increased from 61.6% to 77.0%, mainly in towns of over 20,000 inhabitants. These would have produced concentrated markets for recreational entrepreneurs, though perhaps there was a lessened need for absolute population density because of improvements in transport technology, particularly railways and, to a lesser extent, tramways.[18]

Another important factor was the widespread adoption of Saturday afternoon as a time free from work. Unlike most other goods, sport has a temporal aspect to its demand in that often it is consumed at particular points in time. Thus the time available for the consumption of sport is not just a matter of the volume of free time, but also where those non-working hours are located in the work–leisure calendar. Factory legislation and trade union pressure had established the free Saturday afternoon as a norm in many trades by the 1870s, though unskilled labour in several areas had to wait another decade or so to join their more fortunate brethren.[19] Since electrical technology was not yet capable of illuminating night games effectively and Sunday sport was still taboo, Saturday afternoon provided an ideal time slot for spectator sport.[20]

Entrepreneurs responded to the stimuli. As the economic benefits of industrialisation were passed down to the working class, capitalists saw that money could be made out of man at play as well as man at work. All over the nation, and in a wide variety of sports, grounds were enclosed, stadia erected, and gate-money charged. Sport became an industry in its own right. Heavy investment was made in facilities, and raising the required capital forced many sports clubs to adopt company status with shareholders and limited liability. The covering of overhead and other costs necessitated the holding of events on a regular basis and, to ensure that these could go ahead, advantage was taken of modern technology, in the form of drainage and stand construction, to combat the British climate. To attract larger crowds, the organisation of events was improved, particularly as regards running to time; leagues were introduced to ensure competitive fixtures; and arrangements were made with tram and railway companies to transport spectators to events. Entrepreneurs, club committees, boards of directors and others began to seek the best sportsmen which money could buy, and a willing public, prepared to pay to witness highly skilled entertainers, provided much of the wherewithal to finance this growing professionalism. By 1910 there were over 200 first-class professional cricketers plus several hundred county groundstaff and league professionals; some 400 jockeys and apprentices were seeking rides in horse races; Scottish soccer clubs employed over 1,650 professionals, and south of the Border there were 6,800 registered professionals, many of them part-timers but still earning money from playing sport.[21]

III

The sparsity of quantified data makes it difficult to determine the size of the sports industry.[22] In employment terms, the figures for professionals cited above do not suggest large-scale enterprise, and it can be hazarded that even the addition of those professionals relatively neglected in this study – boxers, athletes, golfers and cyclists – would not alter this view. On the other hand there would be many more – as yet, however, uncounted – workers employed in the servicing of sports consumers, both participants and spectators. Unfortunately census aggregates do not distinguish caddies, greenkeepers, stadium employees, golf course architects, or workers employed by sports equipment manufacturers and retailers.[23]

If output is considered, then there is the question of what should be measured. For participant sports there is at least a tangible product in the form of bicycles, footballs, golf clubs, tennis rackets and fishing rods, though the multiplicity of producers renders it impossible to calculate either the volume or value of production.[24] One estimate is that golfers in Edwardian Britain incurred recurrent expenditure of £4.7m.[25] Another suggests that in the mid 1890s over 1 million cycles were being produced, though many of these were exported and only a proportion would be used for recreational or sporting purposes.[26] William Shillcock, whose firm annually sold 40,000 to 50,000 footballs, claimed that football outfitting was 'a great and profitable industry'.[27] Nevertheless it should be stressed that it was not professional sport which underwrote these markets. It was middle-class participation in golf and tennis which created a market large enough to give commercial viability to factory production.[28] And, in soccer, orders from professional clubs were 'not the backbone of . . . trade' though their patronage influenced others to purchase.[29]

But what of the output of gate-money sport itself? Is the number of matches played or race meetings held a fair indication of output? A better measure, perhaps, is the ability of these games to attract an audience.[30] Some estimates for horse-racing, cricket, soccer and rugby league are provided in succeeding sections of this chapter. However, the data are selective and may not be representative of typical crowds; nor do they allow aggregate attendances for the whole gate-money industry to be calculated.

Then there are the as yet unmeasured economic spin-offs from commercialised sport. Undoubtedly the railways gained as their excursionist traffic rose along with, though not necessarily in proportion to, the growth in sports spectatorship. Like the tram companies, the railways were able to utilise carrying capacity which otherwise, especially on a Saturday afternoon, might have lain idle in the depot. If local-transport historians could be persuaded to add quantification to their bag of tools they could add considerably to our knowledge of the relationship between sport and transport, both inter-urban and intra-urban. The Post Office, too, appears to have benefited from sporting developments, in particular horse-racing, though again complete statistics are lacking. There are, however, some isolated figures for telegraphy and its use at race meetings. On a busy day in the early 1890s, 10,000 messages would be sent to, or arrive at Newmarket and, at the St Leger meeting of 1901, 82 operators despatched 184,000 words of racing news directly from the Doncaster course; no wonder the Post Office created a specialist corps of turf telegraphists.[31] Sport, especially horse-racing and football, also began to feature regularly in the daily and weekly press by the 1880s. Racing tips and football results helped sell papers and in turn the sports received the 'fourth estate benefit' of free publicity.[32] The railways and tram companies, the Post Office and the conventional press, all gained from sport but were not dependent upon it. In contrast the specialist sporting press obviously owed its existence to sport, in particular commercialised sport. Certainly the working man's racing paper was a development of the late nineteenth century, as was the football special, a Saturday evening feature in most towns of any size by the 1890s.[33] Some print-run data exist, but the sporting press remains a very underresearched topic.[34]

IV

Four commercialised sports have been selected for further examination in the ensuing chapters. Two of them, horse-racing and cricket, were traditional sports which had had elements of commercialism associated with them for a long time, but which underwent major organisational change in the late nineteenth century. Soccer, on the other hand, was quite a different game from its folk-football precursor. It changed totally in character and in organisation: the only similarity was the use of a ball. For purposes of analysis, Scottish top-level soccer has been distinguished from the English variety, for, although intrinsically the game was the same, the organisation of the sport north and south of the Border differed in several important respects. Rugby, another hybrid from mob football, dichotomised partly spatially, but essentially between amateur rugby union and professional rugby league. Many of the developments in these particular sports will be detailed later, but the major changes are outlined here to provide a scenario for discussion.

At the beginning of the nineteenth century horse-racing was basically a national sport carried on at local level. Generally meetings were annual affairs intimately associated with local holidays; along with the racing there would be sideshows, itinerant entertainers and other amusements. The degree of commercialisation within racing was relatively low: most spectators did not pay for their pleasure; jockeys generally were little more than liveried servants; and even the best thoroughbred stallion could not obtain a stud fee of more than 50 guineas. By the end of the century racing drew its spectators from far and wide, the carnival atmosphere had been dampened down, and the sport had become much more commercially orientated. Racing companies had enclosed courses and were charging racegoers entry fees; even ordinary jockeys, if these extraordinary individuals can ever be so termed, were earning £1,000 a year;

and a fashionable stallion, able to command 600 guineas a service, could be yielding his owner in excess of £20,000 per annum. Other changes followed in the wake of commercialisation: sprints, handicaps and two-year-old racing began to dominate racecards previously full of long-distance, weight-for-age events; licensed professional officials, working throughout the racing season, generally replaced the amateur starter or handicapper officiating only at his local meeting; and, as already indicated, a racing press developed to throw open the stable doors to the working-class punter. Unfortunately no comprehensive crowd statistics are available for racing, and reliance has to be placed on contemporary comment. This suggests that at the turn of the century race crowds of 10–15,000 were not uncommon; double this could be expected at leading fixtures, and perhaps 70–80,000 at a major public-holiday event.[35] Although the railways undoubtedly played a role in the transformation of racing, the main agent for change was the enclosed racecourse. The pace-setting pioneer was Sandown Park, which held its first meeting in April 1875 as an enclosed course requiring an entry fee from all spectators. Others followed where Sandown had shown the way and within two to three decades racing was taking place at enclosed courses all over Britain. Although Sandown Park had originated as a partnership, it became a limited company in 1885 with an issued share capital of £26,000. Almost all other enclosed courses adopted company status from the beginning, some of them raising substantial sums of capital, such as the £34,000 of Haydock Park and the £80,000 of Newbury, a major development in the early twentieth century.[36] Not all such enterprises succeeded. Portsmouth Park, Hedon Park (Hull) and Four Oaks Park (Birmingham) were conspicuous failures, partly because of an inability to obtain suitable dates.[37] Nevertheless, the majority of the new, enclosed meetings were successful, both from the racing and the financial viewpoint, so much so that many of the older, established fixtures were forced to follow suit and rebuild stands, create enclosures and charge for public admission. Even when they did not enclose to the extent of Sandown and its ilk they offered less free space than before. Primarily this was done to preserve the quality of their racing: they could only hope to attract the best horses by increasing their prizemoney to a level commensurate with that offered by the enclosed meetings, but they could only do this if the funds were available. The best way to ensure that they were was to charge at the gate and this involved some form of enclosure. The choice was simple: either you erected fences or you went to the wall. Most unenclosed meetings either disappeared or struggled along with racing of an inferior character.[38]

That prestige and a good name for racing was insufficient to preserve an open meeting intact is clear from the experience of Newmarket. Here, despite the testing variety of courses and an acknowledged racing reputation, the Jockey Club found that the level and quality of entrants was such as to leave it 'no alternative but to march with the times, to build stands, to make enclosures, to substitute the white rails of modern civilisation for the old-fashioned ropes and stakes of our forefathers'.[39] A few open meetings, however, did far more than merely survive: at Ascot, Epsom, Goodwood, Doncaster and York racing flourished. The charisma of traditional prestige events may have offered some protection, although the prizemoney for the Derby, the blue riband of the turf, had to be raised to a level comparable to the best prizes at the enclosed meetings.[40] Their real protection lay with their position in the social calendar: members and would-be members of high society felt a social obligation to put in an appearance at these meetings. Certificates of social seaworthiness, however, did not come cheaply and the payments of the elite produced ample funds for prizemoney. In 1900 Ascot gave over £37,000 to its 28 races and it was this which was the major attraction for owners.[41] Yet even these important open courses still found 'it necessary from time to time to alter their programmes and keep step in the quick march of the day, lest they too should be fair to take their place in the rear of the companies'.[42]

Gate-money cricket had its origins back in the eighteenth century, but was further stimulated from the 1840s when the peripatetic professional teams took advantage of the railways to tour the country playing local sides, often giving them odds. For two decades or so these touring teams dominated gate-money cricket, but gradually, as new county teams were established and existing ones reorganised, the paying public began to prefer to watch games between teams with which they could identify and where the result was less certain than in the frequently one-sided contests of the wandering elevens. Especial public interest was created by the development of the county championship. The idea of such a competition was first accepted by the counties at a conference called by Surrey in 1873, though for several years it remained a loosely organised tournament, with the final positions often being determined by the sporting press rather than in any formal manner. In fact the championship was not recognised by the M. C. C. until 1894, over two decades after its inauguration. In the meantime, however, it had caught the imagination of the cricket-watching public.

First-class county cricket was at the apex of a cricketing pyramid, the base of which had expanded rapidly from the 1860s under the influence of muscular Christianity and the cult of athleticism. All over England hundreds of clubs were founded, many of them able to attract a substantial proportion of the local population to their matches.[43] Special mention should be made of league cricket, which developed, especially in the 1890s, as a Saturday afternoon spectator sport in the North and Midlands.[44]

Data on county cricket attendances are more readily available than for horse-racing, but there are still deficiencies. One author, working from newspaper estimates, has suggested that county matches drew between 2,000 and 3,000 in the 1840s, 4,000 in the 1860s, perhaps double that in the 1870s and that crowds of 10,000 were not uncommon in the 1880s; attendances then 'kept on rising very steadily . . . until World War One'.[45] These figures, however, are the product of selective reportage and cover only the most popular matches.

More detailed information has been obtained for eight county clubs, but unfortunately pre-1889 data were generally unavailable and there are gaps even in the later period. Nevertheless the information given in Table 6.1a is sufficient to dispel the idea of uninterrupted growth. Table 6.1b points to the quinquennium prior to 1913 as being one of falling paid attendances, but they did not fall significantly below the levels of the early 1890s and, to some extent, the decline might have been offset by higher membership figures. The problem facing the clubs was that as the county championship flourished they had increased their expenditure by employing more professionals and by committing themselves to investment projects in ground facilities, with the result that 'what was formerly considered a good gate is now only fair or moderate'.[46] For too many counties, spending tended to be delicately balanced against income and few of them built up reserves, so that when spectator interest waned they faced financial difficulties. Increasingly, the annual surveys of county cricket in the *Badminton Magazine* and in *Wisden Cricketers' Almanack* revealed deplorable balance sheets, general financial desolation, and lamentations of poverty.

Football changed considerably from its folk version which had been very violent, unorganised, wide-ranging in time and space, and generally held irregularly, save perhaps for being an annual event. By 1914 national authorities were organising the game and setting rules as to its conduct, and matches were being played regularly on defined pitches with a prescribed time limit. Moreover, the earlier game had been essentially for the participants, with whole villages taking part, whereas the new football was, at its highest level, geared towards the paying spectator: only 22 were allowed to play, but there could be thousands watching them.

Table 6.1a *Average attendance at county cricket matches, 1889–1913*

Season	Derbyshire	Essex	Kent	Lancashire	Leicestershire	Surrey	Warwickshire	Yorkshire
1889		1,352		9,948	2,480	9,993		
1890		1,736		12,736	3,353			
1891		1,102		8,728	5,514	8,622		
1892		1,538		12,516	5,433			14,270
1893		4,274		8,840	3,567	9,410		13,780
1894		2,808		18,536	3,646			22,857
1895	3,340	3,760			4,726			12,960
1896	3,084	12,560	7,227		5,823	12,597		15,788
1897	2,496	11,964	9,893		4,526	18,529		20,729
1898	5,014	9,092	11,660		5,525	18,667		21,858
1899	4,568	13,376	7,532		4,436			16,617
1900	3,564	6,742	7,335		3,258			15,586
1901	3,668	9,032	11,218		5,232		5,600	26,411
1902	5,204	6,440	7,862		2,573	11,834	10,050	11,262
1903	3,570		8,782		4,940			21,302
1904	5,404	5,060	11,818					19,760
1905	3,652		10,058			7,335	6,524	12,069
1906	3,944	7,510	13,956			14,726	6,492	17,763
1907	3,004	5,174	12,194			13,131	6,076	14,287
1908	4,200	6,270				10,467	5,262	15,325
1909	2,799	7,004	12,330	9,058			4,792	11,551
1910	3,584	4,178	13,191	6,910			5,464	9,600
1911	3,364	7,906	12,825	7,166			10,392	12,677
1912	1,738	6,088		7,334		6,603	6,509	6,652
1913	4,112	5,316	13,951	6,156		11,535	7,837	11,394

Notes: A common admission fee of 6*d.* was assumed. No account was taken of members attending the games. Derbyshire, Essex, Leicestershire and Warwickshire became first-class counties in 1895.
Source: Calculated from gate-receipt figures in club annual financial statements.

Table 6.1b *Indexes of county cricket attendances, 1889–1913*

Period	Index A (1901 = 1,000)	Index B (1901 = 1,000)
1889–93	640	633
1894–8	908	906
1899–1903	780	809
1904–8	817	798
1909–13	603	616

Notes: Index A is the average attendance of each county weighted by the number of matches played by each county. Index B attempts to fill the gaps in the observations by weighting the annual averages according to the percentage of total attendance in the period 1889–1913 obtained by the club(s) concerned. The figures are then weighted by the number of matches played by each county.
Source: As Table 6.1a.

Although folk football died out, a public-school version emerged. Originally as violent as the plebeian variety, it became less rough and gained some semblance of rules particularly after the middle-class reform of the schools in the 1830s and 1840s. However, the rules varied from school to school, a situation which hindered old boys from different institutions playing together. Attempts to remedy this led to the formation of the Football Association (F. A.) in 1863. A Scottish Football Association (S. F. A.) followed a decade later. By the 1880s all local and district football associations were affiliated to their respective national body and acknowledged its authority.

Initially all matches were friendlies, notwithstanding the spirit in which some of them may have been played, but soon cup competitions were inaugurated to give teams more than just honour to play for. The premier trophy in England, the F. A. Cup, began in 1871 and was followed two seasons later by the Scottish national knockout competition. There was also a plethora of local and regional cup competitions. The progress, or otherwise, of clubs in these tournaments aggravated a situation where 'fixtures had been kept or cancelled pretty much at the caprice of the clubs'.[47] Moreover, the early rounds of cup competitions were often too one-sided to draw the crowds, a situation not to the liking of the professional clubs, to whom 'good gates had become imperative'.[48] Accordingly William McGregor, an Aston Villa committeeman, circularised leading clubs to suggest the formation of what became the Football League, in which teams guaranteed to play each other on a home-and-away basis. Beginning in 1888 with 12 teams, all from the North and the

Midlands, by 1914 it had progressed to two divisions of 20 teams each, with a more diverse geographical coverage.

Again Scotland followed where England had led. In 1887 the S. F. A., feeling that its power could be threatened, had banned Scottish clubs from participation in the English cup. Henceforth there was only one major trophy to compete for at anything more than regional level and it was quite feasible for two leading clubs to meet each other at the very beginning of the competition. The major clubs became increasingly dissatisfied with this situation and, no doubt influenced by the successful inauguration of the Football League, organised a similar league in Scotland from the season 1890/91 on. Of the leading teams only Queen's Park, staunch supporters of amateurism, refused to join as they believed – correctly as it transpired – that the Scottish Football League would pave the way for professionalism.[49] Initially composed of 11 teams, by 1914 the Scottish Football League had expanded to a first division of 20 clubs. A second division had been added in 1893.

For the two decades following the formation of the F. A., soccer was dominated by the old-boy teams, but gradually teams with working-class origins came to prominence, culminating in the victory of Blackburn Olympic over the Old Etonians in the cup final of 1883. Increasingly such teams had been paying their players, illegally at first but with F. A. permission from 1885, and all the initial Football League teams were professional. Yet again Scotland lagged, not following England's lead till 1893.[50] Nevertheless, amateur football continued to expand: indeed working-class amateur clubs were the nurseries from which the most talented were recruited to professional ranks. In aggregate such teams, and their semi-professional brethren, attracted a significant number of spectators but it was the Football League clubs which drew large crowds to individual games.[51]

Early crowd figures are not available on any systematic basis: few statistics have been found in club records and reliance has to be placed on newspaper estimates which themselves are not comprehensive nor always accurate.[52] It has been suggested that the number of large gates, that is those over 10,000, increased in the early 1880s as compared to the late 1870s, but this tells us nothing about typical crowd size, though another source says that in the early to mid 1880s three leading clubs, Aston Villa, Preston North End and Blackburn Rovers, averaged 4–6,000 spectators at home matches.[53] There may have been a temporary stagnation in attendances in the seasons 1886/87 and 1887/88, but then the foundation of the Football League sparked off an upsurge and ground records were broken continually throughout the 1890s.[54] Table 6.2 shows that average

Table 6.2 *Crowd attendances at English first-division League football matches, 1888/89–1913/14*

Season	Number of teams	Aggregate attendance	Average per match[a]
1888/89	12	602,000[b]	4,600
1895/96	16	1,900,000[b]	7,900
1905/06	20	5,000,000[b]	13,200
1908/09	20	6,000,000[c]	15,800
1913/14	20	8,778,000[d]	23,100

Note: [a]Rounded to nearest hundred.
Sources:
[b]H. MacFarlane, 'Football of yesterday and today: a comparison', *Monthly Review*, xxv, 1906, p. 129; [c]A. Mason, *Association Football and English Society, 1863–1915*, Brighton, 1980, p. 168 n. 20; [d]S. Tischler, *Footballers and Businessmen*, New York, 1981, p. 84.

Table 6.3 *Cup final crowds in England and Scotland, 1875–1914*

Period	England Average crowd	Scotland Average receipts (£)
1875–84	4,900	n.a.
1885–94	23,400	792
1895–1904	66,800	871
1905–14	79,300	1,584

Note: Replays have been ignored.
Sources: G. Green, *The History of the Football Association*, London, 1953, p. 592; Annual Reports of the Scottish Football Association.

attendances at first-division matches continued to rise; from 4,600 in the first season of the League to 13,200 in 1905/06 and to 23,100 by 1913/14, by which time 8¾ million spectators were watching the games annually. Cup matches, too, drew larger crowds: in 1888/89 the 31 ties averaged 6,500 as compared to the 19,000 at the 63 matches of the 1905/06 season. First-round games in 1899 averaged 9,800 spectators; by 1913 the average was over 20,600.[55] Cup final attendances, shown in Table 6.3, although perhaps not representative of the game in general, also demonstrate a rising trend. With the crowds came revenue: incomes of a sample of eight clubs in 1913/14 averaged £19,269 and their profits

£5,823.[56] And with profits came spending: Manchester United spent nearly £36,000 on its new stands in 1909, Blackburn Rovers expended £33,000 on its Ewood Park ground in the decade from 1905, and Everton laid out £41,000 at Goodison in the three years to 1909.[57] Not all clubs were successful. Of the 47 whose shareholdings were examined by Mason, 17 had gone out of business by 1914. However, this was less true at the highest levels of soccer: of the 24 clubs which played in the first division of the Football League before 1900 only two, Darwen and Glossop, disappeared from the League altogether.[58]

Crowd figures for Scottish games are not readily available, though it is clear that in the 1870s Glasgow produced the highest attendances in Britain.[59] Cup final receipts, shown in Table 6.3, indicate a rising trend. Isolated figures for Celtic-versus-Rangers matches show that large crowds could be attracted to these Scottish League fixtures: 74,000 at one game at Parkhead in 1912 and 65,000 at Ibrox in 1913.[60] These are scarcely typical Scottish clubs, but ground capacity figures supplied to the Scottish Football Association in application for representative games in 1909, and shown in Table 6.4, suggest that others also had high expectations.[61]

Rugby league was the most regionally concentrated of the sports being examined, restricted as it was essentially to Yorkshire, Lancashire and Cumberland.[62] The catalyst to its development as a separate game from rugby union came with the breakaway of 22 leading northern clubs from the Rugby Football Union (R. F. U.) in 1895 to form the Northern Union (N. U.) which, unlike the national body, would allow broken-time payments to players.[63]

The R. F. U. was founded in 1871 at a time when few working men participated in that sport. By the late 1880s, however, particularly in the north, where many clubs had been founded by businessmen and industrialists, working-class players were having a major impact on the field of play. In the north, too, and perhaps associated with working-class participation, attitudes towards competitions were different. Whereas southern teams rejected the idea of knockout cups, the Yorkshire Challenge Cup was instituted in 1877 followed by Northumberland (1880), Durham (1880) and Cumberland (1882). Lancashire, at this time, stood out. The market signal given by crowds at these cup games – and possibly at Football League matches – encouraged the emergence of leagues in rugby, again only in the north. The Yorkshire senior competition began in 1892 and by the season of 1894/95 it had four divisions, and a similar Lancashire competition had three totalling between them some 81 clubs.

Such cups and leagues, not highly regarded anyway by the R. F. U., led to competition for talented players and claims of professionalism, matters

Table 6.4 *Capacity of Scottish football grounds*

Team	Ground	Stands and enclosure	Total
Queen's Park	105,000	14,588	119,588
Third Lanark	105,000	5,753	110,753
Rangers	47,600	27,000	74,600
Hearts	57,000	3,000	60,000
Partick Thistle	49,000	4,700	53,700
Kilmarnock	26,550	3,950	30,500
Aberdeen	n.a.	n.a.	28,000
Cowdenbeath	13,254	751	14,005

Notes: Celtic did not put in a submission. Third Lanark's ground figure was actually 60,000, with the capacity of a hill to the south estimated at 45,000!
Source: Minutes of Scottish Football Association, 24 November 1909.

even less likely to appeal to the staunchly amateur power brokers on the national body. The split of 1895 was inevitable, though it was not solely on the issue of payments to players. It was also part of the struggle to control the game. Many northern clubs felt that the R. F. U. was unduly influenced by disproportionate southern representation, a feeling aggravated by the absence of any Yorkshireman in the 1894/95 England team. There was also a regional aspect to the power dispute in that the Yorkshire senior clubs objected to the Yorkshire R. F. U.'s attempts to determine the club composition of their competition.[64]

Initially it was the leading northern senior clubs which seceded, but others soon followed in order to preserve their most lucrative fixtures and by 1898/99 98 clubs were affiliated to the Northern Union (to become the Northern Rugby Football League in 1902 and the Rugby League in 1922), with more to come. Expansion was mainly in the northern counties with occasional forays elsewhere. Disputes with the Welsh R. F. U. led to both Ebbw Vale and Merthyr Tydfil joining in 1907/08 and for a brief period – the 1908/09 season only – a Welsh rugby league was formed when Aberdare, Barry, Mid Rhondda and Treherbert participated with the two other clubs. In 1911 Coventry came in, again after a dispute with the national amateur authority.

None of the non-northern teams survived for long, nor did all those in the heartland of the game. The competition of soccer proved too strong for some and others went under when a second division was formed in 1902 which gave many clubs expensive but unremunerative fixtures. Others, however, did prosper. By 1906 Oldham had spent £8,000 on their

Table 6.5 *Rugby league cup final attendances, 1897–1914*

	Challenge Cup	Lancashire Cup	Yorkshire Cup
1897	13,492		
1898	27,941		
1899	15,763		
1900	17,864		
1901	29,563		
1902	15,006		
1903	32,507		
1904	17,041		
1905	19,638		
1906	16,000	16,000 / 10,000	18,500 / 10,500
1907	18,500	14,048	10,500
1908	18,000	14,000	15,000
1909	30,000	20,000	13,000
1910	19,413 / 11,608	14,000	22,000
1911	8,000	14,000	19,000
1912	15,271	20,000	20,000
1913	22,754	6,000	16,000
1914	19,000	18,000	12,000

Source: Rothmans Rugby League 1982–83 Yearbook, Aylesbury, 1982, pp. 127, 150, 157.

ground and had £1,500 invested in loan funds; Hull owed less than £2,500 on their ground improvements of £12,000; and Bradford had facilities worth £25,000 on which their mortgage was only £7,000.[65]

Crowd figures are not available for league matches, although gates of 10,000 are occasionally reported and the president of the Northern Union claimed that 'large' crowds regularly attended ordinary league games and that as much as £710 had been taken at the gate at one of these encounters.[66] Table 6.5 shows that Challenge Cup and County Cup finals attracted significant numbers, though clearly the game was not as popular as soccer.

V

So far, great play has been made of the role of working-class spending in stimulating the development of commercialised sport. Yet, given the nature of the available evidence, to establish that sports crowds were essentially working class is no easy task. It is not sufficient to infer it from the fact that Saturday afternoon matches attracted large crowds and many workers had that time free; or that factory owners and other employers complained of absenteeism on midweek race or match days; or that admission prices were affordable by all except those at the very bottom of the socio-economic scale. There is, of course, considerable contemporary observation: the class-conscious nature of Victorian society encouraged comment on the social composition of crowds, though generally this was only loosely quantified and had an in-built prejudice depending upon how respectable the observer wanted the sport to be. Other data also have deficiencies. The one detailed accident report which has come to light, that for the Ibrox soccer disaster of 1902, is probably class-biased upwards as it occurred at an international rather than at a League game. Bias in the opposite direction can be expected from charge sheets, though this source has not, as yet, been adequately researched. Photographs offer some clues but more knowledge is required as to why they were taken. Accounts which distinguish grandstand from ground receipts could indicate different clienteles but these could be intra-class as much as inter-class. Oral history might help, but has produced little so far.

Despite these problems there is general consensus among historians that the main market for most commercialised sport was the working class, though the degree of their involvement varied. Horse-racing appealed to both high- and low-born, though the enclosed course did attract more members of the middle class than the traditional meetings.[67] Soccer was mainly the prerogative of the upper levels of manual workers and the lower levels of white-collar workers.[68] The county cricket crowd was ranked above that of soccer by William McGregor, despite his anxiety to give his own sport a respectable image.[69] Some support is lent to this view by the fact that only two major cricket grounds, the Oval and Bramall Lane (both also used for soccer matches), were situated in working-class areas,[70] by the long duration of games, and by the complaint that few boys at lads clubs, an institution aimed at working-class youth, had watched first-class cricket but most had seen professional football.[71] It has been suggested that more working men might have been spectators in the north;[72] this might be true, particularly if they had been educated into appreciating the game by watching league cricket. At this stage of knowledge, it can only be speculated that, given its origins, rugby league support was solidly working class.

VI

Sport was only one of several commercialised leisure activities which emerged in the nineteenth century as entrepreneurs discovered that one man's pleasure, at least when aggregated with that of like-minded individuals, could become another man's profit. The popular press was one such development.[73] Another was the music hall, which by the 1890s had generally abandoned its public-house-writ-large image and had instead adopted a conventional theatre-style format and increasingly belonged to a commercial combine.[74] Yet another was the seaside holiday: by the late nineteenth century working-class excursionists and holidaymakers flocked by the million to coastal resorts where their demands created an entertainment industry which included music halls, bands, public houses, beach entertainers, fairgrounds and amusement arcades.[75]

More work needs to be done to establish the respective chronologies of the different forms of commercialised leisure, but it may be that entrepreneurs purveying such products were able to take advantage of a favourable market situation in the 1860s and 1870s when artisans (and perhaps even the semi-skilled) found that their extra spending power had not drawn a sufficient response from the suppliers of consumer goods. A significant extension of the mass market for such goods was delayed until improvements on the supply side in the 1880s brought cheap foreign foods, processed foods, mass-produced footwear and clothing, and a general revolution in the retail and distributive trades.[76] This left an entrée for brewers, who developed the idea of widespread marketing through tied retail outlets and pushed per capita alcohol consumption to a nineteenth-century peak in the 1870s;[77] for newspaper publishers, who began to cater for artisans;[78] for railway companies, who changed their marketing strategies and created an increased demand for their excursions;[79] and for incipient music-hall proprietors.[80] This rise in the consumption of alcohol, public-house and other musical entertainment, railway excursions and cheaper newspapers may have provided a market signal to other leisure entrepreneurs, including those in the embryo sports industry.

Further research is also required on the regional variations in the development of commercialised leisure. London had long provided a mass market and it was there that the music hall first developed. Moreover, the first successful attempts to organise race meetings specifically to make money out of the crowd came in London in the 1860s. Organised by local publicans and bookmakers as a means of selling beer and taking bets, these meetings, on the fringe of the metropolis but beyond the pale of respectability, were eventually put down by parliamentary legislation in 1879.[81] In the meantime Sandown Park, only 13 miles from Hyde Park Corner, had established its enclosed course which, along with Hurst Park, Gatwick and Lingfield, respectively only 15, 26 and 28 miles by rail, catered for the London-based racegoers. Newbury, founded in 1906 by the famous, but then retired trainer, John Porter, also drew on London for the bulk of its spectators.[82] The metropolitan populace appear to have preferred days out to holidays away from home and this might explain why Surrey was the location of four of the five top enclosed meetings as well as the incomparable Epsom gathering.[83] In cricket, both Surrey and Middlesex, and later the London County Club with W. G. Grace at the helm, were also able to take advantage of the size of the metropolitan market.

Nevertheless, it can be argued that, in many respects, Lancashire was to the fore in the emergence of commercialised leisure. It was there that the first holiday industry developed.[84] And there that professional soccer was pioneered: indeed, when the Football League began in 1888, six of the twelve teams hailed from the red-rose county. In rugby the Lancashire senior clubs accompanied their Yorkshire counterparts into the Northern Union. County cricket was played at Old Trafford and Saturday afternoon gate-money cricket was featured in the various Lancashire leagues. The north-western county also had its enclosed racecourses, at Haydock Park and Manchester.

Although more local and regional studies will throw greater light on the reasons for the relative rate of development of commercialised leisure, it is already clear that the losers in the recreational stakes were the rural inhabitants of Britain. Their traditional sports had been undermined; generally their hours of labour were longer and their wages lower than their urban counterparts; and they were too far away from the centres of the new commercialised leisure.[85]

VII

By the late nineteenth century many traditional working-class recreations had virtually disappeared. Some, such as brutal animal sports, had fallen victim to middle-class opposition and more effective policing; others, such as the old-style Lancashire wakes, had been forced to transform because of the competition of the new commercialised leisure activities. Nevertheless, the traditional trio of alcohol, sex and gambling continued to flourish, partly by adapting themselves to changed circumstances.

Although per capita alcohol consumption declined, alcoholic beverages remained the major item of working-class recreational expenditure, so much so that in 1905 10 of the 26 largest British companies were involved in brewing.[86] In fact the struggle between these combines helped keep the public house the most popular place for a Saturday evening's entertainment.[87] Some of their products also went to the working men's clubs, most of which abandoned all pretence of improving the minds of their members and concentrated instead on providing them with cheap drink.[88] Despite its illegality, street bookmaking expanded significantly in the final quarter of the nineteenth century, taking advantage of, and encouraging, the sporting-press practice of publishing starting prices.[89] The emergence of organised professional soccer provided a new vehicle for gambling in the form of the football pools: competitions in which results had to be predicted became a feature of the sporting press in the 1890s, but it was the fixed-odds coupons of the bookmakers which soon came to dominate.[90] Like illegal bookmaking, prostitution, too, was part of the black economy and, though the evidence is unclear, there is no reason to suspect any diminution in working-class brothel-keeping.[91] Sexual licence was also often associated with working-class excursions and seaside holidays.[92]

Indeed, it can be suggested that one reason for the working-class acceptance of commercialised leisure was that it was not offered as a counterattraction to the established triumvirate but was generally prepared to accommodate, or at least tolerate, these traditional activities. Immorality and intemperance were part and parcel of the working-class holiday and also featured at the music hall, if not always in actuality then certainly by innuendo in song and sketch. Drinking also seems to have been an accepted part of sports spectatorship. Racing had long relied upon the rents from beer tents to contribute to the racefund, and, even though this was less necessary once the spectators began to pay at the gate, those same spectators still wished to celebrate with their winnings or forget their losses. Drinks were also served at cricket and football matches but the extent of the consumption is not known. Leicestershire claimed that it was 'impossible to carry on a cricket ground without an hotel' and most counties appear to have held liquor licences.[93] The founder of the Football League argued that 'there is relatively little drinking done at football matches', but he had a vested interest in creating a respectable image for soccer.[94] Similar caution has to be taken with Joseph Ansell's remark that 'it is rare, indeed, for any individual to see a person the worse for drink at a big match'. As both a brewer and chairman of Aston Villa he was unlikely to be an impartial witness.[95] It was claimed that soccer matches helped lessen Saturday afternoon drinking, but the fortunes of a team could well influence the evening's consumption; and what about the alternate Saturday when the team might be playing at the other end of the country?[96] By their nature, sports also encourage gambling. Racing, of course, had a symbiotic relationship with betting and could not afford to do without it. Indeed the executives of the enclosed course filled their racecards with two-year-old, handicap and sprint races geared especially to the gambler.[97] Betting at soccer matches was also commonplace. As the law stood in the late nineteenth century, gambling appeared to be legal at all sports events at which gate-money had been charged. New interpretations of the law in the 1890s, however, made it difficult for bookmakers to operate inside sports grounds (except racing enclosures), but betting on the football terraces seems to have continued.[98] In effect the new commercialised leisure and the traditional recreations were often presented to the consumer as a package, sometimes one planned by the entrepreneurs, on other occasions one created by the consumers themselves.

That alcohol, sex and gambling were associated with the new commercialised leisure naturally enough stimulated, yet again, middle-class attempts to control working-class leisure.[99] The lower classes simply could not be trusted to enjoy themselves without risk to social order or property. There were no objections to the working-class seaside holiday as such. The perceived problem was what the working class did on those holidays. Drinking, nude bathing and promiscuous behaviour under the pier were bad enough, but worse still they did it on a Sunday. Such activities were not only considered degenerating for the working class themselves, but they also spoiled the resort for its residents and their traditionally middle-class clientele. The music hall was castigated on several counts. Songs which defied religion, the state and the established social order were thought likely to aggravate political and social tensions. More narrowly, the halls were seen as catering to the debased tastes of the masses in their vulgarity, in having drink readily available, and in being associated with prostitution. Working-class gambling was also seen as a major problem which needed to be rectified urgently before both family life and the British economy were destroyed. Not surprisingly, commercialised sport was also subjected to attack. There were complaints about the evils of drinking and betting associated with the events, protests over the undermining of the amateur ethos by professionalism, and, perhaps inevitably, dissatisfaction with crowd behaviour.

The reformers achieved some success. By-laws against obstruction had been used to counter street bookmakers but had proved unsatisfactory because of the brief nature of betting transactions. In 1906, however, betting in the street was made illegal nationwide by Act of Parliament. Local authorities also took action. Resorts which desired to maintain their social tone passed, and enforced, by-laws against nude bathing and Sunday non-observance and brought in a system of licences for various entertainments. By-laws, fire regulations and liquor licence requirements were utilised as a threat to keep music halls in line. Counterattractions which tried to reproduce the appeal of the halls purged of their vulgarity and intemperance, however, failed because of their too-obvious patronisation and, perhaps of more importance, because they could not afford to employ star performers as they had no drink sales to inflate their wages fund.

Yet the movement for reform was not just from external pressure groups. In some sections of the leisure industry, the recreational entrepreneurs themselves adopted changes which made their products more respectable and brought economic benefits. Large-scale music-hall proprietors feared that rowdiness could damage their considerable investment in theatre facilities. Hence control agents in the shape of uniformed commissionaires forbade entry to the less respectable, discouraged undue audience participation, and restricted alcohol to the anterooms outside the auditorium. Such internal stimulus to reform was generally the situation in commercialised sport and, as shown later, improvements when they came, stemmed from within the sports, at club or association level, rather than being imposed from outside.[100]

Chapter 7

From sports spectator to sports consumer

In the course of two centuries or so the British economy had been transformed and with it the nature of popular sport. In the pre-industrialised economy working hours were determined primarily by the agrarian calendar, but, although this meant that there was ample time for recreation, energy scarcity rendered participant sport both an irregular and a minority activity. For the majority, sport was something to watch rather than to play, but their poverty prevented them from being paying spectators. Then, although agricultural improvements increased the supply of energy, most of this was expended initially on the extra work effort demanded by the agrarian, and especially the industrial, revolutions. New work patterns also reduced the amount of discretionary free time available to the working class. Additionally, employers sought to discredit traditional sports as being adverse to productivity; and both urbanisation and enclosure reduced the space available for playing games. Nevertheless, traditional sports persisted into the nineteenth century mainly because neither urbanisation nor structural change within the economy had reached levels at which they could not be accommodated. By the mid nineteenth century, rising incomes and improvements in transport technology were laying the foundations for future developments, and in later decades substantial gains in working-class spending power, growing urbanisation, and the concentration of free time into Saturday afternoons, encouraged entrepreneurs to market gate-money sport on a regular basis. Indeed, although further increased supplies of energy facilitated greater sports participation, mass spectator sport became a growth point in the late Victorian economy.

Large crowds at sports events were nothing new but large paying crowds on a regular basis were. Sport, of course, had long been associated with commercialisation, though with related activities such as drinking and gambling rather than the sport itself. By the late nineteenth century, however, sports promoters had taken commercialisation beyond the beer tents and gaming booths. By enclosing grounds they made popular recreation less public than before and forced the sports spectators to pay for their pleasure. The sports entrepreneurs were not alone, and between them, the music hall, the sporting press, and Saturday afternoon sport, provided almost a joint product, one to be consumed along with the traditional ancillary activities of drinking and gambling. In many cases the creation of paying sports consumers resulted in their demands becoming paramount over the inclinations of the actual participants, and the character of several sports was changed simply to attract more spectators through the turnstiles. Apparently market capitalism had taken over from the petty entrepreneur and the noble patron: the consumer was king. Yet, as is detailed in the following chapters, the economics of the sports industry were not so straightforward as this might suggest.

Part III

Sport in the market place: the economics of professional sport

[Are we] to expect daily quotations such as 'Fry rose to a premium in consequence of his fine century; the option of Jackson as a bowler was successful, seeing he took five wickets yesterday; the slump in Hampshires was very severe and not checked by the rumour of the return of Major Poore in August; Ranji's simmered, as he may not appear on Monday; but Spooners were popular, and there was a fair demand for Bosanquets?'

Home Gordon, 'Cricket problems of today', *Badminton Magazine*,
XIX, 1904, p. 197

As an old cricketer, I am entirely out of sympathy with the way in which county cricket is now played, and it has become so entirely a money-making business concern that the true interest of cricket as a sport and a game is fast disappearing.

Mr C. E. Green to Essex C. C. C., 3 December 1912

If professional football is a well-conducted business, it is not a game. If its object is pecuniary, it is not sport.

An Old Player, 'Football: the game and the business', *World Today*,
I, 1902, p. 79

Chapter 8

Profits or premierships?

I

In the period 1875–1914 several major British sports became highly commercialised. This was acknowledged by contemporary observers. As early as 1885 horse-racing was seen as 'becoming, everyday, more of a business than a sport' and, less than a decade later, 'Scottish football [could not] be described as anything else than a big business'.[1] Its counterpart south of the Border was thought by one critic to be 'as sordid a concern of commerce as Pears' soap, or the electric light', and William McGregor, the founder of the Football League, acknowledged that early twentieth-century soccer was 'a big business. The turnover of some of our clubs is considerably larger than the turnover of many an important trading concern.'[2] Even cricket, considered by the run-making intellectual, C. B. Fry, to be 'a cult and a philosophy inexplicable to . . . the merchant minded', had 'become more or less a gatemoney business'.[3]

The question, however, is what sort of businesses had the firms in the sports industry become, or, more precisely, what were their ultimate objectives. There is a major debate among economists of modern sport on this issue. Almost without exception studies of North American sports clubs have argued that they were either profit- or wealth-maximisers, but in Britain many clubs, particularly in football and cricket, have exhibited long-term operating losses, which suggests that either they were highly inefficient profit-maximisers or that some other goal had priority over profits.[4] Utility-maximisation has been suggested as such a target in that, subject to financial viability or a minimum security constraint, clubs sought to win as many matches and championships as they could.[5]

It is commonly accepted by sports economists that consistent winning does not maximise profits, and that attendances will be higher where the outcome of an event is uncertain than where the result is predictable.[6] With given costs – and fixed costs are usually dominant in sports enterprises[7] – the maximisation of profits entails the maximisation of attendances and, although winning teams generally attract more spectators than losing ones, they will not, it is claimed, maximise their crowds if they win too frequently. The less masochistic supporters of the other teams will not turn out to watch certain defeat and even 'champ-followers'[8] might tire of one-sided contests. Thus, even if winning and profits are positively related in the short run, revenue eventually declines with increasing success. Consistent winning, that is successful utility-maximisation, is, for any individual club, said to be a second-best, long-run profit policy. Aggregate league attendances will also be affected by the sustained success of any one club, for, although this keeps open the prospect of victory for that club in a prolonged competition, it simultaneously reduces such a possibility for other teams and may dissuade their fans from attending.[9] Yet a viable league requires returns to the participant clubs sufficient to sustain most of them in their long-run operations: the league must survive so that a product can be marketed. Hence it is argued that club self-interest will be best served by aiming for equality of playing competition between teams so that the results of both individual matches and league championships are unpredictable.

This section of the book is intended to lend a historical perspective to the debate by discussing the profit/utility issue in the context of late nineteenth- and early twentieth-century soccer, cricket, rugby league and, to provide a comparison with the team sports, also horse-racing.

II

After surveying the literature, one economist has maintained that 'it is not clear that we are capable in principle of empirically distinguishing utility and profit maximising behaviour'.[10] One problem is the perceived motivation of spectators. Are they predominantly the economic theorists' disinterested observers or are they generally less dispassionate, partisan supporters committed to seeing their team win? In the former case the creation of a winning team should take second place to maintaining equality of competition (i.e. uncertain results) and other profit-seeking devices, though the issue is complicated by the possibility of the utility-maximiser attempting to maximise the wages fund, which can then be used to improve team quality. In the latter case winning could be considered to be both a utility- and a profit-maximising policy, depending upon the feasibility of spectators accompanying the visiting team and whether or not home and away gates were pooled.[11] There would, of course, be some hardcore fans who would attend home games come what may, but generally the scent of victory would increase the attendance from local supporters.

Nevertheless, it can be suggested that in either case certain distinguishing features can be isolated. First, there is surely a limit to entrepreneurial time and energy, and priorities as to their use have to be established. Hence it can be argued that utility-maximisers will devote more of such resources to producing a winning team than to participating in other revenue-raising activities, with the exception perhaps of donation drives designed to keep the club afloat *after* poor financial results had threatened its survival. Second, profit-maximisers will be more cost-conscious, appreciating that profits are a function of both revenue *and* expenditure. Thus they will be less willing than the utility-maximisers to pay star players their economic rents and more willing to impose restrictions on labour mobility and earnings as a means of holding costs down. Utility-maximisers, on the other hand, might be willing to play uneconomic fixtures designed to improve their win–loss record rather than the balance sheet. Third, whereas utility-maximisers might be willing to run at a loss and rely on donations from supporters for financial viability, profit-maximisers are unlikely to accept lower-than-market returns for more than a limited period of time. Finally there is the matter of profit disposal. Utility-maximisers would tend to use them to increase the wages fund with which they pay or purchase players and be more willing than profit-maximisers to donate a proportion to charity. The latter would distribute the bulk of profits to shareholders or use them to buy grounds and construct facilities there, both of which, unlike player purchase, increase the capital assets of a club and the market value of its shares.

More specifically with regard to player payments, it has been hypothesised that an ideal-type utility-maximiser would develop a tripartite wage structure in order to maximise the playing efficiency of the team.[12] First, players will receive a guaranteed income over a period of possibly three to five years and this income will vary with the perceived skill of the player.[13] Second, the team will be paid by results and receive additional income in the form of uniform – to emphasise the team effort – bonuses for winning matches. Finally, individual players will obtain bonuses for their part in the team's performance, though these will be paid at the end of the season when their relative contribution is more clearly assessed. Those profit-maximisers who see winning as a way of making money might adopt a similar strategy, but not wholeheartedly, as long-term contracts could commit them to unnecessary expenditure. Generally they might also be expected to sell players as a form of revenue production whereas utility-maximisers are more likely to be net purchasers. Utility-maximisers might also be prepared to devote a higher proportion of their financial resources to their wages fund and have less restriction on the size of wages and bonuses paid.

III

As shown in chapter 6, English and Scottish soccer differed in their adoption of the twin spearheads of commercialised sport, a league system and professionalism. They also appear to have differed in their position on the profit/utility spectrum.

No matter what their disgruntled supporters might occasionally have thought, teams played to win: really they had no option as the football authorities would not tolerate anything else. Yet was winning the sole aim of the clubs or did profits and revenue enter into their calculations? Early club advertisements in the *Scottish Football Annual* were concerned with recruiting playing members, but such advertising had ceased by 1885 and possibly around that time gate-money took on greater significance. Aston Villa's committee rejected company formation in 1889 on the grounds that the club should not be conducted as a source of profit to the members, but by 1904/05 it was reporting a profit of over £1,875 to its shareholders.[14]

Experience taught the clubs that winning was more lucrative than losing. As Plymouth reported in 1913: 'in conjunction with the successful playing record the match receipts naturally have increased considerably'.[15] Unfortunately few of the available accounts separate league receipts from cup revenues and only one data set has been traced which covers years with sufficient change in a club's league position for a reasonable comparison to be made.[16] In the three seasons beginning 1906/07 Heart of Midlothian finished ninth, eleventh and twelfth in the Scottish Football League and its share of gate-receipts averaged £127 per game, whereas in 1912/13 and 1913/14, when third place was obtained, the average was £210.[17] Attendance data for English first-division teams showed a rank order correlation with League positions of 0.749 in 1905/06, 0.254 in 1911/12, 0.516 in 1912/13 but only 0.002 in 1913/14, which is inconclusive, though correlations of 0.375, 0.473, 0.391 and 0.367 were obtained when these attendances were compared with average League positions over the preceding five years.[18] What was undoubtedly true was that a good cup run could be very rewarding. Victory in a cup tie guaranteed a further match and spectators appear to have been especially interested in such sudden-death games.[19] Indeed, the Scottish Football

Association was led to comment on 'the number of clubs who have been lifted from poverty to affluence during the past few years through the agency of the Scottish ties', which 'provided more than ever, the most remunerative fixtures in Scotland'.[20] In 1906/07 Hearts obtained £3,750 from 34 League games but £3,669 from only 5 S. F. A. cup matches, including the final.[21] South of the Border, second-division Barnsley gained over £7,000 in its cup-winning year of 1911/12.[22] What is also clear is that there was a quality aspect to attendances and the first divisions of the Leagues attracted larger crowds than second-division and non-League matches.[23]

Clubs felt that it was important to attract spectators. Hence the use of bill-posting and newspaper advertisements to inform the public of the next match to be played: on one occasion Sheffield Wednesday even threatened to supplement what they believed was inadequate advertising and charge their opponents for it.[24] Virtually every prospectus of the clubs also emphasised the availability of railway, and, especially, tramway facilities, and special arrangements were often made with the transport companies regarding fares and travel schedules. Moreover, matches were generally played on a Saturday afternoon so as to maximise the potential market. Sheffield Wednesday, for one, preferred Saturdays: when a cup commitment prevented their opponents from fulfilling a Saturday League fixture at Owlerton, the Sheffield club only accepted Monday as a substitute on the condition that the gates of that match and the reverse Saturday League fixture were pooled.[25] The provision of stands helped make winter viewing more pleasant, but it was also a way of increasing revenue as, even in Scotland where gates were partially pooled, the home team retained the extra fees charged to enter the stands. East Stirlingshire certainly felt that the absence of a stand had a detrimental effect on their revenue and Birmingham claimed that the erection of a new stand could raise their income by £3,000 a year, though this included revenue from the extra ground capacity which would be created.[26]

Interestingly, the differential charge for covered accommodation was the only form of price competition at League games. Prior to the formation of the major leagues, clubs varied admission prices according to the quality of the opposition and occasionally in the light of local economic circumstances.[27] However, both the Football League and the Scottish Football League set a *minimum* entry fee of 6d. for adult males (half price for boys) and no club appears to have gone above this amount as a ground entry charge.[28] Even the Aston Villa versus Liverpool championship decider in 1899, for which the grandstand fee was raised, saw no test of the elasticity of demand at the ground entry gate.[29] Cup ties were different, probably because of revenue-pooling arrangements, but for League matches the situation was that extra was paid only for extra facilities, such as Manchester United's new stand, in which different viewing positions could be had for 1s., 1s. 6d. or 2s. and a reserved seat in the centre for the not inconsiderable sum of 5s.[30] There was indirect price competition in that promotional activities, such as bands before the game and at half-time, reduced the real cost of admission, but these probably influenced only the marginal spectator. There was, however, one major difference between the pricing policies of English and Scottish clubs, in that the former charged women half-price but the latter gave them free entry.[31] It can thus be suggested that the lack of price competition undermined profit-maximisation as a possible objective, though more so in Scotland because of the free entry for females.

All the clubs which adopted limited liability took powers to use their stadia for non-football activities; in practice these were mainly athletics and cycling meetings. Those clubs with superior facilities could also hire their grounds for representative and neutral-ground football fixtures. As Table 8.1 shows, both Rangers and Celtic supplemented their income extensively in such ways, but they may have been special cases as the average for the other Scottish clubs traced was only 1.2% of their income.[32] This contrasts with the English League clubs' average of 3.3%.

Support is lent to the case of Scottish soccer being more inclined towards utility-maximisation by the fact that many clubs played far more matches than they needed to, not only entering a number of competitions in addition to the Scottish Cup and League, but also arranging friendlies when they had no competitive fixture scheduled on Saturdays. This could be interpreted as profit-maximising behaviour in the sense of trying to distribute fixed costs over more output, but costs were fixed to a much lesser extent over the season than at individual games. Players might have to be paid for extra matches, and more ground maintenance would certainly be required. Of course, so long as marginal revenue exceeded marginal costs, playing extra games could still be profit-maximising. There are, however, grounds for suggesting that receipts would not be large at games that were not League or Scottish Cup games. First, spectators were not that interested in friendly matches. Prior to the formation of the Scottish Football League when most games were friendlies, the S. F. A. commented that 'on the majority of their matches clubs actually lose money – the profit coming from the few-and-far-between big gate'.[33] Dumbarton, for one, attributed its new-found prosperity to 'the succession of good matches secured through the Club's association with the Scottish League'.[34] Admittedly, both Rangers and

Table 8.1 *Sources of income of English and Scottish football clubs before 1914 (annual average)*

Club	Number of observations[a]	Gate entry		Stands		Season tickets		Transfers		Other		Total
		£	%	£	%	£	%	£	%	£	%	£
Derby	5	6,362	80.5			696	8.8	649	8.2	195	2.5	7,902
Manchester City	3	6,686	90.2			522	7.0	137	1.9	70	0.9	7,415
Plymouth	3	5,718	88.3			132	2.0	425	6.6	198	3.1	6,473
Preston North End	6	5,403	55.0	2,775	28.2	526	5.4	809	8.2	317	3.2	9,830
Queen's Park Rangers	1	6,825	89.8			93	1.2	550	7.2	137	1.8	7,605
Tottenham Hotspur	7	15,595	87.8			540	3.0	638	3.6	983	5.5	17,756
West Bromwich Albion	1	5,175	78.6			800	12.2	325	4.9	285	4.3	6,585
Celtic	3[b]	3,255	69.3			219	4.7	62	1.3	1,162	24.7	4,698
Clyde	1[b]	1,016	86.8			95	8.1	60	5.1	—		1,171
East Stirlingshire	1	646	71.9			34	3.8	195	21.7	24	2.7	899
Hamilton	1	1,829	93.4			112	5.7	—		18	0.9	1,959
Hearts	5	5,370	73.0	644	8.7	369	5.0	828	11.2	150	2.0	7,361
Hibernian	3[b]	4,412	89.7			125	2.5	329	6.7	55	1.1	4,921
Rangers	3[b]	5,935	86.4			323	4.7	—		611	8.9	6,869
	3[b]	13,024	92.0[c]					34	0.2	1,106	7.8	14,164
St Johnstone	2	569	70.0	80.0	9.8	110	13.4	28	3.4	31	3.8	818
St Mirren	1[b]	4,357	83.1			400	7.6	400	7.6	88	1.7	5,245
Third Lanark	5[b]	2,976	93.1			151	4.7	27	0.8	42	1.3	3,196

[a] Except where indicated the observations are post-1906/07. [b] Pre-1900/01. [c] Gate entry, stands and season tickets.

Sources: Annual Financial Statements of Clubs; *Scottish Sport, passim.*

Celtic did well financially out of 'friendlies' with leading English clubs, but no doubt nationalistic fervour gave these games a competitive edge.[35] There is some later evidence in Hamilton Academical's complaint of 'unprofitable' friendly matches in 1907/08 and in Hearts' profit-and-loss account for 1912/13, which shows a total revenue of only £8 5s. 7d. from friendly matches. Secondly, most other cup games would be of a lower standard than either Scottish Cup or League matches because non-League clubs would often be involved. Finally, many of these games were played on midweek afternoons, and time-off during the week was not the privilege of most supporters. On the basis of matches reported in their annual financial statements, English League clubs do not appear to have pursued additional fixtures as avidly as the Scots, possibly because their League programme was much fuller. In 1899/1900, for example, the Scottish first-division teams played 18 League games whereas the English turned out 34 times. However, this gap then narrowed till by 1913/14 the Leagues were of equal size.

The labour market policies of English and Scottish clubs are inconclusive as regards determining whether or not they were profit- or utility-maximisers. In many respects the English and Scottish clubs adopted similar wage policies. On both sides of the Border income tended to be guaranteed for a season at a time, including summer wages for the better players; wage discrimination was practised within teams; and, although no individual seasonal bonuses have come to light, after five years' service players could be awarded a benefit. However, win-and-draw team incentive bonuses were banned in England from 1901, though after 1910 limited end-of-season payments were allowed for cup matches and for finishing in the top five in the League.[36] The strongest evidence that the two nations were pursuing different objectives was that the English clubs adopted a maximum wage, at least overtly, whereas Scotland allowed the free market to operate. Nevertheless, as shown in Table 8.2, the average Scottish wage bill as a proportion of total expenditure was, at 56.4%, the same as English non-League clubs and only slightly above the English League figure of 53.2%. Moreover, when transfer payments are taken into consideration English clubs were devoting a higher proportion of their spending to players. Indeed, although the available material is extremely limited, the data suggest that English League clubs were net spenders and Scottish clubs were net recipients in the transfer market. However, within the English League several of the poorer clubs only kept themselves afloat by recruiting, training and then selling players.[37] It could be suggested that the religious prejudices of Rangers and Celtic, which prevented them signing the best players available, weakened their

Table 8.2 *Wages and transfer payments as a proportion of expenditure of English and Scottish football clubs before 1914 (annual average)*

Club	Observations[a]	Wages £	Wages %	Transfers £	Transfers %
Derby	5	3,870	51.6	1,020	13.6
Manchester City	3	3,736	48.6	803	10.4
Plymouth	3	3,379	55.4	361	5.9
Preston North End	6	4,739	61.9	824	10.8
Queen's Park Rangers	1	4,138	56.1	528	7.2
Southampton	4	3,098	57.3	393	7.3
Tottenham Hotspur	7	5,240	38.0	3,413	24.7
West Bromwich Albion	1	4,995	66.1	180	2.4
Celtic	2[b]	2,906	51.5	—	—
Clyde	1[b]	795	69.2	—	—
East Stirlingshire	1	402	43.1	—	—
Falkirk	1	2,275	64.1	—	—
Hearts	5	3,731	56.8	496	7.5
Hibernian	3	2,982	68.2	—	—
Rangers	3[b]	2,674	54.6	—	—
	1	5,413	66.3	—	—
St Johnstone	2	411	45.3	93	9.7
St Mirren	1	2,750	52.0	789	15.0
Third Lanark	3[b]	1,360	50.7	—	—

[a]Except where indicated the observations are post-1906/07.
[b]Pre-1900/01.
Sources: Annual Financial Statements of Clubs; *Scottish Sport, passim.*

attempts to maximise utility, but such policies were not hardline before 1914 and, in any case, their sectarian position meant that they were respectively able to attract the best Protestant and Catholic players.[38]

There is fragmentary evidence that some English clubs were profit-oriented, but, without confirmation of the typicality of their behaviour, caution must be exercised in drawing conclusions for the League as a whole. Certainly Arsenal was atypical in moving from Woolwich to Highbury to secure greater support in more populous central London, though many other clubs changed grounds within their locality so as to avoid exorbitant rises in rent and/or to increase spectator capacity.[39] Sheffield Wednesday was another club which adopted profit-maximising attitudes – in charging for practice matches, in refusing shareholders free entry to the stands, and in charging interest on delayed transfer payments.[40] Several smaller English clubs also appear to have been willing to sacrifice their home advantage and switch cup ties to the larger-capacity grounds of their opponents.[41]

Whether or not cups and championships were put before profits, in practice, if the limited data in Table 8.3 are any guide, several clubs, particularly, though not exclusively, in the highest divisions, made profits large enough to justify substantial dividends. In England the Football Association formally imposed a 5% maximum dividend in 1896; in the period 1907/08 to 1913/14 this amount was paid regularly by five, and intermittently by three, of the League clubs whose financial statements were examined in this study.[42] Additionally, many clubs gave a free season ticket to those shareholders who invested at least £10; this could virtually double their dividend, thus making it extremely competitive with the returns on government bonds.[43] In Scotland there was no legislated restriction on dividends, yet relatively few shareholders appear to have received any direct returns. Of the ten teams whose financial statements could be traced, apart from Celtic, only Falkirk (10% in 1907/08 and 1912/13) and St Mirren (5% in 1909/10) paid dividends. Celtic was a major exception as it paid 20% in its first year followed by seven successive years of 10%, then a 12% and a 25% – not bad for a club founded specifically to raise money for a Catholic charity.[44]

Clearly, however, on neither side of the Border was the bulk of the money made by the clubs distributed to shareholders. Where, then, did it go? Some went to charity. The S. F. A. claimed that 'many institutions depend so largely on football for a helping hand' and the president of the Football League opined that 'no sport subscribes more to charity than does football'.[45] Yet most of this money came either from pre-season practice and friendly matches, the proceedings from which the national associations refused to let the clubs retain, or from special competitions organised to assist various charities. Relatively little money went to charity directly from the club accounts, on average much less than 1% of net profits. Some profits went into reserves to cushion the impact of poor financial seasons and possibly to have money on hand for ventures into the transfer market.[46]

Most profits, however, were used to finance ground improvements. In 1912/13 the average book valuation of the ground facilities of the twelve English and six Scottish first-division clubs for whom the information could be traced was £12,540 and £5,046 respectively. Table 8.3 shows that the tangible assets ratio for most English and Scottish first-division clubs, and some second-division English ones, was high enough to offer substantial protection to shareholders and the possibility of capital gains on share transfers.

Net profits as a proportion of share capital of English first-division clubs averaged 43.0% as compared to the 20.3% of their Scottish counterparts. Respective tangible assets ratios were 4.09 (2.58 if Newcastle is excluded) and 1.93. These figures, along with the information on pricing policies, revenue-raising activities and games played, suggest that, as a broad generalisation, clubs in England, at least at the premier level, were more concerned with profit- and wealth-maximisation than those in Scotland.

The real utility-maximisers perhaps were those clubs, both English and Scottish, with ambitions to enter their respective Football Leagues or, even better, gain promotion to the first divisions. Spending money to improve the quality of their teams lowered profits, increased debts, and undermined their tangible assets ratio, but to such clubs expenditure was of less concern than footballing status. Yet in the long run some of these may have been profit-seekers. West Bromwich Albion, for example, averaged net losses of £443 in the four years prior to their promotion to the first division; the next three years then brought average profits of £4,156. Burnley are another instance. They gained total profits of £884 in their second-division sojourn between 1909/10 and 1912/13 before their massive profit of £11,809 in 1913/14, the year in which they finished twelfth in the first division and won the F. A. Cup.[47]

IV

The county cricket club administrators certainly believed that the great majority of spectators came to see their side win. Lord Harris, doyen of Kent cricket, was adamant that 'nothing is more popular than success, and a successful county eleven will draw much better than a non-successful one'.[48] The secretary of Derbyshire, no doubt from bitter experience, maintained that 'the public will not keep up their attendance to see their team lose continually'; the Leicestershire president concurred, noting that 'the repeated failures of the team . . . very materially affected the gate receipts'.[49] Warwickshire epitomises these points: in 1910, when they finished fourteenth, their attendances were the lowest for 17 years, but the following season, when they won the championship, 'people flocked to the Edgbaston ground in such numbers as to relieve the Committee of all anxiety about money'.[50] When a good team went bad, the crowds went with them: in 1910, when Yorkshire finished eighth,

Table 8.3 *Net profits and net tangible assets: English and Scottish soccer clubs, 1906/07–1913/14*

Club[a]	Period	Average net profit[b]		Year	Net tangible assets	
		£	As % of share capital		£	Ratio to share capital
Football League first division						
Blackburn Rovers	1907/08–1912/13	1,550	42.7	1913	14,696	3.77
Bolton Wanderers[c]	1908/09–1913/14	339	9.5	1914	9,847	2.66
Bradford City[d]	1906/07–1912/13	1,211	35.6	1913	8,722	2.42
Bristol City[e]	1907/08–1911/12	62	4.2	1912	700	0.47
Bury[f]	1908/09–1912/13	−523	−29.4	1913	−2,586	−1.45
Liverpool	1907/08–1913/14	2,872	25.2	1914	21,790	1.82
Manchester City[g]	1907/08–1913/14	1,248	104.2	1914	8,643	7.17
Middlesbrough	1907/08–1913/14	1,186	83.8	1914	12,522	8.43
Newcastle United	1908/09–1913/14	1,523	152.3	1914	20,686	20.69
Oldham[h]	1908/09–1912/13	108	8.5	1913	−202	−0.16
Preston North End[i]	1908/09–1913/14	246	12.1	1914	1,592	0.69
Tottenham Hotspur[j]	1907/08–1913/14	3,282	67.3	1914	17,203	3.52
Football League second division						
Birmingham[k]	1907/08–1913/14	−952	−151.8	1914	−7,728	−10.56
Blackpool	1907/08–1913/14	1	0.2	1914	29	0.03
Burnley[l]	1909/10–1913/14	2,551	241.3	1914	15,010	14.17
Derby County[m]	1906/07–1910/11	−292	−36.8	1911	−641	−0.82
Fulham	1908/09–1913/14	−774	−28.5	1914	−1,514	−0.54
West Bromwich Albion[n]	1907/08–1913/14	1,528	297.2	1914	11,013	22.71

English non-League						
Bristol Rovers	1907/08–1913/14	–65	–5.1	1914	–126	–0.10
Queen's Park Rangers	1910/11–1913/14	–387	–35.4	1914	–4,403	–4.03
Southampton	1907/08–1913/14	–268	–63.8	1914	–1,504	–3.49
Stoke	1908/09–1913/14	–216	–19.5	1914	742	0.55
Scottish League first division						
Celtic	1908/09–1913/14	1,241	26.9	1914	15,182	2.95
Falkirk	1907/08–1912/13	292	28.5	1913	1,831	1.66
Hamilton	1907/08–1913/14	–19	–2.1	1914	–370	0.39
Hearts	1906/07–1913/14	421	15.4	1914	6,184	2.23
Hibernian	1906/07–1913/14	536	53.4	1914	3,446	3.80
Motherwell	1909/10–1913/14	297	28.8	1914	1,506	1.47
Partick Thistle	1909/10–1913/14	423	11.2	1914	4,896	1.23
St Mirren	1908/09–1913/14	7	0.4	1914	3,068	1.74
Scottish League second division						
East Stirlingshire	1910/11–1913/14	–10	–2.7	1914	59	0.17
St Johnstone	1910/11–1913/14	–29	–13.6	1914	98	0.36

[a] Clubs were allocated to the group in which they spent most seasons during the time period covered. At least four observations were required for inclusion in the table.

[b] Where possible profit figures have been adjusted to allow for expenditure on the revenue account, which conventionally would be classified as investment; similarly, some anomalous balance sheet items have been removed.

[c] Second division 1909/10. [g] Second division 1909/10. [k] First division 1907/08.
[d] Second division 1906/07–1907/08. [h] Second division 1908/09–1909/10. [l] First division 1913/14.
[e] Second division 1911/12. [i] Second division 1912/13. [m] First division 1906/07.
[f] Second division 1912/13. [j] Non-League 1907/08, second division 1908/09. [n] First division 1911/12–1913/14.

Source: Calculated from Annual Financial Statements of Clubs.

their lowest position for 20 years, *Wisden* was led to comment that 'the ill-success of the Yorkshire team brought about a regrettable apathy on the part of the public at Leeds'.[51] Table 8.4 lends some support to these views in that, for most of the clubs studied, there was a reasonable positive correlation between home gate-receipts and championship performance.[52] One cricket writer summed up the position as one where 'as the business side more completely prevails ... it would be the paramount duty of a selection committee to take no risks, but to provide the team most likely to obtain victory'.[53]

Generally, however, the clubs do not appear to have attempted to maximise their gate-receipts, although they did take some steps in this direction. They were responsible for scheduling their own fixtures and most did try to arrange a crowd-drawing match for holiday periods. They were also aware that poor facilities could adversely influence attendances, but here clubs such as Leicestershire faced a vicious circle of poverty: if you did not have the attendances how could you afford to construct shelters in the sixpenny enclosure or improve the catering facilities?[54] Some clubs were also willing, usually under guarantee, to play a few fixtures away from the main county ground, perhaps, like Lancashire at Blackpool and Essex at Southend, taking advantage of a holiday audience.[55] However, it was not until 1908 that Saturday starts to matches were pioneered by Leicestershire and not till 1910 that Warwickshire introduced the idea of playing from 12.00 to 7.00 to see if an 'artisan attendance' could be attracted in the evenings.[56] Neither policy was widely accepted in the short run. Moreover, although the visiting team generally did not share in the match receipts, clubs did not test the elasticity of demand in either direction and 6*d.* remained the standard charge whether the visitors were county champions or wooden spooners. The only exception at county matches appears to have been the introduction of half-price entry after 4.30: Leicestershire adopted this in 1898 and Lancashire in 1906.[57] Admission prices were doubled for games against the Australians, but the money-hungry, though crowd-appealing, tourists took half the gate.

Indeed, although the Leicestershire club chairman lamented that, in contrast to cricket 'football matches attracted their thousands', it could be that his club was unusual in wanting 'to get at ... the general public'.[58] Perhaps county cricket clubs were aiming at a different market than that supplied by professional soccer. The Warwickshire chairman thought that the two games appealed to different classes and several club secretaries partially attributed the decline in cricket attendances to the rise of motoring and golf, scarcely working-class pursuits in England.[59] For

Table 8.4 *Rank-order correlations between gate-receipts and championship position, 1895–1913*

County	Period	Number of observations	Correlation
Kent	1896–1913	16	0.96
Warwickshire	1900–13	10	0.78
Essex	1895–1913	18	0.66
Lancashire	1895–1913	13	0.52
Surrey	1895–1913	9	0.43
Yorkshire	1895–1913	18	0.24
Derbyshire	1895–1913	18	0.08
Leicestershire	1895–1903	9	−0.13

Note: 1912 was omitted from all calculations due to the wetness of that season. Where the same position was obtained in different seasons the ranking was done on winning percentages.
Sources: Calculated from data in Annual Financial Reports; and *Wisden Cricketers' Almanack*.

many working men a three-day game with no Saturday start must have made it more worthwhile to spend a penny on a paper than sixpence at the gate. In essence many county cricket clubs may have accepted working-class spectators rather than actively sought to attract them. It can be suggested that given both its geographical location – coincident with the early Football League – and its Saturday afternoon setting, it was league cricket which catered for the summer spectating pleasure of the football supporter. It offered cheaper entertainment than county cricket, in terms both of travel and entry fees, and, weather permitting, guaranteed a result.[60]

The weather, in particular wet weather, could exert a major influence on the cricketing and financial fortunes of the county clubs. Rain could wipe out a game completely and, unlike in soccer or rugby, a three-day fixture was difficult to reschedule. It could so reduce the playing time available that an unattractive draw became inevitable or, alternatively, a wicket could become so sticky that the game could be over before the final day. It could also simply render the fireside a more attractive proposition. No wonder, then, that, even when Yorkshire won the championship in 1912, they lost £949 as all but one of 19 home matches had been interrupted by rain.[61] The treasurers of poorer counties, such as Leicestershire, which relied on the Australian tourists or a visit from the London

County Club (provided that W. G. Grace was playing) to put their accounts in the black, must have spent those matches with one eye on the cricket and the other on the clouds.[62] What a disaster the wet summer of 1906 must have been for, even with an Australian touring team, only three clubs made ends meet.[63] Hence all counties paid great emphasis on attracting members, who, hopefully, would pay their subscriptions in advance of the season. Every poor season financially would lead to a membership drive. There was also pressure exerted by the rising costs of first-class cricket, which forced clubs to revise their membership targets. In 1893, for example, Essex reckoned that they required 1,500 members to be viable; by 1905 the figure was 2,000 and by 1910 it was 2,500.[64] Tables 8.1 and 8.5 clearly show that such monies were more significant a proportion of total revenue for cricket clubs than were season tickets for their soccer counterparts.

Some indication of the ideal-type utility-maximiser can be found in the wage and employment policies of the clubs. Certainly wage discrimination was operative within teams. Income was guaranteed to the best players for a season, and later for a full year, at a time, though this was for only a basic groundstaff wage and did not commit the club to paying match fees if the players lost their place in the team. There was in fact a marked reluctance to offer contracts for longer than a year. Lancashire, Leicestershire, Yorkshire and Essex never did, but Warwickshire, after several requests from their star batsman, Willie Quaife, gave in when he threatened to go to league cricket and agreed to a five-year contract subject to his good conduct and continuation of form. Five years later, in 1903, three of their professionals had such contracts and two others had three-year contracts.[65] All teams appear to have offered incentives for winning and also end-of-season bonuses in the shape of talent money, awarded at the discretion of the captain for specific performances during the year. The best players could also look forward to a long-term bonus in the form of a benefit match from which they retained the net proceeds, though they might have to serve the county for 15 years before such a windfall came their way.[66] Nevertheless, despite these elements of utility-maximisation wage policy, the informal acceptance of a conventional limitation to wages and the occasional concern over amateurs' expenses suggest that profit-maximisation via cost control could have been at work.

The evidence is less inconclusive where the revenue-raising activities of the clubs are concerned. The average number of matches played rose until the end of the nineteenth century and then remained stable. The proportion of these which were county championship matches, and presumably more attractive to spectators, shifted upwards, but much of this was due to the increase in championship participants: in effect matches which were previously friendlies became county championship events. Nevertheless, more games could have been scheduled: from 1897/98 on Yorkshire consistently played over 30 matches in each season compared to an average of around 24 for all first-class counties.[67] However, the evidence is that the high number of games played were for utility rather than profit reasons as there was frequent mention of losses on matches in the minute books studied. In 1905 Yorkshire covered their costs on only two of their county matches, and one of them was the traditional August bank holiday Roses game.[68] It was claimed that they played so many matches in order to help out the weaker counties who might find their gates increased by spectators who wanted to see the outstanding team of the era, but it also helped Yorkshire's win–loss record.[69] The white-rose county continually lost money on its second-eleven matches, but felt that it was worthwhile as such games brought on young professionals, gave them match-experienced emergency players, and by playing them on different grounds, stimulated interest in the club across the county.[70] At the other end of the county table, Leicestershire, who maintained that they would 'always put the best team obtainable into the field without regard to the cost', lost money on most of their matches; they also lost most of their matches.[71] Elsewhere both Sussex and Warwickshire found that extensions to their fixture lists brought declining marginal revenue.[72]

Further evidence of a lack of profit-maximisation can be found in the non-cricket sources of revenue summarised in Table 8.5. Only Essex, and to a lesser extent Surrey and Derbyshire, obtained a significant proportion of their revenue from hiring out the ground and other facilities, and Derbyshire's percentage is due more to their low receipts elsewhere.[73] Moreover, Essex which had drawn substantial sums from using its ground for soccer in the winter in the 1890s later reduced such hiring because of the 'very great wear and tear to the ground'.[74] Generally clubs had their facilities and fixed assets lying idle for over half the year; not what might be expected from profit-maximising enterprises.

Nor does the financial experience, as revealed in Table 8.5, suggest that profit-maximisation was a major aim. Of the eight clubs examined, only Surrey, Yorkshire and, to a much lesser extent, Kent made long-term profits. However, although Lancashire sustained heavy losses in the period 1909 to 1914, minute book data suggest that between 1890 and 1908 their average annual net profits topped £1,100. The information lends some support to P. F. Warner, cricket writer and one-time England captain, who summed up the position as he saw it in 1912:

Table 8.5 Sources of revenue and net profits of county cricket clubs, 1890–1914 (annual average)

County	Period	Members' subscriptions		Gate and stands	Other cricket revenue[a]	Donations[b]	Other[c]	Total	Net profit
Derbyshire	1895–1913	£	920	857	68	373	130	2,348	−243
		%	39.2	36.5	2.9	15.9	5.5	100.0	
Essex	1895–1913[d]	£	1,898	1,806	222	315	499	4,739	−211
		%	40.1	38.1	4.7	6.6	10.5	100.0	
Kent	1896–1913[e]	£	2,342	3,347	213	220	100	6,222	+48
		%	37.6	53.8	3.4	3.5	1.6	100.0	
Lancashire	1909–14	£	3,284	2,963	1,089	801	132	8,270	−794
		%	39.7	35.8	13.2	9.7	1.5	100.0	
Leicestershire	1895–1903	£	1,182	1,366	115	386	47	3,096	−188
		%	38.2	44.1	3.7	12.5	1.5	100.0	
Surrey	1890–1914[f]	£	5,152	7,736	509	5	872	14,274	+1,005
		%	36.2	54.3	3.7		5.7	100.0	
Warwickshire	1900–13[g]	£	2,004	2,083	459	54	104	4,705	−53
		%	42.6	44.3	9.7	1.2	2.2	100.0	
Yorkshire	1892–1914	£	2,247	5,809	101	1	291	8,449	+550
		%	26.6	68.9	1.1		3.4	100.0	

[a]Includes printing and refreshment contracts, share of test match proceeds, and sales of match cards.
[b]Includes proceeds from fund-raising balls, bazaars and dinners.
[c]Includes interest, hire of ground and facilities, dividends on investments.
[d]No data for 1903 or 1905.
[e]No data for 1908.
[f]No data for 1892, 1894–5, 1899–1900, 1902–4, 1909–11.
[g]No data for 1902–4.
Source: Annual Financial Statements of the Clubs.

County cricket clubs naturally like to make ends meet, but they are not possessed with an unholy idea that profit is everything and that the game is nothing. 'If we can make a profit on the year's working so much the better; but the first thing is to have a good eleven.' That in so many words is the attitude of a county secretary.[75]

Unlike in soccer there were no shareholders to be considered. Essex had rejected the idea of company formation as a way out of their economic difficulties in 1890[76] and no other club appears to have even broached the idea. Some counties leased their grounds from companies formed by the county committees, but these did not press the clubs for money. When Warwickshire was raising funds to finance the creation of their Edgbaston ground in 1885, Sir Thomas Martineau, a director of the Cricket Ground Company, stated that gentlemen who advanced the requisite money were entitled to expect a fair return but the main object should be 'not to make dividends but to advance the interests and the position of the county club'.[77] This seems to have occurred: from 1907, when official data become available, Warwickshire Cricket Ground Company paid a regular 6% dividend and Hampshire County Cricket Ground Company $3\frac{1}{2}$%.[78] These can be regarded as *rentier* rather than risk-taking returns.

Surpluses were thus not distributed in the form of dividends, nor were committee members in a position to benefit themselves. Direct contributions to charity were also minimal. Some money, though as far as can be ascertained from the financial statements not significant amounts, went 'to foster and encourage the game in the district', a point which *Wisden* had argued in favour of gate-money county cricket as opposed to the earlier private professional speculations.[79] Predominantly this went to subsidise professionals seconded to local clubs, in supplying coaching to promising young players, in encouraging school cricket with trophies, and in occasional donations to clubs. However, the main form of promotion was in showing the flag by playing matches away from the main county grounds. Even this had a possible ulterior motive in that such matches helped attract membership subscriptions from those living some distance from the county headquarters. They could also bring in much needed revenue: when one Manchester member complained that 'if the object of holding county matches in other places than the present county grounds was the encouragement of cricket, there were places more suitable than Blackpool', the chairman replied that 'they must not forget that the match at Blackpool proved a very profitable one'.[80]

Most profit appears to have gone into reserves which were later used to strengthen the playing staff or to improve facilities, primarily for members but also for the public, improvements which, in turn, might encourage further membership and larger attendances. For some counties the construction of ground facilities could be regarded as an operating cost in that it may have been a condition of their lease. Surrey, for example, were granted a 31-year lease of the Oval for £750 per annum providing that they spent at least £10,000 on improvements and additions.[81] At this time only a minority of clubs appear to have owned their grounds and thus it is less likely that the creation of extra facilities would be seen as a means of amassing capital assets, as was the case with several soccer clubs. The relative absence of ground ownership by county clubs could be an indication of a lack of entrepreneurial initiative, though certainly in the case of Yorkshire the geographical size of the county and its dispersed membership would have rendered ownership unviable and politically unfeasible.

When ends did not meet, various financial expedients were resorted to. Essex literally flogged a dead horse, for 7s. 6d. and, to avoid taking out an overdraft, Warwickshire borrowed from Lilley's benefit fund while he was on tour in Australia.[82] Generally, however, when finances were bad committees concentrated on retrenchment. Plans to improve ground facilities were abandoned, repairs were postponed, and maintenance schedules were revised. Inevitably, letting things slide for too long aggravated the situation by 'frightening away those who are satisfied with the actual play as it is, but who are not prepared to be treated worse as spectators of cricket than they are as spectators of any other public performance'.[83] Another solution was to cut back on fixtures and drop the most uneconomic games, though there was no wholesale reduction in matches. Labour bills were lessened by giving up second elevens, reducing the number of groundstaff, not providing lunch for the players, cancelling the engagements of coaches for the young players, and no longer helping out players who were sick or injured. Nevertheless, there were limits to the cutbacks. Although there was some relationship between one season's spending and the previous season's revenue, short of winding-up the club some spending, particularly on labour, was inevitable. Members were too concerned that their clubs would lose matches to allow committee razor-gangs to cut too deep. Although the Lancashire committee of 1913 were determined that 'so long as they remained in office, it [was] in their province to control the expenditure of the club', the subscriptions of the county members proved a strong bargaining weapon and eventually the committee had to satisfy itself with the intention of 'making the expenditure approximately equate with the estimated receipts', but allowing 'that the players shall be treated with at least as great consideration as those of any other county'.[84] Leicestershire had already conceded that 'a cheese-paring policy did not pay in the end' as 'it fostered discontent amongst the staff and players, and produced a feeling of unrest that was detrimental to the best interests of the club'.[85]

Even with the adoption of cost-cutting policies, most counties faced rising expenditure partly because of 'the keen competition which exists among the first class teams' which forced 'the spending of large sums in the selection and training of promising players'.[86] Club financial statements suggest that, on average, the cost of running a county side rose 22% between 1895–1900 and 1907–13.

Most counties, particularly those with a poor championship record, also had but a fleeting acquaintanceship with profits, and several of them lurched from one financial crisis to another. None more so than Leicestershire, which, after nearly going bankrupt in 1899, reported in 1902 that 'the club had passed through the greater part of its difficulties, and with reasonable support should be in a sound financial position in a few years'. Yet by 1905 it faced 'a very serious deficit'. This was offset by donations, but within four seasons the estimated deficit had risen to over £1,000. Again patrons and donors came to the rescue, but by 1912 a special meeting was discussing whether or not to wind up the club.[87] Certainly there was validity in the claim of the Leicestershire chairman that 'first-class cricket cannot be made to pay except in the case of the more thickly-populated counties . . . and if first-class cricket is to exist, not only in Leicestershire, but in other counties, it will have to be subsidised'.[88]

To some extent members were called upon to do this. Many counties emphasised that membership of the county club was a form of social obligation to the county and to cricket. Not all members shared this view. When Leicestershire called for a voluntary doubling of their membership fee in 1901 less than 300 of the 1,100 members responded.[89] Essex fared even worse in 1911 when only 115 members agreed to a similar proposal.[90] Lancashire's members did agree to accept a rise in their subscription from 21s. to 26s., but this was only 25% of the rise which the committee wanted and it took four annual general meetings for even this concession to be achieved.[91] Clearly a grandstand seat at a whole season's home matches for around a pound was too good a bargain to be given up easily.

When all else failed clubs turned to patronage and public appeals. Traditionally club presidents and vice-presidents, often county dignitaries, had dipped into their pockets to bail out clubs when the accounts hit the red. This became less feasible as the size of the deficits rose, and increasingly shilling funds, bazaars and other general fund-raising appeals were used to supplement the donations from patrons.[92]

Derbyshire had been born into debt in 1870 because its membership was so small; by 1887 it had accumulated a deficit of over £1,000 which was liquidated only by the generosity of Walter Boden and the Hon. W. M. Jarvis; thereafter even the liberality of G. H. Strutt, W. H. Worthington and C. Arnold was insufficient to keep the club afloat without regular appeals for donations.[93] Essex was on the verge of dissolution in 1893 when its bankers demanded the settlement of its overdraft; it was saved by donations and interest-free loans from C. E. Green, members of the Buxton dynasty, and C. M. Tebbut. In 1908 J. H. Douglas was rewarded with a place on the committee after he took up the second mortgage rejected by insurance companies; in 1912 C. E. Green liquidated the club's £400 debt so that it could continue free of outstanding liabilities; and throughout the period guarantee funds were organised and called upon.[94] Hampshire's members were constantly called on to rescue the club by making donations and conducting fund-raising campaigns.[95] The Leicester *Daily Post* helped save the local county team by organising a shilling fund which obtained over 15,000 contributions; in addition a bazaar run by the committee raised £1,300.[96] Northamptonshire avoided bankruptcy only thanks to a series of gifts and loans from John Powys, the fifth Baron Lilford.[97] By all accounts Lord Sheffield spent a small fortune trying to sustain the Sussex club; nevertheless, it still required major bazaars in 1894 and 1904 to keep the club afloat.[98] Despite the generosity of loyal patrons, such as C. B. Hollinsworth, Warwickshire was eventually forced to make an appeal for public support in 1902 which met an overwhelming response to the tune of £3,561 and put the club on a sound financial footing for the first time.[99] One year later Worcestershire had to resort to a bazaar to set their accounts straight, a feat previously achieved through the patronage of Lord Dudley.[100]

Profits were thus not the be all and end all of county cricket. The available evidence on wage policies and revenue-raising activities suggests that clubs may have been profit-takers but certainly were not profit-maximisers. Few, if any, clubs put L. s. d. before L. b. w. Potential profits were traded off against other objectives: in some cases winning, in others merely playing the game in the established manner; when Leicestershire won only three games in 1909 the team was still given a vote of thanks as 'one of the most gentlemanly teams that ever came on to the turf'.[101] Most counties could not anticipate winning the championship and, unlike in soccer, there were no other competitions, such as national or regional cups, in which they could participate. All they could hope for was an occasional triumph over one of the Titans and great play was made of such victories in the annual reports. Similarly Leicestershire noted the 'great improvement' in the team's performance when it finished *eleventh* in the championship![102] For these clubs long-run survival may have been the major objective and this was not easy given the economies of cricket. Yet, despite their inherent lack of viability, the clubs were not allowed to collapse, so clearly emotion must often have taken precedence over economics. Cricket in England was regarded as more than a game. As an important national symbol, it was more than a commodity to be bartered in the market place. Some viewed it as a patriotic institution, believing that cricket could 'rank among the links of the chains which unite the Empire' and that 'Kipling and Mafeking have done less for the Empire than cricket'.[103] Others pitched their patriotism at a narrower level, seeing a first-class cricket team as a positive reflection upon their county. For many cricket was character-building: it taught cooperation, self-sacrifice and team spirit; honour and sportsmanship were at the heart of the game; on a 'bumping pitch' in a 'blinding light' cricket was a true test of courage and self-discipline; it extolled comradeship and Christian virtues. It simply represented all that many thought was best in the English way of life.[104] In such circumstances those associated with cricket clubs were prepared to subsidise the sport.[105]

V

Although proponents of amateur rugby maintained that rugby league was 'in many districts a purely commercial speculation' and that the Northern Union ... looked on football 'as a matter of pounds, shillings and pence',[106] failure to gain access to individual club records makes it difficult to ascertain the validity of these assertions. However, in the first season of the Northern Union, except for a few clubs 'to be easily counted on one hand ... the financial results [were] disastrous'.[107] Indeed Manningham, the league champions, had to hold a bazaar to put their financial affairs in order.[108] By 1910 increased support from the public had put 'the great majority of clubs ... in a strong and satisfactory financial position'.[109] Yet what was 'satisfactory'? Data supplied to a local newspaper by the chairman of the Northern Rugby Football League – and reproduced in Table 8.6 – shows that the average profit level of 20 league clubs in 1911/12 was only £174, substantially less than in English first-division soccer, especially when it is noted that only six clubs made more than the average and the data exclude most of the lowest-placed sides.

Table 8.6 *Profitability of rugby league clubs, 1911/12*

Club	League position	Profit (£)
Huddersfield	1	1,249
Wigan	2	c. 900
Hull Kingston Rovers	3	250
Hunslet	4	142
Oldham	5	160
Wakefield	6	−260
St Helens	7	70
Dewsbury	8	109
Broughton	9	90
Hull	10	130
Leeds	11	407
Widnes	12	34
Leigh	13	−167
Halifax	14	−90
Batley	15	200
Rochdale	16	231
Warrington	18	90
Keighley	22	−37
Bradford	26	−52
Bramley	27	19

Source: Yorkshire Post, 13 June 1912.

VI

There were several ways of attempting to make money out of horse-racing. This section concentrates on three of them: ownership of enclosed racecourses, ownership of racehorses, and ownership of breeding stock.

Although a dividend limitation of 10% was set by the Jockey Club, this was still a worthwhile target for the jointstock racecourse companies; and indeed even the average dividend of 7.5% paid in 1913 compared favourably with the consol rate of 3.4%.[110] Free admission at some courses would also have increased the real dividend to shareholders. The financial good fortune of most enclosed courses was primarily because they were able to persuade substantial numbers of racegoers to pay for their viewing. This was done so successfully that change was forced upon the less profit-oriented, traditional meetings and the style of racing in Britain was permanently transformed.

The marketing policy of the companies was geared very much to the working man. The pioneering Sandown Park executive may not have been attempting to tap the working-class market to any depth since their minimum admission charge before 1914 was 2s. 6d., but most other enclosed courses took only 1s.[111] This was still expensive relative to soccer and cricket, but was within the pocket of sufficient working men to satisfy the course directors. Nevertheless, there was no guarantee that the working man would spend his money at an enclosed meeting. Not only had racing to compete against other leisure activities, but, even among racegoers, individual racing companies did not have a captive market: the railways had seen to that. Although the Jockey Club organised the racing calendar so as to prevent serious fixture clashes, courses were still in competition with each other for spectators as the average racegoer had limited funds and leisure time. If he was to be persuaded to pay for his pleasure rather than frequent a meeting which did not charge an entry fee, then the product of the gate-money meeting had to be differentiated from that of its unenclosed rival.

One way was to offer Saturday afternoon racing, a decided product improvement so far as the working man was concerned. Initially this was partly forced on the new courses because many existing meetings, which the Jockey Club gave priority to, would not have a Saturday, traditionally a day for taking horses home from the races. However, as the Saturday half-day become more common, there was an advantage in choosing to race at the weekend. It was also made easier for the racegoer to attend: almost all the new courses had a railway station within a short distance, often with a covered walkway from the platform to the turnstiles. Another attraction was the high-quality horses, themselves attracted partly by the first-class tracks but more by the increased level of prizemoney offered. Primarily, however, the racecourse executives sought their audiences by promoting a new-style racing programme, one dominated by two-year-old races, sprints and handicaps, all of which had a sufficient degree of uncertainty about their result to make for exciting racing and an attractive betting market.

A second group of racegoers which attained significance as paying spectators was women. Prior to the advent of the enclosed meeting relatively few women went racing. Of course, the aristocrats frequented Ascot, where there was the Royal Enclosure to accommodate them; Epsom and especially Goodwood, run under the aegis of the Duke of Richmond, were also part of the elite's social season. Elsewhere, however, even at Newmarket, ladies were rarely seen except for a few in carriages or in private or stewards' stands: respectability inhibited them from utilising the free areas or even the public grandstands.[112] This social parameter was accepted by the racing companies when they attempted to attract female spectators by upgrading the image of their particular form of racing. From its inception Sandown encouraged their attendance by the formation of a racing club, whose members were carefully vetted. Although membership was a male prerogative, those who subscribed at the highest rate obtained two ladies' badges and the others could take in two ladies on the payment of a small fee. Racing clubs were not new, but the earlier ones at Epsom, Stockbridge and Lewes were much smaller and did not admit women.[113] Clubs similar to that at Sandown were established at all enclosed courses. There, the races, luncheon, the musical accompaniment, even just strolling around the lawns and flowerbeds, could all be enjoyed in comfort. By the turn of the century such facilities were attracting several thousand women to the major gate-money meetings.[114]

Except when trying to confuse the handicapper, owners raced their horses to win. Without success on the track there was no possibility of profit; however, with the high prices of well-bred stock and the fees which leading jockeys demanded to ride them, utility-maximisation need not be correlated with profit-maximisation.

Certainly owners appear to have responded to the cash stimulus. In the 1830s both Ascot and Newmarket, despite their social and racing prestige, found difficulty in attracting sufficient runners because of their inadequate level of prizemoney; and in 1842 the York Race Committee established a public subscription for the purpose of making additions to the prize fund as such added money had 'materially contributed to the prosperity of racing at other places'.[115] Similarly in the late 1840s Leicester races failed to attract good horses because of the shortage of prizemoney.[116] By 1885, although 'a few [owners] may race here and there for whim, or a liking to run horses in their own neighbourhood, the majority of them go where the stakes are highest'.[117]

Some owners clearly treated racing as a hobby. None more so than the Duke of Portland, who reputedly gave all his winnings to charity, including the £73,858 which he won in 1889.[118] Indeed, most aristocrats probably raced for pleasure and were prepared to pay for their indulgence.[119] The high proportion of the titled among racehorse owners – perhaps about an eighth in the 1890s – tempted new owners, successful men from industry and commerce, to enter racing in the belief that the ownership of high-quality thoroughbreds indicated not merely wealth but also social position.[120] If they, too, became owners, then not only would their names appear on the racecards alongside those of the nobility, but there was also the chance that introductions in the paddock might lead to invitations elsewhere, an aspiration given support by Edward VII, both when monarch and Prince of Wales, who accepted several of these *nouveaux riches* into his social circle.[121] From the 1880s these millionaires poured money into the sport, willing to lose, it was alleged, £50,000 in a season in search of the social returns from investment in horseflesh.[122] There was also 'an astonishing large number of minor owners racing out of pure liking for the sport, and with small chance of making the game pay'.[123] These might range from the publican who formed a syndicate with a few friends to buy a broken-down plater which the local vet reckoned he could get on its feet again to the traders, grocers and other small businessmen partly imitating their social superiors. Few of this group ever made the big time: in effect they formed a pool of floating owners, coming into racing when they felt they could afford it and going out again when they realised that their pockets could not match their enthusiasm. Yet there were men in racing for the money. Writing in 1890, one commentator noted that for some years past there had been a decided increase in owners 'with whom racing is a trade and a business, rather than a pastime or an avenue to social notoriety'.[124]

Unfortunately it is impossible to quantify the number of the various types of owner for all that is listed are names not motivations. Even the registered names have two major deficiencies. First, many owners raced in partnership and not until 1883 was the registration of such syndicates made compulsory. Even then there is the problem of pseudonyms, for racing under assumed names remained common: 98 owners did so in 1907. Young bloods, anxious that their parents or trustees should not know their degree of involvement in turf affairs, ladies and others not certain of acceptance by the racing fraternity, and gamblers who felt that anonymity would secure better odds, all raced in disguise.

The rise in total prizemoney in the late nineteenth and early twentieth centuries appears to have stimulated a rise in horse ownership. Between 1882 and 1910 prizemoney rose from £413,066 to £511,734 and the number of horses competing for it from 1,916 to 3,875. However, as is shown in Table 8.7, this meant that the prizemoney available per horse actually fell, though even at its nadir of £130 in 1901 it was still above the £124 of the early 1870s.[125]

At the same time, the increased pressure of demand raised the sale prices of thoroughbred racing stock, not so much perhaps at the lower end of the quality spectrum, but certainly for animals with recognised pedigrees.[126] To some extent these prices were pushed up by the *nouveaux riches*, who, unlike many aristocratic owners, were not prepared to wait and breed a good horse of their own. Instead they frequented the sale rings, cheque

Table 8.7 *Prizemoney available per horse, 1882–1910*

Year	No. of horses running	Prizemoney (£)	Prizemoney per horse (£)
1882	1,916	413,066	216
1883	2,070	391,520	189
1884	1,968	393,249	200
1885	2,033	426,142	210
1886	2,072	415,131	200
1887	2,045	415,956	203
1888	2,125	431,530	203
1889	2,100	480,890	229
1890	2,102	446,769	213
1891	2,305	466,308	202
1892	2,559	486,557	190
1893	2,602	460,512	177
1894	2,867	478,934	167
1895	3,086	486,587	158
1896	3,180	488,352	154
1897	3,506	499,586	142
1898	3,500	508,026	145
1899	3,707	503,878	136
1900	3,955	531,907	134
1901	4,019	523,152	130
1902	3,961	533,961	135
1903	3,222	502,650	156
1904	3,017	523,881	174
1905	3,513	524,897	149
1906	3,539	540,279	153
1907	3,455	533,290	154
1908	3,706	541,582	146
1909	3,846	546,100	142
1910	3,875	511,734	132

Source: Calculated from data in *Ruffs Guide to the Turf*, London, 1911.

books at the ready. A few paid high prices for yearlings simply for the publicity, but most were paying in the hope that they were purchasing racing success.[127]

Then there were what can appropriately be termed the running costs of horse ownership. Training bills, entries and forfeits, feeding stuffs, jockeys' fees and presents, travelling costs, stabling at the course, outlays on saddles, cloths and silks, veterinarians' accounts: for some owners the

Table 8.8 *Owners and winnings, 1896–1910*

Year	No. of winning owners	Median winnings (£)	Mean winnings (£)	No. of owners above mean	Maximum winnings (£)
1896	443	341	1,102	73	46,766
1907	460	377	1,159	99	17,910
1910	444	307	1,155	95	35,352

Note: Data refer only to owners who won prizemoney, hence median and mean winnings are inflated.
Source: Calculated from data in *Ruffs Guide to the Turf*, London, 1897, 1908, 1911.

list must have seemed endless. Various estimates in the 1870s and 1880s put the minimum annual requirement at around £300.[128] Contrast this with the prizemoney available per horse and there is no wonder it was argued that 'a thoroughbred in training is an expensive luxury' and that 'racing can scarcely be considered a remunerative enterprise'.[129] Taking the most conservative figures available in 1905, it cost at least £366 to have a horse in training whereas prizemoney offered averaged only £149 per horse, a substantial shortfall.[130]

Tables 8.8 and 8.9 show that some owners won large amounts. Few, however, did so consistently. In 1889 the Duke of Portland won 33 races worth nearly £74,000; in 1897 with a larger and more valuable stable he collected only one race worth £490. Mr L. de Rothschild won £46,766 in 1896 but only £1,150 in 1892, and Mr Hall Walker's winnings of £17,910 in 1907 easily surpassed his £602 in 1903.[131] Most owners lost money. Indeed Table 8.8 suggests that most owners whose horses actually won races – and only 34.4% of horses did so in 1896 and 32.4% in 1910[132] – still managed to lose money: median aggregate earnings probably did not cover the costs of racing even one horse.

Moreover, owners were primarily racing for each other's money as about two-thirds of prizemoney came out of their own pockets in the form of race entry fees and forfeits. In 1913, the first year for which comprehensive, aggregate data are available, English owners supplied 63% of the prizemoney as compared to the 23% of their French counterparts. At no course across the Channel was the proportion higher than 28%, whereas at Manchester owners contributed 50%, at Hurst Park 62%, at Kempton Park 66%, at Newbury 69% and at Sandown Park an astounding 82%.[133]

Table 8.9 *Distribution of prizemoney, 1896–1910*

	£100–49	£150–299	£300–499	£500–999	£1,000–1,999	£2,000–2,999	£3,000–3,999	£4,000–5,999	£6,000+
No. of owners (1896)	117	91	72	78	35	18	9	14	9
No. of owners (1907)	110	87	74	72	53	23	13	12	16
No. of owners (1910)	119	94	71	64	43	20	12	4	17

Source: Calculated from data in *Ruffs Guide to the Turf*, London, 1897, 1908, 1911.

Initially, of course, owners had raced solely for their own money in that the origins of horse-racing lay in one owner backing his animal in a match race against that of another owner: now at least they were obtaining some money from other sources. And certainly, as indicated above, owners were not uninterested in prizemoney. The fact that there was prizemoney meant that some owners would receive a contribution towards their costs and this tempted all owners to believe that it would be them. Nevertheless, it can be suggested that most owners resembled many other middle- and upper-class sportsmen in that, within limits, they were prepared to pay for their pleasure. They were of the same ilk as the yachtsmen who would spend a small fortune trying to win a £50 trophy, as the shooting men whose game would cost well in excess of the shop price, and as the hunting men who laid out substantial sums for no material reward at all.[134] Apparently, then, racehorse ownership can generally be located on the consumption side – conspicuous consumption for some – rather than in the investment sector of the sports industry.

The issue, however, is complicated by two factors: gambling and breeding. It is impossible to be precise about the extent to which owners gambled. There are no quantified data available so reliance has to be placed on contemporary opinion. The impression obtained is that non-gambling owners were in the minority. It was claimed by one reputable turf writer that 'a considerable proportion of the leading owners of horses do not bet at all', but such wealthy owners may have seen no reason to gamble.[135] The same cannot be said of the bulk of losing owners. The very fact that non-betting owners elucidated comment lends support to the Earl of Suffolk's assertion, in his authoritative *Badminton Library* volume on horse-racing, that the great majority of owners gambled to a greater or lesser degree.[136] Those in racing purely for pleasure or status had no need to bet, except to intensify their involvement. Others, however, may have hoped to make the bookmakers contribute to the costs of racing. Whether or not they succeeded is again a matter of opinion rather than of fact, though no one has suggested that in aggregate owners could take more from the bookmakers than they gave to them. Opinions to the contrary are more common. William Day, the famous trainer, maintained that, in general, gambling increased the costs of ownership and that it was 'betting rather than racing [which] ruins the majority of gentlemen on the turf'.[137] Alfred Watson, a leading writer on turf affairs, agreed: 'if an owner bets ... as a general rule he will, at any rate in the long run, find himself a loser by taking the odds'.[138]

There was another way in which owners could attempt to make money. As one contemporary put it, 'horse-racing can be practised ... as a profitable business only by persons who combine horse breeding with horse racing and are content with a few successes at the post to enhance the value of what they offer for sale in the paddock'.[139] Nevertheless breeding, too, could be a gamble.

One problem was that the breeders were not really sure what they were doing. Not until the late nineteenth century, when the work of Mendel on heredity became better known, did racehorse breeders begin to operate on any explicit theoretical basis. Even then there was a good deal of scepticism: if breeding could be pursued scientifically why did the siblings of outstanding horses 'not seldom prove absolutely worthless for racing purposes'?[140] Nineteenth-century breeders appreciated that qualities could be passed on from generation to generation, but they did not understand why; nor did they realise that the female line could contribute as much to the development of the breed as could that of the stallion. The first major attempt to rectify this situation was Bruce Lowe's 'figure system', devised in the 1890s. Its basis was that every mare could be traced back to one of 50 mares in the original *Stud Book* of 1791–1814. Lowe ranked these 50 families according to the number of St Leger, Derby and Oaks winners they had produced. Here, he declared, was a guide to breeding success: the higher a mare's family was ranked, the greater was the chance of producing a top-class racehorse. Unfortunately his conclusion was based on a false premise. The absolute number of classic winners was not a fair guide since there were more brood mares in the top-ranked families than in the lower ones: so not only did these families produce the most winners, but they also produced the most failures. If the proportionate number of major winners was taken, then the top five families averaged 6.7 per 100 brood mares compared to 7.1 for the other forty-five families! There was no magic formula.[141] For the decade or so that it was in vogue the 'figure system' harmed the British bloodstock industry by encouraging breeders to utilise inappropriate selection techniques. On the other hand, and of importance for the future, Lowe's work drew attention to the vital role of the female line in bloodstock development.

Essentially the breeders were attempting to respond to a demand based on pedigree (including ancestral racing performance) and conformation, neither of which could guarantee success on the track.[142] Between 1883 and 1892, 277 well-bred yearlings were each sold for over 1,000 guineas, for a grand total of 462,640 guineas, but between them they won only 203,377 guineas in stakes; only two in five of such expensive animals ever repaid their purchase price.[143]

Although the thoroughbred breeding industry professed that it played a role in improving the quality of non-racing bloodstock, this rationale was weakened as the structure of racing changed under the influence of the enclosed course. Two-year-old racing, sprints and handicaps had little to offer to army remounts or half-bred farming stock: immature horses were too susceptible to breakdown; sprints hid stamina deficiencies; and handicaps offered weak horses a chance of beating better ones.[144] Increasingly the function of breeders was, as an earlier harsh critic put it, to produce winners which 'will in time beget other horses capable of the same splendid and useless triumphs'.[145]

For many of the aristocracy and gentry, horse-breeding was intimately associated with ownership: anyone with money could purchase a horse, but it took talent to give Darwinism a helping hand and breed a classic winner. Most breeders, however, had an eye on the yearling auctions and in the 1870s nine-tenths of thoroughbred horses were produced for sale.[146] Mainly they came from farmers for whom breeding from one or two mares provided a useful income supplement. Others were the 'inferior' or surplus produce of the aristocratic stables. Some also came from the studs of large-scale breeding companies, a movement began in 1852 and rejuvenated in the later nineteenth century as increased prize-money and new owners, wealthy representatives of the industrial and business world, made their influence felt in the bloodstock market.[147]

In assessing whether or not breeders could make money, the owners of mares must be distinguished from the owners of stallions. Data for the former are scarce but roughly it cost between £200 and £225 to bring a horse to the yearling sales.[148] As the average price fetched by an auctioned yearling in the 1890s was around £270, it would seem that there was validity in Lord Durham's claim that 'horse-breeding is a lucrative occupation'.[149] However, the breeder still had to play the odds. Up to a third of the mares covered would not become pregnant, primarily because of the artificial breeding season imposed by the Jockey Club ruling that for racing purposes all horses take their birth date as 1 January in the year in which they were born. This forced breeders to attempt to produce foals earlier in the year than nature might have dictated. In addition to the lower fertility rates caused by the Jockey Club regulation, there was a 20% death rate among foals and a further wastage of 25% before the yearling sales.[150]

What is certain is that few owners would make money from using their stallions for breeding as relatively few stallions went to stud. Only those with good racing records were given any chance to be sires, whereas, with mares, even maidens on the course were allowed to lose that title off the track. In the early 1900s, for example, there were just over 300 stallions registered for thoroughbred breeding (about two-thirds of which would actually sire animals in any year) but well over 1,500 mares being serviced each year.[151] Some stallions would cover only a few mares. However, if a stallion had proved his racing ability, then, providing that he was both potent and amenable to stud duties and that his offspring looked alright and that some of them performed well on the racecourse, his owner could make money. Even in the 1840s the owner of a good, rather than an outstanding, animal could anticipate receiving up to £1,000 if the horse served 40 mares, the traditionally accepted maximum. No wonder John Bowes was disgruntled that his Derby-winning *Mundig* 'had not met his expectations as a stallion'.[152] As racing became more commercialised the rewards increased, especially for the best. By the 1890s a good stallion with a stud fee of 50 to 100 guineas could be bringing in £2,000. And what of an outstanding animal like *St Simon*, who went to stud in 1886 at a 50-guinea fee which had risen to 500 guineas by the late 1890s, and peaked at 600 guineas in 1901? During his stud career he serviced 775 mares and earned his owner at least £250,000.[153] The breeding companies, however, did not share in such bonanzas. Generally the potentially outstanding stallions were retained by private breeders and this, coupled with the unselective mating of the company breeders relative to that of the aristocratic stables, resulted in few classic winners emerging from their studs. In turn this led to the company stallions dropping down the sires' rankings and consequently lower stud fees having to be charged.[154]

VII

This chapter has suggested that there was a range of motivations both within and between sports. Profit-maximising behaviour was perhaps at its extreme in racehorse ownership and breeding, but both these activities were also participated in by utility-maximisers and, in the case of ownership, there was certainly an element of consumption involved in the investment decision. Still with racing, the shareholders in the enclosed courses expected dividends but, as these were limited to 10% by Jockey Club legislation, it may have been *rentier* returns which were being sought. In soccer there seems to have been more profit orientation by clubs south of the Border, though the Scottish situation is complicated by the 'old firm' of Rangers and Celtic. Few, if any, county cricket clubs were profit-maximisers; some were utility-maximisers, but many seem simply to have been intent on survival and avoiding the drop to minor county status. At this stage of knowledge it is hard to say what the aim of rugby league clubs was, but generally their profit levels were not high.

These suggestions cannot be regarded as conclusive, especially as regards team sports. Although it was argued earlier that consistent winning might be a second-best profit policy, most club spokesmen saw victories as the best way to increase attendances. Moreover, they really had no option but to try to win matches. However, there could be collusion between clubs in that the league authorities could impose restrictions designed to maintain equality of sporting competition. This is considered in the next chapter.

Chapter 9

All for one and one for all

I

Sports cartels emerge from the mutual interdependence of clubs in the sense that the revenue of any club depends on the performances of every club. Clubs may be sports competitors but they can be economic partners; and in an effective cartel, although all teams cannot win, all clubs can make profits.

The initial step in determining whether cartels operated in British sport in the period under study is to establish the basic functions of an ideal-type, profit-maximising cartel against which the British sports organisations can be assessed. Four interrelated features can be postulated.[1] First, there has to be a central, decision-making organisation with powers to discipline members for rule infractions. Such powers are necessary because there is an inherent conflict between group and individual club interests in that the costs of reduced uncertainty caused by an overly strong team may be borne primarily by the other clubs. Second, the cartel will act to influence profits by cost-minimising regulations, usually some form of labour market intervention designed to prevent undue competition for players between member clubs. Such devices include limitations on payments to players, territorial restrictions on recruitment, drafting systems, maximum team rosters, impediments imposed on player mobility, and, of course, the size of the league from which the demand for labour is derived. Third, on the other blade of the profit scissors, cartels can attempt to maximise revenue by improving the product offered for sale. This can be done by rule changes aimed at rendering the sport more attractive to spectators, by product diversification in the form of new competitions and special matches, but primarily by promoting equality of playing competition on a match, championship and long-term basis. The cartel thus has to control product quality via league expansion and contraction and by changing league composition.

The cartel can also affect profits by determining admission prices, the location and timing of production, and the number of games to be played. Finally, the cartel has the task of maintaining the viability of the league or sports industry sector, for there have to be sufficient participants to provide saleable products. A champion without challengers has nothing to sell: only the most ardent supporter will pay to watch a team play its own reserves. Here the maintenance of equality of sporting competition has a primary role, but as such equality is hard to guarantee the weaker clubs may often have to be financially assisted by the others via gate-sharing arrangements or other forms of subsidisation. Action may also have to be taken to confront rival organisations in the sport and preserve the cartel's monopolistic and monopsonistic powers.

In many respects sports cartels resemble industrial ones, but there are a few differences. Most clubs have some degree of spatial monopoly and thus there is less danger than with conventional economic cartels of a price-cutting war or a member unilaterally electing to increase output over the prescribed limit. Indeed, it would be very difficult for a club to opt out of a sports cartel and still remain an effective producer in the industry.

II

Horse-racing was controlled by a self-appointed group of socially elite owners. Founded in the early 1750s, the Jockey Club had, by the mid nineteenth century, come to be acknowledged as the pre-eminent authority in racing matters as, over time, racecourse committees had voluntarily adopted the Jockey Club's *Rules of Racing* and increasingly turned to the Club to settle disputes.[2] Compulsion then replaced volunteerism when in 1870 it was ruled that neither the programme, nor the results, of any British flat race would be published in the *Racing Calendar*, the Club's official organ, unless the meeting was advertised as being under Jockey Club rules. Furthermore, a penalty of disqualification was to be imposed on any owner, trainer, jockey or official who took part in such unrecognised meetings.

The Jockey Club was not primarily interested in the costs or profits of those involved in the racing industry, though it did schedule fixtures so as to avoid serious clashes, and its legislation of 1877, which forced course executives to find at least 300 sovereigns added money for each day's racing, served to concentrate racing and secure economies of scale for major courses.[3] However, dividends of the racing companies were limited to 10% and any surplus profits had to be ploughed back into the sport.

As this suggests, the Club's main concern was to preserve the viability of the racing industry. This was why it sought to improve the image of the sport by a two-pronged attempt to cleanse the racing stables. It instituted a system of specialist, licensed professional officials – starters, judges and handicappers – whose use it recommended to racecourse executives, and it developed the use of licences for trainers, jockeys, and even racecourses, which could be revoked, without having to justify the action, should there be a whiff of corruption or incompetence.[4]

A concern for the future of British racing was also why it took action to force racecourses to revise their programmes in the interests of British bloodstock and its presumed contribution to British military and agricultural strength.[5] By the late 1880s all the principal meetings had valuable events for two-year-olds and at most meetings there was more money for sprints and two-year-old racing than for stamina-testing distance races. Although this produced exciting races for spectators, the Jockey Club felt that the concentration was not in the best interests of the bloodstock industry: immature horses were susceptible to breakdown, especially if they raced early in the season, and sprints hid stamina deficiencies. Eventually, in 1899, the Club took action. Severe curbs were placed on two-year-old racing: such races were limited to five furlongs till the Epsom summer meeting and to not more than six furlongs till 1 September; two-year-old horses were not allowed to compete with three-year-olds until June and all handicap races with older horses were forbidden; and until 1 September there were to be no more than two two-year-old races on any card, the maximum thereafter being three. The Club also attempted to make other types of racing financially more attractive: at least half the guaranteed stakes were to go to races other than those for two-year-olds and at least half of that had to be for races of over one and a half miles; and there had to be a minimum of two races of more than a mile aggregating at least two and a half miles, on every daily programme.[6]

This concern for the British bloodstock industry was also demonstrated during the American invasion of the British turf in the late nineteenth and early twentieth centuries.[7] When American horses first arrived in any number they posed a major problem for breeders in that their pedigrees could not always be traced back far enough to show that they stemmed from bloodstock exported from Britain.[8] Thus, if British breeders utilised the American horses, there was no guarantee that the purity of English stock would be maintained. Messrs Weatherby, the publishers of the *General Stud Book*, the *Burke's Peerage* of racing, referred the matter to the Jockey Club, whose stewards, after consulting most of the principal breeders in the country, decided that if eight to nine crosses of pure blood could be proved, a century or more traced back, and the turf performances

of the horse's immediate family be such as to warrant a belief in the purity
of the blood, then the horse could be registered in the *General Stud Book*
as from May 1901.

In 1908, however, a fear that the suppression of racing in many states
would lead to a flood of horses coming to Britain from America stimulated
a reconsideration by British breeders. If American racing did not revive,
then many of the horses might remain in Britain for stud purposes.
Accordingly, with Jockey Club approval, the gateway clause was rescinded and, as from September 1909, no horse was eligible for the *General
Stud Book* unless it could be traced to a strain accepted in earlier volumes.
This did not satisfy the breeding fraternity as the legislation was not
retrospective and thus gave access to the descendants of those American
horses which had gained entry under the clause since 1901. The British
bloodstock industry was a powerful vested interest group within racing
and in the spring of 1913 Lord Jersey was able to persuade his fellow
Jockey Club members to pass a rule which prohibited the acceptance into
the *General Stud Book* of any horse if it could not be traced without flaw,
on *both* the sire's and the dam's side of its pedigree, to horses already
accepted. The stamp of half-breed was thus put on many American horses
with disastrous consequences for American exports of bloodstock. The
British claimed that the Jersey Act was passed to preserve the purity of the
breed, but it came at a time when American bloodstock sales were hitting
at British exports. Certainly American breeders were convinced that it was
designed to make the international bloodstock trade a British monopoly.[9]

III

By the early twentieth century the M. C. C. had full control over
first-class cricket in England: as well as organising the county championship, it coordinated all official tours to and from England and had
responsibility for the administration of domestic test matches. In a way
the M. C. C. had its greatness thrust upon it. Although it had set the rules
of cricket from the late eighteenth century, it took little cognisance of the
county championship and its arrangements until invited to do so by the
participants. The county secretaries had begun to meet regularly to discuss
rules and organisation from 1882 on; five years later the County Cricket
Council was set up in an attempt to centralise the administration of
county cricket, but it was dissolved in 1890 after an acrimonious debate
on a proposal to form divisions with promotion and relegation; in 1894
the county secretaries asked the M. C. C. to define first-class status; and
one year later it took the responsibility of determining the result of the

championship. In 1904 the Advisory County Cricket Committee was established under the aegis of the M. C. C. to provide an avenue for county club opinion into the latter's decision-taking process. Other committees enabled the M. C. C. to maintain control over player qualifications and discipline.[10]

There is little evidence that the M. C. C. and the counties acted as participants in a joint profit-maximising cartel. A failure to improve the cricket product by equalisation of playing strengths is a case in point. The peripatetic professional teams had attempted to render their matches less predictable by allowing their opponents more than the customary eleven players. Such handicapping was never contemplated at the county level so any equalisation of playing strengths required the equalisation of player quality. Here county qualifications had a role. As early as 1873 the counties had agreed that players could qualify for a county either by birth (a distinct advantage to the more populous counties) or by three years' residence (two for amateurs) in their adopted county.[11] The residential qualification was made a uniform two years the following season, but an attempt in 1887 to reduce it to only one year in the interests of the professional players, particularly those born in the minor counties, was defeated overwhelmingly. The fear, as put by the Middlesex delegate, was that 'the county with the largest purse would win the honour of the first position'.[12] From the 1889 season on players were allowed to turn out for their existing county while qualifying for another, something more likely for amateurs, whose other careers may have involved geographical mobility; this practice also assumed the continuation of amicable relations between the club and its departing player.[13] In 1898, following a move by Lord Harris (Kent) to extend the residential qualification to three years, an M. C. C. special committee, with representatives from Kent, Yorkshire, Surrey, Lancashire and the minor counties, decided to adhere to the two years but to tighten up the rule so that residence had to be for more than just the cricket season.[14]

Mobility was also hindered by the convention of players receiving a non-portable benefit for long service with their club. Nevertheless, by the end of the nineteenth century few counties relied solely on players born within their boundaries.[15] Lancashire and Surrey, in particular, drew players from far and wide, though the latter generally recruited youngsters and trained them, unlike Lancashire who sought professionals who had made the grade, either at county or league level.[16] This inter-county flow of players contributed to a concentration of talent in only a few counties. Table 9.1 shows that, although cricketers who played in test matches came from the whole spectrum of first-class counties, three counties were

Table 9.1 *Distribution by county of English test appearances,*
1895–1914

	1895–1904		1905–14	
	No.	%	No.	%
Derbyshire	6	1.7	4	0.8
Essex	5	1.4	29	6.0
Gloucestershire	18	5.0	13	2.7
Hampshire	6	1.7	25	5.2
Kent	12	3.3	48	9.9
Lancashire	53	14.6	51	10.5
Leicestershire	3	0.8	1	0.2
Middlesex	35	9.6	28	5.8
Nottinghamshire	16	4.4	23	4.8
Northamptonshire	—	—	6	1.1
Somerset	21	5.8	8	1.7
Surrey	49	13.5	80	16.5
Sussex	32	8.8	24	5.0
Warwickshire	29	8.0	36	7.4
Worcestershire	10	2.8	14	2.9
Yorkshire	61	16.8	70	14.5
Others	7	1.9	24	5.0
Total	363	100.0	484	100.0

Note: Until 1898 the test teams for home matches were selected by the appropriate ground
authorities, a procedure which may have led to a bias towards local players.
Source: Calculated from data in *Wisden Cricketers' Almanack.*

dominant. Between 1895 and 1904 players from Yorkshire, Surrey and
Lancashire made 44.9% of test appearances and 41.5% in the succeeding
decade. However, as Yorkshire did not recruit externally, the failure to
impose more severe restrictions on mobility cannot wholly explain the
skewed distribution of cricketing talent.[17]

Another failure to equalise playing ability resulted from the manner in
which the composition of the championship was constituted. When the
M. C. C. agreed to an expansion of the championship in the 1890s, it did
not establish strict regulations as to entry, as might be expected from an
administration controlling a cartel: all that was required was the arrangement of fixtures with eight of the existing participants.[18] It should be
stressed that counties had *carte blanche* to organise their fixture lists and

Table 9.2 *Static equality of competition in English county cricket, 1892–1914*

Season	No. of teams	Standard deviation of winning percentages
1892	9	22.6
1893	9	15.8
1894	9	23.1
1895	14	15.2
1896	14	15.8
1897	14	18.6
1898	14	17.4
1899	15	13.5
1900	15	18.2
1901	15	15.8
1902	15	11.4
1903	15	14.3
1904	15	14.8
1905	16	17.6
1906	16	20.3
1907	16	19.3
1908	16	15.6
1909	16	16.4
1910	16	18.5
1911	16	21.0
1912	16	16.4
1913	16	16.9
1914	16	18.4

Note: For the purposes of the calculations draws are classed as a 50% win to both sides.
Source: Calculated from data in *Wisden Cricketers' Almanack.*

Table 9.3 *Championship record of leading counties, 1895–1914*

	1st	2nd	3rd	4th	Top four
Yorkshire	8	4	4	2	18
Lancashire	2	5	1	6	14
Surrey	3	2	3	5	13
Kent	4	2	4	—	10
Total	17	13	12	13	55
Maximum possible	20	20	20	20	80

Source: Wisden Cricketers' Almanack.

there was no requirement for teams to play each other if they did not wish to.[19] The injection of fresh cricketing blood could have served to equalise playing competition had the newcomers replaced teams whose cricketing stars had waned. The pattern, however, was that once counties were in the championship there they remained. Even poor Somerset, who, between 1897 and 1913, had a best position of tenth – and that only once – was allowed to continue. All proposals for two divisions with promotion and relegation, as in English soccer, foundered on the issue of counties having to vote themselves out of the elite group.[20] The newcomers were not all that strong anyway. Although Worcestershire had been minor county champions in the four years prior to their entry, they averaged only tenth position in their first five years of first-class status. Really only Essex, with an average placing of fifth, and possibly Warwickshire, with an average of eighth, justified their elevation. The inclusion of Derbyshire and Hampshire, who both averaged tenth, Northamptonshire twelfth, and Leicestershire thirteenth, merely guaranteed the established, and better, teams more wins rather than closing the gap between the best and the average.

Too many contests remained one-sided affairs, with the weaker team dependent upon the weather to save it from defeat. Table 9.2 measures the static equality of competition in the form of the standard deviations of winning percentages in each championship from 1892 to 1913: the higher the figure, the less equal the teams are. The inequality in county cricket is brought out by a comparison with similar data for English soccer as shown in Table 9.12, especially when the role of the weather in producing draws in cricket is taken into consideration. This high degree of inequality of competition within each season could have been offset by different teams being dominant at different times, that is, there may have been dynamic equality of competition. However, as Tables 9.3 and 9.4 show, the overall superiority of certain counties is unquestionable. In the 20 seasons before 1915 Yorkshire finished in the top three on no less than 16 occasions and had a *mean* winning percentage higher than the *best* seasonal performance of nine other counties; between them, Yorkshire, Lancashire, Surrey and Kent took 55 of the possible 80 top four places. Rank order correlations shown in Table 9.5 suggest that as the competing group was enlarged – from 9 counties in 1894 to 16 in 1905 – positions in the championship became more predictable.

The M. C. C. was also slow to act in the matter of product improvement via a reduction in the number of drawn games. Between 1892 and 1896 the mean percentage of drawn county matches was 21.2, but in succeeding quinquennia it rose to 39.5 and 38.1. Draws in soccer and rugby can reflect closeness of competition, but in cricket they were

Table 9.4 *Winning percentages of English county cricket teams,*
1892–1913

	Period	Mean winning percentage
Derbyshire	1895–1913	27.4
Essex	1895–1913	46.8
Gloucestershire	1892–1913	39.6
Hampshire	1895–1913	36.0
Kent	1892–1913	57.4
Lancashire	1892–1913	62.6
Leicestershire	1895–1913	32.7
Middlesex	1892–1913	56.3
Nottinghamshire	1892–1913	53.4
Northamptonshire	1905–13	42.7
Somerset	1892–1913	32.9
Surrey	1892–1913	63.9
Sussex	1892–1913	45.2
Warwickshire	1895–1913	49.1
Worcestershire	1899–1913	44.8
Yorkshire	1892–1913	70.4

Source: Calculated from data in *Wisden Cricketers' Almanack.*

Table 9.5 *Dynamic equality of competition in English county cricket,*
1871–1913

One-year lag		Ten-year lag	
Period	D. E. C.[a]	Period	D. E. C.[a]
1871–81	0.40	1880–92	0.29
1882–92	0.57	1893–1904	0.31
1893–1903	0.53	1905–13	0.47
1904–13	0.64		

[a]As measured by the mean rank order correlation of championship positions. For the purposes of the calculations newcomers to the championship were omitted when correlations were made with earlier years in which they did not play and championship positions were adjusted accordingly.
Sources: Calculated from data in W. G. Grace, *Cricket,* Bristol, 1891, pp. 408–13; and *Wisden Cricketers' Almanack.*

generally the result of unexciting contests and were less attractive to spectators.[21]

Partly the rise in drawn matches was attributable to an ascendancy of bat over ball due to the preparation of excessively flat batting tracks.[22] In 1905, however, groundsmen were prevented from using anything other than the heavy roller and watering can on the pitch and this may have helped reduce the proportion of drawn games to 27.3% in the period 1907–11.[23] All other attempts to redress the balance in favour of the bowler failed to gain sufficient support. In 1902 a proposal to modify the lbw law so that the ball need not pitch in a direct line between the stumps obtained a majority of votes at the M. C. C. meeting, but not the two-thirds required. Two years later a similar fate befell a proposal to widen the wickets. The stumbling block was that the laws of cricket did not apply solely to the first-class game, but to all grades, and at the lower levels poor pitches meant that the bowlers were in charge and needed no further assistance.[24]

Some draws, of course, were due to the British climate. Yet little was done to combat the weather except after the aquatic displays of 1909 when clubs were given the option of covering the pitch should rain interfere with play.[25] Whether they failed to respond is unknown, but a similar wet season in 1912 saw 47.1% of fixtures ending in draws, the highest pre-war proportion. Little was done about the inefficient use of time, which also contributed to drawn games. One estimate put the loss of play attributed to excessive gaps between individual and team innings, tea intervals, trial balls and bad light appeals at between 65–75 minutes a day.[26] No action was taken by the M. C. C. and it was left to individual clubs, such as Leicestershire, to approach other counties regarding the abolition of the tea interval.[27] The main reaction of the M. C. C. to the situation of drawn games was to institute points for a first-innings lead in such matches in an effort to salvage some spectator interest, especially in rain-affected fixtures.[28] However, this was in 1911, a decade after the idea was introduced into the minor counties championship.

In addition to product improvement, a profit-maximising cartel might well have looked to product diversification, both to attract additional spectators and to encourage further spending from existing consumers. In 1873 the M. C. C., possibly influenced by the example of the Football Association, suggested a knockout competition, but, at this time, the clubs were too concerned with establishing county cricket on a firm footing and the idea was shelved on the ground that 'it may have a tendency to introduce a speculative element into cricket'.[29] The financial problems of the 1903 season, one of the wettest on record, tempted the county committees to discuss another cup competition, this one proposed by C. B. Fry and to include some minor counties, but again the idea fell through as only six first-class counties were willing to enter.[30]

A successful innovation, however, was the regular visits of the Australians. These had begun as private commercial speculations by the Australians themselves, but by the end of the nineteenth century the M. C. C. had taken over the responsibility for inviting the tourists and organising the test matches. So profitable were these international clashes that the number of tests in a series was increased from three to five. Not only the tests proved revenue raisers: crowds flocked to see the antipodean players and most club accounts shifted towards the black when they had a rain-free match against the tourists. However, given that they had the freedom to arrange fixtures – the M. C. C. controlled test matches only – the counties who could offer the largest crowds gained most as 'the Australians always play cricket in a commercial spirit, being keenly anxious for big gates' and would offer them more fixtures than the lesser-supported counties.[31]

A cartel can produce, or preserve, profits by holding down costs. Hence the qualification restrictions imposed on player mobility could be seen as assisting the stabilisation of labour expenses by lessening the chance of an auction for a player's services: if a professional was dissatisfied with the terms offered by his own county, his option was two years in the cricketing wilderness. Although clubs were left totally free to set their wage rates, most seem to have accepted a conventional limit: indeed they consulted each other on the matter.[32] Thus generally the richer counties did not pay higher wages but employed more professionals at the highest rate; they also offered winter pay to more of their players.[33] In the 1890s, however, the counties faced a challenge in the labour market from league cricket, especially in Lancashire, not so much for their star players but certainly for the good journeymen professionals. For these players league cricket was an attractive alternative: there were no residential qualifications; matches were played on Saturday afternoons so there was a possibility of holding a regular job throughout the year; and a good performance, which must have been easier to achieve at league than at county level, would earn a collection from the crowd. Inevitably the possibility of losing players to the leagues, whose 'busy agents . . . [were] always on the lookout for talent', forced the counties to raise the conventional maximum wage, offer more players winter pay, and expand the fixture lists in order to give their professionals sufficient remunerative employment.[34]

As shown in chapter 8, many counties found financial life a constant struggle. One reason for this was the substantial degree of inequality between teams, a direct result of M. C. C. policy. Yet the central body did little to compensate the poorer clubs, even though a lack of subsidisation could have threatened the viability of the competition. In the championship itself matches were arranged on a home and away basis with each club retaining its own gate. Occasionally clubs made arrangements with each other to share the aggregate receipts, particularly if one match was at holiday time, but generally this was between clubs of equal mediocrity and did not involve the major crowd-drawing teams.[35] In 1904 Somerset raised the possibility of pooling gate receipts as a formal policy but did not receive sufficient support.[36] Moreover, there was no transfer fee paid if a player changed counties, for who would risk large sums in the hope that a player would be in form and uninjured two years later: thus no club could finance itself by acting as a nursery for the stronger ones as occurred in soccer at this time. The only concession regarding the redistribution of revenue was in the test area. Until 1899 only the host counties benefited, but then it was agreed that, after sharing the gross gate receipts with the tourists and deducting expenses, the host club should take 20% of the residue (plus all stand receipts) and the remainder was shared between the M. C. C. and the other first-class counties.[37] Table 9.6 suggests that this did not have a major impact on the finances of the clubs concerned. On two occasions for Derbyshire, one of the poorest sides both on and off the field, it became a double-figure percentage of their total revenue but was still insufficient to give them a profit on the season. Moreover, since the tests were allocated by the M. C. C. to a minority of counties, usually among the richest, the greatest benefits from the international fixtures were reaped by them rather than the poorer clubs.[38] Any other subsidisation of the financially weak counties came not via resolutions of the M. C. C., but by donations, usually in the order of £25 to £50, from individual counties to the appeal funds of those clubs in financial strife.[39]

Although there were financial problems within the county championship, there was no major threat of it being rendered non-viable by external competition. Perhaps the Australian incursions could have posed problems, but the M. C. C. took charge and, by restricting the frequency of tours, prevented a crowding-out of the county game. There was no possibility of a rival county competition undermining the championship. The promotion of five counties to first-class status for the 1895 season had destroyed the second-class county championship as it left only Cheshire and Staffordshire. Worcestershire organised a new competition but it died when they, too, entered the first-class fold in 1899. Finally, in 1901, it was

Table 9.6 *Contribution of test match revenue to Derbyshire C. C. C. and Essex C. C. C., 1899–1912*

Year	Tourists	County	Income (£)	Profit (£)	Test revenue (£)	Test revenue as % income
1899	Australia	Derby	2,155	−164	185	8.7
		Essex	6,486	360	185	2.8
1902	Australia	Derby	3,897	−214	195	5.0
		Essex	5,140	10	195	3.8
1905	Australia	Derby	2,372	−196	316	13.3
		Essex	n.a	n.a.	316	n.a.
1907	South Africa	Derby	2,254	−492	124	5.5
		Essex	3,986	−247	124	3.1
1909	Australia	Derby	2,531	−262	308	12.2
		Essex	4,457	−26	308	6.9
1912	Australia \ South Africa ∫	Derby	2,367	−162	157	6.6
		Essex	3,713	−605	157	4.2

Source: Calculated from Annual Financial Statements.

reorganised completely and recognised officially as the minor counties championship by the M. C. C., who formally regulated it.[40] Nothing was done before 1914 about the competition from league cricket, although, especially in Lancashire, it attracted substantial numbers of spectators in aggregate and also provided an alternative market for players, though, apart from Sidney Barnes, not for those of international standard. However, the spectator issue probably affected only Lancashire and they were not unhappy with the use of quality players in the local leagues as, after two seasons, such imported cricketers gained a residential qualification for the red-rose county.[41]

IV

Unlike county cricket and horse-racing, elite English soccer had two ruling bodies. Essentially the Football Association, founded in 1863, set the rules of play (which applied to all levels of soccer) and the Football League, established in 1888, controlled the game's premier championship, though the F. A. also held its own prestigious cup competition and occasionally intervened in the economic activities of the League. The origins of the League stemmed from an idea of William McGregor, a Scotsman associated with Aston Villa, designed 'to improve the present unsatisfactory state of club fixtures and to render them more certain in their fulfilment and interesting in character'.[42] With professionalism 'good gates had become imperative' to the leading clubs, but the multiplicity of local cup competitions, often with one-sided early rounds, could not guarantee this and they also interfered with more remunerative friendly fixtures against other major teams.[43] Hence for the 1888/89 season twelve such clubs, six each from the North and the Midlands, bound themselves to play their full-strength teams in competitive League fixtures.

The two organisations had power effectively sewn up. At its inception the League had declared 'that any offending club or players shall be dealt with by the League in any manner that they may think fit'.[44] Thus any club which was unwilling to accept the League's decisions could forfeit its place in the most financially rewarding and highest-status league tournament in English soccer. Clubs which were unwilling to accept the paramount authority of the Football Association could find it difficult to obtain fixtures at all.[45] The power relationship between the two organisations was complex.[46] Initially McGregor had advocated that the League should govern professional football but, over time, he realised that 'when the League meet, they are actuated by the interests of the League clubs. The general good of football is not then their chief concern' and as such he came 'to see that it is best for the whole government of football to be in the hands of the Football Association'.[47] A similar view was expressed by his successor as League president, J. J. Bentley.[48] Nevertheless, the desire of the League for autonomy in its own affairs, especially as regards financial arrangements, produced friction at times because the F. A. Council was dominated by men from amateur clubs, some of whom, like one-time vice-president, N. L. Jackson, argued that the League was simply a combination of clubs 'formed to obtain the largest amount of gate money they can. It is a purely selfish organisation'.[49]

Certainly some actions of the League lent support to Jackson's assertion of its profit-seeking nature. For example, they seemed more eager than the M. C. C. to secure equality of playing competition. They exercised direct control over the size of the competing group, with changes requiring a two-thirds majority, and they developed quality control through the mechanism of promotion and relegation on merit.[50] Initially the bottom four clubs each season had to apply for re-election. This led to Stoke being replaced by Sunderland in 1890/91 only to regain their place, along with newly elected Darwen, when the League was expanded to 14 teams the following season. One year later a further two places were added but Darwen, who finished last, failed to secure enough votes and dropped to the newly created twelve-team second division. Promotion and relegation between the two divisions was by test matches between the bottom three in the first division and the top three in the lower group; presumably these were intended to assess whether the heirs apparent were good enough to bridge the quality gap. From 1895/96 these sudden-death fixtures were abandoned as being unfair in that a whole season's performances could be negated by the result of one match. Instead, the bottom two from the first division and the champion and runner-up from the second were involved in a peculiar form of mini-league play-off in which each played those from the other division twice and their divisional compatriot only once. This system, too, was abandoned after what seemed very much like an arranged result in the 1897/98 tests when Stoke and Burnley played a goalless draw which guaranteed them both first-division status.[51] Newcastle United and Blackburn Rovers, the other participants, were compensated by an enlargement of the first division to 18 clubs, an expansion urged by Burnley's representative so that there would be more 'League matches [which] always paid' unlike 'friendlies [which] never paid'.[52] From 1898/99 the two top second-division sides automatically replaced the bottom two in the first division and the last three clubs in the lower division, enlarged from 15 in 1893/94 to 16 in 1894/95 and 18 in 1898/99, had to seek re-election as they had had to do since its inception. In 1905/06 both divisions were increased to accommodate 20 teams.

Generally the system of promotion by merit assisted towards attaining equality of competition. Table 9.7 suggests that those clubs which secured positions in the first division performed well enough to justify their elevation. However, the same can be said of the second division and its election system. Votes were cast by all League clubs and they may have had an eye on the potential gates offered by rival candidates. When Lincoln, a founder member of the second division, lost out to Tottenham in 1908/09 one of their supporters bemoaned the fact that his team 'should go under before the encroachment of clubs with their ignoble and sole consideration of the "big purse"'.[53] Yet Lincoln had finished next to last and last in the previous two seasons, whereas Tottenham had a successful record in the Southern League and had achieved several good runs in the F. A. Cup, actually winning it in 1901, and they did manage to gain promotion to the first division at their first attempt.

The Football League was founded at a time when players could easily switch their allegiance from one club to another. To counteract this it was proposed that no player could represent two League clubs in the same season, but this was soon changed to simply having to have League permission, though the clubs involved also had to agree to the move.[54]

Table 9.7 *Performances of promoted and elected clubs in the English Football League, 1891/92–1912/13*

First division

Period	Teams promoted	Teams in division	Average position of promoted teams in first season
1892/93–1897/98	10	16	12
1898/99–1904/05	14	18	10
1905/06–1912/13	16	20	11

Second division

Period	Teams elected	Teams in division	Average position of promoted teams in first season
1894/95–1897/98	9	16	8
1898/99–1904/05	11	18	9
1905/06–1912/13	11	20	9

First division

Period	Teams promoted	Remained in first division at least two seasons	
1891/92–1901/02	20	15	
1902/03–1912/13	22	20	

Second division

Period	Teams elected	Remained in League at least two seasons	Promoted to first division within two seasons
1892/93–1901/02	21	19	3
1902/03–1912/13	13	12	2

Source: Calculated from data in C. E. Sutcliffe, J. A. Brierley and F. Howarth, *The Story of the Football League, 1888–1938*, Preston, 1939.

The League Management Committee said that they would not compel clubs to transfer a player, and the member clubs would not support a proposal of Blackburn Rovers (who had failed to persuade Sheffield Wednesday to release a player) that the League be so empowered.[55]

As far as the League was concerned, once a player had signed for a club they had an exclusive right to his services and he could not play for any other club without their permission. Such a sacrifice of player freedom was seen as essential: 'it will be a bad day for the League, the clubs and the players when freedom all round is given. Teams must be comparatively level to sustain the interest – if they are not, receipts fall off, and without receipts players cannot be paid wages.'[56] Usually the release of a player to another club involved a transfer fee as recompense to the original club for their outlay in training the player and for the loss of his future service: thus the club which lost a player gained funds with which they could strengthen their own playing squad. By 1897 the League was agreeing to set the fee when clubs were willing to trade but could not agree on a price.

Many influential members of the F. A. objected to this 'trafficking' in players and argued that players should be free agents at the end of each season. In 1899 the F. A. Council proposed that the sale of player contracts be prohibited, except for those for whom a fee had already been paid and even here no price increase was to be allowed.[57] The League felt that this would play into the hands of the richer clubs and opposed it vehemently: indeed so strong was their opposition that no agreement could be reached and in 1904, the F. A., tired of the continual bickering, decided to give up all responsibility for further financial arrangements between the League and its constituent clubs and restrict itself to monitoring for sharp practice in such dealings.[58] However, following the transfer of Alf Common from Sunderland to Middlesbrough for £1,000, the first four-figure fee in English soccer, they made one last effort to control transfers by giving three years' notice of the imposition of a maximum figure of £350. However, clubs were prepared to circumvent the legislation by the purchase of makeweight players and the limit operated for only three months.[59]

Although the transfer system offered some protection or compensation to the poorer clubs, unless player payments were limited not only would there be a seller's market for uncontracted players, but there would still be an incentive for players to try and leave a club in search of more money. Such was the competition to secure good footballers that Aston Villa's wage bill, which averaged £626 (31% of total costs) in the four years prior to entering the League, rose to an average of £2,112 (55%) in the four seasons from 1889/90.[60]

Table 9.8 *League and cup record of leading English soccer teams,*
1888/89–1914/15[a]

	League					Cup		
	1st	2nd	3rd	4th	Top four	Winner	Runner-up	Total
Aston Villa	6	6	1	2	15	4	1	5
Everton	1	6	4	3	14	1	3	4
Sunderland	5	3	4	0	12	0	1	1
Newcastle	3	0	2	4	9	1	4	5
Total	15	15	11	9	50	6	9	15
Total possible	27	27	27	27	108	27	27	54

[a]Sunderland entered the League's first division in 1890/91 and Newcastle joined the League
in 1896/97, gaining promotion to division one for 1898/99.
Sources: Calculated from data in C. E. Sutcliffe, J.A. Brierley and F. Howarth, *The Story of
the Football League, 1888–1938*, Preston, 1939; and G. Green, *The Official History of the
F. A. Cup*, London, 1960.

In 1891 signing-on fees were limited to £10, but determined clubs got
round this simply by advancing wages. Two years later an attempt was
made to impose a maximum wage of £140 per annum 'in order to secure
an equitable and permanent basis of remuneration to players, which shall
be advantageous to both clubs and players', but there was insufficient
support: perhaps there were too many utility-maximisers around at this
stage to accept such a cost-reduction policy.[61] Players were still entitled to
a bonus on re-signing for their club but this was legislated against in 1896,
though clubs simply built the money into the wage structure with the
result that 'no rule had so raised the wage list of the clubs'.[62] Finally, in
1900, the Football Association intervened to impose a maximum wage of
£208 a year (or £4 a week) and to outlaw bonuses for match results, which
they felt were detrimental to sportsmanship.[63] At the 1901 annual general
meeting representatives of Aston Villa and Liverpool attempted to rescind
the rule but could not get a sufficient majority and the new rule became
operative for the 1901/02 season. Amendments were moved at succeeding
annual general meetings but to no avail. Increasingly League clubs were
accepting the view of a leading member of their Management Committee
that 'if football has to be governed as a business, a maximum wage
becomes a necessity' and thus when, in 1908, the F. A. Council proposed
the abolition of the maximum wage it was defeated after the delegate from

Table 9.9 *Distribution of English international soccer caps, 1888/89–1913/14*

	1888/89–1893/94	1896/97–1901/02	1902/03–1907/08	1908/09–1913/14
(a) No. of caps awarded	209	231	231	308
(b) Caps to Football League players	152	169	203	295
(c) Caps to players from Aston Villa, Everton, Sunderland and Newcastle United	22	30	52	54
(c) as a percentage of (a)	10.4	13.0	22.5	17.5
(c) as a percentage of (b)	14.5	17.8	25.6	18.3

Source: Calculated from data in *Rothmans Football Yearbook 1977–78*, London, 1978.

Table 9.10 *Distribution of Scottish international soccer caps, 1890/91–1913/14*

	1890/91–1895/96	1896/97–1901/02	1902/03–1907/08	1908/09–1913/14
(a) No. of caps awarded	198	198	198	198
(b) Caps to Scottish-based players	195	176	137	149
(c) Caps to Scottish League players	95	126	135	149
(d) Caps to players from Celtic, Rangers and Hearts	59	101	90	98
(e) Caps to English-based players[a]	3	22	61	49
(f) Caps to players from Aston Villa, Everton, Sunderland and Newcastle United	—	7	44	26
(d) as a percentage of (a)	29.8	51.0	45.5	49.5
(d) as a percentage of (b)	30.3	57.4	65.7	65.8
(d) as a percentage of (c)	62.1	80.2	66.7	65.8
(f) as a percentage of (e)	—	31.8	72.1	53.1

[a] There was an S. F. A. policy of selecting only home-based Scots until 1895/96 and, prior to 1893/94, different teams were selected for the three international matches each season 'as it was thought desirable to spread the honour of representing the country among as many players as possible' (*Scottish Football Annual 1878/79*, p. 81).

Source: Calculated from data in *Rothmans Football Yearbook 1977/78*, London, 1978.

Table 9.11 Winning percentages of English first-division football teams, 1888/89–1914/15[a]

Team	No. of seasons in first division	Period[b]	Mean winning percentage	Highest winning percentage	Lowest winning percentage
Accrington	5	1888/89–1892/93	42.6	54.5	36.4
Aston Villa	27	1888/89–1914/15	58.8	78.3	43.2
Birmingham	6	1901/02–1907/08	48.1	57.4	39.5
Blackburn Rovers	27	1888/89–1914/15	51.5	67.1	39.7
Bolton Wanderers	22	1888/89–1914/15	45.9	61.7	31.6
Bradford City	7	1908/09–1914/15	51.1	59.2	44.7
Bradford Park Avenue	1	1914/15	53.9	53.9	53.9
Bristol City	5	1906/07–1910/11	47.6	63.2	35.5
Burnley	{ 11	1888/89–1899/1900	44.5	57.4	29.5
	{ 2	1913/14–1914/15	52.0	56.6	47.4
Bury	17	1895/96–1911/12	44.9	57.4	27.6
Chelsea	6	1907/08–1914/15	43.4	51.3	36.8
Darwen	2	1891/92–1893/94	26.5	31.7	21.2
Derby	{ 19	1888/89–1906/07	47.7	68.3	34.1
	{ 2	1912/13–1913/14	45.4	55.3	35.5
Everton	27	1888/89–1914/15	56.9	70.5	45.5
Glossop	1	1899/1900	26.5	26.5	26.5
Grimsby	2	1901/02–1902/03	42.0	47.1	36.8
Leicester Fosse	1	1908/09	32.9	32.9	32.9
Liverpool	19	1894/95–1914/15	50.8	67.1	36.7
Manchester City	14	1899/1900–1914/15	51.4	64.7	40.8
Manchester United	9	1906/07–1914/15	55.1	68.4	39.5

Middlesbrough	13	1902/03–1914/15	46.5	56.6	38.2
Newcastle United	17	1898/99–1914/15	55.3	69.7	42.1
Newton Heath	2	1892/93–1893/94	26.7	30.0	23.3
Nottingham Forest	18	1892/93–1910/11	47.1	58.3	32.9
Nott's County	23	1888/89–1914/15	44.1	59.1	26.5
Oldham	5	1910/11–1914/15	53.9	59.2	44.7
Preston North End	22	1888/89–1914/15	52.3	90.9	36.8
Sheffield United	22	1893/94–1914/15	52.8	70.6	42.6
Sheffield Wednesday	22	1892/93–1914/15	52.1	69.1	35.3
Small Heath	2	1894/95–1895/96	37.5	41.7	33.3
Stoke	18	1888/89–1906/07	41.8	54.5	26.9
Sunderland	25	1890/91–1914/15	59.2	80.8	38.7
Tottenham	6	1909/10–1914/15	42.3	48.7	36.8
West Bromwich Albion {	15	1888/89–1903/04	52.6	56.8	27.3
	4	1911/12–1914/15	52.6	56.6	50.0
Wolverhampton Wanderers	18	1888/89–1905/06	48.9	63.6	30.3
Woolwich Arsenal	9	1904/05–1912/13	46.3	57.9	23.7

[a]League fixtures only.
[b]Where teams were absent from the first division for five seasons or more a separate entry has been made.

Source: Calculated from data in C. E. Sutcliffe, J. A. Brierley and F. Howarth, The Story of the Football League, 1888–1938, Preston, 1939.

Table 9.12 *Static equality of competition in the English Football League, 1888/89–1914/15*

Season	First division		Second division	
	No. of teams	S. E. C.[a]	No. of teams	S. E. C.[a]
1888–89	12	18.0		
1889–90	12	15.6		
1890–91	12	12.4		
1891–92	14	16.6		
1892–93	16	11.4	12	17.6
1893–94	16	12.4	15	19.6
1894–95	16	12.4	16	16.5
1895–96	16	12.9	16	17.2
1896–97	16	10.9	16	13.7
1897–98	16	9.3	16	17.3
1898–99	16	8.2	18	17.0
1899–1900	18	10.9	18	17.6
1900–01	18	9.0	18	11.6
1901–02	18	5.6	18	13.7
1902–03	18	8.5	18	14.3
1903–04	18	10.6	18	12.3
1904–05	18	12.9	18	18.1
1905–06	20	8.3	20	16.2
1906–07	20	9.2	20	12.6
1907–08	20	6.3	20	13.0
1908–09	20	7.1	20	9.2
1909–10	20	9.7	20	13.0
1910–11	20	9.8	20	10.4
1911–12	20	7.7	20	11.2
1912–13	20	12.0	20	9.3
1913–14	20	7.1	20	11.3
1914–15	20	7.8	20	11.3

[a]As measured by the standard deviation of winning percentages each season. Draws were classed as a 50% win to both sides.
Source: Calculated from data in C. E. Sutcliffe, J. A. Brierley and F. Howarth, *The Story of the Football League, 1888–1938*, Preston, 1939.

Staffordshire, in reality from Wolverhampton Wanderers, maintained that 'it would mean ruin for the poorer clubs' who, 'with little money, but any amount of enthusiasm, must have a chance to carry off the highest honours'.[64] The richer clubs could not persuade the others to remove all

Table 9.13 *Dynamic equality of competition in the Football League first division, 1889/90–1914/15*

One-year lag		Ten-year lag	
Period	D. E. C.[a]	Period	D. E. C.[a]
1889/90–1897/98	0.40	1889/90–1905/06	0.19
1898/99–1905/06	0.25	1906/07–1914/15	0.26
1906/07–1914/15	0.23		

[a]As measured by the mean rank order correlation of championship positions. For the purposes of the calculations newcomers to the championship were omitted when correlations were made with earlier years in which they did not play and championship positions were adjusted accordingly.

Sources: Calculated from data in C. E. Sutcliffe, J. A. Brierley and F. Howarth, *The Story of the Football League, 1888–1938*, Preston, 1939.

wage restrictions and settled for, and eventually obtained, bonuses for winning F. A. Cup matches, talent money for finishing in the top five of the League, and an extra pound a week for long-serving players.[65] By this time many of the clubs which had advocated the total abolition of wage restrictions had changed their minds. Union militancy had forced men such as John McKenna of Liverpool to revise their thinking in the light of 'the exorbitant demands of players'.[66]

Despite these interventions in the labour market by both the League and the F. A., four clubs were still able to win more often than others. Table 9.8 shows that Aston Villa, Everton, Newcastle United and Sunderland enjoyed a disproportionate share of playing success. Although, as Table 9.9 demonstrates, they never secured more than a quarter of England's international players, they were, as Table 9.10 shows, able to strengthen their squads with star players from north of the Border. Nevertheless, they did not totally dominate English soccer, particularly on a match-by-match basis. It is clear from Table 9.11 that several other clubs had mean winning percentages almost as good as the famous four, and that in terms of highest winning percentages most first-division clubs had at least one very good season. The weaker sides dropped down into the second division to be replaced by teams who certainly in the short run were capable of performing better in the higher grade. The measures of both static and dynamic equality of competition, presented in Tables 9.12 and 9.13, quite clearly show that English soccer was more competitive than county cricket and lend some support to the view of T. H. Sydney

(Wolverhampton Wanderers) that the imposition of the maximum wage 'had worked well because clubs were of a much more equal playing strength than ever they were before'.[67] There was a wider disparity of playing talent in the second division, though even here only 9 out of the 64 entrants had a mean winning percentage of less than 40%.[68]

Initially the League faced some competition in the market for spectators in that some clubs failed to give priority to League fixtures. Fines imposed for the cancellation of League matches soon brought them into line.[69] Clubs were then forbidden to arrange any other matches before the League fixture card was completed.[70] However, they were still free to choose the dates of their games and some were leaving Saturdays free for cup ties. This was stopped in 1892, though it was later agreed that the first round of the F. A. Cup be left free and the Birmingham and Lancashire Associations were assured that they could play their cup semi-finals and finals on Saturdays. In 1897 a fixture committee was established to arrange all matches, though clubs could request specific days, with ballots for the first Saturday of the season and for disputed claims to holiday dates.[71]

The major competition, however, was in the labour market, where non-League clubs frequently poached League players with offers of high wages but refused to pay the League clubs for the players' contracts. The initial reaction of the League was the institution of a boycott against such clubs, thus denying them lucrative fixtures against League opposition.[72] This forced Ardwick for one to offer to retransfer a player to Burnley, but many other ambitious clubs found it no deterrent to be placed on 'the list'.[73] The F. A. successfully lobbied for the boycott to be rescinded for cup games but otherwise it remained in operation until 1896.[74] In the meantime many of the major poachers had actually joined the League and become subject to its authority. Others had formed the Southern League: indeed its establishment in 1894 was a direct result of the boycott being applied to Millwall, who then sought to develop competitive league fixtures in the south of England.[75] Arrangements were made with the Scottish Football League, in 1897, to recognise each other's registrations but not with the Southern League till 1909.[76]

From its beginning the Football League was acknowledged as the premier competition and other clubs constantly sought to participate.[77] The extension to two divisions and the increase in the number of teams accommodated many of the serious aspirants, so that the only real challenger within England was the Southern League. Nevertheless, as Table 9.9 shows, the great majority of English international players were being selected from Football League teams, and the Southern League was aware of its subordinate position, attempting in 1900 and again in 1909 to join the League, either as a southern-based second division or even as a third division.[78] The latter proposal came after League clubs had rejected the notion of a third division 'owing to the small number of applicants and the calibre of the clubs'.[79] Nonetheless, the Southern League was not brought into the fold, despite their plea that the acquisition of 20 of the strongest clubs outside the League 'would accordingly materially assist in the solution of financial problems'.[80] The reasons for their rejection can only be speculated upon. Perhaps it was a fear of increased travel costs; or maybe existing clubs preferred to risk re-election than the drop in status which relegation would bring; or possibly the Southern League had brought it on itself by suspending both Queen's Park Rangers and Tottenham Hotspur when they applied for individual Football League membership.[81]

Initially it had been proposed that gates be pooled but this was quickly changed to a retention of home gates with a guarantee of £12 to the visiting club, a figure which soon became dwarfed by gate-receipts and hence the idea of a guarantee was dropped, except where some distant clubs made their League debuts and had to compensate the others for increased travel costs.[82] West Bromwich Albion had proposed an equal division of receipts but this was defeated by seven votes to five, though clubs were given permission to make individual pooling arrangements; in 1891 a proposal for 25% of gross takings to be pooled for *all* clubs to share was rejected; and a similar fate befell Preston's resurrection of the West Bromwich proposal in 1908.[83]

Although the setting of a minimum entrance charge prevented clubs engaging in potentially ruinous price competition, it could have acted against the interests of the weaker clubs, who may have wished to test the elasticity of demand for their inferior product. To prevent undue competition for spectators within the League, it was decided in 1891 not to admit any club whose ground was within three miles of that of an existing member.[84] Yet when Chelsea, Clapton Orient and Tottenham Hotspur objected to Arsenal's proposed move to Highbury, the League declined to intervene on the grounds that 'there is ample population and opportunity'.[85] Possibly the League saw little necessity to maintain policies designed to keep its members afloat as gates for most of them were rising anyway. Member clubs do not appear to have been concerned about letting Stoke, Darwen, Port Vale and a few others disappear from the League because of financial problems, presumably because there were clubs of a reasonable quality to replace them. Certainly the response to a call by the League for voluntary contributions to assist clubs in a poor financial position was such as to call forth a scathing comment from N. L. Jackson that 'only self-interest, or self-preservation will persuade the richer clubs to devote a portion of their wealth to keeping their poorer brethren alive'.[86] Nevertheless, there were examples of individual clubs occasionally assisting others, as when Aston Villa donated 100 guineas to West Bromwich Albion's appeal fund.[87] The transfer system did operate to help clubs, some of whom 'derived considerable pecuniary advantage from training young players and then selling them to the more prominent clubs'.[88] Indeed teams such as West Bromwich Albion, Bury, Blackpool and Barnsley survived only because of their earnings in the transfer market.[89] Although a limit on transfer fees could have operated as a cost-reduction mechanism, the richer clubs were prepared to pay, and the poorer to accept, larger fees for players, the loss of whom probably undermined their chances of winning but helped solve financial difficulties. However, when the viability of the whole League was threatened by the fall in attendances after the outbreak of the First World War, a League Relief Fund was quickly established by means of a $2\frac{1}{2}$% levy on club gates and a sliding scale of wage cuts ranging from 15% for those on £5 a week to 5% for those who earned between £2 and £3.[90]

V

The Scottish Football Association was founded in 1873. By 1906 116 clubs and 11 major associations had affiliated, but not until 1912 did the Scottish Junior Association align itself with the S. F. A. 'thus tending to lengthen, strengthen and centralise the government of Association Football, and bring this Association into line with the other national associations'.[91] With this major exception the control of Scottish football had long been in the hands of the S. F. A. One test had come in 1887 when Queen's Park and Partick Thistle were drawn against each other in an F. A. Cup tie which would, of course, be played in Scotland. In the event of a dispute who would adjudicate, the F. A. or the S. F. A.? An International Board meeting then decided that each national association within the United Kingdom had the right to complete control over its own clubs. The reaction of the S. F. A. was to order all its affiliates to withdraw from membership of the F. A. and to prohibit any Scottish club from competing for any national trophy outside Scotland.[92]

The Scottish Football League was founded in 1890. As in England, it was established to schedule regular competitive fixtures between the leading clubs (apart from Queen's Park, who elected not to participate until the season 1901/02). The League did not attempt to challenge the authority of the S. F. A. and remained 'loyal adherents of the Association, subordinating League interests where there was the semblance of conflict'.[93] However, the S. F. A. made decisions on such matters as the length of the playing season and the punishment of sent-off players, both of which had consequences for the League. It should also be noted that the S. F. A.'s governing committee was composed predominantly of representatives from non-League clubs.

There seems to have been little attempt by the League to equalise playing strengths between teams save for the adoption of the rule which tied a player to the League club for which he first signed: there were no recruitment zones or qualification periods and, unlike in England, no maximum wage. The richest clubs were thus free to offer the highest signing-on fees, wages and transfer fees, and it is clear from Table 9.10 that player talent gravitated to Celtic, Rangers and Hearts: from 1902/03 to 1913/14 virtually two-thirds of all caps to Scottish-based teams came from these three clubs.

Nor was there any major effort to control the quality of teams in the first division by any systematic scheme of promotion and relegation. The bottom three teams each season simply had to apply for re-election in competition with any aspiring club. This continued even after the establishment of the second division in 1893, from which there was no automatic promotion. In the first decade of the League several sides failed to secure re-election, including Vale of Leven, cup finalists seven times, Renton, twice cup winners, and Dumbarton, winners of the first two League championships. Whether these clubs were voted out because, with their virtual village populations, they could not offer sufficient gate-money to satisfy the other teams must remain a matter for conjecture. They certainly did not have the resources to retain their best players; both Vale of Leven and Dumbarton had two poor playing seasons before they departed and Renton's last season's winning percentage of 11.1 was the third-worst in League history. The worst, Abercorn's 8.3%, also resulted in non-re-election, but not Dundee's 9.1%, which on the basis of their other performances seems to have been an aberration. After 1901 an expansionist policy, from 10 clubs in 1901/02 to 20 by 1913/14, meant that re-election was generally forthcoming, only Port Glasgow Athletic disappearing from the competition after gaining a percentage of 16.2, the second-worst of the pre-war period.[94] The other side of the bawbee was that the winner of the second division did not always secure election to the first division. In fact on only six occasions between 1893/94 and 1913/14 was the champion team promoted.

With promotion and relegation not based solely on merit and with a

Table 9.14 *Static equality of competition in the Scottish Football League, 1890/91–1914/15*

Season	First division		Second division	
	No. of teams	S. E. C.[a]	No. of teams	S. E. C.[a]
1890/91	10[b]	28.4		
1891/92	12	22.0		
1892/93	10	19.0		
1893/94	10	20.4	n.a.	n.a.
1894/95	10	21.5	n.a.	n.a.
1895/96	10	19.4	10	n.a.
1896/97	10	22.7	10	20.3
1897/98	10	16.8	10	16.5
1898/99	10	27.2	10	21.3
1899/1900	10	22.5	n.a.	n.a.
1900/01	11	17.9	n.a.	n.a.
1901/02	10	17.6	n.a.	n.a.
1902/03	12	19.3	12	17.1
1903/04	14	19.1	12	22.9
1904/05	14	15.4	12	20.1
1905/06	16	15.6	12	21.4
1906/07	18	13.8	12	20.2
1907/08	18	17.0	12	19.8
1908/09	18	16.0	12	22.5
1909/10	18	14.6	12	20.4
1910/11	18	15.3	12	22.6
1911/12	18	11.0	12	17.7
1912/13	18	13.7	14	20.2
1913/14	20	16.3	12	16.8
1914/15	20	15.4	n.a.	n.a.

[a]As measured by the standard deviation of winning percentages each season. Draws were classed as a 50% win to both sides.

[b]Initially there were eleven teams but Renton were expelled from the Scottish Football Association for playing a match against Edinburgh Saints, in reality St Bernards, who had already been suspended by the S. F. A. for professionalism (S. F. A. Annual Report 1890/91). Renton had played five League matches and these results were cancelled (M. Golesworthy (ed.), *The Encyclopaedia of Association Football*, Newton Abbot, 1977, p. 183).

Sources: Calculated from data in S. F. A., *Scottish Football Annual 1899*; *Scotsman*, passim; *Evening Times Football Annual 1915*.

Table 9.15 *Dynamic equality of competition in the Scottish Football
League first division, 1893/94–1914/15*

One-year lag		Ten-year lag	
Period	D. E. C.[a]	Period	D. E. C.[a]
1893/94–1901/02	0.61	1902/03–1907/08	0.28
1902/03–1905/06	0.54	1908/09–1914/15	0.33
1906/07–1914/15	0.55		

[a]As measured by the mean rank order correlation of championship positions. For the
purposes of the calculations newcomers to the championship were omitted when correlations were made with earlier years in which they did not play, and League positions were
adjusted accordingly.
Sources: Calculated from data in S. F. A., *Scottish Football Annual 1899*; *Scotsman*,
passim; *Evening Times Football Annual 1915*.

Table 9.16 *Playing record of leading Scottish soccer teams,
1890/91–1914/15*

	League				Cup		
	1st	2nd	3rd	Top three	Winner	Runner-up	Finalist[a]
Celtic	12	7	2	21	9	4	14
Rangers	7	6	8	21	4	3	8
Hearts	2	5	4	11	3	2	5
Total	21	18	14	53	16	9	27
Total possible[b]	25	25	25	75	24	24	48

[a]The 1909 cup final between Celtic and Rangers ended in a draw and in a riot so the cup was
withheld that season. However, it has been included in the calculations.
[b]There was no cup competition in the season 1914/15.
Source: Rothmans Football Yearbook 1977–78, London, 1978.

Table 9.17 *Winning percentages of Scottish first-division soccer teams, 1890/91–1914/15*[a]

Team	No. of seasons in first division[b]	Period	Mean winning percentage	Highest winning percentage	Lowest winning percentage
Abercorn	4	1890/91–1896/97	27.7	38.6	8.3
Aberdeen	10	1905/06–1914/15	50.7	70.6	39.5
Airdrieonians	12	1903/04–1914/15	53.8	63.3	34.6
Ayr United	2	1913/14–1914/15	53.3	63.2	43.4
Cambuslang	2	1890/91–1891/92	39.2	55.6	22.7
Celtic	25	1890/91–1914/15	74.9	91.7	58.3
Clyde	{ 8	1891/92–1899/1900	27.2	45.6	11.1
	9	1906/07–1914/15	50.9	70.6	26.5
Cowlairs	1	1890/91	16.7	16.7	16.7
Dumbarton	{ 6	1890/91–1895/96	51.0	84.1	18.5
	2	1913/14–1914/15	40.1	44.7	35.5
Dundee	22	1893/94–1914/15	49.7	70.6	9.1
Falkirk	10	1905/06–1914/15	58.9	76.4	38.3
Hamilton	9	1906/07–1914/15	39.7	50.0	30.4

Hears	25	1890/91–1914/15	60.0	86.1	35.0
Hibernian	20	1895/96–1914/15	54.3	84.1	36.5
Kilmarnock	16	1899/1900–1914/15	41.3	50.0	25.0
Leith Athletic	4	1891/92–1914/15	37.6	56.8	18.5
Morton	15	1900/01–1914/15	42.0	71.1	18.5
Motherwell	12	1903/04–1914/15	40.1	54.4	26.9
Parrick Thistle	16	1895/96–1914/15	40.8	61.8	11.8
Port Glasgow Athletic	8	1902/03–1909/10	31.3	41.2	16.2
Queen's Park	15	1900/01–1914/15	33.2	44.2	17.1
Raith	5	1910/11–1914/15	38.4	42.1	35.3
Rangers	25	1890/91–1914/15	73.3	100.0	54.5
Renton	3	1891/92–1893/94	33.5	47.7	11.1
St Bernards	7	1893/94–1899/1900	40.5	63.9	25.0
St Mirren	25	1890/91–1914/15	46.2	55.6	28.9
Third Lanark	25	1890/91–1914/15	50.0	82.7	30.6
Vale of Leven	2	1890/91–1891/92	21.0	30.6	11.4

[a]League fixtures only.

[b]Where teams were absent from the first division for five seasons or more a separate entry has been made.

Sources: Calculated from data in S. F. A., Scottish Football Annuals 1890–9; Evening Times Football Annual 1915; Scotsman, passim.

labour market that was not tightly controlled, there was little likelihood of sporting equality being attained. Indeed Table 9.14 shows that the Scottish League championship was generally an unequal contest, especially when a comparison is made with the Football League data in Table 9.12. In no season was the static equality of competition lower in the Scottish first division than in its English counterpart: in fact the mean Scottish figure of 18.3 was higher than that of any season south of the Border. Similarly the mean static equality of competition in the Scottish second division of 20.0 ranked above the most unequal season in either of the English divisions. As demonstrated in Tables 9.13 and 9.15 the dynamic equality of competition was also higher in Scotland. Moreover, an examination of the top League positions and Scottish Cup finalists, shown in Table 9.16, clearly exhibits the playing dominance of Celtic, Rangers and, to a lesser extent, Hearts. Only in three seasons of the first quarter-century of the League did they not fill at least two of the top three positions and on six occasions they obtained all three places; neither Celtic nor Rangers ever finished lower than fifth, and that on only three occasions between them; and in the 24 cup finals up to 1914 these three clubs provided a finalist in all but three years and, excluding the abandoned final of 1909, won the trophy 16 times. No English club exerted such a dominance. Table 9.17 reinforces the view in respect of Celtic and Rangers. Not only did they win three points out of every four played for, but their average performance ranked above the best seasonal performances of 23 of the other 28 clubs which played first-division soccer. Moreover, Celtic's worst performance of 58.3%, in 1890/91, topped the best performance of 15 clubs, and Rangers' poorest season, 54.5%, in 1891/92, was better than the best attempts of 12 other clubs.

It may be that the basic objective of the Scottish Football League was survival: simply to keep itself viable in order that its members would have a recognised major championship to compete for. Such a policy might require income redistribution between clubs so as to keep the constituent members financially afloat. As early as 1880 the S. F. A. had decided that gate-money at cup ties should be shared equally between the two clubs, but the League rejected this and opted for a two-thirds to one-third arrangement in favour of the home team.[95] Not till 1905 was the principle of equal division accepted, and this still favoured those clubs with the largest aggregate home support. Moreover, all that was shared was the basic gate-money; stand receipts were retained by the home club, which was, of course, to the advantage of those sides which could afford to provide such spectator facilities. A proposal by St Mirren in 1893 that stand receipts be included in the money to be divided failed to be carried, because 'the leading clubs consider the non-drawing elements in the League are sufficiently well remunerated at present'.[96] It could be that more equitable income redistribution was viewed as unnecessary in that adequate substitutes were forthcoming for any teams which fell by the wayside: prior to 1901 the ten new entrants to the first division performed creditably with an average winning percentage of 46.1 in their first season – 50.3 if Abercorn's disastrous 8.3 is discounted. However, the five newcomers in the next four years averaged only 30.9%, which may have tempted the rethink on gate-division.

The other route to League survival lay in the elimination of rivals. As in England, the expansion in the number of clubs and the extension to two divisions – at one swoop, taking half the teams from the Scottish Alliance League – served to head off major challengers. Certainly the League was able to recruit the best playing talent: the last non-League international cap awarded was in 1903/04. In fact the most important league outside the Scottish League was the Inter-City one, which was actually composed of members of the Scottish League![97] It began as a four-club Glasgow League in 1894/95, with Clyde joining Queen's Park, Celtic, Rangers and Third Lanark in 1896/97 and Partick Thistle being added in 1898/99. However, the following season saw the Edinburgh duo of Hearts and Hibernian replacing the Glasgow latecomers and the competition being renamed the Inter-City League. The idea behind both leagues had been to fill in blanks in fixture schedules with competitive matches as, in those days, Scottish League games were finished by the early new year. In 1902/03 the Inter-City competition expanded to include all first-division sides except Kilmarnock, Port Glasgow and Morton, though each team played the others only once. However, the venture lasted only two seasons and then reverted to a Glasgow League only and was finally disbanded in 1907. The increased number of matches required by an expanding Scottish League had made it difficult to find suitable dates for other fixtures.

VI

The Northern Rugby Football Union, established in 1895 after the breakaway from the English Rugby Football Union, remained the controlling authority of all rugby league, amateur and professional, throughout the period studied, a position analogous to that of the Football Association. Initially, it also organised the major league competition, but, in June 1900, 14 leading clubs set up the Northern Rugby Football League to run the senior professional league competition. However, this organi-

Table 9.18 *Playing record of leading rugby league teams, 1895/96–1914/15*

	Northern Union and Northern League			League play-offs		Yorkshire or Lancashire Senior competition		Yorkshire or Lancashire League	Challenge Cup		County Cups	
	1st	2nd	3rd	1st	2nd	1st	2nd	1st	1st	2nd	1st	2nd
Oldham	2	2	1	2	3	2	3	2	1	2	3	2
Wigan	2	3	2	1	4	1	—	6	—	1	4	2
Huddersfield	4	—	—	3	1	—	—	4	2	—	4	1
Total	8	5	3	6	8	3	3	12	3	3	11	5
Total possible	12	12	12	9	9	7	7	16	19	19	20	20

Source: Rothmans Rugby League 1982/83 Yearbook, Aylesbury, 1982.

Table 9.19 *Winning percentages of Northern Rugby League teams,*
1905/06–1914/15

Team	Period	Mean winning percentage	Highest winning percentage	Lowest winning percentage
Aberdare	1908/09	5.9	5.9	5.9
Barrow	1905/06–1914/15	39.3	66.7	19.6
Barry	1908/09	16.7	16.7	16.7
Batley	1905/06–1914/15	51.7	76.7	39.7
Bradford	1905/06–1906/07	51.1	58.8	43.3
Bradford N.	1907/08–1914/15	32.7	53.1	11.1
Bramley	1907/08–1914/15	19.2	35.9	5.0
Brighouse	1905/06	15.4	15.4	15.4
Broughton R.	1905/06–1914/15	56.5	78.3	32.4
Castleford	1905/06	20.0	20.0	20.0
Coventry	1910/11–1912/13	14.3	20.6	1.9
Dewsbury	1905/06–1914/15	47.9	69.1	38.3
Ebbw Vale	1907/08–1911/12	33.1	52.1	18.3
Halifax	1905/06–1914/15	59.4	83.8	34.4
Huddersfield	1905/06–1914/15	68.4	88.2	40.6
Hull	1905/06–1914/15	54.3	72.1	34.4
Hull K. R.	1905/06–1914/15	60.9	73.5	45.3
Hunslet	1905/06–1914/15	58.0	79.7	19.6
Keighley	1905/06–1914/15	47.5	72.9	47.5
Leeds	1905/06–1914/15	58.2	76.5	32.8
Leigh	1905/06–1914/15	45.7	80.0	26.7
Liverpool C.	1906/07	1.7	1.7	1.7
Merthyr Tydfil	1907/08–1910/11	33.0	63.9	11.9
Mid Rhondda	1908/09	30.6	30.6	30.6
Millom	1905/06	20.0	20.0	20.0
Morecambe	1905/06	15.4	15.4	15.4
Normanton	1905/06	20.8	20.8	20.8
Oldham	1905/06–1914/15	72.6	90.6	50.0
Pontefract	1905/06–1906/07	39.5	41.1	37.5
Rochdale H.	1905/06–1914/15	45.3	73.5	18.8
Runcorn	1905/06–1914/15	42.2	76.7	1.9
Salford	1905/06–1914/15	50.1	79.7	33.3
St Helens	1905/06–1914/15	47.4	65.4	26.6
Swinton	1905/06–1914/15	44.3	57.8	31.7
Treherbert	1908/09–1909/10	12.5	25.0	0.0
Wakefield T.	1905/06–1914/15	52.7	75.0	39.7
Warrington	1905/06–1914/15	54.9	65.0	43.8
Widnes	1905/06–1914/15	45.8	68.3	26.8
Wigan	1905/06–1914/15	77.8	87.5	66.2
York	1905/06–1914/15	30.9	42.2	17.7

Source: Calculated from data in *Rothmans Rugby League 1982/83 Yearbook*, Aylesbury, 1982.

sation bowed to the ultimate authority of the N. R. F. U. and in turn it was delegated powers regarding qualification of players, engagements, protests, championships and transfers in its own competitions.[98] Between them the two authorities had full disciplinary powers over players and clubs.

One difference between regulations covering player recruitment and mobility in rugby league as compared to soccer was the imposition of a maximum player roster of 75.[99] Although it seems too large to have been an effective deterrent to the concentration of the best players in one team, it should be noted that at one time Halifax attempted to have 400 players registered.[100] The residential qualification for overseas players initially was set at one year but was increased to two years in 1912.[101] Attempts were also made to regularise the competition for players from Australasian touring sides by barring a club from obtaining the services of any player approached by them before the end of the tour.[102] Transfers could be prevented if a player's existing club objected to the proposed move, but an inquiry could be requested by either the player or his potential employer.[103] Although broken-time payments had been limited to 6s. a day, once professionalism was accepted there was no maximum wage. The regulations did little to prevent the concentration of sporting talent. Players from Wigan, Oldham and Huddersfield filled exactly half of the 208 places available in Great Britain teams between 1904 and 1914.[104] As Tables 9.18 and 9.19 show, these same clubs had the highest mean winning percentages and were also top of the rugby league honours board.

Tables 9.20 and 9.21 demonstrate that the structure of the various league competitions did not promote equality of competition. During its first season the N. R. F. U. was composed of 22 teams, each playing the others home and away. At the end of that season eight new clubs joined and the competition was divided into separate Lancashire and Yorkshire Senior Competitions. Despite numerous applications to join there was no automatic relegation of the bottom teams, despite some atrocious playing records. Morecambe, with an average winning percentage of 13.4, finished in last place in three consecutive seasons before they were dropped; and, across the Pennines, Liversedge survived despite three last positions, a second last, and a winning percentage of 15.7 over the four seasons. Many leading clubs became dissatisfied with the geographical restrictions of the county-based leagues and for the 1901/02 season established a breakaway 14-team Northern Rugby Football League. To avoid allegations of a closed shop they agreed that the bottom team each season should be replaced by the winner of a play-off between the

Table 9.20 *Static equality of competition in rugby league,*
1896/97–1914/15

	Northern Union	
	No. of teams	S. E. C.[a]
1895/96	22	15.8

	Senior Competition			
	Yorkshire		Lancashire	
	No. of teams	S. E. C.[a]	No. of teams	S. E. C.[a]
1896/97	16	16.9	14	19.7
1897/98	16	16.9	14	21.5
1898/99	16	18.6	14	24.1
1899/1900	16	19.3	14	22.2
1900/01	16	20.7	14	21.9

	Northern Rugby League					
			First division		Second division	
	No. of teams	S. E. C.[a]	No. of teams	S. E. C.[a]	No. of teams	S. E. C.[a]
1901/02	14	16.2				
1902/03			18	12.5	18	18.5
1903/04			18	15.7	17	22.9
1904/05			18	14.4	14[b]	20.7
1905/06	31	19.6				
1906/07	26[c]	20.7				
1907/08	27	19.5				
1908/09	31	20.9				
1909/10	28	21.6				
1910/11	28	17.3				
1911/12	27	20.6				
1912/13	26	20.4				
1913/14	25	17.9				
1914/15	25	18.8				

[a] As measured by standard deviation of winning percentages each season. Draws were classed as a 50% win to both sides. Points deducted for irregularities have been reinstated.
[b] Birkenhead resigned after four matches and their games have been discounted.
[c] Pontefract resigned after eight matches and their games have been discounted.
Source: Calculated from data in *Rothmans Rugby League 1982/83 Yearbook*, Aylesbury, 1982.

Table 9.21 *Dynamic equality of competition in rugby league,*
1896/97–1914/15

Competition	Period	D. E. C.[a]
Lancashire Senior	1896/97–1900/01	0.54
Yorkshire Senior	1896/97–1900/01	0.67
First Division	1902/03–1904/05	0.55
Second Division	1902/03–1904/05	0.43
N. R. F. L.	1905/06–1914/15	0.63

[a]As measured by the mean rank order correlation of league positions from one season to the
next. For the purposes of the calculations newcomers were omitted when correlations were
not possible and league positions were adjusted accordingly.
Source: Calculated from data in *Rothmans Rugby League 1982/83 Yearbook*, Aylesbury,
1982.

champions of the respective Senior Competitions. This did not appease
the excluded Yorkshire teams, who resolved not to play any fixtures
against the N. R. F. L. teams, but they soon found that this hurt them too
much financially. After only one season the N. R. F. L. was expanded to
two 18-club divisions with a seasonal interchange of two clubs from each
division. For the three years in which this system operated the first division
had the lowest static equality of competition recorded before 1914.
However, many second-division clubs found themselves in financial
difficulties; their matches lacked the drawing power of star clubs and
players but involved just as much travelling as first-division fixtures.[105]
Reconstruction was forced upon the N. R. F. L., though many first-
division clubs were reluctant to support a scheme which was, in the words
of the Northern Union president, 'primarily . . . for the amelioration of
less important organisations'.[106] What emerged was a single-division
league, open to any club which could arrange home and away fixtures
with ten other members. With 31 members in both 1905/06 and 1908/09
the league must surely have been one of the largest in the world. As there
was no obligation to play all other teams, the championship was decided
on the percentage of games won. However, when Leigh won with 80.0%
from 30 games, accusations of an easy fixture list led to the introduction of
a top-four play-off.[107] From 1907/08 a county championship was inaugurated within the existing system, each eligible side having to play all its
county colleagues twice. In addition an acceptable programme necessitated at least four home and away fixtures with other N. R. F. L. clubs. A
proposal that these matches should specifically be based on the previous

season's league positions, with teams playing those of similar standing, failed to gain a sufficient majority.[108]

Profits via cost reduction were the province of the individual club and its housekeeping, though as a group they voted South Shields out of the N. R. F. L. in 1904 because its drawing power did not compensate for the travelling expenses involved.[109] However, the controlling bodies did aim to make profits via innovation. The inauguration of the Challenge Cup in 1897, its county equivalents in 1905 and the league play-off system all served to generate spectator interest, as did the 1907/08 tour by New Zealand organised under the auspices of the N. R. F. U.[110] From the beginning, in contrast to established rugby, which was 'not made for the public', the rugby league advocates were determined to cater for spectators by rendering their game 'more attractive'.[111] Hence by 1907, when the Northern Union declared itself 'well satisfied with the result of alterations of [its] rules', the number of players had been reduced to 13, the scoring of tries was rewarded more than the kicking of goals, line-outs had been abandoned, and kicking directly into touch was being penalised.[112]

Despite the inequality of sporting competition, the controlling bodies in rugby league did little to assist the financially weak clubs.[113] When it was believed that two Welsh clubs would participate in 1908/09, the N. R. F. L. decided to allow them £10 towards the expenses of each visit north, but this was reduced to £5 after other Welsh teams elected to participate and, despite appeals from Merthyr Tydfil, it remained at that level even when all but Merthyr and Ebbw Vale had dropped out.[114] One of those which gave up, Aberdare, applied to the N. R. F. L. for financial assistance but was turned down.[115]

Almost all the 15 clubs which dropped out of the N. R. F. L. after its reconstruction into a single division had poor playing records: their average winning percentage in the new league was just 25.6. More significantly, eight of them were newcomers to the N. R. F. L., which suggests that the pool of viable entrants had been drained: in fact no newcomer won even a third of its matches. Disregarding the special circumstances of Bradford Northern, formed from the ashes of the disbanded Bradford club, there was only one new entrant from within the traditional boundaries of rugby league. This was Liverpool City, which had the magnificent official winning percentage of zero![116] Elsewhere there was too much competition from clubs affiliated to the English and Welsh Rugby Unions. In the years immediately following the split over broken-time payments the amateur hard line on northern leprosy had backfired in that several leading clubs had opted to join the new organisation in order to preserve their most lucrative fixtures.[117] In later years, however, attempts to expand the new code into fresh areas failed, partly because soccer had established itself as the major winter spectator sport, but also, especially in Wales, because of widespread shamateurism. Despite the propaganda effects of playing test matches at the Chelsea and Queen's Park Rangers football grounds, the attempt to establish a club in London failed and that in Coventry lasted only three dismal seasons.[118] The lesson taught by South Shields and Coventry was learned. When proposals were raised regarding the promotion of the game in the West Country it was advocated that this 'be done by the formation of a Western League, as it would be unwise for individual clubs to join the Union from so great a distance'.[119] Yet even a local competition could not ensure survival. At one stage there was a six-club Welsh league, operating within the N. R. F. L., but by 1912/13 all these teams had given up the game.

VII

Central controlling bodies existed in all the sports studied here, though the M. C. C., at least overtly, exerted much less power than either the Jockey Club or the various football authorities. Yet it is hard to envisage most of them as controlling economic cartels designed to maximise profits. Indeed both the Football Association and the Jockey Club imposed dividend limitations on football clubs and racing companies respectively. The main objective of the Jockey Club appears to have been to keep the racing and thoroughbred-breeding industries viable as a whole rather than acting in the financial interests of individual members of those industries, few of whom actually participated in the decision-making process. The M. C. C. was unrepresentative of the county clubs and, perhaps because its decisions could affect cricket world-wide and at all levels, was reluctant to take an active leadership role in promoting change.[120] It acted to set rules and control some activities of group members, but generally behaved more like a private club than as an administrative body and left the county clubs to operate more or less independently in economic matters. In English soccer the Football League, much more a collective decision-making body than the Jockey Club or the M. C. C., took steps to promote equality of competition, control costs and head off competitors, all of which suggest a degree of profit-maximisation. However, the dual-authority system which existed in soccer meant that the F. A. was able to limit the dividends paid to shareholders. North of the Border attempts at group profit-maximisation were less evident: in fact Celtic and Rangers dominated Scottish soccer tournaments far more than did teams in any other sport. In rugby league there was no attempt to equalise playing competition except for the few seasons in which a first division operated.

Chapter 10

Paying the piper: shareholders and directors

I

One line of inquiry into the causes of different economic attitudes within the sports industry is to examine who owned and controlled the constituent firms. Much of the background of those involved remains to be traced at the local level, but, as the sports industry was not immune from the general incorporation movement in British industry, some aggregated information can be provided here on shareholders and directors in sports enterprises, particularly English and Scottish soccer clubs.[1] The data presented concentrates on occupations, though, of course, these can be utilised as a guide to social class.[2]

For the purposes of analysis eleven broad categories of occupation were distinguished: aristocracy and gentry; upper professional; lower professional; proprietors and employers associated with the drink trade; other proprietors and employers; managerial and higher administration; clerical; supervisors, foremen and inspectors; skilled manual workers; semi-skilled manual workers; and unskilled manual workers.[3] The allocation of shareholders and directors to these categories met with some problems, though none severe enough to vitiate the analysis. No occupations were given for the very few female shareholders, so where possible – with apologies to feminist readers – they were allotted to the category of the male resident at the same address. The most serious problem was the blurring of the demarcation lines between groups. The professional groups were reasonably unambiguous, but lower management and higher supervisory occasionally overlapped and there was some difficulty in distinguishing skilled manual workers from the semi-skilled, particularly where localised specialist trades were concerned. Worse still were occupations recorded simply as 'baker', 'tailor' etc., which could be either proprietors or artisans. Addresses and checks with later registers enabled some to be identified more accurately and the remainder were allocated to the proprietorial group.[4] This was done because one objective of the analysis was to determine the level of working-class involvement and thus it was deemed best to bias all assumptions against such participation, particularly as there was probably an element of upward social bias in the data in that the occupations were self-assigned by the shareholders.[5]

II

Although the identity of the original club members may remain a mystery, it is possible to say something about the social composition of membership of Scottish soccer clubs at the time that they adopted company status, for several of them issued either free proprietary shares or fully or partially paid-up ordinary shares to existing members as compensation for goodwill and the takeover of club assets. A search of the shareholders' registers revealed comprehensive lists of members for Hearts, Kilmarnock and St Johnstone, and less detailed ones for Hamilton and Motherwell. Unfortunately neither of the latter gave any information on occupations and these could be traced only for those members who bought additional shares, 71 out of a membership of 187 for Hamilton and 97 out of 440 for Motherwell. No membership lists were found for either Celtic or Rangers, but their proprietary shares were easily distinguishable in the registers. Partick Thistle's members were given only one free share and an extraction of those shareholders with one, six, eleven etc. shares possibly identified 177 out of 182 members. A similar exercise for Dumbarton and St Mirren, who offered their members two shares on special terms, possibly traced 224 and 406 out of their respective memberships of 322 and 554.

From the aggregate information shown in Table 10.1 and the individual club data in Appendix 1a it is clear that the members were overwhelmingly local, with over 98% of them living within 25 miles of their team's ground. It is also apparent that the majority of members came from various strata of the manual working class. Overall 61.7% of all members traced came from these social groups and, of individual clubs, only Rangers, with 41.7%, had less than half its membership derived from manual occupations. Nevertheless, as roughly 80% of the occupied male population in Scotland could be classed as manual workers, they were underrepresented in football club membership. This was attributable to the relatively low proportional involvement of the unskilled and semiskilled. Possibly this has something to do with the costs of membership: in 1890 Hearts, for example, charged a 5s. entrance fee and a similar amount for the annual subscription. It may have been easier to lay out 6d. a time

Table 10.1 Occupational analysis of shareholders in major Scottish soccer clubs before 1915[a]

Occupational category	% occupied males in 1911	Members[b] No.	Members[b] %	Shareholders[c] First division No.	%	Other No.	%	Total No.	%	Shareholdings[d] First division No.	%	Other No.	%	Total No.	%
Aristocracy and gentry	n.a.	6	0.3	5	0.3	—	—	5	0.2	320	1.0	—	—	320	0.9
Upper professional	1.2	69	3.0	59	3.1	26	6.3	85	3.7	1,554	4.9	70	2.6	1,624	4.8
Lower professional	1.2	84	3.6	105	5.4	12	2.9	117	5.0	1,697	5.3	71	2.7	1,768	5.3
Proprietors and employers associated with the drink trade	9.2	99	4.1	242	12.5	42	10.1	262	11.3	10,036	31.4	460	17.2	10,496	31.2
Other proprietors and employers		190	8.2	237	12.3	72	17.4	309	13.3	6,500	20.4	406	52.6	6,906	20.5
Managers and higher administration	0.3	69	3.0	66	3.4	18	4.3	84	3.6	1,245	3.9	39	1.4	1,284	3.8
Clerical	7.1	333	14.3	273	14.2	45	10.9	318	13.7	2,694	8.4	178	6.7	2,872	8.5
Foremen, supervisors and inspectors	0.7	41	1.8	34	1.8	10	2.4	44	1.9	245	0.8	33	1.2	278	0.8
Skilled manual	38.9	1,132	48.7	711	36.9	159	38.4	870	37.5	6,060	19.0	364	13.6	6,424	19.1
Semi-skilled manual	29.6	236	10.1	159	8.2	24	5.8	183	7.9	1,426	4.5	49	1.8	1,475	4.4
Unskilled manual	11.8	67	2.9	38	2.0	6	1.4	44	1.9	150	0.5	4	0.1	154	0.5
Total traced	100.0	2,326	100.0	1,929	100.0	414	100.0	2,321	100.0	31,927	100.0	1,674	100.0	33,601	100.0
Untraced or unspecified		1,051		150		7		157		1,275		10		1,285	

[a] Individual club data can be found in Appendix 1a.
[b] At the time that the clubs adopted company status.
[c] At the time that the shares were first issued. Two clubs, Aberdeen and Hamilton, who gained first-division status two years after adopting company status, were allocated to the first-division category.
[d] As [c] and converted into £1 units.
Sources: Occupational structure based on Census of 1911; club data from shareholders' registers in Companies Registry, Edinburgh, and Scottish Record Office, Edinburgh.

to see a match than the lump sum which membership required. The disproportionate representation of the professional classes, managers and administrators, and foremen and supervisors, may be a function of the absolutely small numbers involved and the difficulties of adequately distinguishing these groups in a census based on industrial rather than on occupational classifications.[6] The involvement of clerks, however, requires a comment. A detailed study of Birmingham in England has shown that clerical workers in that city were to the fore in the organisation of sports clubs and associations, partly because they gained the Saturday half-day holiday before many other workers, but also possibly because they had better book-keeping and administrative ability.[7] Whether such a situation existed in Scotland must, in the light of current knowledge, remain a matter for conjecture.

A significant proportion of members made a financial commitment to their teams when company status was adopted. Of those that can be traced, although only 38.5% of Hamilton's members accepted their partially paid-up shares, the respective percentages for Kilmarnock and St Mirren were 67.6 and 73.1. No figures were available for Kilmarnock, but additional shares were taken by 15.3% of Hamilton's membership and 44.4% of St Mirren's: the higher figure for the latter club might be attributable to the lower share price asked, 5s. as compared to £1. Of the five clubs traced which gave their members fully paid-up shares, the proportion of the membership which bought additional shares varied little between clubs, ranging from Partick Thistle's 18.1% to Rangers' 26.0%. As these figures suggest, despite many members being willing to purchase shares, the involvement of members was insufficient to dominate the shareholders' registers. Apart from Celtic and Partick Thistle, previous members formed a minority of shareholders in each club and, in all cases except Celtic, held a minority of shares.

The switch to company status thus brought new men into the clubs. Like the previous members most of them were local, but there were two major differences in their occupational composition. First, there was a significant rise in the proportion of proprietors and employers – from 12.5% to 21.2%. The increase was particularly marked for those in the drink trade, whose involvement jumped from 4.3% to 11.7%. For all clubs, including those for which membership details were unavailable, proprietors comprised 24.6% of shareholders and held 51.7% of shares; overall the drink trade element comprised 11.3% of shareholders and held a remarkable 31.2% of shares. Although the patrons and superfans among these businessmen would have been looking for social returns or psychic income, generally even those wanting financial rewards from their investment would have had to seek them indirectly, since few clubs promised dividends in their prospectuses, but most stressed that the establishment of a quality football team in the area would attract spectators whose spending would benefit local businessmen.

The second significant change which followed company formation was the decline in the proportionate involvement of the manual working class – from 61.7% of members to 41.2% of shareholders.[8] There was, however, considerable variation between clubs regarding this group's participation; Motherwell's shareholders comprised 65.9% manual working class, but those of Partick Thistle were only 22.6%. The variation was not explicable in terms of differences in the occupational structure of the areas from which the shareholders were drawn.[9] Nor was there any obvious relationship between manual working-class shareholding and what a club offered in terms of voting rights or cheap season tickets. Two other factors, however, were influential. The percentage of manual working-class members showed a 0.53 product moment correlation with the percentage of shareholders who were similarly recruited: in other words, a previous large working-class membership heightened the likelihood of having working-class shareholders. However, the most influential variable appears to have been the price of shares. Clubs which sold £1 shares had on average only 34.0% of their shareholders emanating from the manual working class; if the price was 10s. the percentage rose to 43.1; and if merely 5s. was asked the proportion reached 49.2%. Significantly the lower prices did not lead to large shareholdings by the manual workers: their mean-value shareholding of £1 shares was £13.23, of 10s. shares £2.39, and of 5s. shares a mere £1.19. Typical shareholdings for the latter two groups ranged between 10s. and £1, which suggests that many manual workers simply regarded shareholding as an extension, or a little more than the equivalent, of membership. The larger shareholdings for the £1 shares are partly a function of the minimum subscriptions demanded by some clubs, but are mainly the result of Rangers' and Celtic's financial dominance: without these two clubs the manual worker's average shareholding of £1 shares was £4.66. Why it was £25.12 for Celtic and £20.88 for Rangers is a matter of speculation. Both clubs were successful in playing and in financial terms, and certainly Celtic offered the prospect of high dividends. The real answer, however, may lie in their unique position as rallying points for staunch Protestantism and Irish Catholicism: both Rangers and Celtic were more than just football clubs.

In the light of the data on shareholdings, it can be argued that the higher share prices discouraged some manual workers from becoming shareholders in their local club. Nevertheless, especially when it is remembered that the data are biased against their involvement, the fact that the manual working class comprised 47.3% of all shareholders and held 24.0% of all shares is remarkable. Indeed a comparison with other companies in the Scottish sports industry, shown in Appendix 1b, brings out the peculiar attraction which soccer had for the Scottish working class. Although the sample was non-random,[10] it is significant that only one company, the Aberdeen Cycling and Athletic Association, had a comparable percentage of manual working-class support. This also was the only company in the sample which specifically did not promise any dividends.[11] Possibly here is the key to explaining working-class shareholding. Perhaps many still saw the soccer club as a voluntary association rather than as a capitalistic enterprise. To them shareholding probably was more consumption than investment. It was just an extension of their involvement as members or as fans: dividends were less important than a cheap season ticket and voting rights at the annual general meeting.

III

Unfortunately English and Scottish football club memberships cannot be compared as too little information appears to exist on the former. Sheffield United issued special shares to existing members of the Sheffield United Cricket and Football Club which show that it was a predominantly middle-class body, though possibly this was influenced by the cricket section as the shareholders in the two county cricket ground companies shown in Appendix 1d also contained very few of the working class. The Sheffield Football Club, a different organisation, was also mainly middle-class, but as only 13 of 18 newly enrolling members were traced, and this for 1870, its utility for comparative purposes must be questioned.[12]

For shareholders, however, some interesting comparisons can be drawn between clubs north and south of the Border. It is apparent from the individual club data (see Appendix 1c) that English soccer club shareholders, like their Scottish counterparts, were overwhelmingly drawn from the local populace. This contrasts with some of the other English sports companies shown in the very limited sample (see Appendix 1d), not so much with Rochdale Hornets, a professional rugby team with strong working-class financial involvement, but certainly with the racecourses and, to a lesser extent, the county cricket ground companies. It can be surmised that local identification was important to the soccer shareholder and clearly there was little or no blind investment.

In other respects, however, as is shown in Tables 10.1 and 10.2, English soccer shareholders differed from the Scottish. Different population

Table 10.2 *Occupational analysis of shareholders in major English soccer clubs before 1915*[a]

Occupational category	% Occupied males	Shareholders[b]								Shareholdings[c]							
		First division		Second division		Other		Total		First division		Second division		Other		Total	
		No.	%	No.	%	No.	%	No.	%	No.	%	No.	%	No.	%	No.	%
Aristocracy and gentry	n.a.	92	2.7	12	0.9	110	4.9	214	3.1	2,704	6.9	350	3.1	1,328	9.9	4,382	6.9
Upper professional	1.0	256	7.5	53	4.1	112	5.0	421	6.1	4,245	10.9	974	8.6	1,046	7.8	6,265	9.8
Lower professional	3.2	162	4.8	51	4.0	105	4.7	318	4.6	1,387	3.6	251	2.2	710	5.3	2,348	3.7
Proprietors and employers associated with the drink trade	6.5	250	7.3	79	6.1	152	6.8	481	6.9	5,993	15.4	1,488	13.2	2,043	15.2	9,554	14.9
Other proprietors and employers		728	21.4	253	19.6	345	15.3	1,326	19.1	12,697	32.5	3,851	34.1	3,287	24.4	19,835	31.1
Managers and higher administration	3.7	245	7.2	82	6.4	138	6.1	465	6.7	2,439	6.2	732	6.5	945	7.0	4,116	6.5
Clerical	4.6	526	15.5	134	10.4	361	16.1	1,021	14.7	3,397	8.7	575	5.1	1,320	9.8	5,292	8.3
Foremen, supervisors and inspectors	1.3	74	2.2	26	2.0	43	1.9	143	2.1	445	1.1	123	1.1	126	0.9	694	1.1
Skilled manual	29.8	845	24.8	453	35.1	644	28.6	1,942	28.0	4,920	12.6	1,907	16.9	1,913	14.2	8,740	13.7
Semi-skilled manual	40.3	157	4.6	94	7.3	172	7.7	423	6.1	697	1.8	976	8.6	673	5.0	2,346	3.7
Unskilled manual	9.4	67	2.0	53	4.1	66	2.9	186	2.7	132	0.3	75	0.7	64	0.5	271	0.4
Total traced	100.0	3,402	100.0	1,290	100.0	2,248	100.0	6,940	100.0	39,056	100.0	11,302	100.0	13,455	100.0	63,813	100.0
Untraced or unspecified		282		40		348		670		4,474		184		2,538		7,196	

[a] Individual club data can be found in Appendix 1c.
[b] At the time that the shares were first issued. A few clubs who were non-League at this time but who gained entry to the Football League within two years were allocated to the second-division category.
[c] As [b] and converted into £1 units.
Sources: Occupational structure based on Census of 1911; club data from shareholders' registers in Companies House, London, and Companies Registry, Cardiff.

structures may account for the differential representation of the aristocracy and gentry and the management sections, but they cannot explain the
significantly lower participation from the manual working class for, with
approximately the same proportion of the occupied male population, the
English manual workers comprised 36.8% of shareholders and held
17.8% of the shares in contrast to the Scottish percentages of 47.2% and
24.0%. This is not attributable to voting rights, which actually were more
favourable to the small shareholder in England (see Tables 10.3 and 10.4).
Possibly club membership was less working-class in England and thus had
less flow-on into shareholding. A plausible explanation, however, can be
found in the size of shares. As in Scotland, the share price was an
important variable in working-class share purchases: twelve clubs which
charged £1 averaged 35.4% working-class shareholders whereas seven
which offered 10s. shares averaged 47.0%. Thus the answer to the
differential working-class participation north and south of the Border
may be that in aggregate English clubs offered less cheap shares than did
the Scottish. Even so, it should be stressed that working-class shareholding in English soccer clubs was significantly higher than in the sample of
cricket and racing companies.

The other major difference between the English and Scottish experiences lies in the proprietory group, though not in their overall contribution, which was similar, but in the contrasting participation of the
drink trade, which owned 31.2% of shares in the Scottish clubs, but only
14.9% in the English. Whether this was partially attributable to differences in occupation structures is a matter for conjecture.[13]

IV

What remains to be examined is the occupational composition of those
who controlled the clubs and whether this changed with the switch from
club to company status. Unfortunately, although directors are well
covered in the company returns, relatively little information is available
on club committees prior to company formation.[14] All we have for
Scotland, apart from Hutchinson's detailed but unpublished study of
Heart of Midlothian, are a few references in some of the prospectuses.[15]
Table 10.1 shows that those committees for which information is available were dominated by manual working men and by employers and
proprietors. However, as the data refer to only three clubs – Hearts, East
Stirlingshire and St Johnstone – no firm conclusions should be drawn.
Nevertheless, these data, plus additional comments from the prospectuses
of Dumbarton, Motherwell, St Mirren, Partick Thistle and Hamilton,

Table 10.3 *Aspects of shareholding in Scottish soccer clubs*

Club	Size of share	Voting rights	Proxy votes	Directors' qualification
Aberdeen	10s.	n.a.	n.a.	n.a.
Airdrieonians	£1	n.a.	n.a.	n.a.
Ayr United	10s.	n.a.	n.a.	n.a.
Celtic	£1	{ Proprietary shares 1 vote per share { Ordinary shares 1 vote per 10 shares	yes	5 shares
Clyde	£1	n.a.	n.a.	n.a.
Cowdenbeath	5s.	n.a.	n.a.	16 shares
Dumbarton	£1	{ Members shares 1 vote per 2 shares { Ordinary shares 1 vote per 5 shares	yes	Enough shares for 2 votes
Dundee F. and A. C.	£1	1 vote per share	yes	5 shares
Dundee	£1	1 vote per share	yes	n.a.
Dundee Hibernian	£1	1 vote for first 10 shares, then 1 vote for each 5 shares up to 100 shares, then 1 for every 10 shares	yes	20 shares
East Fife	5s.	n.a.	n.a.	10 shares

Club	Par value	Voting	Proxy	Qualification
East Stirlingshire	5s.	As Dundee Hibernian	yes	10 shares
Falkirk	10s.	n.a.	n.a.	n.a.
Hamilton Academicals	£1	1 vote per shareholder plus 1 vote for each additional 5 shares	yes	10 shares or an original member's share
Heart of Midlothian	£1	1 vote per share	yes	n.a.
Kilmarnock	£1	1 vote per shareholder	no	5 shares or 2 if an original member
Motherwell	£1	1 vote per shareholder plus 1 vote for each additional 5 shares up to a maximum of 5 votes	yes	10 shares or 1 member's share
Partick Thistle	£1	1 vote per share	yes	10 shares or 1 member's share
Rangers	£1 / £5 proprietary	1 vote for each £5 worth of shares	yes	1 proprietary share or 25 ordinary shares
St Johnstone	5s.	n.a.	Chairman to decide at meeting	1 original in own right
St Mirren	10s.	1 vote per shareholder	n.a.	10 shares or 2 if an original member

Sources: Memoranda of Association of the Clubs.

Table 10.4 *Aspects of shareholding in English soccer clubs*

Club	Size of share	Voting rights	Proxy votes	Directors' qualification
Aston Villa	£5	1 vote per shareholder	no	2 shares
Blackburn Rovers	£1	1 vote per shareholder plus 1 vote if holding at least 25 shares	no	25 shares
Blackpool	£1	1 vote for 1–4 shares plus 1 vote for each share over 5	n.a.	10 shares
Bolton Wanderers	£1	1 vote for 1–5 shares plus 1 vote for each additional 5 shares	no	25 shares
Bradford City	£1	1 vote for 1 share plus 1 vote for each additional 5 shares	n.a.	10 shares
Burnley	£1	1 vote per shareholder	no	10 shares
Derby	£1	1 vote for every share up to 10, then 1 for every 5 shares up to 50, then 1 for every 25	yes	25 shares
Eastville Rovers	£1	1 vote for every 5 or proportion of 5	no	1 share
Everton	£1	1 vote per shareholder plus 1 vote for 20 or more shares	n.a.	5 shares
Fulham	10s.	1 vote for each shareholder plus 1 vote for 5 shares plus 1 vote for each additional 10	no	3 shares
Leicester	n.a.	1 vote per share	yes	20 shares
Manchester City	£1	1 vote per shareholder	no	100 shares
Manchester United	£1	1 vote per share	yes	3 shares

Club	Share value	Voting rights	Qualification required	Qualifying shares
Middlesbrough	£1	1 vote for each share up to 10 plus 1 vote for each additional 5	n.a.	5 shares
Portsmouth	£1 (A) / 8s. (B)	1 vote for each 'A' share; 1 per 'B' shareholder plus 1 vote for each 5 above 5 shares	yes	100 'A' shares
Queen's Park Rangers	10s.	1 vote for each share up to 10, plus 1 for each 5 up to 50, then 1 for each 25	yes	20 shares
Reading	10s.	1 vote per shareholder	no	10 shares
Sheffield United	£20 / £10	1 vote per shareholder	no	1 share
Small Heath	10s.	1 vote per share	yes	2 shares
Southampton	£1	1 vote for each shareholder plus 1 vote for 5 shares plus 1 vote for each additional 10	no	10 shares
Stoke	£1	1 vote per share	yes	5 shares
Tottenham	£1	1 vote per shareholder plus 1 vote for 5 shares plus 1 vote for each additional 10	no	10 shares
Wednesday	£5 / £10	1 vote per shareholder	no	n.a.
West Bromwich Albion	£1	1 vote per shareholder plus 1 vote for every 5 shares above 5	no	n.a.
West Ham	10s.	1 vote per shareholder	no	10 shares

Sources: Memoranda of Association of the Clubs.

suggest that going limited did not lead to immediate changes in the decision-taking personnel, though usually the powers of the old committee were diluted by an extension of the numbers on the board. This continuity between the committees and the first directors possibly accounts for the substantial representation of manual workers on the early Scottish boards, some 28.8%, though proprietors and employers now reached 38%, including 17.2% from the drink trade. Even more striking is that the position had not changed substantially by 1914. The representation of the manual working class remained strong. Table 10.5 shows that, for clubs for which data on board membership is available both for the initial year of company formation and for 1914, there was a rise in the proportion of proprietors and employers from 40.7% to 44.8%, but only a marginal downward shift in manual working-class directorships – from 30.4% to 28.8%.

English soccer club directorates have already been analysed by both Mason and Tischler, the former applying a twelve-category analysis to as many clubs which adopted company status before 1914 as he could trace, and the latter concentrating on those teams which played in the first division of the Football League before 1914 and using a narrower five-category classification.[16] Rather than duplicate their efforts, further analysis was restricted to boards of directors as they were in 1901. In order to facilitate comparisons, Mason's and Tischler's categories were reclassified using the occupational groups applied in the earlier analysis of shareholders. Inevitably this resulted in some inconsistencies as compared to the 1901 analysis. In both cases subgroups of the manual working class and of professional occupations had to be combined, and in Tischler's case some professionals had to be transferred to other categories. The drink trade category is inflated for Tischler by the inclusion of the tobacco interests and for Mason by the addition of the food trade. The clerical group is also inflated for Mason because all the financial/commercial group were allotted to it: correspondingly the professional sector could be understated. Despite these problems, the results of the reclassification shown in Table 10.6 are reasonably consistent. The main unexplained inconsistency is the professional category of Tischler, which is higher than in both Mason and Vamplew; this may be associated with the first-division status of Tischler's sample, but it may also owe something to different definitions of a profession.

Generally the English boards reflected shareholdings rather than shareholders. As might be anticipated, the directorates were dominated by proprietors and employers, more so than in Scotland, but surprisingly, in view of their possible organisational ability, clerks were represented less

Table 10.5 *Occupational analysis of directors of Scottish soccer clubs before 1915*

Occupational category	Committeemen		Original boards of all clubs traced[a]		Original boards of clubs traced for 1914[a]		Boards of 1914[b]	
	No.	%	No.	%	No.	%	No.	%
Aristocracy	—	—	—	—	—	—	1	0.8
Upper professional	—	—	7	4.3	4	3.0	6	4.8
Lower professional	—	—	7	4.3	4	3.0	7	5.6
Proprietors and employers associated with the drink trade	1	4.3	28	17.2	27	20.0	25	20.0
Other proprietors and employers	6	26.1	34	20.9	28	20.7	31	24.8
Managers and higher administration	—	—	8	4.9	7	5.2	5	4.0
Clerical	2	8.7	28	17.2	20	14.8	14	11.2
Foremen, supervisors and inspectors	3	13.0	4	2.5	4	3.0	—	—
Skilled manual	10	43.5	42	25.8	38	28.1	34	27.2
Semi-skilled manual	1	4.3	5	3.1	3	2.2	2	1.6
Unskilled manual	—	—	—	—	—	—	—	—
Total traced	23	100.0	163	100.0	135	100.0	125	100.0

[a]For Hearts this is the board of the restructured company.
[b]As they existed after the annual general meeting of that year.
Sources: Lists of directors in the Companies Register, Edinburgh, and the Scottish Record Office, Edinburgh.

Table 10.6 Occupational analysis of directors of English soccer clubs before 1915

Source[a]	Vamplew 1901 24		Mason 1888–1915 46		Tischler 1888–1914 28	
Period Number of clubs covered	No.	%[b]	No.	%[b]	No.	%[b]
Aristocracy and gentry	11	4.7	32	4.6	19	4.0
Upper professional	31	13.4	} 110	15.8	} 116	24.4
Lower professional	11	4.7				
Proprietors and employers associated with the drink trade	27	11.6	89	12.8	69	14.5
Other proprietors and employers	84	36.2	279	40.0	187	39.3
Managers and higher administration	20	8.6	35	5.0	17	3.6
Clerical	23	9.9	70[c]	10.0	29	6.1
Foremen, supervisors and inspectors	2	0.9	?	?	4	0.8
Skilled manual	20	8.6	56	8.0	} 35	7.4
Semi-skilled manual	3	1.3	22	3.2		
Unskilled manual	—	—	4	0.6		
Total traced	232	100.0	697	100.0	476	100.0
Untraced or unspecified[d]	11		43		15	

[a] All three breakdowns were based on the returns of directors filed by the clubs and now held in the Companies Register, Cardiff. The classifications of A. Mason, *Association Football and English Society, 1863–1915*, Brighton, 1980, p. 43, and S. Tischler, *Footballers and Businessmen*, New York, 1981, pp. 72, 76, were adapted to the occupational categories used for the analysis of shareholders in Table 10.1.

[b] For purposes of comparison the percentages are of those allocated to the occupational categories used here.

[c] Overestimated as it includes all those in financial/commercial occupations.

[d] As in Table 10.1, but signifies 'other' as well as untraced or unspecified.

than north of the Border. The major difference between the two nations, however, was the relative low participation rate of the working class in England, far less than might be expected given the degree of working-class shareholding, and voting rights which favoured the smaller shareholders, who were, in practice, the manual working class. A possible reason for the differential involvement in England, as compared to Scotland, is that the shareholding qualifications required of English club directors were generally higher than for their Scottish counterparts and few English clubs allowed special directors' qualifications for pre-existing club members.[17] Although some of the qualifications required by English clubs may have been designed to minimise working-class participation, they contrast favourably with the racing companies: Newbury, Haydock Park and Sandown Park all demanded £500 shareholdings from their directors.

Both in Scotland and England, directors as a group took steps to maintain their control over their clubs. First, they were generally careful not to let their proprietary ratios fall below 50% and normally maintained them at much higher levels. These ratios show the aggregate of equity capital, reserves and retained profits as a percentage of total funds employed by the club; hence, the lower the ratio is, the more the club is financed by external debt and the greater the risk is of control being lost by the existing board. Second, directors in all clubs maintained the right to veto the transfer of shares without having to specify reasons for their refusal to approve the transaction. This could have served to prevent individuals building a shareholding power base from which to challenge the board. Third, as is shown in Tables 10.3 and 10.4, many clubs allowed the use of proxy votes at their annual general meetings and directors were in the best position to collect such votes to back themselves and their policies: all they needed do was attach a voting slip to the agenda circulated to each shareholder in advance of the meeting. Finally, on average, Scottish boards held 24.7% of the company's stock, and English directors 16.3%, which gave them substantial voting power in their own right.

Whether individual directors could control clubs is a matter for conjecture. On the basis of a study of the board composition of Liverpool, Chelsea and Manchester United, Tischler has concluded that particular directors, respectively John Houlding, Henry Myers and J. H. Davies, exerted virtual unilateral control of those clubs.[18] Club histories lend support to this view.[19] However, Tischler then makes a quantum leap in historical inference to suggest that 'affluent men actually controlled the larger teams' and that 'the consent of the team's majority stockholder' was necessary for policies to be adopted by the board.[20] Korr has shown that the latter point was not necessarily true, for in West Ham's case A. F. Hills, who possessed 600 of the 1,442 shares issued, did not even have a seat on the board;[21] nor for that matter did Huddersfield's major shareholder. As to the former claim, if such domination occurred, then it was by virtue of personality as much as funds, for initially, at least, few directors had shareholdings large enough to exert dominance simply by the size of their financial commitment.[22] In Scotland the mean holding of the director with the largest investment in each club was only 8.1% of all shares, and in England it was even lower, a mere 4.6%. Loans to the clubs could also be a way of strengthening directorial influence, but the existing financial statements do not reveal any such direct dealings, though certainly directors often acted as guarantors for bank overdrafts.[23]

V

Whether the occupational composition of shareholders and directors influenced club policies is difficult to determine. Indeed the attempt at assessment here raises as many questions as it answers. As regards shareholders, much will depend upon whether or not they anticipated that dividends would be paid or assets accumulated and this requires the discovery of more prospectuses than the author was able to trace. Nevertheless, some tentative conclusions can be advanced. In chapter 8 it was suggested that, generally, English first-division clubs were more profit-oriented than others in either England or Scotland. The data on which this hypothesis was based was predominantly post-1905, but, if the suggestion holds true for a slightly earlier period, then the data in Tables 10.1 and 10.2 lend support to the idea that the occupations of share-holders might be a relevant variable in that English first-division teams in aggregate had the least working-class involvement, both in numbers and in volume of shares held.[24] They also had the highest participation by entrepreneurs not in the drink trade except for Scottish non-first-division clubs, and the latter's figure is explicable in terms of a few large shareholdings. More work on shareholders in non-League teams outside southern England might enable the apparently high involvement of the gentry in that category to be put into perspective. Comparisons within Scotland are virtually meaningless because of the low capitalisation of non-first-division teams. What is significant is the much higher involvement of the drink trade in Scottish soccer as a whole as compared to England.

As shown in Table 10.7 the differences are even more apparent at board level. An analysis of 1914 directorates shows that Scotland had sig-

Table 10.7 *Comparison of directorates in English and Scottish soccer in 1914 by occupational group (%)*

	English first division	English second division	English non-League	Scottish first division	Scottish second division
Aristocracy and gentry	4.3	2.9	11.1	1.1	—
Upper professional	13.8	8.7	7.8	6.9	—
Lower professional	6.9	8.7	5.6	6.9	2.6
Proprietors and employers associated with the drink trade	14.7	10.1	6.7	21.8	15.8
Other proprietors and employers	36.2	40.6	28.9	21.8	31.6
Managers and higher administration	13.8	4.3	8.9	4.6	2.6
Clerical	7.8	7.2	13.3	9.2	15.8
Foremen, supervisors and inspectors	—	2.9	2.2	—	—
Skilled manual	2.6	13.0	13.3	25.3	31.6
Semi-skilled manual	—	1.4	2.2	2.3	—
Unskilled manual	—	—	—	—	—

Sources: List of directors in the Companies Registers, Cardiff and Edinburgh, and the Scottish Record Office, Edinburgh.

nificantly more working-class and drink trade directors. Hence in Scotland it is possible that a flow-on of the working class from club committees may have encouraged a policy of utility-maximisation. Working men with an intense loyalty to a club with a successful playing record – and few unsuccessful clubs adopted company status – could have been determined to maintain that record and hence be more concerned with *their* club winning games than making money. A similar utility-maximising policy may have emanated from the drink trade. To that group home crowds were all important: attendance at away games was immaterial to their business receipts. And, so far as they were concerned, home attendances would be greater if there was a winning team to support. In England, however, other types of businessmen were more prominent and they may have preferred the club to maximise profits, possibly to pay dividends but more likely to be ploughed back into the enterprise in the form of new equipment and improved facilities, for which some of them would have been able to contract. It is also clear that by 1914 working men had little say in English first-division boardrooms.

The situation no doubt is more complex than is revealed by this unsophisticated analysis. Some sweeping assertions have been made regarding the motivation of particular occupational groupings. However, men became soccer club directors for a variety of reasons which need not necessarily correlate with their occupations. In Scotland there was the possibility of payment. Celtic always paid their board and in 1913 the seven directors each received £50.[25] In England such honoraria were banned but, as also in Scotland, there was the possibility of renting land and premises to the club and of obtaining contracts for building, equipment, outfits and catering. Some, to the disgust of William McGregor, did join boards 'for the money [they] indirectly make out of it'.[26] A survey of articles of association showed that in Scotland only Aberdeen and Dumbarton specifically forbade directors from contracting with the club and that in England only Newcastle did likewise, though it was allowed if the director contracted as a member of a company not as an individual.[27] Such benefits would, of course, be available only to particular members of the board and it needs to be checked whether market rates were charged.

What of those who joined overtly for non-economic reasons? If Tischler is correct, some would be appointed as nominees of influential directors. Others looked for 'the pleasing prominence a position on the directorate brings':[28] indeed in 1905 the president of the Football League maintained that 'in most towns it is considered a distinct privilege to be on the board of the local club directorate, and the position is as eagerly sought after as a seat in the council chamber'.[29] Being associated with the local team must have brought an element of community prestige and this would have been heightened if the club was a successful one. No doubt local political figures could benefit from giving such patronage.[30] It can, however, be suggested that for some directors there might also be economic spin-offs: the 'free' advertising from such prestige could bring custom to both businessmen and professionals. More research is required at the local level before any firm conclusions can be drawn. The success which directors had in their own businesses, or the size of their enterprises, might well be more significant variables than the type of business or occupation pursued. It may also be the case, of course, that they just loved the game.

Chapter 11

Winning at any cost?

I

Generally economists have argued that attendances at sports events will be higher the greater is the degree of uncertainty about the result. This is not necessarily true for any given home game in team sports, but has more relevance as regards the home and away gates aggregated together and, although untested, it has *a priori* relevance to horse-racing because of the associated betting market. Equality thus has economic value.

Contemporary statements suggest that this uncertainty hypothesis had its supporters in the period under study. The Football League itself noted that 'the meeting of a strong and weak club . . . does not form an effective draw' and one well-versed cricket writer pointed out that:

beyond doubt the apathy shown by spectators everywhere may in great measure be set down to the conviction that Yorkshire always had matters their own way . . . whether this prolonged and immense superiority benefits the game is a debateable matter. A keen competition between several counties struggling for first place until the very last fixture arouses more enthusiasm.[1]

The evidence presented in Table 11.1 does not lend strong support to the uncertainty hypothesis, but, it must be stressed, the results are from an unsophisticated statistical approach which merely produces rank order correlations between attendances and closeness of competition (as defined by relative end-of-season championship positions). Nevertheless, it is not calculated truths which determine a club's policy; what they believe to be true is far more significant.

However, it was not within the province of the individual horse owner or sports club to produce closeness of competition. They had no option but to adopt an overt policy of trying to win as often as possible; otherwise they would face trouble both from the sport authorities and, in the case of clubs, from their supporters. Clubs, at least, faced the paradox of success: too many victories could prove Pyrrhic in revenue terms. Even

Table 11.1 *Uncertainty and attendance in English county cricket*

Home gate			Home and away gate		
County	Observations	Correlation	Counties	Observations	Correlation
Yorkshire	23	.41	Kent v. Surrey	8	.50
Surrey	11	.40	Yorkshire v. Warwickshire	11	-.07
Kent	16	.09	Yorkshire v. Surrey	10	-.21
Warwickshire	11	.09	Yorkshire v. Leicestershire	8	-.21
Leicestershire	9	-.19	Yorkshire v. Kent	13	-.33

Sources: Calculated from data in Annual Financial Statements of the clubs.

horse owners could fail to maximise their incomes if the prizemoney obtained failed to compensate for the shortened gambling odds on near certainties. Short of refusing to sign the best players or employ the leading jockeys, or perhaps transferring star players to the weaker teams, there was little that the individual club or owner could do to equalise playing strengths and racing probabilities. Such was virtually the prerogative of the clubs in aggregate or of the bodies controlling the various sports.

Yet it can be suggested that this was not a major objective of the sports organisations studied here. The Jockey Club in fact forced the racecourse executives to cut the volume of two-year-old races and increase the amount of distance events, thus reducing the degree of uncertainty in horse-racing. In county cricket there is no way that the freedom given to clubs to arrange their own fixtures can be reconciled with the promotion of equality of competition. In rugby league, too, the relative free choice regarding the fixture schedule once a single division was established also undermined any efforts to create uncertainty. Scottish soccer was the most unequal of all the sports studied, with its first division having a mean static equality of competition of 18.3, marginally above cricket's 17.3, but far exceeding the English Football League's first-division figure of 10.5. English soccer most nearly equated to the ideal-type profit-maximiser and, although the Football Association stepped in to prevent clubs paying dividends of more than 5%, they did not attempt to stop them accumulating assets; so by 1914 several first-division teams had tangible asset ratios higher than for any other sport examined.[2]

It is possible that the major objective of the controlling bodies was to ensure the survival of their competitions, and indeed they have attained a remarkable longevity, particularly when their experience is contrasted with that of conventional business cartels, which have been notoriously unstable.[3] One way was to head off challenges from actual or potential rivals. The Jockey Club maintained their monopoly of respectable racing by their £300 added-money rule and the threat of disqualification from all recognised racing of participants in unauthorised events. In contrast the football authorities, of all codes, expanded their competitions to bring in clubs which offered a product of comparable quality. Monopsonic power was used to hold down costs, and hence assist the viability of the industry, not just by maximum-wage legislation, as in English soccer, but also by restrictions on the mobility of players which reduced their bargaining power relative to that of their employers. Powers of a different kind, those to control the conduct of their sport, were taken, and used, by all the authorities except the M. C. C. in an attempt to see that spectators were not driven away by corrupt practices rendering the results certain to some. No authority went so far as to enforce the full pooling of revenues, though Scottish soccer eventually did adopt a $\frac{2}{3}$:$\frac{1}{3}$ policy on gate-takings. Scottish soccer was actually in a unique position because of the crowd-drawing dominance of Rangers and Celtic. In Scotland, as elsewhere, the dispersion of major sports grounds meant that the market for soccer was fragmented, but to a lesser degree than in English soccer and cricket because of the concentration of clubs in the Central Lowlands belt and, particularly, in Glasgow. Although the matches of Rangers and Celtic can in no way be considered as substitutes for each other, it is conceivable that developments in intra-city transport enabled the 'old firm' to attract fans who otherwise might have supported the other Glasgow teams. On the other hand, railway specials allowed them to take some of their vast support with them to away games, thus boosting the finances of the clubs visited. From this viewpoint the very success of Celtic and Rangers which contributed to their huge followings also helped to keep the other clubs viable.

Cricket appears to have been in a different situation to other sports. The distances between county grounds, coupled with the long duration of matches, sheltered counties from any rigours of internal competition for spectators. Certainly the expansion of the championship worked to improve the winning record of the initial clubs rather than defend the competition against potential rivals. Only Lancashire faced severe competition for spectators from league clubs, though all the counties found that their labour bills were increased by competition for players from the leagues, which, unlike the counties, did not demand residential qualifications. Little leadership was offered by the M. C. C., which, unlike other sporting bodies, made no effort to change equipment or rules in the interests of brighter play.[4] Most efforts to attract larger crowds by such innovations as Saturday starts were left to the initiative of individual clubs with no direction from above. Possibly the M. C. C. shared the view of the Yorkshire secretary that 'the financial side of a county club is a matter solely for the county club itself. Each county must work out its own salvation in this respect.'[5] The leading clubs were too concerned with winning to consider fully the plight of their weaker brethren. Apart from occasional donations and some redistribution of test match revenue, they were left to solve their own financial problems, basically by patronage and public appeals. No wonder that cricket struggled to maintain 16 first-class county clubs in contrast to the larger number of soccer and rugby teams and racecourses.

II

The preceding discussion is not to deny that some individual clubs were profit-maximisers, but, if they were, they operated within the parameters determined by the controlling bodies, and accepted regulations which, with the exception of English soccer, did not encourage group profit-maximisation. Given the revenue-sharing arrangements, or rather the lack thereof, it was in the best financial interests of most clubs to win as many games as possible in order to attract the partisan home supporter and to hope that they played well enough also to attract the connoisseur of the game: in effect different markets were being supplied with the same product. Uncertain results may well maximise aggregate attendances but the away gate was of little concern to all but Scottish football clubs. Nevertheless, the expectation of a close game might well tempt more supporters to travel with the visiting team, but uncertain results can go either way and too many in the wrong direction could reduce local support and undermine a club's long-term viability. Hence clubs generally preferred to attempt to maximise their playing efficiency and risk too successful a season along with diminishing financial returns rather than attempt to profit-maximise and risk losing too many matches. In any case, although consistently winning teams may not have earned maximum profits, they seldom lost money. Moreover, at least in the English second division, consistent winning was the way to gain entry to the more profitable first division.

The basic problem with utility-maximisation, as compared to profit-maximisation, is that sport is a zero-sum game, so that, whereas it would be possible for all participants to make money, it is impossible for all pursuers of utility to achieve their objectives: for every winner there must be a loser. However, perhaps utility can be redefined to be considered as doing one's best within a budget constraint, a limiting factor which can vary considerably between clubs and perhaps reduce the chances of some clubs of being consistent winners.

Nevertheless, even in Scottish soccer, the most unequal of the sports studied, there was no absolute barrier to sporting success. Although Celtic, Rangers and Hearts dominated the League and cup honours board, they did not invariably make a clean sweep. Of the 20 first-division clubs in 1914/15 only eight had not finished in the top three sometime and, of these, only four had never reached a Scottish cup final. Running close to the 'big three' perhaps became accepted as a criterion of success by the weaker clubs. Moreover, there were other trophies to be won and a club regularly playing first-division football should have had the quality to win

a city, county or local charity cup from time to time.[6] At worst, perhaps
something could be salvaged from a poor playing season by a morale-
boosting win over local archrivals.

County cricket clubs stood alone in having only one trophy to play for.
Most counties could not envisage ever winning the championship and all
that they could hope for was an occasional victory against one of the
Titans. Perhaps for the majority of counties, playing the game in the
accepted manner and surviving to enjoy the status of being a first-class
club was reward enough.

Yet even clubs with such limited perceptions of utility could not neglect
commercial considerations. Whatever their motivation, profit, or rather
revenue, could not be ignored. Over time the costs of participation in all
the sports studied rose substantially. As one observer noted regarding
cricket on the eve of the First World War:

The day has gone when a modest income from a few matches will maintain a
modern county club, very often burdened with the maintenance of a large ground
all the year round, with the salary of a staff of professionals, with the match
expenses of amateurs, with responsibilities, liabilities, insurances, and growing
taxation never dreamed of years ago.[7]

Hence the increased concern of county clubs with the state of their balance
sheets, which led to first-class cricket being labelled as a 'money-grubbing
business' which 'apart from the M. C. C. has become a money-making
concern'.[8] Yet really cricket was more than just a commodity in the
market place. Many of the game's supporters were willing to subsidise it
for reasons of civic pride, county allegiance, or even national jingoism. It
had become so much an integral part of English mores and tradition that it
was not viewed primarily as a business proposition, and these social
values of the game clearly hindered the response of those in charge to
market signals.[9]

III

Although money was being made out of man at play in late nineteenth-
and early twentieth-century Britain, it can be suggested that, despite the
emphasis on private rather than public funding, profit-maximisation was
not necessarily the aim of all those who invested in the sports industry. At
one end of the spectrum of motivations were those, such as boxing
promoters and some owners of thoroughbred racing, and especially
breeding, bloodstock, who sought direct profits. Yet even in this category
there were *rentiers* satisfied with the safe return rather than the high-risk,
high-yield investment.

Others sought profits from sport more indirectly. As well as the businessmen who patronised works teams as part of their industrial welfare policies, these included the penny capitalists and wealthier organisers of illegal off-course betting; cycle manufacturers who regarded the sponsoring of meetings and riders as a form of advertising; and those builders, caterers and sports outfitters who took shares in football clubs in expectation of contracts. Another major group of football shareholders who looked to benefit indirectly was the drink trade, who hoped that fans would celebrate their victories or drown their sorrows in public houses owned by men who supported their club financially. Transport enterprises expected to benefit from sports passenger traffic and hence extended facilities to football grounds and racetracks, occasionally also sponsoring races at the latter. Another example of a symbiotic relationship was that with the press, which provided free publicity for sports events and in turn found ready customers among sports fans.

A third category of sports investor seems to have been either uninterested in profits or gave priority to other objectives. As suggested earlier in this chapter, many gate-money sports clubs looked to winning first and revenue second. Other examples of such non-economic investment in sport can be found at all levels of society. Some upper-class and middle-class expenditure can be viewed as consumption, sometimes of the conspicuous variety, despite its apparent investment nature: clearly, in racecourse ownership, there was a strong social-status element to the heavy expenditure involved. Other members of the middle class laid out substantial sums to purchase social exclusivity in their capital-intensive and land-extensive golf clubs. Yet others were prepared to underwrite their local or county cricket team for reasons of civic or county pride. Some of those who subsidised cricket may have been among that group who sought to use sport as a means of social control of the lower orders by investing in municipal facilities and sponsoring teams. Even some of the working class were prepared to purchase a few shares in their local soccer club with no regard to financial reward: to them shareholding was simply an extension of being a fan.

Part IV

Playing for pay: professional sport as an occupation

What goes against the grain is the false pretence of the whole system, its paltry snobbishness. Our best man – choose whomsoever you please – would lose caste if he declared himself a professor; as if professionalism carried with it a sort of social degradation.

M. Cobbett, *The Man on the March*, London, 1896, p. 282

The ideal formation of a pastime, and sometimes also of a sport, is professionalism leavened by amateurism. In the hunting or shooting field we see this is the case, where the master and his whips or the host and his keepers unite to show us the best of sport; and, still closer to our argument, we witness it in the Yorkshire cricket team with its professionals combining with the unsullied amateurism of Lord Hawke.

A. R. Haig-Brown, 'The lesson from New Zealand',
Badminton Magazine, XXII, 1906, p. 48

I am convinced that open professionalism is better than bogus amateurism. And in clubs whose members are drawn mainly from the working-classes, only one or other of these alternatives is possible.

J. J. Bentley (1902) quoted in P. M. Young, *Bolton Wanderers*,
London, 1961, pp. 44–5

Heaven save us from strikes, lockouts and unions in cricket – where the only strike in the game should, and always must, come from the full face of the bat.

Athletic Chat, 6 June 1900

Chapter 12

The struggle for recognition

I

The emergence of professionalism in sports such as football, rugby and cycling was very much a product of the wave of commercialisation which engulfed the leisure sector in the late nineteenth century. The same economic tide also left its mark on sports with a longer tradition of professionalism, such as cricket and horse-racing. Change was accompanied by controversy and almost every sport had its debate on the merits, or otherwise, of recognising professionalism and on the safeguards which would have to be imposed should it be accepted.

The essential difference between amateurs and professionals in nineteenth-century Britain was social rather than economic.[1] No one labelled as professionals those early nineteenth-century, socially elite sportsmen who rowed or raced against each other for money prizes, or backed their sporting prowess with heavy wagers. Nor, at this time were they classed as amateurs: the contradistinction to professional was gentleman. However, as active sports involvement became more broadly based, the middle class added the organisation of sports bodies to its administrative portfolio and began to set rules regarding participation, rules in which birth and background became important parameters in the protection of middle-class sporting preserves. The concept of the amateur which developed was thus a by-product of changing circumstances in British sport. The ensuing struggle by professionals for recognition as legitimate sportsmen can perhaps be seen as part of the wider class confrontation taking place in society at this time.

II

The first men to be paid for playing cricket were those estate workers who, in the early eighteenth century, were found employment as gardeners and gamekeepers by their patron so that he could utilise their more obvious talents in his cricket team.[2] Clearly such men played at and under the orders of their social superiors. There were some freelance professionals who played where and when payment was offered, but even they had a servant–master relationship with their employer of the moment. In the nineteenth century, however, the demise of aristocratic paternalism in wider society led to a decline in upper-class patronage of cricket and a temporary change in the status of the professional player, not so much for those who were employed as coaches and bowlers by clubs, schools and universities, but certainly for the leading players who joined the various itinerant professional teams. These men were much more their own masters: indeed several members of the All England XI run by fellow-professional, William Clarke, quit to form a rival United XI of England because Clarke did not pay them enough.

In the 1870s county cricket revived and eclipsed the touring elevens as spectator attractions and once more the professionals were playing alongside men of higher social class. The county committees were determined that the professionals, having lost their independence, should again know their place. It was acknowledged that they were indispensable to the county game as few amateurs could afford, or were willing, to devote sufficient time to the acquisition of the necessary skills, particularly bowling, and even fewer could play throughout the season.[3] Nevertheless, it was deemed important that professionals be seen to be subordinate to the amateur players. This was done partly by nomenclature: in cricketing parlance amateurs were termed gentlemen which had obvious social connotations. It was also done by symbolic subordination in that amateurs and professionals ate, travelled, dressed for the game and even entered the field of play separately.[4] Moreover, amateurs had their initials before their surnames on the scorecards whereas professionals generally had theirs placed after. Subordination was more than symbolic as the captain of a county team was almost always an amateur of some social standing: indeed Leicestershire went so far as to select Sir Arthur Hazelrigg as captain though he had never played in a first-class match, had not made a university trial or even his public-school eleven.[5] Additionally most of the professional staff were expected to help prepare the pitch, and the bowlers among them had to turn up to give batting practice to the amateur members of the county club.

Horse-racing was another sport with a long tradition of professional-ism.[6] In the early days of the sport, owners generally rode their own horses, though soon some of them realised that they could increase their chances of winning by employing specialist jockeys to ride for them. Until the early nineteenth century most jockeys were merely riding grooms, liveried servants beholden to a specific employer. However, as commercial attitudes strengthened within the sport, independent jockeys emerged and by the later part of the century the leading riders were able to pick and choose for whom they rode. This led to some disquiet based on status considerations. One critic voiced outrage at the 'school of skinny dwarfs whose leaders are paid better than the greatest statesmen in Europe . . . the commonest jockey-boy in the company of mannikins can usually earn more than the average scholar or professional man', and Lord Suffolk argued that 'it is impossible that jockeys can be kept in their proper position when successful members of the riding fraternity are enabled to realise fortunes of £100,000 or more within a dozen years of their first appearance in the saddle'.[7]

Increased commercialisation also led to fewer amateurs being able to ride against professionals for, as the value of racing bloodstock increased, the Jockey Club acted to prevent unskilled riders from putting valuable horseflesh at risk. From 1879 all gentlemen who wished to race with professional jockeys had to obtain a licence from the Jockey Club and these were not granted readily.

Most amateurs in fact preferred National Hunt racing as the heavier weights which the horses carried allowed them to ride without too great a sacrifice of the good life. Moreover, there were many races over fences which were restricted to gentlemen riders, though, as the term implies, there were social qualifications for such jockeys. Up to 1866 the term was somewhat elastic and covered a multitude of sinners. There was probably an element of truth in the story of the 'gentleman' rider at a Yorkshire meeting in 1836 who had no doubts as to his eligibility: 'I subscribes to a pack o' dogs. I hunts three days a week. I drinks wine to my dinner. And I keeps a mistress!'[8] The formation of the National Hunt Committee brought stricter regulations in that a qualified amateur rider had to belong to one of a select list of clubs, or be an officer of either service on full pay, a magistrate, a peer, or bear a courtesy title. Persons of lower social standing could be balloted in, but they had to be nominated by men holding the club or commission qualification. There had been modifications to these rules by the end of the century, particularly after the reorganisation of the National Hunt Committee in 1883: the list of approved clubs was extended, farmers (and their sons) with a minimum occupation of 100 acres became eligible, but those seeking entry by ballot had to be proposed and seconded by members of the National Hunt Committee itself.[9]

Professionalism in rowing actually pre-dated amateur participation.

Whereas amateur racing developed in the early nineteenth century, the annual Doggett Coat and Badge race had been instituted for Thames watermen back in 1715.[10] Professionals, however, were clearly men who made their living out of fishing or ferrying goods and passengers rather than men who raced for money. No one regarded the Oxford or Leander crews who raced each other for £200 a side in 1831 as professionals: indeed a newspaper headline of the time described the race as a match between London and Oxford amateurs.[11] Eight years later, when the Henley Regatta was established, events were restricted to amateurs and, although no definition of amateur was given, it was implicit in the clause which considered as eligible 'any crew composed of members of a College of either of the Universities of Oxford, Cambridge, or London, the schools of Eton and Westminster, the officers of the two brigades of Household Troops, or of members of a club established at least one year previous to the time of entering'.[12] By 1861 the *Rowing Almanack* had a similar definition, though with the addition of a class-ridden clause specifically excluding 'tradesmen, labourers, artisans or working mechanics'.[13] Nevertheless, there was no national controlling body and no authorised version of what constituted an amateur.

This situation was not rectified until the late 1870s. In 1878 the newly formed Metropolitan Rowing Association issued a formal definition of amateurism which stimulated the Henley authorities to announce, in 1879, that no person should be considered an amateur who had ever competed in an open competition for a stake, money, or entrance fee; who had ever competed with or against a professional for any prize; who had ever taught, pursued, or assisted in the practice of athletic exercises of any kind as a means of gaining a livelihood; who had ever been employed in or about boats for money or wages; or who was or had ever been by trade or employment for wages, a mechanic, artisan or labourer. This negative definition was then adopted by the Metropolitan Rowing Association, which became the accepted governing body for British rowing, as was acknowledged when they changed their title to the Amateur Rowing Association in 1882.[14] Those working-class rowers who wished to compete without turning professional were left to found their own organisation, the National Amateur Rowing Association, in 1890.[15]

Up to 1894 the Amateur Rowing Association deemed everyone a professional if they were not qualified to be amateurs, but in that year it was decided to interpret professional 'in its primary and literal sense' as one who made money by rowing, sculling, or steering. Hence three categories of oarsmen were created, namely amateur, non-amateur and professional.[16] Mechanics, manual labourers and the like were no longer classed as professionals but they were still not allowed to compete at regattas held under Amateur Rowing Association regulations.[17] The 'mechanic's clause', however, was subject to interpretation. One principle which emerged was that an apprenticeship was not grounds for a disqualification even if it involved manual labour for money, but that to do the same work after an apprenticeship was completed was a bar to amateur oarsmanship.[18] Nevertheless, a hard line was generally taken. Even in the 1920s Jack Kelly, an Olympic gold medallist, was banned from rowing at Henley as he had once been a bricklayer.[19]

Professionalism also had a long history in athletics.[20] Its origins lay in aristocrats and gentlemen backing their footmen and messengers to outrun those of fellow members of the leisured class. Over time, however, this type of professional was replaced by men who performed endurance feats against the clock or who competed for money prizes at specialised meetings, such as the Fell gatherings or Highland games. This 'foot-running' or 'pedestrianism' was distinct from 'athletics', which developed in Britain in the 1860s. In fact the Amateur Athletic Club, formed in 1866 by athletes from London and the universities, specifically aimed 'to afford as completely as possible to all classes of gentleman amateurs the means of practising and competing against one another, without being compelled to mix with professional runners'.[21] Nor were they to mingle with working men, as in 1867 the mechanic's clause was added to the Club's definition of an amateur. However, although the Club itself remained exclusive, its annual championships were open to all except overt professionals and thus the winners became accepted as national champions.[22] The rival to the A. A. C. as a potential national controlling body for athletics was the London Athletic Club, itself initially so status-conscious that 60 members resigned when the entry of a tradesman was accepted for a meeting.[23]

When both these clubs were formed most athletes, and certainly the best of them, emanated from the universities, but over the next decade athletics became popularised. Civil servants, clerks and businessmen swelled the ranks of the L. A. C. and, especially in the north, working-class runners began to take up the sport. By the late 1870s a crisis was at hand. The Northern Counties Athletics Association, founded in 1879, was pressing to have its more liberal definition of an amateur accepted nationally, the L. A. C. was threatening to hold its own national championships, and the A. A. C. itself was almost defunct. The twelve events at its championships had attracted only 26 entries and it was alleged that the Club had only three active members – the secretary, the pony and the heavy roller![24]

The situation was ripe for the emergence of a new controlling body and in 1880, following a meeting of leading clubs held under the aegis of Oxford athletes, the Amateur Athletic Association was established.[25] It dropped the 'mechanic's clause', made no reference to 'gentlemen', and adopted the N. C. A. A. definition of an amateur as 'one who has never competed for a money prize or staked bet, or with or against a professional for any prize, or who has never taught, pursued or assisted in the practice of athletic exercises as a means of obtaining a livelihood'.[26] Apart from banning them from meetings under its own jurisdiction, professional athletes were left alone, with any supervision being entirely in the hands of the promoters of the particular meeting.

Amateurs and professionals were also segregated in boxing. A few 'amateurs' probably faced up to professionals in the boxing booths of travelling shows, and certainly a few talented performers used the amateur ring as a step towards professional circles. Otherwise the two branches of boxing remained virtually separate sports.

No doubt in the early eighteenth century young sporting gentlemen sparred with professional prizefighters in the gymnasia run by the paid exponents of the noble art, but prizefighting itself was left to the professional pugilists.[27] In fact there was no organised boxing as a sport for amateurs until mid-Victorian times. Although gentlemen amateurs probably fought each other from time to time and rustic fairs witnessed bouts between rural youths eager for glory rather than cash, it was not until 1867 that a few clubs held the first national amateur boxing championships under the auspices of the Amateur Athletic Club, with cups provided by Lord Queensberry. These Queensberry championships continued till 1885, for the last five years running in parallel with those of the Amateur Boxing Association (founded 1880), whose rules allowed more in-fighting.[28]

In the meantime professional boxing, having adopted the rules to which the Marquis of Queensberry lent his patronage, was rising out of the ashes of prizefighting. Yet, unlike in the amateur sector, there was no controlling body to oversee the development of the sport: promoters were free to decide if bouts should be decided on points or by knockout, whether they should be fought with gloves or bareknuckle, and to foist them on an unsuspecting public as being for titles or championships.[29] The National Sporting Club, a private organisation founded in 1891 to promote and encourage the development of professional boxing, instituted the Lord Lonsdale Championship Challenge belts in 1909, which did something to regularise the notion of title matches, but, despite its pretensions, the Club did not control British boxing.[30]

Cycling was one of the first new sports to accept the professional. From its inception in 1877 the Bicycle Union allowed professional riders to become members.[31] Moreover, in order to publicise the sport it actively promoted a series of races between leading amateur and professional cyclists. Both these moves were, of course, anathema to the athletic clubs who had been the initial promoters of amateur cycle-racing. An even greater shock to traditionalists, however, was the definition of amateurism adopted by the Union in May 1878:

That a professional bicyclist is one who has ridden a bicycle in public for money, or who has engaged, taught, or assisted in bicycling or any other athletic exercise for money, and that a bicyclist who shall have competed with a professional bicyclist for a prize knowingly and without protest (except at a meeting specially sanctioned by the Union), shall also be considered a professional bicyclist. Any person not included in the above definition shall be considered an amateur bicyclist.[32]

The Union was thus the first national sports authority to define amateurism without any reference to social status.

Athletic clubs had been to the fore in the promotion of cycle-racing: in fact the recognised national amateur bicycling championship had been organised by the Amateur Athletic Club at their Lillie Bridge track since 1871. Thus in order to establish its position as the sole authority in cycling, so far as racing was concerned, the Bicycle Union had to challenge the athletic establishment.[33] Almost immediately it declared that the Lillie Bridge championships were no longer bona fide and replaced them by events of its own.[34] It did not attempt to isolate cycling from athletics and many athletic clubs continued to hold cycle races as part of their programme because they helped to attract the crowds. When the Amateur Athletic Association took control of British athletics it insisted on exercising control over cycle-racing held as part of athletic meetings. In 1885 matters came to a head and, after a vehement dispute, the National Cyclists' Union, as it had become, was acknowledged as having the sole right to control cycle-racing.[35] Although it did not promote professional racing, the Union established a licensing system for all riders in order to regulate both branches of the sport. Nevertheless, despite its acceptance of professionalism, the Union recommended that professionals and amateurs should not race against each other.[36] In fact professional cycling went on its way very much as an adjunct to the bicycle and cycle accessory industries, with most riders virtually mobile advertisements for their sponsor or employer.[37]

Although golf did not establish itself on any scale in England until the latter part of the nineteenth century, professional golfers had existed in

Scotland for a long time. Generally they played money matches with a patron against another pro–am partnership or against other professionals for stakes provided by a backer.[38] By the middle of the century most of them also undertook other tasks, either as caddies or, for the more fortunate, as professionals attached to clubs looking after the greens and making and selling golfing equipment.[39] As golf began to boom in England the Scots responded to the market opportunity and, unlike in soccer, the English middle class welcomed this flow of talent across the Border. As demand for club professionals outpaced supply, caddying fell to irregularly employed young boys and, later, as other sectors of the market were stimulated by the upsurge, specialist greenkeepers emerged and equipment companies began to manufacture standardised parts which the professional assembled.[40] His major role at the club became that of 'professor', teaching members the rudiments of the game. Perhaps this was why one commentator believed that the status of the golf professional had risen.[41]

Nevertheless, the great majority of professionals were dependent upon club members for their livelihood: few professionals could earn a living from competitive play. Matches, generally financed by backers, continued to be played, but tournaments, both match and increasingly stroke play, came into prominence.[42] A very few were restricted to professionals; more were solely for amateurs, defined as

a golfer who has never made for sale golf clubs, balls, or any other article connected with the game; who has never carried clubs for hire after attaining the age of fifteen years, and who has not carried clubs at any time within six years of the date on which competition begins in each year; who has never received any consideration for playing in a match or for giving lessons in the game; or for a period of five years prior to September 1st, 1886 has never received a money prize in open competition.[43]

However, there was no unbridgeable chasm as in athletics and the *open* championship meant precisely that. Like cricketers, amateurs and professionals competed on equal terms. However, also like cricketers, professionals were kept firmly in their place, which was most definitely not the members' clubroom.[44]

Allegedly the first professionals in English football were two Scots, James Lang and Peter Andrews, who came to Sheffield to play for the Heeley Club around 1876.[45] Others followed and by the early 1880s many Scots were crossing the Border, ostensibly in search of more regular employment but also out to make money from playing football. They did not venture south unsolicited: the Lancashire clubs in particular actively recruited in Scotland and the Scottish press carried many advertisements of jobs available in Blackburn, Burnley and other cotton towns for men blessed with footballing talent.

Increasingly the Committee of the Football Association came under pressure from those who wished to preserve the game for amateur players and in 1882 it passed a rule which empowered it to expel any club which paid its players more than actual expenses or wages actually lost. No serious effort, however, seems to have been made to enforce this regulation until after the local Sheffield, Birmingham and Lancashire associations held their own inquiries and punished some transgressors. At this time active resistance to professionalism was stronger at the regional than at the national level and the F. A. Committee appears to have preferred to ignore the issue till its hand was actually forced. Even then its subcommittee appointed to investigate the twin problems of importation and professionalism stated in February 1883 that it had not obtained sufficient evidence to render a report.[46] Perhaps too many clubs followed Bolton's lead and prepared a fresh set of books for inspection.[47] Maybe the investigators should have followed the line pursued by some of the clubs. In 1883 Nottingham Forest put up placards offering a £20 reward to anyone who could prove that some of the Wednesday's players were professionals and the Wednesday club itself wrote to opposition players asking them if they had been paid to play.[48] Wednesday also took precautions regarding the status of its own players by cautioning them to refrain from playing in matches organised by private parties, since a failure 'to hold themselves aloof from ill temptations thrown out . . . would constitute them professionals at once'.[49] It was around this time that the F. A. actually obtained sufficient information to show that a player named Beresford had been offered financial inducement to join Accrington. In this case action was taken: Beresford was suspended and Accrington expelled.[50] At least something had been done at the national level.

By now protest upon protest was being lodged with various regional associations regarding the amateur qualifications of participants in local cup competitions. It was only a matter of time before the same occurred in the national tournament. The inevitable came in January 1885 when Upton Park, a London amateur side, claimed that Preston North End, one of the leading teams in the country, had fielded professionals in their fourth-round F. A. Cup tie. At the subsequent inquiry Major William Suddell, cotton manufacturer and organiser of the Preston team, not only openly admitted paying his players but also maintained that this was common practice.[51] Preston were disqualified, but clearly this would not be the end of the matter. The issue was now out in the open and a decision had to be made as to the direction in which football was to go.

At a general meeting of the F. A. in February 1884 an abortive proposal to legalise professionalism led to the formation of yet another sub-committee, this one charged with formulating rules 'for the repression' of veiled professionalism and the importation of players. In June regulations were adopted which forbade clubs from paying 'wages lost' for more than one day in any week and which made it compulsory to issue written receipts. Moreover, in a reversal of natural justice, the F. A. Committee was empowered to call upon suspected clubs and players to prove their innocence.[52] Finally, in an effort to stop importation, only Englishmen were to be allowed to play for English clubs in F. A. Cup ties.[53] Nevertheless, it still appeared that the F. A. wanted to leave the initiation of action to the clubs, and even then to keep it low key by recommending that they should simply not play those other clubs who apparently engaged professionals.[54]

Then, in October, a circular was issued which required that clubs entering the F. A. Cup make a return of all their players who were not English or who had joined the club from another district. Among the information requested were details of the player's earnings, both before and after his move, and a statement of the reason for his mobility. Almost immediately many northern clubs threatened to secede and form a British Football Association. Although they were persuaded not to break away, no doubt their threat forced some F. A. committeemen to reconsider their position and, after two proposals to accept professionalism had gained absolute, but not the necessary two-thirds, majorities, a third attempt in July 1885 was successful. Nevertheless, professionalism was to be controlled stringently. Fuller details are given in Appendix 2d, but essentially birth and residential qualifications were imposed – though not for long. A reconstitution of the F. A. Committee gave more power to the professional clubs and in May 1889 these conditions were abolished.[55] Once again footballing Scots began to move south and within a year 230 Scottish professionals were registered with English clubs.[56]

Once professionals were accepted in football there does not appear to have been any serious attempt to subordinate them, as in cricket. Some individuals tried, as when Lindley and Walters, amateurs in the English team versus Ireland, refused to travel on the same boat or stay in the same hotel as the professionals, but after 1898 there were no such distinctions at the international level.[57] Professionals, however, were forbidden by both the F. A. and the Football League from representing their club at the committee or board level, at least until they had finished playing, and then only with special permission.[58]

As professional teams came to dominate the F. A. Cup, the Football

Association instituted the F. A. Amateur Cup in 1894. Despite this, many amateurs, especially in the south, felt that the F. A. had become too concerned with issues of professionalism to the detriment of the amateur game. A particular irritant was the introduction of the penalty kick, designed to punish the professional foul but applicable to all levels of soccer. The old-boy sides from the public schools refused to have such awards in their Arthur Dunn cup competition on the grounds that it cast doubt on their gentlemanly conduct.[59] For this they were reprimanded by the Football Association.[60] Eventually the southern amateurs rebelled: the Surrey and Middlesex associations refused to allow professional clubs to affiliate, and when the F. A. insisted the amateurs seceded and formed their own national association.[61]

Official resistance to paid soccer players proved more obdurate in Scotland than south of the Border and the recognition of professionalism in Scottish football lagged almost a decade behind its acceptance by the F. A. in England. Founded in 1873, the Scottish Football Association espoused a utilitarian view of sport and saw the ultimate aim of football as being 'to maintain the superiority of British nerve and muscle, and to promote the healthful conditions of town and country alike, and to produce in the inhabitants of our native land, a bold, athletic, and manly race . . . [and] to preserve that Scottish bone and muscle which has so often proven its worth on many a hard-fought field of war, and of industry, throughout the world'.[62] Professionalism, defined as 'having engaged in open public sports for money', was banned and the rule was enforced: Vale of Leven, a leading side, were excluded from the Scottish Cup in 1875 because their captain had run for money prizes.[63]

Many clubs initially supported the functional view of soccer – their advertisements for members in the early editions of the *Scottish Football Annual* stressed 'healthful recreation' and rarely mentioned playing success – but by 1881 the secretary of the S. F. A. was alleging that some of them were paying players in order to attract spectators by a high standard of play. There was a touch of Calvinism about his added complaint that some of the gate-money raised was being used to finance 'indiscriminate feasting and debauchery after matches'. He was adamant that professionalism had to be resisted for 'football is nothing if it is not a game for amateurs'.[64] Words were backed by action and in 1884 the Association's constitution was altered to include a threat of two years' disqualification for any player 'found guilty of receiving remuneration for their services beyond their reasonable and legitimate expenses': two players were in fact suspended that season and the offending club expelled from the Association, though later one player and the club were reinstated.[65]

The decision of the English F. A. to recognise professionalism in 1885 shocked its Scottish counterpart. Only two years before, the Scottish Association had called for close cooperation with the southern body in its efforts to suppress professionalism 'as an unmitigated evil'.[66] The Scottish organisation not only refused to follow the English lead, but immediately barred any players under its jurisdiction from playing with or against professionals.[67] For a while this attitude threatened the future of both the home internationals and the lucrative Anglo–Scottish club fixtures, but eventually the Scots were placated by an English promise of residential qualifications on Scottish players who moved over the Border and an agreement that each home association had complete autonomy to define professionalism as regards the players under its jurisdiction.[68] It was with smug satisfaction that the annual report for the following season recorded an international victory over the predominantly professional Welsh side as 'showing that amateurism still holds the sway'.[69]

Some Scottish clubs did not appear to share the ideals of their ruling body. They felt that payments to players were necessary to prevent, or at least to retard, the flow of indigenous footballing talent across the Border. In 1887 the S. F. A. clarified its position and announced that amateurs could receive hotel and travelling expenses and broken-time payments of up to 5s., though not for more than one day in any week.[70] It also decided to investigate the strong rumours of veiled professionalism and called in the books of 28 clubs for examination. Most were in good order but a few led to suspensions.[71] Punishment, however, failed to deter professionalism and in 1890 the books of 45 clubs were examined with the surprising, but carefully worded, conclusion that 'on the testimony of the books submitted, with the explanation given, professionalism does not exist in Scotland' – this, despite over 200 players being dealt with for irregular expenses! Clearly the state of the book-keeping – which would probably not have been tolerated in the businesses of many of the committeemen – gave ample opportunity for payments to players to be hidden. Apart from the mutilated books and those specially written up for the investigation, there was a general failure to record stand receipts, to retain gate-money vouchers, or to check players' claims for travel and lost time.[72]

The tide could not be stemmed. Increasing pressure was put on the S. F. A. to alter its stance, especially once the Scottish Football League began operations. Finally, in 1893, the Association bowed with the wind of change and sanctioned the employment of professionals in Scottish soccer. Immediately 50 clubs registered 560 professionals and within two seasons 89 Scottish clubs had 936 professionals on their books.[73]

Rugby was late to embrace professionalism and this occurred only after a schism which irreconcilably split the organisation of the game.[74] By 1890 rugby was firmly established in the industrial areas of northern England and the northern counties dominated the county championship, with Yorkshire winning in seven of the first eight years and Lancashire securing the one missed by the white-rose county. Undoubtedly some of this northern superiority was attributable to working-class players who were able to play only because they received covert broken-time payments.[75] In September 1893 the Yorkshire representatives to the Rugby Football Union attempted to legitimise this practice by proposing that such payments be allowed for bona fide loss of earnings. The supporters of pure amateurism, however, had arranged for a strong turnout at the meeting and had also collected a substantial number of proxy votes. Not only was the Yorkshire proposal defeated, but soon afterwards an amended by-law was instituted which declared that 'only clubs composed entirely of amateurs shall be eligible for membership': what had been an unwritten law was now embedded in the constitution of the Rugby Football Union. The counterattack did not end there. Although a 'manifesto' issued in late 1894 failed to gain sufficient support at the county level, in September 1895 the annual general meeting of the R. F. U. carried a set of resolutions designed to purge their game of professionalism once and for all. Money could be given to players solely in recompense for genuine travelling expenses; anything else would label a player as a professional and would result in the expulsion of himself and those who played with him. So strict were the new regulations that players were deemed professionals if they did paid repair work to club facilities or if they were awarded medals without the formal permission of the R. F. U.[76]

No doubt the passage of these resolutions was eased by the prior defection of eleven of the twelve leading Yorkshire clubs who, in anticipation of the new legislation, had established the Northern Rugby Football Union a month previously. They and their Lancashire counterparts were adamant that the 'cast iron rules framed by the Rugby Union for an ideal amateurism [were] totally unworkable in this part of the country where we have to rely on the working-class player'.[77] Initially the Northern Union was content to legalise broken-time payments up to a maximum of 6s. a day. Before long, however, some clubs began to exceed this figure and inevitably, as the diehard adherents to the R. F. U. had prophesied, professionalism was recognised, though it was of a peculiar kind. Under the enabling legislation of 1898 no one could play as a professional who was not in full-time employment in another job: moreover, to keep the image of professionalism less tarnished, jobs such as working in a public house, billiard-marking or bookie's runner were not acceptable. The 'work clauses' were enforced and players were suspended for failing to find full-time employment, for changing jobs without notifying the Union, for taking time off prior to playing, even if only to visit sick relatives, for not working for three days after their own sickness, and, of course, for following a proscribed occupation.[78] It can be seen in its extreme form in the fining of Broughton Rangers, Challenge Cup winners in 1902, for not having their players work on the morning of the final.[79] Checking the eligibility of their players from week to week caused many headaches for club secretaries and the 'work clauses' were attacked regularly at the annual general meetings of the Northern Union, but not until 1905 did the advocates of abolition gain the necessary votes.[80] Although this opened the way for full-time professionalism, such a movement did not develop on any scale, possibly because of the relatively low level of earnings for most players in the game.

A firm stand against the rebels was maintained by the R. F. U. Anyone playing with a Northern Union player was automatically labelled a professional and themselves liable to contaminate the amateur standing of others. This led to one view that 'of all the epidemics of modern times, Northern Union leprosy is the most insidious in its attacks'.[81] Most hardline of all on the question of amateurism were the Scottish Rugby Union. They threatened to cancel their match against England in 1908 because the R. F. U. had approved 3s. a day allowance to the Australian touring team in 1908/09, a payment which the Scots reckoned was 'tantamount to professionalism in a very insidious form'. They also refused to play the Australians, although three years earlier they had played the New Zealanders, who had received a similar allowance: perhaps their demand to the New Zealanders for the return of the match ball was a protest against veiled professionalism rather than Scottish parsimony.[82]

III

Social prejudice permeated all the major criticisms of sports professionalism. Often this masqueraded as sporting idealism, though some opponents openly admitted to class bias, believing that professionalism lowered sport to the level of a trade and that merely to play alongside players was sufficient for some gentlemen to 'hazard their self-respect' and that it was 'degrading for respectable men to play with professionals'.[83]

Others felt that professionals did not play the game, that they had turned play into work, consumption into production, and made winning so important that in order to secure victory they would resort to foul play and sharp practice.[84] Their lack of education meant that they had not 'the same sense of honour as the public school boy'.[85] Although C. B. Fry, who played with and against professionals in both cricket and football, reckoned that 'even in the worst days the case against the standard of sportsmanship among professionals was usually much overstated', it remains true that certainly in soccer foul play was part and parcel of the professional scene.[86] Nevertheless, professionals had no monopoly of sharp practice or violent play. At Henley, in 1868, the Brasenose four had their cox jump overboard just after the start and with a lessened load easily won their race.[87] In amateur rugby union one commentator noted that 'things have reached a pretty pass when public school boys, past and present, hand out of the scrum, or continue their run after knowing they have stepped into touch'.[88] And what of W. G. Grace himself, who ran out an Australian player who had merely moved down the wicket to pat down a rough patch.[89] Nor was intentional rough play confined to professionals: amateur rugby, in particular, both at school and club level, was prone to excessive violence.[90]

Where the critics of professionalism had a stronger case was in their belief that men who were paid to win could also be paid to lose.[91] Once sport became part of the struggle for existence, then it was more likely to lead to temptation and the race need not necessarily go to the swiftest. The history of the turf is replete with such instances and it is not coincidence that one meaning of 'jockey' is to cheat or deceive: indeed it is noticeable that honest is a rare word in racing parlance, being used deliberately about only a few jockeys with the implicit assumption that it was not applicable to the majority. Yet generally it was not professionalism *per se* which was responsible for corruption, but the gambling associated with a particular sport. Cricket, golf and tennis had their professionals but relatively little gambling and virtually no corruption. Amateur athletics had its book-maker and its share of abuses.[92] Nevertheless, generally it was professional rather than amateur sportsmen who were tempted into misconduct and, in order to protect their sports, the authorities had to police them and use disciplinary measures as a deterrent.[93]

A moral judgement also made from a class standpoint was that professionalism was wrong because it attracted spectators who might otherwise be playing themselves.[94] Instead of healthy recreation such passive observers risked colds and worse on wind-blown, rain-drenched terraces, leading one extremist to suggest that the number of lives 'indirectly sacrificed to football must be enormous'.[95] There is, however, no evidence whatsoever that those watching sport would, in the absence of professionalism, have been actively participating in sport. It is equally valid to argue, as did Ernest Needham, the captain of Sheffield United, that by providing Saturday afternoon entertainment football kept many working men out of the public houses and gave them some fresh air.[96]

Worse still, from the class-prejudiced viewpoint of the critics, was that the spectators lionised their sporting heroes, making them better known than politicians and encouraging the popular press to feature sport more than political news.[97] It irked them even more that the loyalty to their clubs of such feted, but mercenary, players could be transient. What *esprit de corps* could there be when 'lean and sinewy players change ownership after the manner of fat and beefy cattle'?[98] If allegiance could be bought and sold, then the rivalry was that of money not of localities.[99] Although one critic miscounted when he remarked that 'there is no stranger sight in the world to be seen than the populace of an English town becoming frenzied with delight over the victories of eleven hired Scotch players', it remains true that Tottenham Hotspur, the London-based winners of the F. A. Cup in 1901, consisted of five Scots, two Welsh, one Irish, and three players from the North of England, and that the only southerner in the final actually played for Sheffield United.[100] Yet it should be noted that the Corinthians, the leading British amateur side, could hardly stimulate local patriotism, composed as it was of players from the universities and several public schools.[101]

Envy of the more efficient coupled with a fear of being beaten by their social inferiors also motivated some to oppose professionalism, for, if professionals were allowed to compete, amateurs might no longer rule the sporting roost, at least not without a good deal of hard work.[102] There was precedence for such beliefs as professional jockeys had dominated the turf for decades.[103] So it proved in other sports. Although a few amateurs in golf performed creditably against professionals at the highest level, almost all course records were set by paid players.[104] In soccer, professional teams came to dominate the F. A. Cup and the S. F. A. Cup competitions and by 1900 professional players were predominant in the international teams. In cycling, initially, amateurs could hold their own against the professionals, but by the 1890s this was true only if they devoted their whole time to training.[105] In cricket, the gentlemen could make a match of it against the players, but this was really because prominent amateurs played just as much cricket as the professionals.[106]

Gentlemen amateurs objected to the development of professionalism as it damaged their self-interest. They did not criticise professionals outside the leisure sector; few of them would have preferred to consult an amateur solicitor or surgeon. Nor did they castigate professional artists or entertainers, who were not seen as a threat to amateur painters or singers. However, professional sportsmen, equally artists and entertainers, were condemned. Most amateurs could not hope to beat the professionals and this fear of the loss of their traditional sporting mastery led to actions designed to keep a sport, or a section of it, exclusive to amateur participation or, where this failed, to keep the professional element under strict control. This was attempted by legislation from those who controlled particular sports; by the master–servant relationship between the teaching professional and those who paid for instruction; and by the paternalism and discipline proferred to those players who performed at the behest of their employers.[107]

IV

In the early nineteenth century, being an amateur had generally required the possession of certain social qualifications, but by the end of the century many sports had adopted various, more functional definitions of amateurism. This caused problems for those middle-class sportsmen who could not afford either the time or the money to play for nothing but whose fear of losing social status rendered them unwilling to turn professional. Although some of them faced up to socio-economic reality and bowed out of sport, others continued to play, ostensibly as amateurs, but actually deriving an income from their sporting activities, details of which were often veiled by the obscurity of private arrangements.[108] Possibly much of the money they received was genuine reimbursement of expenses, though even this was a departure from absolute amateur standards. Once expenses of any kind were paid, then pure amateurism had had its day. Not being able to afford to play was similar to not being able to afford a holiday or other luxuries, and receiving expenses was really akin to changing occupations. Moreover, once expenses were given to those who otherwise could not afford to play, it was only a matter of time before other amateurs also received them, particularly in team sports where players travelled and ate together. Indeed by 1900 most sets of amateur regulations sanctioned the payment of hotel and travelling expenses. For the bibulous and gastronomic amateur this could finance a high standard of living. Few seem to have questioned the generous hospitality enjoyed by middle-class rugby teams on their Christmas or Easter tours, or by the Corinthians, that outstanding amateur soccer team, on their regular trips around Britain and on the Continent.[109] Accustomed consumption habits meant that what was 'no substantial reward to men of one class' in fact was so 'to those of another':

If the University oarsmen have their boats and oars paid for by their club, and their hotel bills at Putney defrayed by the same means, it would be hard to say that by so doing they lose their right to be called amateurs; yet if a body of pitmen are boarded and lodged for a month at the seaside at the expense of their football club, the amateur footballer would call them 'pros' and would point out that they are getting an excellent gratuitous holiday out of the sport they follow.[110]

The home of shamateurism was English county cricket, especially towards the end of the century when most counties lengthened their fixture lists and hence increased their demands on the time of their amateurs. The M. C. C. had always been reluctant to define amateurism, though in 1878 it had declared that

no gentleman ought to make a profit by his services in the Cricket Field, and that for the future, no cricketer who takes more than his expenses in any match shall be qualified to play for the Gentlemen against the Players at Lord's; but that if any gentleman feels difficulty in joining in the match without pecuniary assistance, he shall not be debarred from playing as a gentleman by having his actual expenses defrayed.[111]

Nevertheless, a blind eye appears to have been turned to 'men who without the visible means of spending the entire season in recreation, must pay their way in life by what they receive under the guise of expenses'.[112] When the Australian, L. S. Poideven, offered to qualify for Warwickshire in 1902, he was told that there would be 'very considerable difficulty' in making the payments he suggested to a supposedly amateur cricketer and that, at the time, there was no possibility of creating an assistant post of any kind, but if he chose to come to Birmingham for his medical studies he would be provided with 'a very liberal allowance for expenses'.[113]

Certainly on those occasions when the amateurs' 'reimbursements' were accidentally delivered to the wrong dressing-room, the professionals became well aware of who was being paid the most.[114] Sometimes the expenses were inflated by super broken-time payments to cover losses incurred by a player's business in his absence.[115] These were denounced scathingly by one supporter of pure amateurism:

You can't be looking after the 'shop' much while you are engaged from Monday morning to Saturday afternoon in the cricket field, and a funny sort of business it must be that will stand letting slide from the beginning of May till the end of September ... Where, then, is compensation in hundreds and thousands of pounds ... justified, except as a market transaction?[116]

Other amateurs were given nominal employment as assistant secretary to the club and the like. Archie MacLaren was persuaded not to leave Lancashire by being appointed as 'cricket instructor', a position carrying

£450 per annum for five years, though there is no evidence that he ever did anything but captain the side.[117] Leicestershire purchased the services of V. F. S. Crawford from Surrey by offering him the post of secretary at £175 per annum plus his cricket expenses and appointing an assistant 'who shall have full control of the secretarial business'; Crawford was also left free to take up any employment outside the cricket season.[118] Even the M. C. C., whose firm line on amateur expenses was a stumbling block to representative tour selection, created the post of financial secretary in a successful attempt to persuade one amateur to go to Australia.[119] Although *Wisden* maintained that not more than half a dozen shamateurs were making anything out of the game, others felt that the number was considerably more.[120]

The greatest shamateur of all was W. G. Grace. His cricketing records were almost matched by his financial ones. His county, Gloucestershire, paid for a locum for his medical practice during the cricket season and his match stipend was in the order of £50 a game.[121] Rumours of the amount of expenses he received eventually resulted in the Surrey county secretary issuing a statement that the committee had paid him only £10 per match to cover his costs when playing for either England or the Gentlemen at the Oval and that 'beyond this amount Dr Grace has not received directly or indirectly, one farthing for playing in a match at the Oval'.[122] No comment was made by Gloucestershire. Whatever the truth of these particular rumours, there is no doubt that the Doctor made money from his cricketing prowess. In 1873/74 he obtained £1,500 plus expenses for taking a team to Australia: the professionals each received £170 and expenses. Eighteen years later he demanded, and received, £3,000 plus expenses for a similar venture. Possibly this money could be regarded as broken-time payments and compensation for the employment of a locum, but the ethics of an amateur pocketing nearly £1,500 from a testimonial in 1879 and over £9,000 from another in 1895 are unfathomable.[123] Overall between 1870 and 1910 he earned around £120,000 directly or indirectly from cricket.[124] Even *Wisden* was forced to acknowledge that 'Mr W. G. Grace's position has for years, as everyone knows, been an anomalous one, but 'nice customs curtsey to great kings' and the work he has done in popularising cricket outweighs a hundredfold every other consideration':[125] no fall from grace here apparently. Caste rather than money earned from the game was clearly the distinction between gentleman and player.

The Rugby Football Union, too, was willing to bend its rules when it suited them to do so. In 1897 the Welsh Union sanctioned a testimonial to Arthur Gould, the Welsh captain, who had retired after a record 27 international caps. They even contributed £50 of the £600 collected, which was used to purchase the title of Gould's rented house. The R. F. U. decided that this smacked of professionalism and banned Gould from association with the game. Although initially the Welsh Union was willing to reconsider its involvement in the testimonial, hamfisted diplomacy by the R. F. U. provoked them to push ahead, and indeed it was the president of the Welsh Union who presented Gould with the deeds to his house.[126] So far the R. F. U. had adhered firmly to its professed principles, but then at the general meeting in September the ban was rescinded 'under the exceptional circumstances of the case'.[127] The other home Unions were slower to forgive and both Scotland and Ireland refused to play matches against Wales, the former for two seasons and the latter for one. The year that Scotland resumed its internationals against Wales saw Gould featured in advertisements for Fry's chocolate, but then so was C. B. Fry, that amateur sportsman *par excellence*![128]

National Hunt racing was the other sport in which middle-class shamateurism developed on any scale. Admittedly some clerks of the course took a lenient attitude to gentlemen riders of obscure pedigree, but mainly it was the economic qualification which was abused, with supposedly amateur jockeys obtaining retainers and liberal fees when they were not legitimately entitled even to out-of-pocket expenses. It was open to owners, however, to object to the prerequisites of suspect gentlemen riders, and one such objection to Mr Frank Lotan at Melton brought the whole issue into the open. Following the reorganisation of the National Hunt Committee in 1883, the regulations were tightened, but still some owners were willing to condone shamateurism by purchasing the services of men qualified to ride both on social grounds and by 'never having ridden for hire'; their way round the regulations was to lay a bet, with the proceeds going as a present to the rider.[129]

Not all shamateurs came from the middle class. Many working men found that amateur sport could be quite lucrative, particularly athletics, cycling and Welsh rugby. Although the Welsh and English Rugby Football Unions had agreed to a common set of tightened regulations regarding professionalism, in 1900, there is little doubt that veiled professionalism was 'rampant in the Rhondda Valley' where working-class players were paid both to play and to offset the lucrative offers made to them by the Northern Union clubs.[130]

Shamateurism was encouraged in athletics by the limited number of professional meetings organised: possibly only the Scottish circuit of Highland games offered an opportunity for regular professional earnings. In contrast amateur athletic meetings were frequent enough to enable 'many of the leading amateurs [to] make a living out of athletic sports'.[131] Some did it by selling the prizes which they won; others via the betting coups engineered by their backers; and for the best of them, who were in high demand by promoters, there was appearance money and inflated expenses.[132] The Amateur Athletic Association attempted vainly to thwart the shamateurs by limiting the value of prizes to £10, though this was still a substantial amount; by insisting that all prizes worth £5 or over had to be inscribed, which would both reduce their resale value and possibly make it easier to trace those trading in prizes; and by threatening to suspend any athlete caught taking expenses from a promoter. However, with promoters and shamateurs condoning each others' actions, all legislation proved ineffective and 'a great many athletes who passed as amateurs . . . were professionals in truth and fact, who made a living out of the sport'.[133]

Cycling, too, had its share of working-class shamateurs, though to a lesser degree than in athletics as professionalism was a viable proposition for the better riders. Some shamateurism followed the pattern of athletics. A. W. Harris won £2,000 worth of prizes before the National Cyclists' Union pressured him into becoming an open professional.[134] The main guise, however, was the so-called 'maker's amateur'. In a period of rapid technological change some good working-class riders accepted bicycles from publicity-conscious manufacturers in order to compete more effectively with their wealthier opponents. Other tyre-tied amateurs went further and accepted money so that they could take time off work to train. The N. C. U. refused to distinguish between those riders who received assistance in order to pursue their love of sport and those who merely loved money, and eventually declared the 'maker's amateurs' to be professionals and thus excluded them from amateur races.[135]

Chapter 13

Earnings and opportunities

I

It is generally accepted that professional sportsmen came from the
working class: indeed, in the light of the discussion in the previous
chapter, this is virtually a tautological statement.[1] Of their geographical
origins there is less certainty. Most jockeys hailed from rural areas,
perhaps a consequence of racing stables being located in the countryside;
some aspirants had urban backgrounds, but too often their small stature
owed more to nurture than to nature and a few months of fresh air and
good food soon ruined their chances of a career in the saddle.[2] Country
towns and villages remained the dominant source for county cricketers,
though increasingly the flow was from the north and the Midlands rather
than from the southern counties.[3] Inadequate playing facilities in the cities
may have restricted the emergence of cricketers, but soccer players could
develop their ball skills in the back streets and thus many of them may
have come from urban areas: more will be known when Osborne
completes his computerised study of Football League and Southern
League players.[4] What Table 13.1 shows is that the north of England and
Scotland were the main recruiting areas of the English Football League,
but that southerners did make more of a contribution to the Southern
League. Nevertheless, it should not be assumed that this inferred local
recruitment: Table 13.2 makes it clear that the majority of players came
from outside the region in which they played.

In the initial days of professionalism, and earlier, soccer teams often
advertised for players in the sporting press and in the 1890s resorted to the
services of football agents who touted their clients around the clubs.[5] The
role of such agencies declined as clubs established their own scouting
networks: Sheffield Wednesday, for example, employed two peripatetic
scouts at 10s. a week plus expenses and were also willing to pay a spotter's
fee to others who recommended worthwhile players.[6] Allegiance and

Table 13.1 *Geographical origins of footballers playing in England in 1910*

	Football League				Southern League	
	First division		Second division			
Area of origin[a]	No.	%[b]	No.	%[b]	No.	%[b]
Southern England	27	5.1	18	5.3	70	18.2
London	13	2.5	19	5.5	58	15.1
South central England	47	8.9	52	15.2	70	18.2
North central England	163	30.9	98	28.6	49	12.7
North-east England	80	15.2	67	19.5	50	13.0
North-west England	52	9.9	37	10.8	38	9.9
Wales	11	2.1	4	1.2	4	1.0
Scotland	124	23.5	44	12.8	45	11.7
Ireland	7	1.3	2	0.6	1	0.3
Overseas	3	0.6	2	0.6	—	—
Total traced	527		343		385	

[a]Birthplace.
[b]Of the total traced.
Source: Calculated from information supplied by Professor John Osborne, Dickinson College, Carlisle, Pennsylvania.

convenience might bring ambitious footballers almost automatically for trials with their local professional clubs, but reliance on such recruits could prove uneconomic because of the investment wasted in training those who did not make the grade.[7] Celtic, however, abandoned their policy of purchasing ready-made players from other clubs and elected to train young recruits, but by the time this decision was taken, in 1902, the best Catholic talent was probably already gravitating their way.[8] Because of the qualification rule county cricket teams mainly concentrated their recruiting efforts within their own borders, though they did advertise further afield. Most appealed to members to recommend promising players and held pre-season trial matches.[9] Additionally, old professionals and, occasionally, the county coach would be despatched on periodic talent-spotting sojourns.[10] Club and ground matches and second-eleven fixtures were also seen as a means of discovering and assessing young cricketers.[11] The system was not foolproof – pre-season was perhaps not the best time to expect good form to be displayed – and Warwickshire no

Table 13.2 *Geographical recruitment of footballers playing in England in 1910*

| | Football League | | | | Southern League | |
| | First division | | Second division | | | |
Area of origin[a]	No.	%[b]	No.	%[b]	No.	%[b]
Local (10–12 miles)	116	22.0	45	13.1	88	22.9
Within region	122	23.1	85	24.8	72	18.7
Distant	289	54.8	213	62.1	225	58.4
Total traced	527		343		385	

[a]Birthplace.
[b]Of the total traced.
Source: Calculated from information supplied by Professor John Osborne, Dickinson College, Carlisle, Pennsylvania.

doubt regretted more than once that they let Sidney Barnes go and did not even give Wilfred Rhodes a trial.[12] As far as can be ascertained, few, if any, trainers adopted the methods of cricket and soccer clubs and recruited boys as apprentices via organised scouting. Nevertheless, the stable doors were open to all who had the basic prerequisite of diminutive size. Few trainers objected to taking on an extra apprentice who could be employed as cheap labour and who, if he had the talent to win races, could also supplement the stable's income.

Learning by doing was the primary method of improving youngsters recruited by the county cricket clubs. Most young bowlers found plenty of work at the nets but unsupervised practice rarely makes perfect and coaches were appointed to pass on the benefit of their experience.[13] Other players were seconded to the large groundstaff at Lord's, where they would receive instruction and also get match practice thanks to the M. C. C.'s heavy schedule of fixtures.[14] Second-eleven county games also proved beneficial in affording 'facilities for young players to gain experience', as did club and ground matches and the farming-out of players to local clubs, though to a lesser extent because of the shorter duration of their games.[15] Essex found their second-team matches 'beneficial for the training of young players for the County XI' but gave them up for financial reasons.[16] Yorkshire and Lancashire were willing to stand the cost in order to 'boast of a contingent of young players capable at any time of filling the gaps which must inevitably occur in the county ranks'.[17] Little is known about soccer training for young signings, but there appears to have been no coaching, not much use of a ball, and an emphasis on fitness rather than on skills or tactics.[18] Racing trainers, however, offered budding jockeys formal indentures by which, in return for cheap stable labour and a proportion, often a large one, of any riding fees, they promised to teach them how to ride.[19]

II

Net practice, trial matches and training gallops all provided a screening mechanism to sieve out those who would not make the professional grade. In cricket, of the 44 colts who applied to Yorkshire in 1895 only 3 eventually played for the county; of the 50 applicants in 1904 7 made the county ranks but only 3 of these lasted more than one season; the 1910 trials brought in 39 aspirants, 5 of whom made the breakthrough to the first team, all lasting two or three seasons.[20] Even if appointed to the groundstaff there was no guarantee that a player would get a game for the county: in 1898 Lancashire had 23 professionals but only 16 played in a first-class fixture.[21] In soccer, too, many never got the chance to demonstrate their skills at the highest grade. Of the 261 new signings by English first-division clubs for the season 1893/94, 91 never kicked a ball at League level.[22] Table 13.3 suggests that this was not unusual: of the 502 registered first-division professionals in 1891/92 214 (43%) did not play a League match and 20 years later 503 (49%) of the 1,022 registrants had a similar experience. Such labour-hoarding forced the Football League Management Committee to institute a six months' limit after which a club had to cancel a player's contract if he had neither been played nor paid.[23]

Getting a chance to pit themselves at the highest level thus was not easy. Even when they had the opportunity many failed the test. Boys who were competent horsemen on the training gallops somehow never learned to ride a race; others, no matter how keen and educable, lacked the qualities which separated the men from the lads. Of the 187 apprentices registered in 1900 only 75 (40%) became licensed jockeys and a mere 48 (26%) rode as such for more than one season.[24] The three-day county cricket game demanded better skills, more concentration and greater fitness than the one-day club fixtures and stars in these games could not always make the transition and establish themselves in the county team. Table 13.4 shows that, in the seasons analysed, 30–40% of professionals played fewer than six games. Similarly, in soccer, of those who actually got a game about a quarter played fewer than five matches.

Table 13.3 *English first-division soccer appearances, 1891/92 and 1910/11*

		Matches played						
Season	Registered players	0	1	2–4	5–9	10–19	20–9	30–8
1891/92	502	213	26	50	38	65	109[a]	
1910/11	1,022	515	46	83	67	120	92	103[b]

[a]The maximum possible was 26, achieved by 21 players.
[b]The maximum possible was 38, achieved by 10 players.
Source: Calculated from Football League Registration Books.

Table 13.4 *County cricket appearances by professionals, 1898–1912*

	Matches played						
Season	1	2–5	6–10	11–15	16–20	21–5	26+
1898	29	24	28	30	25	14	6
1905	8	47	23	24	39	18	19
1912	28	29	21	17	62	23	11

Source: Calculated from data in *Wisden Cricketers' Almanacks.*

In some sports such as golf the professional could enter himself in tournaments, but in team games and in horse-racing it was a matter of catching a selector's eye or impressing an owner with one's riding style. In both Kent and Yorkshire cricket it was customary for the captain to select the team.[25] Lancashire's captain had some discretion when the county was on its southern tours but was instructed that the team should not 'be arbitrarily interfered with'.[26] Normally, however, the power lay with a selection committee, often an unwieldy one – at one stage Leicestershire's included nine members – and sometimes with no input from the captain.[27] A match committee drawn from soccer club directors appears to have chosen the teams both north and south of the Border; the manager did not become a significant figure until the inter-war years.[28] In horse-racing the owner made the decision as to who should ride his horses, though he might listen to advice from his trainer.

Generally, especially where winning was deemed important, selection was on perceived merit, although fans might consider some perceptions to be grossly distorted. However, there were apparent instances of discrimination of both the positive and negative variety, though even here they may have reflected conceptions of productivity or performance differences. Considering Victorian and Edwardian social prejudices, it is no surprise that women were virtually excluded altogether from participation in professional sport. The Football Association did not recognise women footballers even as amateurs until the second half of the twentieth century and the thought of silk-breeched lady riders would have caused apoplexy, or worse, in Jockey Club circles.[29] In the 1890s the English Cricket and Athletic Association Ltd launched women's exhibition cricket matches, but the venture was short-lived and the standard nowhere near that of men's county games.[30]

Nationality, too, sometimes influenced selection decisions. Scottish golfers were in high demand by English clubs mainly because of skills developed by virtue of the earlier establishment of the game in Scotland.[31] Table 13.1 shows that there was also a significant flow of soccer players across the Border, partly due to an appreciation of the ball skills of the Scots but also attributable to the pull of differential wages and perhaps a push from the religious bigotry of the leading clubs.

Professionals also faced competition from amateurs in some sports. Amateur soccer players, even top-line ones, were not sought by the clubs as they could not be tied down by the retain-and-transfer system, and at the turn of the century only a dozen or so were playing for League teams.[32] Many county cricket teams, on the other hand, reserved places for amateurs, especially in the university and public-school vacations; even Lancashire, hardly hostile to the professional, met at the start of the season to ascertain which amateurs would be available.[33] Given amateur 'expenses' this was hardly a cost-saving policy and perhaps owed something to the more flamboyant and entertaining style of the amateur, whose performance was not constrained by fears of losing his livelihood along with his wicket. Many well-coached amateur batsmen would be well able to compete on merit against the professionals. All teams, however, relied on professional bowlers: the hard grind of practice and play seems to have reduced the amateur challenge in this area and in 1905 only 18.8% of overs bowled in first-class county matches were sent down by unpaid players.[34] Nevertheless, on average, amateurs comprised almost a third of county sides in 1912, the proportions ranging from Somerset's 60.9% to Yorkshire's 15.9%, not coincidentally the least and most successful teams in pre-1914 county cricket.[35] Recognition of the playing success of the professionally dominated elevens helps explain the overall decline in places going to amateurs – from 44.6% in 1894 to 32.4% in 1912 – though the withdrawal of amateurs into country house cricket away from the increased pressures of championship matches must also have contributed.[36] Amateurs were no problem to the professional jockey. The introduction of a licensing system for *all* riders, paid or unpaid, in 1879, with its requirement of demonstrated competence, and perhaps also its status implications, served to reduce the number of gentlemen riders willing to compete against the professional. However, in the late 1890s even leading British jockeys felt the influence of transatlantic competition as diminutive Yankee invaders took the British turf by storm with their revolutionary riding style and racing tactics.[37] Although initially they met with prejudice and even scorn, their abilities soon became recognised and owners bargained for their services, especially after the Prince of Wales gave them the seal of approval by offering Tod Sloan, the first to make his mark, a retainer of 6,000 guineas.[38] Their success level was astonishing. In 1900 five of the leading ten jockeys were American, including Lester Reiff, who won the championship. They did not merely win a large number of races, they also had high winning percentages: in 1900 Danny Maher, Johnny Reiff and J. H. 'Skeets' Martin all topped 20%, Lester Reiff had 26%, and Tod Sloan almost 27%. No wonder that owners preferred to employ American riders and 'that English jockeys had become exceedingly doleful with the conviction that they were to be swept practically out of existence'.[39]

III

So far as the British jockeys were concerned, the labour market in horse-racing was crowded enough without the addition of the Americans. Indeed there was a permanent excess supply of jockeys.[40] Rarely were there more than a score of runners in a race, but there were twenty times this number of riders looking for a mount. A fixture clash could double the opportunity for a ride, but, in the interests of the race organisers, the Jockey Club took care to minimise such occurrences.

The opportunity for employment as a soccer professional at the highest level increased with the expansion of both the English and Scottish Football Leagues. The number of registered professionals in Scotland rose from 560 in 1893/94 to 1,754 in 1913/14.[41] In England there were 1,092 paid players in 1889, about 4,500 at the turn of the century and approximately 7,000 in 1914, though only 2,500 of these were full-time.[42] Good players were in short enough supply to keep their wages up to the maximum allowed by the F. A., but the bulk of professionals could not hope to make a living out of football. Partly this was because attendances outside the major leagues – and sometimes within them – could not justify high wages, but it was also because in the lower grades of soccer there was a vast reserve army of labour. Not all the amateurs playing football in 1909 would have had the talent and the inclination to turn professional but, out of an estimated 300,000 players, some surely would.[43]

Opportunities for employment in first-class cricket also expanded as the number of counties competing in the championship increased, but the absolute number of employers still remained small and some degree of monopsonistic power stemmed from the qualification rule. However, this was offset for some cricketers by the development of league cricket, though many leagues expressly forbade clubs to play more than two professionals at a time, and for others by the expansion in club and school coaching positions at home and abroad.[44]

IV

Restrictions on the mobility of professional sportsmen could prevent them taking advantage of market opportunities. In fact mobility was practically impossible for the apprentice jockey, even though things had changed from the first half of the nineteenth century, when for most practical purposes the apprentice could be regarded as his master's property. Nevertheless, stable discipline could not tolerate boys changing their employers at whim and few trainers would take on a runaway unless his late master had been consulted; eventually the Jockey Club formalised this practice and banned from Newmarket any trainer who took on a boy who had run away from another stable.[45] Once out of their indentures, however, jockeys were free to choose their employers unless tied down by a retainer, but this restriction was well-paid compensation for the loss of mobility.

To some extent the qualification rule in county cricket acted as a deterrent to mobility, especially for established players. To be reduced to groundstaff wages for two years whilst qualifying by residence could not have been a pleasant prospect, though good players could sometimes strike a better bargain. Thanks to a patron, Leicestershire were also able to offer a 30s. a week position outside the cricket season to attract Whiteside from Lancashire, and that county agreed to give Mold weekly winter pay of 25s. in partial compensation for missed match fees.[46] The deterrent thus was not absolute. Even in the 1880s Surrey recruited 7 players from elsewhere and Yorkshire supplied other counties with 13 players, 10 of whom had first-team experience; and in the 1890s Leicestershire, for one, were seeking to discover the terms on which professionals from outside their borders would be willing to qualify and also asking their own players who were being tempted elsewhere 'to put their requirements' in writing.[47] By the end of the century only Kent and Yorkshire maintained a policy of playing only cricketers born within their boundaries.[48] However, the impression gained from a reading of the Lancashire and Leicestershire minutes is that, in switching counties, individuals generally bettered themselves only because one employer was willing to play them in more matches than another: certainly before the mid 1890s there does not appear to have been any significant bidding-up of match fees to attract or retain players.

The labour market for professional footballers in England changed significantly in the period studied. Initially, because of the illegal nature of professionalism, players were practically free agents: a club could retain its players only so long as it was prepared to make veiled payments. By 1914 a series of restrictions, in particular the retain-and-transfer system, had severely curbed the economic freedom of the player. At the close of each season clubs would prepare a list of players whom they wished to retain and a second list of those who were offered for transfer. Those on the retained list could reject the terms offered and they had a right of appeal to the League Management Committee; but generally if 'reasonable wages' (usually defined as similar to the previous season's) were offered, and certainly if the maximum wage was specified, the appeal would go in the club's favour.[49] Moreover, during the period of the appeal the player did not receive any wages. Transfer-listed players also were not paid and they had the additional problem in that their clubs, although no longer wishing to employ them, generally still demanded fees to let them go elsewhere. An appeals procedure developed and the results, shown in Table 13.5, support the Management Committee's claim that 'in many instances fees are fixed that the clubs can never hope to realise' and the possibility that the transfer list was being utilised as a short-run cost-saving mechanism.[50]

What had developed in League soccer both north and south of the Border was a unique set of limitations on free labour mobility. After their initial decision to join a club, players were no longer free to choose their employers. Unless, like Whitehead of Blackburn Rovers, they had the initiative to write a freedom-of-movement clause into their contracts – not that many clubs would accept this – they could not insist on being allowed to join another club, even if that club was willing to pay a transfer fee.[51] One knowledgeable club director, however, did claim that if a player was determined to move to another club he would get there 'sooner or later', and the experiences of Sheffield Wednesday with Stewart in 1908, Lyall in 1909 and McConnell in 1910 lend support to this view, though the negotiations could be protracted.[52] If their own club no longer wished to employ them, they were still not free to go elsewhere: unless a club was prepared to pay the transfer fee asked they would be unemployed footballers. Admittedly, a club could not transfer a player against his will, but if he refused to go his career could be over.

Tables 13.5 and 13.6 suggest that the mobility of players, either enforced or voluntary, was substantial, especially as the English figures before 1909 do not include moves to the Southern League. In fact, in 1910, approximately 15% of registered professionals in Scotland, and possibly an even higher proportion of Football League players, were transferred.[53] Although there was a net outflow of footballers from Scotland, many of them, designated 'returned players' in the S. F. A. figures, came back north, either because they did not make the grade or to complete their careers in less alien territory.

V

Being a professional sportsman was not just a matter of turning up for the game and collecting the money. Like the military, paid players often spent more time preparing for conflict than actually facing the opposition, though the amount of practice and preparation varied from sport to sport. This activity could influence their actual performance and hence be a major determinant of their income, for ultimately sport, perhaps more than any other occupation, involves payment by results.

Cricketers, particularly bowlers, had a lot of extra work to do. Prior to the season, and during the season on non-match days, they had to report to the ground by 10.30 or 11.00 and, after completing groundstaff chores, had to be prepared to bowl to amateur members of the county club in the afternoon and late into the evening, as well as give net practice to the county batsmen.[54] Presumably this was also regarded as training for themselves. Essex, for one, allowed occasional leave of absence providing that an efficient substitute was provided, and Warwickshire excused Hargraves and Lilley, both senior professionals, from bowling at the nets – even though Lilley was a wicketkeeper – but it cost them £15 each to secure their release.[55] Generally, however, during the season the cricketer put in almost as many hours as any other skilled working man.

Stable jockeys and those employed to ride trials might have to rise much earlier than other professional sportsmen but they would not have to do

Table 13.5 *Football League transfers, 1903–12*

| Year[a] | Total number of transfers | Applications for reduction in fee[b] | | | |
		Total	Voluntarily reduced	In favour of player	In favour of club
1903[c]	152	20	3	13	4
1904	195	26	3	19	4
1905	217	49	14	19	16
1906	259	64	25	25	14
1907	238	81	18	40	23
1908	314	108	27	47	34
1909	221	121	44	36	41
1910	337	281	61	156	64
1911	366	297	50	166	81
1912	332	274	36	164	74

[a]Data not available before 1903.
[b]Does not infer that a transfer actually occurred.
[c]From May.
Source: Calculated from Minutes of Football League Management Committee.

much training. Even for apprentices life in the stables was not hard, though the hours were long. However, apart from a few blessed with natural lightness, all jockeys had to watch their weight. Racing, like cricket and soccer, had a close season, but, freed of Lent-like restrictions, many jockeys took to good living in the winter months and then had to shed a stone, two stones, or even more.[56] During the season there was the constant temptation to take an extra ride a pound or so below their normal racing weight, and getting even ounces off a fit man is never easy. For most jockeys masochism was a professional necessity. The basic method of reduction was a combination of sweat and diet. For those who could not face tramping across country wearing heavy clothes, there was the Turkish bath, but this tended to sap their strength. Although some jockeys could afford to eat well, none dared do so during the season. Fred Archer earned more than any other sportsman, but his standard fare while riding was warm castor oil, an occasional strip of dry toast and either half a glass of champagne or half a cup of tea with a drop of gin in it.[57] For seven to eight months of the year most jockeys relied on eating very little and combating even that with purgatives.

Footballers perhaps had the easiest time. Most contracts required players to keep themselves in a fit condition, but the actual training does

Table 13.6 *Transfers registered with the Scottish Football Association,*
1893/94–1913/14[a]

Season	Within Scotland	To outside Scotland	From outside Scotland	Total transfers
1893/94	54	10	n.a.	64+
1894/95	43	31	23	97
1895/96	74	27	23	124
1896/97	70	43	17	130
1897/98	89	33	20	142
1898/99	145	44	19	208
1899/1900	107	29	16	152
1900/01	101	23	6	130
1901/02	96	17	9	122
1902/03	145	23	3	171
1903/04	177	22	7	206
1904/05	111	21	8	140
1905/06	215	34	13	262
1906/07	235	38	14	287
1907/08	227	} (51)[b] {		278
1908/09	228	} (50)[b] {		278
1909/10	176	36	n.a.	212+
1910/11	170	44	n.a.	214+
1911/12	176	40	17	233
1912/13	144	35	20	199
1913/14	299	46	30	375

[a]Includes Scottish junior clubs who employed professionals as well as Scottish Football League.
[b]Total number of transfers involving clubs outside Scotland.
Sources: Annual Reports of Scottish Football Association.

not appear to have been arduous.[58] Possibly after a heavy defeat a full day's training would be called for, but generally only a few hours would be undertaken. A typical programme would involve no Monday training unless there was a midweek engagement.[59] Training days would not necessitate attendance at the ground until 10.00 a.m., reason enough for a working man to aspire to be a professional soccer player. Normal training would consist of a brisk five-mile walk, though not too brisk if the West Bromwich team were at all typical, for they wore three-piece suits complete with watch chains. The alternative in inclement weather would be skipping or Indian club and punchball work. Ball practice occurred only once a week.[60] Perhaps the relative lack of training stemmed from the early years of professional football when most players were part-timers with little opportunity to train; those were the days when Sheffield Wednesday was reduced to sending its players a circular 'requesting' them to keep fit for an important cup tie.[61] By the mid 1890s most leading teams employed only full-time professionals as they were not willing to risk a player being unable to turn out for a midweek fixture, or not getting away early enough from work to catch the Saturday morning train to an away fixture, or, worse still, becoming involved in an industrial accident.[62] Certainly one ex-player who became a club director reckoned that the prime function of organised training was simply to keep the players from having too much time on their hands.[63]

VI

Although the basic riding fee, as legislated by the Jockey Club, remained at three guineas for a mount and five for a win, the actual rewards to the more successful of these diminutive men were large. There may have been an excess supply of ordinary jockeys but the demand was for the most talented. The increased economic rewards available to owners and breeders tempted the more commercially minded owners to bid more for the services of the best jockeys; in turn this forced the aristocratic and nouveaux riches owners to enlarge their 'wages fund' so that they could bargain effectively in the competition for riders.

Handsome retainers began to be paid for a claim on the services of a skilled jockey. Not only did this ensure that he would ride his employer's horses; it also kept him off those of rival owners. Such restrictions on economic freedom became increasingly expensive as racing became more commercialised. Whereas leading riders in the 1830s were lucky to obtain annual retainers of £100, in 1881 Fred Archer received £3,600, and later that decade Tom Cannon was given £15,000 for a three-year contract.[64] Many of the top jockeys obtained substantial sums for second or even third call on their services: in 1910 the gifted Danny Maher totalled £8,000 in retainers from three separate owners.[65] Then there were presents. Unlike the early nineteenth-century riding groom who, if successful, could have expected a side of bacon or perhaps a sack of potatoes, scarcely gifts to be appreciated by a weight-watching jockey, the late nineteenth-century professional rider could anticipate doubling his fees with presents from winning gamblers, and large presents from owners became the norm for winning big races.[66] This was most certainly associated with increased commercialisation within racing, but perhaps there was also an element of conspicuous consumption as nouveaux riches owners sought to impress society with their wealth.

Between them presents and retainers produced additional income for top-rank jockeys 'before which even 2,000 guineas in bare riding fees shrinks into insignificance'.[67] Even before racing came under the influence of the enclosed course, one or two jockeys had made £5,000 in a season; Nat Flatman, for one, had done it as early as 1848.[68] However, in the last two decades of the century, on the not unreasonable assumptions of a £1,000 retainer and 5% of prizemoney won, at least ten jockeys would have earned such a sum or more. Allegedly the best of the riding fraternity could 'realise fortunes of £100,000 or more, within a dozen years of their first appearance in the saddle'.[69] Even a moderately successful rider could bank on £1,000 in a good season.[70]

Once he reached, or neared, the pinnacle of his profession the star jockey could entrench himself. The high demand for such riders enabled them to increase their earnings by expanding their workload, an option not open to lesser horsemen. Success brought the offer of more rides and thus the chance to reinforce that success. Every extra mount they took of course meant one less opportunity for someone else to gain money or experience. Table 13.7 shows that the vast majority of jockeys rode no winners at all; that relatively few rode ten or more winners in a season; and that the leading dozen, perhaps 3% of registered riders, consistently rode more than half of the total winners – at least until the introduction of the apprentice allowance. Hence the distribution of incomes among riders was significantly skewed: high economic rents accrued to an elite group but the bulk of riders probably earned more money from riding trials at two guineas a time than by performing on the racetrack. For many the basic riding fee was inadequate to keep them in racing as they were offered too few mounts.

The good jockey, however, could taste the fruits of success early in life. Almost overnight young men could burst from poverty and obscurity into wealth and fame. In 1905 Elijah Wheatley rode 124 winners and thus headed the jockeys' championship while still an apprentice.[71] Also in the early twentieth century Frank Wootton retired, still a minor but having won a St Leger and amassed £30,000.[72] Such instances no doubt enticed many boys into becoming apprentices and thus aggravated the oversupply situation in the labour market.

Apprentices made little money. Fred Archer was to earn somewhere between £8,000 and £13,000 a year at the height of his career, but his indentures gave him 9 guineas per annum in his first year rising to 13 guineas in his fourth and fifth; a stable lad doing a similar job could expect three to four times as much.[73] Moreover, if an apprentice showed promise as a jockey the fees for any rides could be pocketed by his master, supposedly as a reward for teaching the boy to ride.[74] Certainly there were

Table 13.7 *Distribution of winning rides, 1879–1909*

	No. of jockeys and apprentices winning						% of races won by leading 12 riders
	0[a] races	1–4 races	5–9 races	10–19 races	20–9 races	30+ races	
1879	n.a.	71	20	12	10	14	55
1889	n.a.	54	10	10	5	16	61
1899	306	71	14	9	8	14	62
1909	309	50	18	12	13	17	49[b]

[a]Some riders may have had no mounts.
[b]The reduction is attributable to the apprentice allowance.
Source: Calculated from data in the *Racing Calendar*.

trainers whose views on apprenticeship were dominated by such financial considerations: Tom Jennings, for one, practically established a racing school in order to supplement his income in this way.[75] Some owners, however, might put something in the bank for a winning apprentice, enough perhaps to whet the boy's appetite for what the future might hold.[76] In effect the apprentice paid for his own training by working for less than the market rate for stable lads. Trainers were not willing to incur the costs of teaching jockeyship to the apprentice when, once through his indentures, the youth could offer his acquired skill to the highest bidder.

The qualification rule meant that effectively most cricketers faced a single prospective purchaser for their services at county level. Nevertheless, the data in Tables 13.8 and 13.9 suggest that over time there was some improvement in basic groundstaff wages, perhaps attributable to competition from league cricket: Leicestershire certainly raised the pay of some of its professionals in the face of offers from league clubs.[77] Moreover, particularly for those players attached to the M. C. C. groundstaff, there was the possibility of tips for bowling to members in the nets.[78]

Generally groundstaff wages were not paid when the professional played in a county match; for this they received a separate fee but had to finance their own travel and accommodation. Lancashire's experience supports the claim in *Wisden's Cricketers' Almanack* for 1897 that such match payments had not risen in proportion to the growing popularity of the game during the previous 20 years.[79] Indeed the fee for Lancashire's players remained unchanged from the mid 1880s to 1897, though occasionally an extra pound would be paid for a potentially hard game.

Table 13.8 *Basic wages of Lancashire cricketers, 1883–1901*

Weekly wage (£ s. d.)	1883	1889	1895	1901
3. 0. 0		4	12	17
2. 15. 0			1	
2. 10. 0		2	2	1
2. 7. 0	1			
2. 5. 0	1	1		
2. 0. 0	1		2	4
1. 15. 0		1		1
1. 5. 0			1	
1. 0. 0				1

Source: Minute Books of Lancashire C. C. C.

Table 13.9 *Basic wages of Leicestershire cricketers, 1896–1911*

Weekly wage (£ s. d.)	1896	1902	1911
4. 0. 0		1	4
3. 0. 0		3	
2. 10. 0			1
2. 5. 0	1	3	2
2. 0. 0		1	1
1. 15. 0	2		
1. 10. 0	3	2	
1. 7. 6	1		
1. 5. 0			4
1. 0. 0			1

Source: Minute Books of Leicestershire C. C. C.

Apart from that, £4 was earned for home games, £5 for away ones, and £6 for matches in the south and west. In 1898 the fee for home fixtures was raised to £5, and £6 was paid for all away games.[80] Such rates appear to have become the norm around the counties.[81] However, earnings rose more than match fees as there was a trend towards fuller fixture lists.

Additionally there was the possibility of productivity payments in the form of winning bonuses and talent money. All counties appear to have added an extra £1 to the match fee in a successful game, and championship-winning sides received bonuses from grateful committees.[82] Talent money was awarded for specific individual performances. Most counties operated a marks system whereby the team captain awarded points for outstanding achievements. To prevent matters getting out of hand financially most also fixed the aggregate sum to be distributed: hence Lancashire's players shared £100 in 1912, but impoverished Leicestershire could only afford £75 in 1908 and £50 the following season.[83] Yorkshire, however, equated each mark with 5s. and allowed Lord Hawke to award as many as he thought fit.[84] Collections were also sometimes made: generally they raised a few pounds but occasionally much higher sums were realised, most notably when Tom Hayward received £131 for a test century against the Australians on his home ground.[85] Initially, Warwickshire's professionals – apart from a few with performance bonuses written into their contracts – had to rely on collections for talent money. Despite the inequity of this as regards players who starred in away matches, in front of alien crowds, early suggestions for a formal system of marks were rejected. Even when it was introduced, talent money often fell victim to economy drives and when the players shared £60 in 1909 it was their first payment for five years.[86] However, when they won the championship in 1911 they obtained £300.[87]

The great financial breakthrough for the professional cricketer was the introduction of winter pay. The first-class season was short, rarely lasting 20 weeks, so, apart from the more successful players who traded on their names in sports outfitters and other businesses, prior to the 1890s most cricketers had to seek remunerative employment for the rest of the year – not an easy task when notice had to be given come the start of the next season. Despite protests from the Warwickshire committee, who feared that he might be injured, Dick Lilley played professional soccer 'because it helps me get a living in the winter'.[88] Although counties often asked committeemen and patrons to assist players to find work, many professionals had 'a bad time in the winter' and the subsidy given by out-of-season pay must have been a godsend.[89] Lancashire had paid Mold 25s. a week in the winters of 1888/89 and 1889/90 to preserve his residential qualification, but this was an isolated occurrence and Surrey are generally considered to have pioneered winter wages on any scale when, in the early 1890s, they gave their best players 30s. a week and £1 to their other capped professionals. They were followed closely by Yorkshire, who paid their regular players £2 a week. Other counties then felt compelled to follow suit.[90] Kent decided in 1897 that winter pay was 'justified by the action already taken in other counties'.[91] Lancashire had already given the two Tinsleys £1 a week each after the 1893 season, but, as Table 13.10 shows, even in 1895 only these two players received winter pay. By 1898/99, however, they were paying over £250 in total to eleven

Table 13.10 *Winter pay of Lancashire cricketers, 1883–1901*

Weekly wage (£ s. d.)	1883	1889	1895	1901
1. 15. 0				1
1. 5. 0		1		
1. 0. 0			2	8
10. 0				4
Nil	3	5	16	11

Source: Minute Books of Lancashire C. C. C.

professionals 'to keep the club in line with the other counties as regards the payment of winter wages'.[92] From 1906 £2 per week was paid out of season to all Lancashire's recognised county players.[93] To the club winter pay was a method of retaining those players whom they feared might go elsewhere. To many players the issue was simple: as one wrote to the Lancashire committee: 'if you will not give any winter pay I can't afford to sign'.[94]

By 1900 a good professional could be earning £275 a year.[95] Star players did not get higher wages than fellow cricketers who could command a regular place in the county side. Indeed Lancashire's policy of standardising the wages of recognised county players was one reason why Barnes opted to leave.[96] However, leading players could earn more than the others if they participated in a representative fixture, which for most of the late nineteenth century paid £10 and twice that amount from 1899.[97] Better still, if their county would let them go, was selection for an overseas tour, especially before the coming of winter pay; those who voyaged to Australia in 1882 cleared about £200, about two-thirds of what Grace's professionals made 15 years later.[98] Yet test team positions were scarce and, especially for domestic series, professionals faced strong competition from amateurs who, in successive decades from 1876, took 58.2%, 32.2%, 42.4% and 34.4% of home test places and 21.6%, 34.2%, 36.4% and 25.0% of those played abroad.[99]

Apart from tours and tests, which in any case were irregular occurrences, the seasonal earnings of star players were not much above those of the regular county players. The real opportunity to cash in on their status came with the benefit, when they would generally be offered the choice of a county match, from which they would retain the gate receipts less the county's expenses associated with that match and the return fixture. Subscription lists would also be opened so that members especially could pay their financial respects. If the player was popular, the weather kind, and the supporters generous, then substantial sums could be raised relative to annual earnings. George Hirst, for whom everything went right, obtained £3,703 in 1904, a record benefit at the time. Table 13.11 suggests that there was a rising trend in the amounts raised, though it was still better to play for Yorkshire than for Derbyshire, whose highest pre-war benefit was Sugg's £264. However, the benefit did not guarantee that a player would be enabled 'to live comfortably for the rest of his life' as bad weather or a batting collapse could seriously affect attendances or the length of the game.[100] Poor Wheeler of Leicestershire changed his mind and opted for the game against Derbyshire rather than Yorkshire and had a net return of 4s. 8d.: the club then made him a £25 grant.[101] Yorkshire brought in a Benefit Augmentation Fund, into which they deposited £200 annually, to protect their players from such disasters.[102] Generally, however, the benefit made 'the difference between the gains of the few who are very successful and the many who are only moderately so'.[103] To obtain a benefit a player had to remain loyal. Briggs of Lancashire, when approaching his 15th season with the club, was told that his application was 'premature', though he was awarded one a year later.[104] On average Yorkshire's professionals served 13 years before obtaining their benefit matches.[105] If the recipient had to wait so long, even a benefit of £1,500 is only a deferred payment of just over £2 a week, summer and winter. Nevertheless, this extra pay was more than most groundstaff would earn from cricket over the year.

Information on soccer players' wages is plentiful but unsystematic.[106] It is, however, clear, even from this scattered material, that wages for skilled footballers were on an upward trend in the 1890s. Before the inauguration of the Football League top players earned between 30s. and £2 a week, though many were paid by the match rather than by the week. By 1893 outstanding players were obtaining between £3 and £4, with others of reasonable ability typically making £3 a week in winter and £2 in the close season. Because of the longer playing season summer wages were not the problem which winter payments were in cricket. By the late 1890s stars could be earning £6–£7 and others up to £4. Not all this was net gain to the players as they had to become full-time professionals and, in most cases, lose their other sources of income.

The rise reflected the increased funds available to clubs from gate-receipts: more matches were being played and the average attendance was increasing. No other club overtly followed Small Heath's initial policy of remunerating players according to the takings at the gate, but, in effect, this is what happened: William McGregor maintained that the pro-

Table 13.11 *Cricket benefits, 1860–1909*

	Yorkshire[a]		All counties[b]		All counties[c]		Selected counties[d]	
	No. traced	Average (£)	No. traced	Average (£)	No. traced	Average (£)	No. traced	Average (£)
1860–9	n.a.	n.a.	2	249	n.a.	n.a.	n.a.	n.a.
1870–9	6	422	9	366	4	419	n.a.	n.a.
1880–9	4	557	6	708	9	657	n.a.	n.a.
1890–9	4	1,586	10	816	15	1,420	6	540
1900–9	5	2,344	2	1,566	13	1,997	14	817

Sources:
[a] *Yorkshire C. C. C. Year Books.*
[b] W. F. Mandle, 'The professional cricketer in England in the nineteenth century', *Labour History* XXIII, 1972, p. 11.
[c] *Wisden Cricketers' Almanacks.*
[d] Annual Reports of Derbyshire, Kent, Lancashire, Leicestershire and Surrey.

fessional's 'wages rose in relation to the amount of ability he displayed. Such ability being represented, more or less, by the magnitude of the crowd which that ability drew.'[107]

The imposition of the maximum wage, even if not fully effective, meant a wage reduction for some top players in England. Unless wages for less-skilled players were reduced in proportion – and Sheffield Wednesday's books suggest that they were not – the maximum wage legislation served to lessen the skew of earnings among professional footballers. Nevertheless, this was still significant. In 1910, of the 6,800 registered professionals in English soccer only 573, all in either the Football or the Southern League, received the maximum wage, though the implication of these figures is that for the bulk of regular League players, especially in the first division, the maximum wage was the standard wage.[108] Good players were in short enough supply to keep their wages up to the maximum, but the bulk of professionals could not hope to make a living out of football.

Some players, especially those from Celtic, Rangers or Hearts, were able to benefit from the absence of a maximum wage in Scotland. Bobby Walker, Hearts' famous international player, was paid £6 per week whether he played or not.[109] Most leading players, however, obtained only £4.[110] Still Rangers' second-team players were on higher wages than Partick Thistle's first team.[111] At the other end of the Scottish wage scale, second-division players earned so little that they had to apply for a reduction in the 6d. a week union fees.[112] Cowdenbeath's part-timers, this being the dominant form of second-division contract, were paid only 15s. a week during the season.[113]

In practice the maximum wage proved somewhat elastic. The Players' Union said that clubs broke the rules when it suited them.[114] McGregor, on the other hand, maintained that the limit was breeched less than most people believed, though even he had 'no doubt that isolated players [were] getting more than the maximum wage'.[115] However, as in cricket, the main way of increasing the star's earnings was via the benefit. The F. A. allowed clubs to grant these to players who were retiring through injury or age or to those with five years' continuous service, a much shorter period than that required of cricketers.[116] The sums raised were also substantially less. The typical Sheffield Wednesday benefit in the decade before 1914 brought the player between £150 and £250, though in the other clubs a guarantee of £500 was often given.[117] In the Southern League perhaps £100 could be expected.[118] The matches played were usually friendlies rather than League games, but were easier to organise and slot into the timetable than were the three-day cricket fixtures. Theoretically any player could obtain a benefit; in practice they generally went to the star rather than the journeyman professional.

Top players would also have the chance of representative games either for their country or in inter-League fixtures. Payment for internationals in 1887 was only £1 but this had risen to £4 by 1908.[119] Inter-League games in the early 1890s brought a guinea and third-class rail fares, but later this was changed to a choice of £3 or 10s. 6d., travel costs and a medal.[120] Even though competition from amateurs was less severe than in cricket, opportunities were limited: between 1908 and 1914, apart from the two annual inter-League fixtures and the three home internationals, there were only seven other international games for English players. Some popular professionals would also be able to augment their incomes by advertising, usually for football gear or tobacco products, or by writing or putting their name to newspaper columns, as some 80 players did in 1914.[121]

Even ordinary players had the chance to make more than their basic wage after the F. A. agreed that from 1910 bonuses could be paid for cup tie wins and talent money for a top-four League position.[122] Till then, of course, a good cup run in the era of the maximum wage had brought no additional legal reward, though it had swelled the bank account of the club. There were also occasional perks in the form of a limited number of free tickets, which could be sold, and close-season tours – in 1909 Everton ventured as far as Argentina.[123] In both cases the football authorities kept a firm eye on what the players received. Any player found reselling tickets at more than face value was in trouble and, after Newcastle gave their players £1 a day for a 19-day Continental tour plus £14 10s. for entertainment and also paid for the travel, accommodation and tips, the Football League decided that professionals must not be allowed to profit from a tour.[124]

Initially, broken-time payments in rugby league were fixed at a maximum of 6s. a day, but by the end of the century, when professionalism had been accepted, good players were receiving from 30s. to £4 a week, though no close-season money was allowed.[125] In 1913 the payments system was rationalised to suit the semi-professional nature of the game, with match fees generally replacing weekly wages.[126] Before 1914 there was only one overseas tour, to Australia. In addition to all travelling expenses, reasonable hotel bills, football outfits and laundry costs, players received 10s. per week shipboard and £1 a week on land. A further £1 a week was paid to the families of married men. Finally, one-third of any profits was to be divided among the 27 tourists as the committee saw fit.[127]

Skewed income distributions are to be expected amongst professional sportsmen for sport is a competitive process in which rewards are distributed unequally on the basis of performance. The degree of skewness varied between sports. It was at its most extreme in horse-racing, where one jockey could make over £8,000 in a year whilst others might only get half a dozen rides. At least in both soccer and cricket many of those who had little opportunity to play in the first team still had a weekly wage packet while the season lasted. However, whereas apprentice jockeys earned less than cricket groundstaff, and many riders obtained lower incomes than fringe first-team soccer, cricket or even rugby players, successful jockeys earned far more than stars in those games. To some extent this was a function of the volume of funds available to pay performers in the different sports. Unlike the others, horse-racing was closely associated with gambling and hence the returns of the owners, out of which jockeys would be paid, were not totally dependent on prize-money. Budgetary constraints were perhaps more severe in soccer, cricket and rugby league, where the wages funds were more dependent upon gate-money and subventions from directors, members and other patrons. Possibly pay differentials between the sports also reflected the relative ease with which remuneration based on merit can be allocated in an indi-vidual-based sport such as horse-racing: the spoils simply go to the winner. In team sports, however, it is difficult to ascertain the specific contribution made by members of the side. Jockeys could also increase their income by accepting more mounts: even one on a retainer could ride for other owners if his own employers did not require his services in a particular race. In the other sports it was only the cricket groundstaff who could work overtime: the severe mobility restrictions on other players drastically curtailed their opportunities to play extra matches.

Chapter 14

Close of play

I

Constant insecurity was the hallmark of a career in professional sport. Every day the professional sportsman faced the possibility that there would be no work tomorrow: losing in a tight finish, a poor afternoon in the field, being the victim of a nasty tackle could all lead to non-selection. Accentuating the anxiety was the annual trauma of contract renewal, for few employers in the sports industry were willing to 'guarantee' work for more than a year. In horse-racing a few outstanding riders managed to obtain retainers for a two- or three-year period, but most were for a single season. The majority of jockeys, however, did not hold retainers and had to join the demeaning, and often demoralising struggle for mounts on a day-to-day basis. In soccer the retain-and-transfer system operated on an annual basis – in 1891 the Football League Management Committee specifically forbade the signing of players for more than one season at a time[1] – and, if not retained, the unwanted footballer had to hope that some other club would be willing to pay for what was a rejected product. Sheffield Wednesday did concede one of their players a two-year contract after he had been a first-team regular for a couple of seasons, but when this led to further demands a board decision was made not to sign any player for longer than twelve months.[2] Cricketers, too, generally obtained only annual contracts, sometimes with a guaranteed number of matches, though in 1898 Willie Quaife, Warwickshire's star batsman, after several requests and a threat to go to league cricket, persuaded the county to grant him a five-year engagement. By 1903 three Warwickshire professionals had such contracts and two others had three-year appointments, though all of them had a saving clause for the club as to the contracts being subject to good conduct and continuation of form.[3] Leicestershire gave Knight, one of their England players, a three-year 'certain' guarantee and attracted Gill from Somerset by the promise of a four-year contract.[4]

Of course in having even limited tenure the professional sportsman was better placed than other working men. In few other trades, however, would he be subject to an annual review of his performance and a prediction as to his future capabilities. No professional sportsman could simply go through the motions: there was no place to hide on the sports field. Every time he played, his performance was open to public scrutiny and, should he fail to come up to par, he faced, not the castigation of a foreman or supervisor, but vocal condemnation by thousands of spectators as well as the prospect of losing his place in the team, and with it his earning power.

Moreover, his was a precarious existence as he had little control over his own destiny. Even if he was performing well there was no guarantee that he would continue to be selected. Seniority offered no security. There were always rivals for his position and should a newcomer prove to be a better player or rider – or, rather, should the selection committee or owner believe so – then he might be discarded. Sheffield Wednesday, for one, often deferred re-engagements until they had first sought specific players in the transfer market. New faces in the committee room could also lead to player redundancy. Others became victims of technological change: jockeys unable to cope with the monkey-on-a-stick riding style of the American invaders, and bowlers figuratively, and perhaps literally, brought to their knees by the lifeless pitches prepared by groundsmen in the 1890s.

All sportsmen, of course, had built-in obsolescence. Although it varied between sports and between individuals, eventually experience no longer compensated for ageing muscles: physiological attrition always won the final game. For many sportsmen, however, physical problems ended their careers even more prematurely. By the nature of their occupation professional sportsmen needed to be fit, yet injuries often befell them because they played sport. Although it cannot be quantified, professional football does not seem to have been more dangerous than the amateur game:[5] professionals had too much at stake to set out deliberately to maim each other. Indeed the Football League, in congratulating its members on the lack of serious injuries in 1891, claimed that 'the higher the quality of football the less liability is there of accidents'.[6] Nevertheless, the socially sanctioned violence on the field meant that injuries inevitably occurred, leading clubs to employ doctors, hire physiotherapists, and send players for specialist treatment: Matlock House in Manchester became well known as a footballers' hospital.[7] Treatment, however, was not always successful. Peter McWilliam of Newcastle United was injured playing for Scotland against Wales and never played again.[8] His was not a solitary case. There are several examples in the Sheffield Wednesday books alone of players giving up the game because of injury. In any event once a player had a recurrent problem, even if it responded to treatment, he was a marked man. Fred Spiksley, an England international and scorer of two goals in an F. A. Cup final, found only four seasons after his memorable performance that his re-signing was 'subject to engagement terminating in case he breaks down';[9] another Wednesday player, Topham, had his basic wage reduced to £1 a week because he had 'so many injuries'.[10]

Horse-racing was an even more dangerous sport. Coming off at 30 miles per hour or thereabouts, often without warning, resulted in several deaths and many serious injuries. More jockeys, however, found their careers ended by a different physical problem, that of pushing the scales down too far. Apart from a few blessed with natural lightness, all jockeys had to diet in order to maximise their riding opportunities. Masochism was virtually a professional necessity.[11] Those who failed to control their weight and retired were perhaps lucky. The appalling end of Fred Archer, champion jockey for 13 consecutive seasons, came during delirium brought on by excessive dieting. He had been riding at 9 st. 4 lb. and had to get down to 8 st. 6 lb. for the Cambridgeshire. Despite starvation and devastating doses of purgative he still put up a pound overweight. His ensuing weakness laid him open to a chill and later typhoid. On the anniversary of his wife's death he shot himself, a victim of dieting, illness and melancholy.

Other hard-dieting jockeys killed themselves just as surely as if they, too, had put a revolver to their heads. Attempting to stave off, or starve off, the inevitable so weakened their constitutions that they became easily susceptible to illness: indeed tuberculosis was almost an occupational disease.[12] The same was true of cricketers. The cricket season was not only at the height of summer, and long hours in the cold and damp conditions of an English spring or autumn led to several deaths from consumption and rheumatism.[13]

Other career-damaging events beyond the influence of the individual sportsman included the financial state of his employers. A soccer club might have to sell his services in order to move their accounts nearer the black; he might be the marginal player when the county cricket team embarked on a wave of retrenchment and be sacked 'solely on grounds of economy'; or the owner who paid his retainer might suddenly decide that the costs of horse-racing had become prohibitive.[14]

Some professionals fell victim to moral crusades rather than economy drives. In the early 1880s Nottinghamshire claimed that at least two Lancashire bowlers had unfair actions and they refused to play the county if Crossland, the more suspect, was selected. Initially Lancashire stood by their man, perhaps because in 1882 he took 112 wickets at an average of only 10.06, and even chose him to play for England against Australia in 1884. However, they did not re-engage him as a ground bowler and when, perhaps in umbrage, he wintered away, ironically in Notts, he lost his residential qualification.[15] Similarly, Mold, a man who had played first-class cricket for over twelve years, was thrown out of the game when the county captains decided on a campaign against unfair bowling.[16] Lancashire offered him a groundstaff appointment – 'it being understood that he is not to play in county matches' – and he left the game.[17] With him went Tyler of Somerset and Geeson of Leicestershire.[18]

Mold and Crossland were unfortunate. Others had only themselves to blame. Some had no self-discipline to survive professionally and missed training or turned up late for matches, offences for which no degree of skill could compensate. A few, predominantly jockeys, were found to be corrupt and were cast temporarily or permanently into the sporting wilderness.[19]

'Civility' was a vital ingredient in the recipe for professional survival.[20] Everton soccer club, for example, dispensed with the services of Thomas Chadwick because of his 'gross insubordination' when making demands of the club.[21] In cricket, too, there was a limit to what a club would stand from a professional player. Although Quaife received no more than a reprimand from the Warwickshire committee for his occasional utterances against the social standing of the professional, they were more severe with Dick Lilley. After 20 seasons with the club and 35 games for England, the old pro finally rebelled at the amateur-dominated power structure in the sport and openly usurped his captain's authority on the field. He refused to apologise and out he went.[22] Insubordination also cost one of Derbyshire's best batsmen his place in 1902.[23] At Old Trafford the Lancashire committee found Sidney Barnes' strident demands for the money which he felt was commensurate with his ability too much to take and he was allowed to go to league cricket.[24] In horse-racing several young riders were spoiled by early success. After winning a few races they gained false ideas of how good they were. If they did not price themselves out of the market by excessive demands, they lost mounts by offending potential patrons who may have accepted familiarity from a champion jockey but certainly not from a recent graduate of the stables.[25]

Other professionals were victims of self-indulgence, especially regarding alcohol. Considering the nagging insecurity of their working lives and the constant, tortuous slimming process, it is not surprising that many jockeys took their calories in liquid form to the detriment of their

Table 14.1 *Career lengths in English League football*

		Years registered[a]										
		Total	1	2	3	4	5	6	7	8	9	10	11+
New signings in 1893/94	No.	261	111	88	27	12	12	3	3	3	1	1	—
	%	100	42.5	33.7	10.3	4.6	4.6	1.1	1.1	1.1	0.4	0.4	0.0
Registered for Sheffield United or Sunderland in 1901/02	No.	71	32	4	5	5	2	4	3	1	4	2	9
	%	100	45.1	5.6	7.0	7.0	2.8	5.6	4.2	1.4	5.6	2.8	12.7

[a]Career length includes seasons with other Football League clubs but not with non-League teams.
Source: Calculated from data in the Registration Books of the Football League.

judgement and their careers. Lifting his elbow too much on the eve of the 1873 Derby cost Jem Snowden a winning mount and the money which would have followed and, although he had his successes, eventually years of drinking caught up with him and he died in poverty.[26] In cricket many county administrators complained about fans buying drinks for the players: in 1890 the Warwickshire secretary actually appealed to the public not to treat the county's professionals.[27] This was the same season that the Yorkshire chairman claimed that the 'demon drink' had cost his side the championship.[28] No doubt there is an element of truth in the apocryphal view that, before Lord Hawke became captain, Yorkshire's first eleven consisted of ten drunks and a parson; and it has been alleged that Peel, who, like many bowlers, was fond of his ale, was dismissed for being so much under the influence that he watered the wicket in unorthodox fashion![29] Footballers, too, could overimbibe. In 1902 the Heart of Midlothian goalkeeper let in seven goals when in a 'peculiar condition' and on seven other occasions players were disciplined for drunkenness while training or travelling.[30] Several of Sheffield Wednesday's players were also disciplined by the club for excessive drinking which had affected their match performance; and, when one of them was also found guilty of being drunk and disorderly, the club imposed a month's suspension in addition to the magistrate's sentence and, shortly afterwards, put him on the transfer list.[31] Whether professional sportsmen drank more or less than the population at large is unknown. Their working hours meant that many had more opportunity to do so and probably, especially for the more successful, there were worshippers willing to buy it for them. In the longer run, however, they paid for it.

II

This section brings together some limited quantitative data on career lengths in four professional sports, English League soccer, rugby league, county cricket and horse-racing. The information for each sport is not totally comparable because of varying coverage, but it still allows some points to be made about attrition rates between, as well as within, the different sports.[32]

The shortest careers appear to have been in soccer. Table 14.1 analyses the length of registration within the Football League of all new players signed by first-division clubs in the season 1893/94. Almost half these players did not have their contracts renewed at the end of their first season – most of them had not even played a game – and over three-quarters failed to last more than two years. Of the 261 signings a mere 23 were playing top-grade soccer four years later and only one lasted a decade in the game. However, a later sample – of all the players registered for Sheffield United and Sunderland in 1901/02 – suggests that these high attrition rates of the early years may not have been maintained, though it still exhibited a very high fall-out after only one season.[33]

Surprisingly, in view of the greater physical contact, rugby league players may have lasted longer at the top. The data in Table 14.2 is similar in format to that of Table 14.1, but is for all players first registered in 1903/04, the year in which registration data are first available. In contrast to soccer's 13.5% (though the limited later soccer sample figure is much higher at 39.4%), 47.2% of rugby professionals lasted more than three years in the sport. Possibly there is some upward bias in the rugby calculation as it excludes players whose teams left the Northern Rugby Football competition: presumably they may have been less likely to have made their mark in the sport. Again, in contrast to the early soccer figures, 42 players were still on the books of Northern Rugby Football League clubs ten years after they first signed professional forms; however, the actual percentage of 15.4% of the traceable entry is almost identical to that of the later soccer sample.

Table 14.3, based on the experiences of three leading counties, shows that only 45.5% of county cricketers who made their debut in the 1880s and 1890s lasted into a fourth season. This figure, however, is inflated relative to both soccer and rugby as it only includes men who played at least once for their county. Nevertheless, those cricketers who managed to secure a regular place in the county team could anticipate up to a decade at the top, with a possibility, particularly for batsmen, of playing into their forties.

It is clear from Table 14.4 that early attrition rates were high in horse-racing. Of the 187 apprentices registered in 1900, only 75 became jockeys and only 23, or 12.3% of the original entry, lasted beyond a third season as a licensed rider. Weight problems and accidents ended the careers of some, but for most it was a matter of too few rides and too many losers rendering the basic riding fee too small a source of income. However, although the typical jockey's career was short, it was possible for a jockey to have a lengthy professional riding life providing that calories did not thicken his waistline or injury befall him. Of the group studied, fifteen lasted over a decade, six of these for more than two decades, and one topped thirty years in the racing saddle.

III

There is little information available on what happened to professional sportsmen after they retired.[34] This is particularly true for the great

Table 14.2 *Career lengths in rugby league*

		Years registered								
		Total	1–3[a]	4	5	6	7	8	9	10	11+
New signings in 1903/04[b]	No.	271	143	10	8	33	4	8	23	9	33
	%	100	52.8	3.7	3.0	12.2	1.5	3.0	8.5	3.3	12.1

[a]The nature of the source material did not allow a more detailed breakdown.
[b]Does not include 72 players who signed for clubs which later left the first-grade competition.
Sources: Calculated from data in Minutes of Northern Rugby Football League Management Committee, 1903/04; and Northern Rugby Football League Registration Books, 1906/07–1915/16.

Table 14.3 *Career lengths in county cricket (Surrey, Yorkshire and Lancashire)*

		Seasons engaged					
		Total	1	2–3	4–5	6–9	10–19	20+
Players making debut 1880–1900[a]	No.	222	94	27	21	31	42	7
	%	100	42.3	12.2	9.5	14.0	18.9	3.2

[a] Surrey and Yorkshire 1880–1900, Lancashire 1888–1900.
Sources: Calculated from data in P. Thomas, *Yorkshire Cricketers, 1839–1939*, Manchester, 1973; A. B. de Lugo, 'Surrey county players', in Lord Alverstone and C. W. Alcock (eds.), *Surrey Cricket*, London, 1902; scores of Lancashire Cricket Club, 1888–1914; and *Wisden Cricketers' Almanack.*

Table 14.4 *Career lengths in horse-racing*

	Apprentices registered in 1900	No. who became licensed jockeys	Number of years licensed				
			1	2–3	4–9	10–19	20+
Number	187	75	27	25	8	9	6
% of apprentices	100	40.1	14.4	13.4	4.3	4.8	3.2
% of jockeys	—	100	36.0	33.3	10.7	12.0	8.0

Source: Calculated from data in the *Racing Calendar.*

majority who failed to establish themselves. It can be speculated that some failed jockeys became stable lads, that some not-quite-good-enough cricketers remained with the county as practice bowlers, and that many unsuccessful soccer professionals opted for reinstatement as amateurs, often 'with a speediness of conversion rivalled only by the Salvation Army',[35] but for most rejected professionals there is simply no knowledge as to what they did next. What should be stressed, however, is that the typical professional sportsman's career was so short – indeed most were never in the game long enough to call it a career – that the opportunity costs of attempting to make the grade were low.

For those who did make it, at least for a while, there may have been employment problems after their retirement from sport. Even if they had a trade to go back to, and many did not, they might have to retool themselves and they would be competing against contemporaries who had had time to establish themselves in the occupation. Some who had emerged from the ruck might find that 'the really good player is remembered, and that this recognition may be of use to him in after [sporting] life' by enabling him to secure a public-house tenancy or establish a shop.[36]

Those who had to leave their sport because of injury were doubly hit: not only did they lose their income from sport, but they may have been incapable of earning a living from manual labour, the obvious avenue for the poorly educated but physically fit ex-sportsman. Jockeys and cricketers could seek assistance from the benevolent funds established respectively by the Jockey Club and the M. C. C. and, in having such a source of aid, albeit sparse, available to them, were in a better position than the average working man.[37]

Given that their skills were specific to sport many tried to remain associated with it. Some continued to play but moved down a grade, taking up league cricket or semi-professional soccer. For cricketers there were also openings as coaches, either to clubs or public schools; football, however, remained the teaching province of the amateur.[38] County cricket clubs also often recommended ex-players for the umpires' list, though this did not guarantee them either acceptance or engagements. If they were taken on, then a median career of eleven years could be expected with match fees of £5 (£6 from 1895).[39] Others who became entrepreneurs might receive contracts for supplying clubs with cricket or football gear or, as with Whitlam of Lancashire, for printing match cards.[40] Nevertheless, such employment opportunities were limited: there would always be more players leaving the game than new ancillary jobs being created. Some jockeys – perhaps 7% if the inter-war years are any guide[41] – progressed to becoming trainers, but there is no indication that their riding experience guaranteed them success in a field where increasingly business sense was becoming more important than horse sense. Most ex-jockeys who remained in racing were probably relegated to being stable lads, or eking out an existence by riding an occasional gallop, hanging around stables and racecourses for odd jobs, or even begging from the crowds at race meetings.

Few jockeys made provision for the future. For too many the end of riding meant poverty. Henry Luke, winner of the Two Thousand Guineas in 1876, died in the workhouse at Sandbach; Jem Snowden, who at times had earned thousands, died so poor that a few Yorkshire trainers had to pay for his funeral expenses.[42] Jockeys underwent dangerous and, for some, severe toil to earn their living, but then, once the racing season was over, they dissipated most of their earnings on leisure and pleasure. It was observable that most jockeys failed to sustain their careers, so why did the attitude to eat, drink and be merry prevail? Perhaps they rationalised that they would not be the ones to fall by the wayside or possibly the dismal future was simply too horrific to be contemplated.[43] It may, of course, have had nothing to do with being a jockey. A similar pattern of working-class sportsmen rising in their profession, dissipating all that they earned, and dying in poverty has been found among eighteenth-century prizefighters and mid twentieth-century American boxers.[44] Moreover, judging from the appeals made by destitute former employees to Sheffield Wednesday, Lancashire C. C. C. and Essex C. C. C., it may also apply to late nineteenth-century cricket and football.[45] Possibly this reflects class background rather than being specific to these occupations, for several modern studies have suggested that in general the manual working class puts a premium on immediate pleasure and makes relatively little provision for the future.[46]

It was not only money which the professional failed to hang on to. Sportsmen could be catapulted from obscurity to fame and could equally quickly return to the unknown. Teams, clubs and sports have an existence beyond the careers of the players. For most of the crowd it was a case of 'the king is dead, long live the king', and the exploits of the retired were relegated to a fading communal memory, to be resurrected, and embroidered, to the detriment of later players when they failed to come up to spectator expectations. Possibly most fans might not even recognise the old pro out of uniform next to them on the terraces. Sporting fame was a rapidly depreciating currency. Consider poor John Thewlis, a Yorkshire stalwart for 14 seasons, who was so forgotten by his ex-employers that they did not even know if he was alive when a journalist sought an interview some years after his retirement from county cricket.[47] Or George Fordham, rider of over 2,000 winners, idol of the masses, and fawned over by his upper-crust patrons. On his deathbed he was grateful for his few 'fair friends, considering all others gave me up and at any moment I may go'.[48] He was only 50 years old and had been third leading jockey in the country when he gave up riding but four years before his death.

Chapter 15

Not playing the game: unionism and strikes

I

Power relationships in commercialised sport were skewed against the professionals. Admittedly some top-class jockeys found that they held the reins, partly because they were frequently proved right in their choice of race tactics, but also because 'the supply of men between 7 stones and 8 stones possessed of the needful skill and experience [was] extremely limited, and [so] people think it diplomatic in consequence to put up with this, that and the other'.[1] These men could always find employment with a rival owner and hence their peccadillos were often tolerated by employers who would not have accepted similar behaviour from others in their pay. Generally, however, the pendulum of sports power swung towards the employers, men whose notions of industrial relations were dominated by paternalism: employees would be looked after if they behaved themselves and they should be grateful for what they were given.

Clubs could be 'good' to their players. The provision of leisure facilities at the ground, winter employment, excursions, and the payment of doctors' and hospital bills, often in excess of what a player obtained in wages, all testify to that. Individual examples of club generosity include Sheffield Wednesday sending the injured Robertson, accompanied by his wife, to the seaside to recuperate; Leicestershire doing the same for the consumptive Jayes and later paying for his sojourn in a Swiss sanitorium; and Lancashire financing the long-serving Richard Pilling's journey to Australia in an attempt to beat the respiratory affliction which eventually killed him.[2] Lancashire's committee also felt they were being 'responsible' in investing benefit monies on the behalf of the cricket professionals, as did Lord Hawke, who insisted that half, later two-thirds, of any Yorkshire professional's benefit proceeds should be retained by the club at least until the player retired.[3] Surrey C. C. C. adopted a similar policy, though, fortunately for Bobby Abel, he managed to persuade the financial committee to withdraw his money from Mexican 4% scrip in 1909, five years after he last played for the county but thankfully before the Mexican Revolution.[4] West Ham United went so far as to hold wages in fund for those professionals who exhibited a drinking problem.[5] Clearly such employers believed that the sports professional could not be trusted to handle his own financial affairs, a belief reinforced by the many, and generally unsuccessful, applications from players for loans. Hopefully, when, on the eve of the marriage of the club's goalkeeper, the Heart of Midlothian chairman 'took the opportunity of giving him some advice' along with a £10 wedding present, it was financial in nature; even paternalism must have its limits![6]

Paternalism, however, had its unsmiling face. Impudence, ingratitude, indiscipline – all, of course, subjectively interpreted – and any insistence on players' 'rights' were not tolerated. The Heart of Midlothian chairman demanded that the club trainer immediately report 'any player misbehaving or who refused to obey orders'.[7] A random selection of instances from the Sheffield Wednesday minute books shows that players were suspended for missing training, not attending reserve games after being dropped from the first team, and uttering bad language during the game. Discipline could also come in other guises. Holbern, who had a poor conduct record, had great difficulty in getting his benefit granted and Miller's misconduct was utilised as an excuse for refusing him a percentage of his transfer fee.[8] Several other players who fought running battles with the administration simply found that a dictated peace treaty put them on the transfer list. According to the Football League regulations clubs could terminate any agreement with a player on only 14 days' notice if he was guilty of serious misconduct or the breaking of disciplinary rules. As this could be done 'without prejudice to the club's right to transfer fees', in some cases money could be made by clubs when disposing of their dissidents.[9] Many county cricket committees shared the precept of Lord Hawke, arbiter of Yorkshire cricket for many years, that 'the man who is a pernicious example ought to be sacked, no matter how skilled he may be as a cricketer'.[10] Woodcock was dropped by Leicestershire 'in consequence of reports as to his conduct' and Warwickshire told Grundy that he would not be re-engaged unless his behaviour improved.[11] Long service was no protector of the petulant as poor Lilley discovered following his outburst at Edgbaston.[12] Similarly R. G. Barlow's services were dispensed with by Lancashire when, after being stood down in the game against Essex in order to give a younger player a trial, he replied that 'if he did not play in that match he would not play again'. Significantly the county chairman reckoned that 'had his manner been a little courteous . . . he might have been played again'.[13] Only when A. G. Hornby, Lancashire's captain and his partner 'of long ago', requested that Barlow be reinstated did the committee change its mind and then 'solely out of deference to [his] personal desire'.[14]

Some sports employers, soccer club directors in particular, also attempted to control the lives of their players off the field. Possibly in the belief that the devil finds work for idle feet, West Ham imposed an 8 p.m. curfew on their sick and injured players.[15] Several other clubs claimed that they would only employ footballers of good character.[16] Bristol Rovers stipulated that all their players must be total abstainers and Sheffield Wednesday went so far as to forbid its players to even lodge in licensed premises.[17] The latter also took a strong line regarding the part-time employment of its professional staff, and any player who took a job in a public house was given the option of passing balls or pulling pints. There were no exceptions: even F. H. Crawshaw, considered respectable enough to be club captain, was refused both re-engagement and a transfer, in effect putting him out of the game, because he became a publican.[18] Cricketers, too, were expected to toe the moral line. Warwickshire got rid of Teddy Diver after he was cited in a divorce case, though he had already angered the establishment by a demonstration at Essex against the symbolic subordination of the professional.[19] Leicestershire, for one, felt that guidance should be given and thus sought to appoint a captain 'who will be likely to take a sympathetic interest in the players both on and off the field'.[20]

Employers were not the only form of authority to which professional sportsmen were subject. The ruling bodies of individual sports could exercise a significant influence over a sportsman's earning capacity. In rugby league it was extra-curricular earnings which were affected: no one was allowed to be paid for playing rugby unless they were in full-time employment outside the game, but, in an effort to keep the professional image untarnished, certain jobs were proscribed.[21] Other sports, as has been shown, had restrictions of varying severity on the free operation of the labour market.[22] Additionally the sports authorities assumed the right to discipline players for misconduct, acting as both judge and jury and with the ultimate sanction of excluding a player from his chosen career.[23]

The sports authorities were not inherently opposed to the professionals. Indeed they stepped in to remedy some of the worst features of the master–servant relationship which had developed in many sports. Football League players who felt that their transfer fees were unrealistic had the right to appeal to the League Management Committee, who in many cases adjudicated in their favour.[24] The Committee was also instrumental in bringing about a regulation to the effect that if a player did not get a game within six months of signing for a club his registration could be cancelled.[25] In Scotland the S. F. A. advised players to be 'careful to see that they had proper agreements with the clubs employing them' and advertised that any professional who considered himself in any way aggrieved by his club could appeal to the S. F. A. Council.[26] The N. R. F. U. also intervened occasionally to force clubs to fulfil their agreements with players, as when Swinton dropped Thomas but were compelled to continue to find him employment at 30s. a week as was specified in his contract.[27] The Jockey Club took action to compel owners to deposit riding fees with the stakeholder before a race was run, so as to prevent jockeys, who feared that they would not get paid, from being tempted to make up their wages by gambling, an offence which would have cost them their licences.[28]

There was little to balance the scales of power back towards the professionals. Ultimately any professional who felt aggrieved could resort to law, though the courts were never really a refuge of the working class, and few sportsmen seem to have exercised the right. Footballers may have been intimidated by the F. A. rule which forbade any player from taking legal action against his club without the prior consent of the F. A. Council.[29] Warwickshire's cricket professionals did attempt to negotiate through a solicitor, but the club refused to countenance this.[30] Nor could the professional, or ex-professional, gain entry to the ruling bodies and attempt to change things from within. Sir Frederick Wall, one-time F. A. secretary, summed up the situation:

Professionalism has never been a success without rigid control, because the power of money becomes too strong. Jockeys are not elected members of the Jockey Club, and professional cricketers are not made members of the M. C. C. The question is not one of class but of control.[31]

By the late nineteenth century the option of players forming a cooperative and in effect employing themselves was also gone. Threshold costs were prohibitive, at least at the level of competing with county cricket or first-grade soccer. Moreover, once the national ruling bodies had established themselves, all self-help ventures were frowned upon and participants in these were banned from officially sanctioned events: possibly some ranked professionals appeared heavily disguised as cricketing 'clowns' or soccer-playing 'Zulus' (from Sheffield!), but generally, like unregistered race meetings, these events were for the 'also-rans' of the game.[32] In racing itself professional jockeys were not allowed to own racehorses and the only jockeys permitted to ride their own animals at official meetings came from that group of amateurs termed 'gentlemen riders'.[33]

II

Considering the circumstances outlined in the previous section, it is not surprising that on occasions professional sportsmen withdrew their labour in protest at their working conditions. One of the most interesting strikes, that most visible aspect of industrial conflict, was that in 1890 by the Celtic football team for higher wages. They were being paid 30s. a week, but demanded more when three players were attracted back from England by an offer of double this amount. The Celtic committee acceded and henceforth all regular first-team players received £3 a week.[34] This does not seem out of the ordinary – except perhaps in that the players won – until it is remembered that professionalism was illegal in Scottish soccer before 1892. Another successful combination occurred in cricket when seven Nottinghamshire players in 1880 asked for, and obtained, £20 a man to play against the crowd-drawing Australian team: the professionals who had not signed the petition were given £21! Next season the same 'malcontents' requested employment in every match and guaranteed benefits after ten years' service. This was too much for the Nottinghamshire committee and, strengthened by the support of both Surrey and the M. C. C., who refused to select any of the maleficent seven for representative games, they stood firm. Eventually five of the players backed down.[35] Perhaps the most famous cricket strike was that in 1896, when practically on the eve of the final test match at the Oval, five players, four of them from the host county, demanded £20 instead of the usual £10 for playing. Despite the growing – and immense – crowds being attracted to the games, rewards to test professionals had not been raised for over a decade. Three of the Surrey men recanted and were allowed to play, but the other, Lohman, intimated that he would have to consult his colleagues before doing so and hence he, and Gunn of Nottinghamshire, were replaced. Surrey had only just agreed to pay more to their county professionals but that was their own decision, unprompted by any action on the part of the players. In contrast this was an untimely demand from 'greedy' professionals. To emphasise their position of power the Surrey committee then gave £20 to all those selected, including the reserves.[36]

Further research, particularly at club level, is required in order to determine whether such flashpoint combinations were the tip of a sporting disputes iceberg. More work is also needed on other aspects of labour conflict in the sports industry – on matters such as industrial sabotage, absenteeism, and protracted contract negotiation. What is clear, however, is that in an age when other workers were joining unions in unprecedented numbers – from 1,559,000 in 1893 to 4,145,000 in 1914[37] – sports professionals demonstrated a marked reluctance to do likewise. Only in soccer was there an effort before 1914 to establish a permanent union organisation.

The first attempt came in 1893, when W. C. Rose, the Wolverhampton Wanderers goalkeeper, circulated all first-division captains proposing the formation of a union 'to protect professional interests'.[38] Nothing came of this, but five years later a National Union of Association Players was set up, with John Bell, the Scottish captain of Everton, as chairman. It focused on the retain-and-transfer system, attracted some support, and even established a branch in Scotland, but it became defunct by the end of the century.[39] A more permanent venture began towards the close of 1907 with the formation of the Association Football Players' Union.[40] Why it began at this time is unclear. One historian of the Union has speculated that perhaps it had something to do with the adoption of company status and the loss of personal contact with players by the club committees, now replaced by boards of directors.[41] Yet this was nothing new by 1907 and it is more likely, in chronological terms, that it had to do with the passing of the Trade Disputes Act of 1906, which clarified and publicised the legal status of trade unions, and with a realisation that the League clubs were no longer likely to overthrow the maximum-wage legislation. The major objective of the A. F. P. U. was 'to promote and protect the interests of the members by endeavouring to come to amicable arrangements with the governing football authorities with a view to abolishing all restrictions which affect the social and financial position of players, and to safeguard their rights at all times'.[42] Additionally they intended to offer legal assistance, to help find employment, and to render temporary financial assistance to players and their families.[43] These functions were to be financed by a 5s. entrance fee and a 6d. per week subscription during the playing season.[44]

Initially there was little overt opposition from either the F. A. or the Football League: indeed the F. A. offered recognition to the Union, several club directors accepted Union vice-presidencies, and the boards of Manchester United and Newcastle allowed their teams to play a match to raise funds for the Union's provident fund.[45] Later, however, attitudes changed. In 1910 the League accused the Union of disloyalty when it urged its players to wear Union badges in defiance of the League's wishes; and by 1915 the League Management Committee declared that, on the basis of their 'past experiences of conferences with the representatives of the Players' Union', they could 'never imagine the Union being of any practical service to the game [because] it is indisposed to be of any practical assistance to the clubs and governing bodies'.[46] In other words, the Union had tried to look after the interests of the players, particularly as regards the abolition of the maximum wage, the application of the Workmen's Compensation Act to football players, and the abandonment of the retain-and-transfer system. So far as the authorities were concerned benevolent activities were fine, but attempts to improve employment conditions merely antagonised those in charge.

Efforts to enforce the application of the Workmen's Compensation Act, along with the payment of wage arrears to some members, produced a major confrontation with the F. A. in 1909.[47] When the Union threatened to go to law on the issues, the F. A., determined not to have its position undermined, pointed out that this required the prior consent of the F. A. Council. The Union committee retorted that they were 'not convinced that they [were] expected to regard seriously the opinion that a football player forfeits a common legal right on entering into a professional legal engagement with a football club'.[48] The gloves were off. The F. A. Council, fearful that its authority was in danger of being usurped, responded by withdrawing its recognition of the Union. In retaliation the A. F. P. U. executive opted to strengthen the position of the Union by seeking to affiliate with the General Federation of Trade Unions. This raised the possibility that soccer players could be called out in sympathetic strikes, a not unrealistic scenario considering the growing militancy of trade unions. In the next move, the F. A. demanded that all Union committeemen – later expanded to all members – resign from the Union or have their registrations cancelled.[49] H. L. Mainman, the aptly named Union chairman, and H. C. Bloomfield, the secretary, soldiered on but were banned from all football or football management. The other committeemen, all players, resigned under protest, feeling that 'their adherence to the Union would not be of any great benefit under the circumstances'.[50] Nevertheless, it appeared that the Union might call a strike on its own accord, let alone in support of other unionists. The clubs were aghast: they reacted individually by such actions as Sheffield Wednesday's refusal to discuss benefits 'until the trouble with the Players' Union is settled' and collectively at the League level by unanimously agreeing 'to remain loyal to the F. A. and give them their unqualified support'.[51] Union representatives met with J. C. Clegg of the F. A., but, so far as the Union was concerned, it was 'to all intents and purposes useless'.[52] The F. A., with League support, was not going to bend and so the Union, after a ballot of members and 'in the interests of peace and harmony', resigned from the G. F. T. U.[53]

It is difficult to reconcile this backdown with the claim of one historian that the Union had gained a victory.[54] Admittedly it succeeded in having itself once again recognised by the football authorities; it managed to get suspensions arising out of the dispute lifted; and it gained permission to represent its members before the courts providing that it first presented any dispute to the F. A. Council and gave them reasonable time to try and resolve the matter. Additionally discussions were promised on the two major planks of Union policy, the abolition of the retain-and-transfer system and the abandonment of the maximum wage. Yet the concessions gained virtually only restored the status quo and the later negotiations did little to disturb it.

Initially, despite its long-term commitment to the abolition of the maximum wage, the Union opted for what was seen as more attainable targets, such as 'talent money' paid at the end of the season for 'good conduct and skill' and bonuses for winning or drawing matches.[55] However, when in 1908 the F. A. Council, tired of the endless debate and friction between clubs, proposed the dropping of wage restrictions, the Union abandoned its attempt at piecemeal attrition and rallied to the F. A. flag only to discover that the wind of change had blown out almost before the banner had been unfurled.[56] Although the removal of wage restrictions remained Union policy, the executive agreed to accept 'any scheme that tends to improve the now-existing conditions'.[57] Hence all that emerged from the post-dispute negotiations was a Football League concession of the possibility of a pay rise of 10s. a week after a player had been with a club for two years and a further 10s. after four years' continuous service, plus limited end-of-season bonuses to players from teams which finished in the top five League positions or won F. A. Cup ties. At most a long-serving player with a side able to 'do the double' could earn £102 above the normal annual maximum of £208; however, none of these extra payments were compulsory.[58]

The industrial attack on the retain-and-transfer system also proved fruitless. One approach was to accept the system, albeit reluctantly, and to campaign for the security of longer contracts and free transfers, or a percentage of the transfer fee for those who were not retained.[59] Only the last point was achieved and even that was circumscribed in that the transfer had to be at the club's, not the player's, request and the percentage related only to any increase in the transfer fee; it was in fact in lieu of the player's claim to a benefit and again it was optional.[60] Really, though, the Union wished to throw off the shackles of an iniquitous system which did not allow players to choose their employer or to accept an offer of improved working conditions elsewhere. Their chance came with the Kingaby case, in which, with the assent of both the F. A. and the Football League, a legal test was made of Aston Villa's right to apply the retain-and-transfer system to one of their players.[61] The decision, in 1912, came down in favour of the status quo much to the relief of the clubs, who believed that 'had they lost the League would have been at the mercy of the players' Union'.[62] The Union was left with a heavy bill of £725 and efforts to finance this led to another showdown. The League, not wishing to be 'unnecessarily harsh', granted permission for a fund-raising match to be played between English and Scottish Union members, but this was withdrawn when the Union refused to accept an F. A. dictum that the benevolent fund of the Union should be used solely for welfare purposes, some such money having previously been transferred to the general fund to help meet costs.[63] In the ensuing debate, A. S. Owen, who had become secretary when Bloomfield retired, published a vitriolic attack 'on the honour and honesty of the Football League Management Committee' which was so outrageous that the rest of the Union executive disassociated itself from the statement, apologised to the Committee and, in return, obtained permission for the match.[64] After Owen was censured, he resigned and took up a position in Budapest.[65]

Eventually active interest in the Union declined. It had claimed a membership of 900 in April 1908 and one of over 1,300 from 70 clubs in December of that year.[66] By September 1910 membership was 510 (from only 46 of the 158 clubs which employed professionals), but it then increased to 625 in April 1911 and to 853 a year later.[67] Of these, 173 were the result of a successful campaign to recruit players from Scottish clubs. Ultimately, and amicably, the Scots developed a separate organisation on the recommendation of the Scottish Football Association, which feared demarcation disputes with the F. A. if problems north of the Border were taken up by an English-based union.[68] This Scottish Union, however, was dissolved after only two years.[69] In the meantime, as shown in Table 15.1, the English membership of the A. F. P. U. was on the slide, dropping to 442 by April 1913, with a further 'considerable falling off' reported in October.[70] This was reflected in the Union's financial position: to save money the secretary volunteered to use a room in his own house as an office and to do his own typing unless the work was of an exceptional nature.[71]

The Union may have helped distressed members and their families, but apart from successfully assisting in 60 disputes with clubs it achieved little

Table 15.1 *Membership of Association Football Players' Union, 1910–13*

	September 1910		April 1911		September 1911		April 1912		September 1912		April 1913	
	Players	Clubs	Players	Clubs	Players	Clubs	Players	Clubs	Players	Clubs	Players	Clubs
Football League first division	282	16	335	16	259	17	361	19	164	13	133	11
Football League second division	109	15	119	15	116	14	141	14	172	17	133	15
Other English leagues	119	15	171	20	144	23	178	21	183	14	176	18
English registrations	510	46	625	51	519	54	680	54	519	44	442	44
Scottish League	—		—		10	1	173	13	111	10	25	5
Total registrations	510	46	625	51	529	55	853	67	630	54	467	49

Note: The number of clubs refers to those which had at least one player in the Union.
Source: Subscription Register of A. F. P. U.

on the industrial front.[72] Negotiations for contracts remained on an individual basis, with hardly any of the framework set by the Union. Indeed as unions elsewhere in the economy became more militant the A. F. P. U. retreated from conflict. Finally, it failed to stop the imposition of wage cuts at the outbreak of war or have them converted to deferred pay.[73] It could not win. The Trade Disputes Act of 1906 may have conceded the right to strike, but the F. A. had the ultimate weapon in its ability, and willingness, to deregister players who did so.

III

The A. F. P. U. did little towards improving the terms of employment of their members, but in itself this particular performance cannot explain the relative lack of permanent union organisation in other sports at a time when industrial workers were unionising at an unprecedented rate. Possibly rugby league players, as part-time sportsmen, were poor union material, but why did not jockeys and cricketers follow the example of soccer players and unionise?[74] Certainly most cricketers had earnings high enough to afford membership subscriptions.

A major prerequisite of unionism is the establishment of a community of interest. This would not be easy in professional sport, particularly the individual type, where one man's success is inevitably someone else's failure. Professional sport is also the province of elitism: many try but few make it to the top. Nevertheless in theory, and certainly in belief, any one could get there if they had the talent. New entrants who turned professional with the intention of becoming stars would be unlikely to be attracted by unionism until hard experience forced them to face the reality of blocked upward mobility, and by then many would have quit the game. Without the stars sports unions had little bargaining power; average players could always be replaced. It is notable that the few successes at collective bargaining at club level involved leading performers. Only if there were issues which affected the star players was there a basis for successful unionism.[75] Such matters would include restrictions which prevented the sportsman from earning his economic rent, for these would irritate the champions as well as the men who would be kings. It is perhaps significant that the early football unions which failed to establish any permanency pre-dated the maximum wage and that Scottish soccer, where there was no such limitation on earnings, also proved a poor field for more than temporary unionism.

Certainly there were fewer restrictions on the mobility and earning power of cricket players and jockeys than on English footballers.

Admittedly cricketers faced the problem of two years out of the game if they wished to change county clubs, but, nevertheless, they were at liberty to choose their employers and they did have the option of a reasonably remunerative position in league cricket. Moreover, they did not suffer the indignity of being bought and sold in a transfer market. Jockeys could be prevented from riding for other employers, but owners paid them handsome retainers for such a restrictive practice.

As for earnings neither jockeys nor cricketers faced maximum-wage legislation: indeed for jockeys the only limit was the depth of the owner's purse. There was little common interest between the top echelon of jockeys and the vast reserve army of underemployed riders. Any combination of jockeys – if such a thing existed – would be a ring rather than a union, rumours of which invariably concerned top riders who could exert the power of their riding oligopoly to keep the spoils for their select group.[76] The run-of-the-mill jockey perhaps had more need of unionism, but, in such a highly competitive trade, no union could guarantee him a ride. Moreover, the Jockey Club had already legislated minimum riding fees and had taken action to ensure that owners handed them over.

Officially cricketers, too, had no maximum wage, though in practice a conventional limit to match payments was in operation. There was the possibility of a benefit in the long term, though this also applied to footballers. Nevertheless, in practice, win bonuses, talent money, tours, and the fact that cricketers were paid by the match rather than by the season, eased the restriction and pushed the cricketer's earnings above those of his football counterpart. His situation was well summarised by Wisden, in 1897, which, whilst admitting that earnings had not gone up in proportion to the popularity of cricket, maintained that 'to represent the average professional as an ill-treated or downtrodden individual [would be] a gross exaggeration . . . there is plenty of room for further improvement, but, taken all round, things are certainly far better than they were'.[77] Additionally the cricket professional was in a unique and peculiar working situation in that not only was he employed by men of a superior social class, but he also plied his trade alongside them. Whether this affected his attitude towards unionism is conjectural but it was claimed, though for different reasons, that the employer–employee relationship in cricket was not that of industrial capitalism:

Professional cricketers ought to remember that their relation with County Committees is not the ordinary commercial relation of labour and capital, where labourers and capitalists alike seek remuneration, and where in many people's opinion the labourer is fully entitled, by striking, to get his fair share of the profits. In county cricket the Professional, who is the labourer, makes a profit: ·the

Committee, which is the capitalist, does not, but merely seeks to encourage and support the game.[78]

IV

In soccer the A. F. P. U. set out to perform simultaneously the function of collective-bargaining agency and benevolent society. Here it had the advantage over both cricket and horse-racing in being part of a relatively new professional sport, for in the others the welfare aspect had already been partially taken on by the sports authorities.

The M. C. C. had established a Cricketers' Fund in 1848 'for the purpose of giving donations in cases of illness and accident'. It was under the sole control of the M. C. C. committee and served as a disciplinary weapon as it was designed 'to encourage good conduct on the part of professional players, both of the ground, and who had been engaged in matches by the M. C. C.'.[79] Interestingly, it replaced a reward fund for outstanding performances by professionals playing at Lord's: batting and bowling were now deemed less worthy than good behaviour. It was to be financed by an annual donation of £10 from the M. C. C. and any other money which members cared to subscribe. Whether or why this fund collapsed is unknown, but later a Cricketers' Fund Friendly Society was set up by the professionals themselves, financed by games between the United and All-England teams, as well as by a small subscription.[80] However, wrangles between members of the professional elevens and the fall in the popularity of such teams reduced the importance of the Fund, which by 1872 had a mere 26 members and an annual income of only £98.[81] Possibly it had been affected by an initiative of the M. C. C. which, five years earlier, had established another Cricketers' Fund, with first claim going to professionals on the Lord's ground but secondarily 'for the relief of all cricketers who, during their career shall have conducted themselves to the entire satisfaction of the Committee of the M. C. C.'.[82] What happened to both these funds is unclear, but in 1886 Lord Harris, the president of the M. C. C., developed a scheme to solicit support for a Cricketers' Fund Friendly Society and put it on a sound financial basis.[83] In addition to subscriptions, donations and an annual sale of bats used by famous players, regular matches were held to finance this fund which, in 1890, was paying up to 30s. a week allowance to sick and injured professionals.[84] Some county clubs, Kent especially, also established funds for the 'means of assisting decayed cricketers'.[85]

Horse-racing had the Bentinck Benevolent Fund. As a tribute to Lord George Bentinck's efforts in the 1840s to remove corruption from racing, turf patrons had subscribed £2,100, which he donated to the Jockey Club to form the nucleus of a fund which would provide assistance to distressed jockeys and their dependants. It was later supplemented by the Rous Memorial Fund, another sum raised in honour of a turf reformer. All fines imposed by the Jockey Club were added to these funds. Although the restricted resources of both funds meant that only small pensions and disbursements could be offered, in having such a source of assistance available to them jockeys were in a better situation than the average working man.[86] Possibly this changed with the passing of the Workmen's Compensation Acts of 1897 and 1900, for these did not apply to jockeys on several counts: many earned above £250 a year; they worked on premises not under the control or management of the person who employed them; and most were casually employed for a purpose unconnected with their patron's trade or business.[87]

The Football League actually sought counsel's opinion as to the liability of member clubs under these Acts, but he held that professional footballers were not 'workmen' as defined in the legislation. The League 'acted upon this expert opinion while at the same time considering sympathetically any cases which came within the scope of their assistance or guidance'.[88] They did in fact canvass insurance companies on behalf of the clubs, but, finding the rates too high, established the Football Mutual Insurance Federation, comprising teams from the Football, Southern and Scottish Leagues.[89] However, as it was not compulsory for clubs to join, it still left a welfare gap to be filled by the Players' Union. In 1912, however, the courts ruled that footballers were manual labourers and had to be insured under the National Insurance Act.[90] Possibly this undermined the A. F. P. U.'s benevolent activities and contributed to the decline in Union membership.

V

Despite the need for a countervailing force to protect the interests of sports labourers, several factors hindered the development of unionism by professional sportsmen. The geographical dispersion of clubs and the high rate of labour turnover made organisation difficult, but perhaps the main reason was the lack of a community of interest amongst professionals, even in the same sport, a deficiency accentuated by the competitive nature of an occupation which always has to have winners and losers. Moreover, given the shortness of careers in sport, too many individual professionals were out to maximise their earnings, with no time to spare any thought for collective action, except perhaps at the club level where there would be relatively easy communication between players. Only in English soccer, where restrictions prevented stars from earning their economic rents, was there an incentive for *all* players to band together. The pre-emption of welfare functions by employers and sports authorities could also have weakened moves towards unionisation. Perhaps, too, for many professionals there was a good deal of job satisfaction: the public exhibition of one's skills and the adulation of the crowd yield psychic income which, if coupled with an emotional attachment to the game or loyalty to one's club, could have undermined the influences pushing for unionism.[91]

Chapter 16

Labour aristocrats or wage slaves?

The earnings of successful professional sportsmen were high relative to other working-class incomes.[1] No working man, no matter how skilled, could hope to match the money of top jockeys, and even the £4 a week of the professional footballer would be envied by most workers. On such an economic criterion there would be a strong claim for at least the higher echelons of professional sportsmen to be categorised as members of the labour aristocracy, that 'distinctive upper strata of the working class, better paid, better treated, and generally regarded as more respectable and politically moderate than the mass of the proletariat'.[2] Yet, as this definition implies, the issue was not just one of earnings. As a group the labour aristocrats are considered to have differed from other sections of the working class in job security, life style, political attitudes, relationships with employers, and their willingness and ability to unionise and organise other cooperative enterprises.[3] On these grounds it is difficult to include sportsmen within the ranks of the labour aristocracy, though far more biographical research is needed before firm conclusions can be drawn.

Sportsmen had little long-term job security, simply because ageing muscles brought declining physical prowess which, apart from a few jockeys and the exceptional cricketer, generally failed to be offset by experience and tactical nous. There were also more immediate problems caused partly by injuries, an occupational hazard, but mainly by the lack of any power to restrict entry to the profession. Admittedly, unlike the factory workers whose jobs would go if their enterprise proved unprofitable, footballers, and especially cricketers, could continue to be employed despite unfavourable financial statements. However, a jockey without a retainer was no more than a casual labourer, albeit a skilled one. Sportsmen's employers tended towards paternalism and kept a firm control over the determination of working conditions; moreover, the free operation of the labour market was circumscribed by restrictions which adversely affected the bargaining power of the players. Very few professionals found sport to be a means of further social or economic advancement: the vast majority had a brief glimpse of fame and fortune and were then absorbed back into the mass of the working class.

Working-class experiences are not confined to the workplace, but unfortunately little is known currently about where sportsmen lived and whom they married, two significant indicators of social distance. Nor, since their political affiliations have not yet been well researched, would it be wise to generalise from the few examples available. What is clearer is that there was a social divide between professional sportsmen and the middle class, many of whom viewed such professionals, especially jockeys, as unrespectable, and even those who played alongside them on the cricket field insisted on symbolic separation. It is equally clear that leading sportsmen were idolised by many of the working class, though whether as representatives of their class or of their community is a matter for conjecture.

The major impediment to enlisting sportsmen in the ranks of the labour aristocracy is their failure, except in soccer, to unionise; and even in soccer less than 10% of professional players joined the organisation. Nor is there evidence that they participated in friendly societies or other voluntary working men's associations. The sporting professional possessed no clear sense of class identity; his trade was far too competitive.

It may be, of course, that historians have set the qualifications for membership of the labour aristocracy too stringently and that indeed few occupations would fit the ideal type. Nevertheless, at this stage of knowledge, it is hard to ennoble professional sportsmen. They shared some common experiences and were a distinct group with respect to potential earning power, gender, and generally age, but they were united only on the field of play.

It is easier to make a case that some professionals, particularly in team sports, were akin to bonded men, or, as the secretary of the Association Football Players' Union put it, 'the professional player is the slave of his club and they can do practically what they like with him'.[4] Certainly the employers in soccer stated that they were 'determined to be the masters', and experiences in cricket suggest that county committees shared this view.[5] The economic freedom of professionals was curtailed severely: soccer players faced a maximum wage; both they and cricketers were subject to mobility restrictions; and jockeys were prevented from owning horses or attempting to make money by gambling, unlike almost everyone else in horse-racing. It could be argued that these limitations were compensated for by generally higher incomes than other working men, but studies have shown that, despite their high earnings, modern professional sportsmen are still exploited economically in that they fail to obtain their marginal-value product.[6] There is no reason to suppose that things were different historically.

Part V

Unsporting behaviour

Every sport which comes to the state of merely being a resource for betting will arrive eventually at a condition of rottenness which will make it the despair of a reformer.

M. Shearman, *Athletics and Football*, London, 1888, p. 239

In British professional running and rowing it is generally admitted that the race is not always to the swift, but it is not uncommonly predestined by the blessed gods who wield the pencil.

H. Graves, 'A philosophy of sport', *Contemporary Review*, LXXVIII, 1900, p. 888

Glasgow people are very impartial in their applause, and when any good bit of play was shown on the English side it was at once recognised by the well-behaved spectators.

Scottish Football Association Annual 1877/78, p. 68

The Referee Committee note with regret that objectionable practices by spectators at matches are on the increase, and urge on all clubs the immediate necessity for taking strong measures for the suppression of same.

Minutes of Scottish Football Association, 26 October 1910

Chapter 17

Ungentlemanly conduct

I

The rewards to the successful in professional sport, and equally the failure to obtain them, can tempt participants to go beyond the violence and dispossession sanctioned by the rules. Thus many late nineteenth-century commentators feared that, unless it was strictly controlled, sports professionalism would inevitably lead to corruption and misconduct:

It is not good that a game should be made a matter of money. Evil passions are excited; the temptation to unfairness is increased; rowdyism comes in.[1]

As soon as any sport has become so popular that money is to be made out of it, and men engage in it upon whom the loss of reputation has little effect, it may be prophesied with certainty that abuses will arise.[2]

Experience shows that whenever, in any sport, an entrance has been opened for making money without amateur supervision, the element of corruptibility is sure to step in, with disastrous effects.[3]

The history of prizefighting was testimony to what could happen to a sport if professionalism got out of hand. Increasingly from the 1820s on, fights became unpredictable — not, however, due to closeness of competition, which might have been acceptable, but because of corruption, which was not. Despite the pretensions of the Pugilistic Club, the sport had no real ruling body and no steps were taken to rectify the situation. Once fighters failed to perform to their abilities the odds no longer reflected probability and the gambling gentry withdrew its support. Unfortunately for prizefighting this coincided with an assault on the sport by those determined to civilise society. As upper-class patronage declined the way was open for pugilism to be hounded into extinction, only lingering on till the 1860s as a financial prop of the underworld, a sport increasingly conducted by delinquents for delinquents.[4] Fears that such might also be the fate of their sport produced an initial hostility towards professionalism by most amateur sports authorities, later to be replaced –

and then only in some sports – by a grudging acceptance providing that it was subject to stringent regulations.[5]

With the major exception of cricket, the controlling bodies in professional sports all assumed the power to suspend participants for misconduct and took steps to have the penalties recognised by other sports authorities both in Britain and abroad. In cricket, however, the exemplary influence of playing alongside amateurs was considered sufficient to keep the game clean and other disciplinary matters were left in the hands of the individual county committees. Additionally all sports utilised control agents – referees, umpires and other officials – to enforce adherence both to the rules of the game and as to how it should be played.[6]

Soccer (and rugby) referees had the power to send off players for misbehaviour on the field of play, an action which usually resulted in at least one month's suspension during which no wages could be paid.[7] To ensure fair play neutral referees were appointed, but they had to be seen to be impartial: the Football League warned clubs not to allow referees to have lunch with either players or club executives; not to write to congratulate referees who had secured a place on the official list; and not to pay referees more than their set fee and travel expenses. For their part referees were told not to speak to players during the game and they were also banned from writing for the press or from betting on football matches.[8] Scottish referees were also advised, in a well-intentioned but poorly phrased statement, 'to avoid intercourse with players prior to a match'![9] Initially the Football League refused to entertain any complaints about a referee's competence: indeed apologies were often demanded from those rash enough to question the official's judgement. When the Darwen committee made 'an outrageous and totally unfounded' accusation that the referee in their match against Bolton was inebriated, they were ordered to make a full retraction in several newspapers. The League Management Committee also refused to recognise Mr A. F. Reeves as the secretary of Stoke until he made ample apology and withdrew his 'serious imputations' against a referee.[10] Later, possibly because fewer members of the Management Committee were then themselves referees, but more likely because of the growing financial importance of match results, the League authorities became less dogmatic about a referee's omniscience. In 1897, following repeated protests about particular officials 'note was taken to avoid as far as possible their appointments in matches of complaining clubs'.[11] By 1900, although the referee's views were still accepted on specific decisions, such as penalties, goals, the state of the pitch and the accuracy of the timing, when his general competence or efficiency was questioned, particularly by more than one club, observers were sent to report on his matches. This new policy resulted in incompetent referees being suspended, removed from the list, or being given a hint to retire, as with the official who 'while in West Yorkshire and Lancashire for the purpose of acting as a referee in certain matches during Christmas Tide did not keep himself in the condition that the F. A. and Football League would have the right to expect from persons who are appointed to such responsible positions'.[12] Nevertheless such officials were in the minority and generally the Management Committee continued to support the referee: in the season 1912/13, for example, of 54 complaints only one resulted in the suspension of a referee.[13] By this time referees underwent a stiff selection procedure and had to work their way up to League level by performing satisfactorily in lower-grade matches.[14]

Although nominated to the first-class panel by specific counties, usually ones for which they had played, cricket umpires rarely appear to have been accused of partiality. Their role was virtually confined to responding to appeals from players: only in determining wides, no balls and other illegal deliveries could they take the initiative. They were not expected to enforce on-field discipline: perhaps as ex-professionals they were not trusted to do so and such matters were left to the amateur captains 'in whose hands the ultimate fate of the game must rest'.[15] A compulsory eyesight test was introduced in 1907.[16]

Referees and umpires were paid for what they did. In contrast, amateurism reigned supreme among racing stewards. Throughout the period studied these were selected from the local aristocracy and gentry, a hangover from the pre-railway era when patronage from such people was vital to the success of a meeting. Interestingly, although other racing officials were not allowed to bet on races in which they were involved, no such restriction applied to the stewards: gentlemen by definition were deemed incorruptible. Many stewards accepted the honour of nomination but failed to attend the meetings; others turned up but performed their duties in a perfunctory manner.[17] In the opinion of many racing men justice would be better done, and seen to be done, if stipendary stewards were appointed, either to replace or assist the local honorary officials.[18] These stewards, by travelling the country and attending race meetings regularly, could have form at their fingertips and be aware of inconsistent running. Nothing was done in this regard, but, after a debate emanating from a query by Lord Hamilton of Dalzell, stewards did begin to act on their own initiative rather than wait for an objection to be raised by an owner or trainer.[19]

II

Penalties for foul riding could not be expected to be a fully effective preventative measure simply because, in a tight finish, excitement and desperation could easily rule the head. Most serious misconduct in racing, however, was premeditated and hence amenable to a rational weighing of the potential costs if found out against the known benefits if the coup was achieved. Overall it would appear that racing's association with gambling kept the incentives to corruption high.

The excess supply in the labour market did not help. Clearly for most jockeys 'money [was] to be made with greater certainty by foul means than by fair'.[20] Apprentices might have little option but to be dishonest: if they wanted mounts, and what apprentice did not, then they had to ride to orders and these were not always to win.[21] Young jockeys, whose basic work was seeking work, also might have to lose or starve even more than their occupation necessitated. Others, although less desperate for rides, chose the crooked track. Even such a well-known rider as Charley Wood obtained minimal damages in a libel action such was his 'general character as a dishonest jockey': Wood was third-ranked jockey in the country when he was warned off for illegally owning horses in partnership with Sir George Chetwynd.[22] Nevertheless, many commentators believed that, as a group, jockeys had become less dishonest: even such a stern critic of racing morality as L. H. Curzon accepted that the great majority of riders were 'beyond suspicion'.[23] If fewer jockeys were falling to temptation it was probably associated with the Jockey Club gaining control over British racing and instituting a licensing system for jockeys in 1879. However, those who lost their licences were allowed to apply for their reinstatement and, for those jockeys with influential employers, the warning-off was seldom permanent.[24] Several attempts were made to get Wood reinstated after the Chetwynd affair and eventually in 1897 the Jockey Club relented. Lord Durham, a Club steward and the man virtually responsible for having Wood warned off, wrote to bury the hatchet:

If you are going to ride at Lincoln I should be pleased to give you your first mount and would put in a horse for you to ride in the Trial Stakes – you would thereby have public proof that I feel confident that you will do your best to reinstate yourself as a jockey.[25]

Wood had been put out of the saddle for five years, a not inconsiderable financial penalty. He had in fact learned his lesson and became a successful and honest jockey, but some others who were let back incurred suspicion again.[26] Clearly the deterrent effect of a warning-off was diluted by forgiving sinners their trespasses.

Turf corruption was aggravated by the American invasion. Most trainers who crossed the Atlantic had no qualms about using dope which, although legal at the time, made a farce of handicapping and undermined the rationale of racing, which was to select the best horses for breeding as judged by the racetrack test. Some of these trainers also went outside the rules of racing by arranging to have their horses pulled.[27] The American seat, which made it more difficult to control a horse, was blamed for many riding offences by the visiting jockeys, but some was due to a disregard for the rules, even by men at the top of their profession. Lester Reiff, champion jockey in 1900, was warned off in October 1901 for not trying to win at a Manchester meeting.[28] A year earlier, Tod Sloan, the man chiefly responsible for popularising the new style of riding in Britain, was barred from racing because of his betting activities.[29]

As this suggests, the Jockey Club did attempt to rid the turf of its worst abuses, but critics still thought that it was too timid to provide 'good government on the turf'.[30] More should have been done and it should have been done earlier. In many instances legislation only followed actions so flagrant that even the eyes of the 'three blind mice', as the Club stewards were being irreverently called, were opened. Doping is a case in point. Despite growing public unrest, the Club did nothing until the trainer George Lambton doped five of his own rogue horses, creatures that had shown no form whatsoever but which, when running with the assistance of drugs, gained four first places and a second. He had informed his brother, Lord Durham, a leading member of the Jockey Club, of his intentions, so the Club was forced to take notice and in 1904 doping of a horse was made a turf offence. Nevertheless, eradication of the practice was not easily attained, particularly before the development of the saliva test in 1910.[31]

A more vigilant racing press assisted the Jockey Club in its attempts to improve the conduct of racing and to some extent this was achieved. Writing in the mid 1890s, Alfred Watson, a leading writer on turf affairs, maintained:

a few rogues are still to the fore, sometimes in prominent places, and not a few others have conveniently elastic consciences, together with excessive liberal ideas of what is permissible, but I do believe that there is far less rascality on the turf than there used to be.[32]

It may be, as L. H. Curzon opined, that roguery was merely pushed underground: that racing changed only from being overtly corrupt to being covertly corrupt.[33] Yet, if this was true and the public remained ignorant, surely those in racing would suspect what was happening and, if they sensed widespread malpractice, surely racing would not have expanded as it did.

Football's major on-field problem was violent play. The introduction of the penalty kick, sending-off, suspensions and fines were all designed as deterrents, but on the day players would find that referees differed in their distinction between hard and rough play, and some heat-of-the-moment violence was inevitable in a body contact sport. Off-field offences were not solely the fault of the professional. In the early days of the Football League 'those who ran the clubs, the secretaries, and the players all conspired to harass the League by either flouting the rules, indifference, neglect or secret violation'.[34] Although the volume of malfeasance was later reduced, the minute books of the Football League Management Committee continued to illustrate the fact that some club officials would attempt to evade cartel regulations by falsifying registration forms, fielding ineligible players, poaching and approaching players at other clubs, and paying signing-on fees and wages above the permitted level.[35] Fines on the clubs concerned do not appear to have been an effective deterrent – at most they represented a 10,000 gate – but suspensions from football management, increasingly utilised from the early 1900s on, may have had some influence on those directors who were superfans or who sought status from board membership. More impact could have been obtained by deducting League points from clubs whose officials transgressed, but there was a marked reluctance to adopt such a policy.[36]

Allegations of attempted match-fixing were treated seriously and were fully investigated. Most were considered unfounded but a few, very few, were substantiated. Billy Meredith, the Welsh winger, was put out of the game for a season (a surprisingly light penalty) for allegedly offering an Aston Villa opponent £10 (a surprisingly low amount) to throw a game against Manchester City.[37] More severe retribution was dealt to Colonel T. Gibson Poole, the chairman of Middlesbrough. He offered £30 to Charles Thompson, the Sunderland captain, to arrange to lose the Teesside derby so as to boost Poole's chances at a forthcoming parliamentary election. Thompson informed his own chairman, who reported the matter to the F. A., and both Poole and A. D. Walker, the club secretary, who had acted as intermediary, were suspended *sine die* from organised football.[38]

Of the sports examined, cricket alone remained above suspicion. It was 'the pure game . . . untouched by the lowering tendencies of the betting-ring and its degrading accompaniments'.[39] Here 'no whisper of matches being sold for money is ever heard . . . no charge of cheating is brought against players'.[40]

III

Although reliance has to be placed on contemporary observation, there would seem to be some correlation between the rewards sought from a sport and the degree of corruption within it. Despite improvements, racing remained the most corrupt sport, mainly because of its association with gambling, though the situation was aggravated by the timidity of the Jockey Club. The banning of gambling, as was done both in soccer and cricket, might have helped the situation but was not really an option. Potential financial gains in soccer were less than in racing and so was corruption. Matches were played on merit, though misconduct, particularly rough play and illegal payments, remained a problem. In cricket, playing the game was generally felt to be more important than any financial considerations. The whites of the players reflected the pristine nature of the sport: indeed 'it's not cricket' had entered the language as a cry against unfair conduct.[41]

Chapter 18

The madding crowd

I

Almost any event in Victorian England which brought together a large gathering of people could result in crowd disorder. Violence frequently broke out at all sorts of mass meetings 'from Salvation Army processions to demonstrations of the unemployed, industrial disputes, . . . eviction scenes, Orange celebrations, public hangings'.[1] Sports crowds were no exception.

Spectators frequently got out of hand at mid Victorian horse-racing. Trouble seems to have been commonplace at several London meetings in the late 1860s: at Bromley a pitched battle was fought between welshing bookmakers and angry punters; at Streatham a rioting mob tore up railings and flung them at a jockey accused of not trying; and at Enfield a similarly suspected rider was saved from lynching only by the intervention of armed racecourse officials.[2] The disturbances at some metropolitan meetings became so bad that in 1879 parliamentary legislation was used to suppress them.[3] Provincial meetings, too, had their disturbances, particularly when backers felt that they had not had a fair run for their money or when bookmakers welshed on winning bets.[4] No wonder that J. H. Peart, right-hand man of the famous trainer, John Scott, unfavourably contrasted the English situation with that at Chantilly, where 'the arrangements on the racecourse are far beyond what they have in England. The roughs are kept in their proper place, and there was no hustle or confusion, and no fear of being robbed of your wallet.'[5] Soccer, too, had its crowd problems. Several researchers have demonstrated that 'spectator disorderliness at football had occurred on a substantial scale in the three and a half decades before the First World War'.[6] Cricket, however, despite a few instances documented below, does not appear to have experienced the kind of crowd violence frequently observed at soccer matches and race meetings.[7]

Sports promoters had sound economic reasons to fear crowd disorder. Commercialisation had led to heavy investment in ground and course facilities, and valuable property was at risk if crowds got out of control. Additionally, there was the threat to gate-receipts if spectator misbehaviour deterred other paying customers from attending: after Glasgow Rangers' first game at Ibrox in 1887 one sporting newspaper commented on 'the very large number of the better classes that turned out to see the game. It behoves the Rangers to do everything in their power to retain the patronage of these people ... and they can only do so by keeping the rowdier portion of the crowd in order.'[8] Ultimately, of course, the authorities, either legal or sporting, could close a ground or racetrack if there was too much disorder. As indicated above, some metropolitan racecourses had already fallen victim to parliamentary legislation, and the football authorities of both codes made it clear that they held clubs responsible for crowd misbehaviour and that they would close grounds if spectators got out of hand.[9] Over time, of course, increasing gate-receipts made this a severer penalty. Clearly a strategy for crowd control had to be devised.

II

Yet what the club directors or course executives could do was not clear. Even today the causes of sports crowd disturbances are not fully understood or agreed upon, though most modern studies suggest that it is probable that deep-rooted social strains and structural tensions produce conditions conducive to disorder.[10] Certainly it can be argued that the working-class sports fan often became the sports fanatic because of deprivation or alienation. He was more than just a spectator, more than merely a consumer of the sports product.[11] Deprived of power and esteem at work, he found a surrogate identity as a member of a large group; as a partisan team supporter he could bask in the reflected glory of a winning team. Alternatively he could seek to control his fate by using his skill to select winning horses. Although he himself could rarely triumph over social and economic institutions, his team or racing selection could defeat its opponents. Sport also allowed the working man openly to challenge authority by barracking the referee, umpire or racing official. To many such men sport performed a compensatory function, as was acknowledged by the Scottish Football Association, who endorsed the view that 'football has brought them to a happier life, and has breathed into them interest in, and enthusiasm for, something different from the common experiences of their existence; it has helped them to a taste of the extreme pleasure of forgetting themselves, and their hard lot, and their squalid surroundings, and their general discomfort and poverty'.[12] The intense role of sport in such persons' lives meant that their reactions to sports events became highly emotional, none more so perhaps than the consumptive Sheffield Wednesday supporter who struggled to the cup final at Crystal Palace and then returned home to die, surrounded by his team's colours, content that they had won the trophy.[13]

Even if the sports promoters had appreciated the sociological and psychological roots to sports crowd disorders, there was little which they could have done to rectify the situation. Hence they concentrated on a variety of measures designed either to reduce the triggers to disorder or to contain any disturbances which did break out. This was not problem-free as the motivations of sports crowd rioters could differ considerably and thus require different control measures. Indeed a recent work by social psychologists has classified sports crowd disorders into five major categories, depending upon the apparent motivation of those involved, all of which could be found at the sports events being examined here.[14]

The first category, frustration disorders, occurs when spectators' expectations of access to the game, or the way it will be played or adjudicated, are thwarted. A classic example of this took place at Hampden Park on 17 April 1909. Glasgow Celtic, bidding for a third successive League and Cup double, were replaying the Scottish Cup final against their traditional rivals, Glasgow Rangers, many of whose supporters felt that they had been robbed of victory in the original final. At full time in the replay the scores were level and, due to a false press report, many fans expected extra time to be played. When it became apparent that this was not the case jeering began, soon followed by an invasion of the field by an estimated 6,000 disgruntled spectators. A few policemen attempted to stem the flow but they were beaten savagely. Reinforcements were able to prevent the mob from reaching the dressing rooms, but that was all they could accomplish. Rioters tore out the goalposts, ripped up the nets, and smashed down fencing. Bonfires were made out of the broken barricading, and the uprooted goalposts were used as battering rams against the turnstiles and payboxes, which were also then set on fire. The arrival of the fire brigade signalled further trouble and the firemen were attacked and their hoses slashed. Ultimately some 200 policemen were fighting the mob. Not till two and a half hours after the match ended were the rioters forced out of the ground and the fires brought under control. Much of the stadium was damaged: 5 gates and payboxes with 22 turnstiles had been destroyed, the terracing on the north side had suffered severely, a substantial proportion of fencing had been smashed and burned, and a large part of the playing area had been scarred by fire and broken glass, in all some £1,000 worth of damage. Casualties were heavy, with 58 policemen and 60 others having to receive hospital treatment.[15]

This was the worst case of frustration violence before 1914, but it was not an isolated occurrence. At Everton, in 1895, two contingents of police had to use their batons to clear the ground of rioting fans following the referee's abandonment of a game because he felt that the pitch had become unplayable.[16] In cricket, at the Middlesex versus Lancashire match of 1907, the crowd, exasperated by a failure to let them know when play was to start after a delay for rain, invaded the playing area and tore up the pitch, an incident described by a contemporary as a 'miniature riot'.[17]

Perceived injustice can also be a source of frustration as when a bookmaker refused to pay winning clients or when partisan fans and gamblers believe that an incompetent or biased official has cost their team or horse victory. Another type of frustration disorder is stimulated by a feeling that someone has not tried their best, as with the Australian cricket team at the Oval in 1884, who were far too transparent in their attempts to prolong a match so that they could obtain another day's gate-money.[18] Or as in the 1896 University match at Lord's when, in an incident which shocked the cricketing world, the Cambridge captain instructed his bowler to send three balls straight to the boundary in order to avoid having to enforce what was then a compulsory follow-on.[19]

Most disorder traced was either caused by frustration or was confrontational in nature, the latter category stemming from the emotional attachment of supporters to their team. Given the appropriate circumstances, smouldering resentment between rival religious, geographic, ethnic or national groups can easily spark into open hostility, particularly when the divisions are readily identifiable and the fans are congregated in large numbers. Where supporters have developed a strong sense of collective identity, then 'us' versus 'them' conflict situations can erupt into disorder, with matches becoming symbolic struggles for supremacy between, say, Protestant and Catholic, or one area of the city and another. Derby matches were an obvious setting for confrontational disturbances, particularly 'in the North [where] football . . . is something more than a game [and] . . . awakes local patriotism to its highest pitch'.[20] For example, in 1880, a time when Darwen and neighbouring Blackburn Rovers were fierce rivals, the spectators divided over an incident involving Marshall of the home side and Suter of Blackburn, and the subsequent riot forced the abandonment of the game.[21]

The other types of identifiable disturbance were less common before

1914 but nevertheless were present. In the third category, expressive disorder, the intense emotional arousal which accompanies victory or defeat, particularly if it is exciting or unexpected, triggers uninhibited behaviour in which members of the crowd become completely abandoned. Cup matches, with their sudden-death exit from the competition, are a likely source of expressive disturbance. So it was when Blackburn Olympic, essentially a working-class team, beat the Old Etonians in the 1883 cup final and took the trophy to the north for the first time: their supporters reputedly went mad with excitement, particularly as the result had been snatched during extra time.[22]

The fourth category, remonstrance disorder, occurs when a section of the crowd uses a sports event as an arena for the expression of political grievances, as in the early twentieth century when suffragettes turned to militant action. Sport was a bastion of male chauvinism and exclusiveness and thus was an obvious target: racecourses, bowling greens, soccer grounds, cricket pitches and golf courses all had their turf torn up and their buildings set on fire. And it was at a sports event, the 1913 Derby, that the suffragettes found their martyr when Emily Davison threw herself under the King's horse and was killed.[23]

The most difficult category of disorder to identify is that of outlawry, which occurs when groups of violence-prone spectators use sports events to act out their anti-social activities by attacking officials, by fighting, and by destroying property. Such crowd violence is seen as the work of a delinquent or criminal element. Historical examples are not easy to pinpoint as this type of rioter would doubtless join in most other disturbances. A possible indication of their existence comes from a critic of those professional sports organised for betting purposes who claimed that such sports attracted 'a varying but always large blackguard element', 'a mob of loafers' and 'a base rabble', and that 'disorder and attacks on the police are not things of rare occurrence among the rougher spectators'.[24] Another critic of racing crowds castigated the railways for 'facilitating the movement of bands of indolent roughs'.[25] A further lead is the comment on soccer crowds that 'it all depends upon the measure of civilisation in your locality whether there is or is not a good deal of fighting after the match'.[26] The problem here is that these descriptions are labels applied by outside, and perhaps prejudiced, observers who can perceive only indirectly the motivations of the people involved. How much experience they had had of the working class *en masse* is unknown, nor is it clear whether the same observers would have castigated middle-class student high jinks as vociferously as they condemned working-class sports hooliganism.

III

What is apparent from the above categorisation is that no single method of control can cope with all the varieties of disorder, and that action which might be suitable for one situation could be inappropriate in another. To some extent the sport promoters learned this lesson by trial and error, and measures for crowd control took time to evolve, but by the end of the nineteenth century five major strategies had been devised: improvements in the conduct of the sport, improvements in the organisation of the sports event, crowd segregation, control of ancillary activities, and the use of control agents.

In most cases efforts to improve the conduct of a sport came from the national controlling bodies, and not always with the prime aim of improving crowd behaviour. Nevertheless, with less malpractice to anger the crowd, the spectators' propensity to riot might be reduced. As detailed in the previous chapter, the sports authorities achieved some success in stamping out corruption and premeditated misconduct. However, legislation could do little to curb spontaneous heat-of-the-moment violence in a contact sport such as soccer. Moreover, the power given to the referee could actually precipitate disorder because of the number of decisions which he had to make during the game, any one of which could spark a riot. Even though refereeing standards improved with the introduction of examinations, eyesight tests and official lists, little could be done about the partiality of the fans. When the Football League Management Committee circularised referees and requested them to cut down on violence in the game, they were told to distinguish between 'robust' and 'rough' play, a distinction no doubt much easier for the partisan supporter to make than the appointed match official.[27]

The improved organisation of sports events did much to reduce the chances of frustration disorder. A simple but effective improvement was to have races and matches start on time. Traditionally race meetings had commenced in the morning and the times of the afternoon races had depended on the quality of the luncheon partaken by the race committee. Even then the method of starting races with a shout of 'no' or 'go' was apt to lead to false starts. The enclosed courses ran to a much stricter timetable, thanks to the employment of professional starters and, from the late 1890s, the use of the starting gate.[28] Darkness sometimes forced the abandonment of soccer matches, usually because the visiting team had turned up late. In 1892 the Football League warned that teams not arriving in time for the scheduled kick-off were 'open to a charge of objectionable conduct', and thereafter offenders were usually fined.[29] If a late start led to an abandonment, then a replay was usually ordered, with the offending club paying some financial penalty. Initially, however, only the unexpired time was replayed, which led to some ludicrous situations as when Stoke, 4–2 down to Wolves, had to journey to Wolverhampton to play only three minutes.[30] Later the League Management Committee began to use its discretion either to let the score stand at the time of the abandonment or to insist on the whole game being replayed. In cricket the spectator's complaint was not so much starting time, but the delays which occurred between innings or between the fall of wickets. Generally, however, this did not lead to more than verbal abuse.[31] Another organisational problem which could anger the crowd was the fielding of weak teams, either because first-team players were being rested prior to an important game or because teams turned up short-handed. At Blackburn, on Christmas Day 1890, over 3,000 spectators turned up in anticipation of an exciting first-team friendly match between the home side and local rivals, Darwen. Blackburn, however, had a hard League match due on Boxing Day at Wolverhampton and fielded what was virtually their second team. Darwen responded by taking their players from the pitch and replacing them with their reserve eleven. The crowd was not amused. Hundreds swarmed onto the ground to uproot the goalposts, while others attacked the grandstand, smashing windows and tearing up carpets in the section occupied, and presumably now vacated, by the Blackburn directors.[32] That teams should be at full strength was one of the original rules of the Football League and clubs which broke this rule were fined, sometimes as much as £250, which was the equivalent of a 10,000 gate. When it was a matter of not having enough players, initially it was the player who failed to arrive who was fined, but by 1904 the emphasis had shifted to disciplining the club for not having sufficient reserves available. As with late starts, these policies seem to have been successful and by 1914 such abuses were rare.[33]

The most effective segregation policy, so far as disorder at sports events was concerned, was the absolute exclusion of undesirable spectators. Traditionally segregation at race meetings had been a matter of employing a few burly pugilists to keep the 'riff-raff' out of the stands; with the development of the enclosed course, however, the lower elements of the racing world were not even to be allowed on the course. In soccer, too, the authorities insisted that clubs exclude known troublemakers and, in cricket, this seems to have been done voluntarily. Northamptonshire, for example, decided to refuse entry to two men who, after a 'very careful investigation', they decided had led the crowd in a demonstration against poor umpiring decisions.[34] Such policies of exclusion became easier with the adoption of the turnstile in the late nineteenth century. This technology also enabled entry to be controlled to the various enclosures, stands and terraces at sports grounds. Such segregation within the crowd was aided in all sports by differential pricing. Another method adopted in both racing and cricket was the reservation of particular areas for club members, entry to which was controlled by strict social vetting and high subscription costs. In soccer, club membership was more open socially, but apart from directors and their friends, viewing privileges were restricted to first claim on seats for those with season tickets. Physical segregation and differential pricing were primarily economic policies designed to increase returns by supplying different spectator markets, but they did have the indirect effect of making it easier to contain disorder to the areas in which it broke out, and perhaps also enabling it to be put down more readily.[35] Unfortunately it is also possible that segregation may have encouraged disorder. Crowd density is a significant influence on spectator behaviour and it may have been intensified in certain areas; moreover, if segregation led to the grouping-together of similarly motivated, one-class spectators, then, as communication is easier when people have pre-existing group ties, the dynamics of crowd disorder could spread faster.[36] The soccer authorities were also insistent that fans be kept off the playing area, partly to prevent matches having to be abandoned because of encroachment but also to lessen the chance of assault on players or officials.[37] This was not an easy task in the early days, when many clubs, even those with enclosed grounds, did not separate the spectators from the pitch by anything more than a painted line. However, they began to take action when fines were imposed and replays were ordered because encroachment had interfered with games and, at stadia where invading spectators committed assaults, railings or fences were demanded on penalty of ground closure. The problem in cricket was that the playing surface itself might be damaged and in the early twentieth century some counties began to restrict spectators from trespassing on the pitch even during the intervals between play.[38]

Most sports promoters also took action to try to control the drinking and gambling associated with their sport. A reduction in gambling, or at least more stringently regulated gambling, could lead to fewer precipitating events, and less alcohol might prevent some sections of the crowd from becoming too uninhibited and possibly also result in a less false perception of occurrences on the field. Nevertheless, drinking remained an accepted part of sports spectatorship and thus, even when access was limited by the ground or course authorities, was a possible contributory factor to crowd disturbance. Racing had a symbiotic relationship with gambling and could not afford to do without it, but, with the emergence of the enclosed, gate-money course, gambling was restricted to betting on the races and the cardsharps, thimblemen and even/odd table operators were no longer welcomed. There seems to have been no gambling problems at cricket matches, but certainly in soccer some spectator misconduct was associated with betting.[39] In 1892 the Football Association required clubs 'to take all reasonable measures to prevent gambling by spectators' and five years later, following several court decisions, bills were posted on all grounds pointing out the illegality of gambling on the terraces.[40] Firm action by the clubs and police drastically reduced the volume of betting taking place at the grounds, but could not eliminate it.[41] Moreover, in the immediate pre-war years coupon betting developed. Thus spectators could well have had a bet on the match which they were watching and this could have adversely affected their behaviour.[42]

Preventing betting at matches, keeping the crowd segregated, ejecting or prohibiting troublesome spectators, and stopping field invasions and encroachment, necessitated the use of control agents in the form of gatemen, stewards and police. Their basic function was to enforce compliance with regulations and to deter miscreants, but the stewards and police were also there to contain any trouble which did break out, as they most certainly did at Blackburn in 1900 and Stockport in 1912.[43] Gatemen at the enclosed race meetings improved in calibre once they became subject to Jockey Club licence, and the best of them would be employed at many meetings; by travelling the racing circuits they were able to familiarise themselves with defaulting bookmakers and itinerant troublemakers.[44] Gatemen at cricket, and especially at football matches, possibly found such identification easier because of the more regular nature of their events. Law and order outside the grounds and racecourses was part of the normal duties of the police, but payment had to be made for their use inside. The English soccer authorities expected clubs to provide sufficient police protection to keep the crowd in order, but in Scotland the decision as to numbers was left to the relevant police department.[45]

IV

Crowd disorder could not be totally eliminated. Not all the triggers to disturbance could be removed. Little could be done, for example, about heat-of-the-moment violence on the field of play. Nor were the perceptions and attitudes of the partisan spectator likely to be influenced by legislation from the sports authorities or entreaties from the clubs, particularly when drinking and gambling remained an accompaniment of both horse-racing and soccer. For example, even though the Football Association acknowledged that the directors of Sheffield Wednesday had done all that they could to ensure proper conduct at the match against Preston in 1906, local supporters had still assaulted the visiting Preston team on their route from the ground to their hotel.[46] It is also possible that some of the measures intended to solve disorder may actually have worsened the problem. Improved organisation helped swell attendance figures, but increased crowd size and density could have aggravated spectator disorder. Segregation of the crowd could also have increased crowd density in some parts of the grounds.

Nevertheless, it would appear that a combination of repressive and reformative measures by sports promoters and authorities attained some degree of success in improving crowd behaviour. Actions taken to improve the conduct and organisation of sports events did much to reduce the triggers to frustration, confrontation and expressive disorders; segregation of various sections of the crowd and the absolute exclusion of troublesome spectators reduced the danger of confrontation and outlawry disorders; and the stricter controls on gambling and drinking, coupled with the deterrent effect of control agents, lessened the possibility of all kinds of disturbance, except perhaps for remonstrance disorders. If trouble did break out, then the segregation of the crowd, the restricted availability of alcohol, and the presence of the police, generally acted to weaken the contagion dynamics of disorder and to contain the disturbance.

There is some evidence to suggest that crowd behaviour improved at the more commercialised race meetings and soccer matches.[47] By the turn of the century one knowledgeable commentator could claim that 'ruffianism [was] practically unknown' at the enclosed racecourses and in soccer the measures taken 'had the effect of practically putting an end to disorder upon our leading grounds'.[48] Certainly at League club grounds there was a decline in the number of incidents deemed serious enough to warrant Football Association censure. This was especially so when consideration is taken of the number of games played: if the incidents per game are indexed at 1,000 in the period 1895–1901, then the figure for 1904–8 is 779, and for 1909–14 only 464.[49]

The behaviour of cricket crowds, however, allegedly worsened. In the late 1890s one commentator noted 'a marked deterioration . . . in the behaviour of spectators at cricket matches . . . they hoot and yell or applaud accordingly as one side or other drops catches or makes other mistakes in the field' and another maintained that the crowd 'certainly has never been so outspoken in its marks of disapprobation'.[50] Things did not improve. In 1903 Leicestershire felt obliged to display a notice which threatened that 'any person using bad language or addressing unseemly remarks to the players or umpires will be expelled'.[51] An 'undoubted feature' of the 1905 season was 'the increasing desire of spectators to express distaste', and in 1909 it was claimed that 'the practice of guying slow play is on the increase'.[52] The main reason for this was that the wishes of the spectators were not being adequately considered. In particular no official steps were taken over slow and negative play, or time-wasting, both of which were rendering the game less entertaining.[53] Cricket was bringing trouble on itself by taking the crowd's admission fees and then not giving value for money.[54]

But was the conduct of cricket crowds really all that bad? What was being complained of was verbal not physical aggression and such barracking was commonplace and generally accepted as part of the game in both racing and at least *English* soccer.[55] The cricket authorities refused to accept that the paying spectator was not content to remain a passive observer. Their attitudes were epitomised in the remarks of one-time England captain and pillar of the cricketing establishment, P. F. Warner, that the spectator

should not, for instance, boo or jeer at the players. The only time he has a right to act thus is when a player has been obviously guilty of an unsportsmanlike or ungentlemanly action, or is clearly not trying. Then I think he might justifiably express his disapproval in an obvious manner, though the better and more dignified course would be to leave the ground. Too often spectators, ignorant of the finer points of the game, cheer ironically, and even make rude remarks. These people should be dealt with firmly, and told that they will not be allowed to stay in the ground if they persist in their attitude, their sixpence being returned to them. It is contrary to the dignity of any cricket ground to allow the cricketers to be subjected to undeserved censure.[56]

'The truth of it', Warner maintained, 'is that the attitude of the public towards cricket has changed'.[57] What he failed to add was that it was equally true that the attitude of the cricket authorities had not.

Why cricket crowds never became as violent as those at race meetings and soccer matches is a matter for conjecture. Certainly the absence or low level of gambling on cricket reduced one stimulus to disorder. Possibly another answer lies in the larger middle-class element among cricket spectators, for whom structural strains relating to social or economic deprivation might be less intense than for working-class football fanatics or turf gamblers: there seems general agreement that cricket spectators were less partisan than football followers.[58] Or it might simply be a function of the relatively drawn-out nature of cricket matches generally resulting in less tension among the crowd, particularly among one which was usually seated, as this reduces body contact between spectators and also more clearly demarcates personal territory, both factors which lessen the scope for offence to be taken.

Whether sports crowd behaviour would have improved anyway is questionable. It has been argued that in the second half of the nineteenth century rioting was eliminated from English social life, mob disorder conquered and that 'violence, crime and disorder declined to levels unimagined before and, certainly since'.[59] This seems too sweeping. Richter has shown that election violence by rowdy mobs continued through the Victorian and Edwardian eras and has claimed that this political disorder was 'only one manifestation of [a] violent society'.[60] It may be true, as Bailey suggests, that riots in the late nineteenth and early twentieth centuries posed no substantial threat to social order, but this does not necessarily mean that they were less violent than before.[61] Certainly if the social tension and structural strains thesis has any validity, it might have been anticipated that sports crowd behaviour, particularly by working men, would have worsened rather than improved.[62] The working class was becoming increasingly aware and resentful of its relative social, economic and political deprivation. This led to it generally becoming more militant. In political life trade unions swung to the left and the Labour Party was established; in the social sphere class consciousness became more pervasive than before; and in the economic arena trade union membership accelerated, industrial relations became more bitter, strikes, often accompanied by violence, were more frequent, and the degree of labour unrest was unprecedented.[63] Sports fans were not immune from such influences. That crowd behaviour at some commercialised sports events appears to have improved must owe something to the actions taken by the sports promoters, particularly when crowd conduct at their events is contrasted with that of soccer clubs not belonging to either the Football League or the Scottish League, who were the ones primarily being censured by the national and local associations, and with the situation in racing, where 'outside the enclosures the unfortunate state of our racecourses is too notorious to need comment'.[64]

Part VI

A second overview

Athleticism can put into play the most noble as well as the most vile passions; it can develop disinterestedness and the sentiment of honour as well as the love of gain.

Pierre de Coubertin, *Mémoires olympiques*, Paris, 1931, pp. 22–3

Chapter 19

An industrial revolution in sport

During the eighteenth and nineteenth centuries popular sport in Britain was influenced significantly by economic development, particularly industrialisation. The demands of the Industrial Revolution changed working-class leisure by reducing the amount of free time available and by contributing to the pressure which altered the character of many traditional sporting pastimes. Later, however, the productivity-raising innovations associated with industrialisation enabled both incomes to be increased and leisure time to be extended. These parallel developments stimulated a demand for commercialised spectator sport, a demand enhanced by growing urbanisation, which offered entrepreneurs concentrated markets.

What should be stressed is that it was not until the economic benefits of industrialisation filtered down to the mass of the population that a large and regular paying clientele could be relied upon for sports events. Thus the rate of economic development in Britain inevitably restricted the scale of commercialised sport till the late nineteenth century. Income levels in the eighteenth century were such that popular sport, at least at the spectator level, was generally dependent upon patronage; most onlookers could only afford to view what was offered free of charge. Where payment was required events were infrequent and attempts to hold them more regularly failed because of a lack of consumer spending power. Industrialisation eventually brought rises in real income, but the Industrial Revolution was a much more drawn-out process than its nomenclature implies and, although industrial workers made real-income gains from the 1820s on, they remained a distinct minority of the occupied population well beyond that date. Moreover, not until the widespread adoption of steam power in the mid nineteenth century did productivity increases allow a general reduction in industrial working hours. Hence the situation by 1840 was one of a growing group of industrial workers with rising incomes, but generally without the leisure time of their counterparts in more traditional occupations, who, however, lagged behind the industrial employees in earning power. From then on, individual economic advancement joined forces with railway development to stimulate the development of a market for spectator sport and, by the late nineteenth century, commercialised sport was a growth point in the British economy.

Indeed it can be claimed that sport itself had undergone an industrial revolution. Certainly eighteenth-century, and possibly even early nine-teenth-century, spectators may have had some difficulty in recognising much that was familiar had they been transported forward in time to be part of the vast throng watching the F. A. Cup final at Crystal Palace, an Ashes test match at Old Trafford, or a race meeting at one of the ubiquitous enclosed courses. They may have discerned an element of mob football in a rugby game but hardly so in soccer, where skill and tactics had replaced brute force and ignorance; overarm bowling on a manicured pitch would be a far cry from single-wicket matches at the back of the alehouse; and what had happened to the portly owner-riders in the stampede of two-year-olds carrying lightweight professional jockeys? Elsewhere, gloved combatants were less bloodied than their prizefighting predecessors; golfers far outdrove their forebears, thanks to modern technology; and, unrecognisable to ancient eyes, two- and four-wheeled racers chased around specially constructed tracks. Some of these changes might have been appreciated but perhaps less so the greatest change of all – that now they had to pay for the pleasure of being sports spectators.

This industrialisation of British sport can be charted as the working-out of supply and demand in the market place. Favourable changes in demand parameters, particularly time and income, encouraged the injection of factors of production into the supply of sport and the application of modern technology in the form of drainage and stand construction to combat the weather and allow regular and more intensive use of facilities. Those involved in the burgeoning sports industry did not merely play games. Like other businesses sports organisations were involved in purchasing equipment, in renting or buying premises, in recruiting, training and paying personnel, in promoting their product, and in generating revenue.

Yet the relationship between sport and commerce was a complex one for, unlike much conventional business, including other suppliers of commercialised leisure, many sports promoters were not necessarily in pursuit of profit. Admittedly some bloodstock breeders and racehorse owners were in their sport for the economic rewards, but others of the racing fraternity expended their money more as consumption than investment. This lack of profit orientation applied even more to gate-money team sports: here English soccer clubs tended most towards being profit-maximisers but even they generally fell far short of the ideal type. Although revenue was important to ensure a club's financial stability, for most committees or boards profits took second place to playing performance.

Like its economic counterpart, the industrial revolution in sport had social ramifications. As professionalism impinged on amateur fields gentlemen were forced to retreat before the players, though they did not always go quietly. Even more vociferous were the large crowds attracted to commercialised spectator sport: clearly working-class consumption of this particular brand of popular culture had bypassed the supposed sporting virtues of muscular Christianity.

Social historians have recognised such consequences stemming from the industrialisation of British sport, but economic historians have too often marginalised sport and neglected it; for example, sport has rarely featured in the discussion of Britain's economic performance in the late nineteenth century, and of the role of the entrepreneur and the development of new industries at that time. One reason for this could be the 'peculiar economics' prevailing in many of the markets for sport and sportspersons. It is high time that economic historians cast off their profit-oriented blinkers and studied the development of an industry to which conventional economic analysis is not always applicable. The industrial revolution in sport deserves similar attention to that which has been given to its economic namesake.

Appendices

Appendix 1: Shareholders and shareholding in Scottish and English sport

APPENDIX 1a   An occupational and spatial analysis of members and shareholders in Scottish soccer clubs before 1915[a]

	Aberdeen		Airdrieonians		Ayr United		Celtic						Clyde	
Members or shareholders[b] / Public or private company / Size of share / Year[c] / Nominal capital	S/h Public 10s. 1903 £1,500		S/h Private £1 1902 £1,000		S/h Public 10s. 1910 ?		Members 1897		S/h Public £1 1897 £5,000		S/h Public £1 1897-8 £5,000		S/h Public £1 1908 ?	
	No.	%[d]	No.	%	No.	%	No.	%	No.	%	No.	%	No.	%
Members or shareholders by occupational groups[e]														
A	—	—	—	—	—	—	1	0.5	—	—	—	—	—	—
B	10	3.6	1	11.1	4	11.4	4	2.1	1	1.4	1	1.9	—	—
C	7	2.5	—	—	1	2.9	10	5.3	2	2.7	—	—	1	3.1
D	22	8.0	1	11.1	4	11.4	21	11.1	18	24.7	17	32.7	6	18.8
E	33	12.0	5	55.5	8	22.9	25	13.2	17	23.3	12	23.1	11	34.4
F	6	2.2	—	—	4	11.4	8	4.2	2	2.7	1	1.9	4	12.5
G	47	17.1	1	11.1	4	11.4	11	5.8	2	2.7	3	5.8	4	12.5
H	5	1.8	—	—	—	—	—	—	—	—	—	—	—	—
I	113	41.1	1	11.1	9	25.7	63	33.2	24	32.9	14	26.9	6	18.8
J	17	6.2	—	—	1	2.9	29	15.3	4	5.5	3	5.8	—	—
K	15	5.5	—	—	—	—	18	9.5	3	4.1	1	1.9	—	—
L Total traced	275 (12)	100.0	9 (1)	100.0	35 (2)	100.0	190 (12)	100.0	73	100.0	52 (2)	100.0	32	100.0
Shareholdings by occupational groups[e]														
A	—	—	—	—	—	—			—	—	—	—	—	—
B	103	7.0	1	7.1	25	11.2			300	6.4	350	7.0	—	—
C	64	4.4	—	—	5	2.2			50	1.1	50	1.1	5	1.9
D	272	18.5	1	7.1	50	22.3			2,090	44.5	2,180	43.8	77	30.0
E	262	17.8	10	71.4	65	29.0			1,140	24.3	810	16.3	115	44.7
F	50	3.4	—	—	17	7.6			110	2.3	300	6.0	22	8.6
G	226	15.4	1	7.1	11	4.9			230	4.9	265	5.3	21	8.2
H	11	0.7	—	—	—	—			—	—	—	—	—	—
I	405	27.5	1	7.1	47	21.0			474	10.1	796	16.0	17	6.6
J	33	2.2	—	—	2	0.8			270	5.7	270	5.4	—	—
K	45	3.1	—	—	—	—			35	0.7	10	0.2	—	—
L Total traced	1,471 (61)	100.0	14	100.0	222 (7)	100.0			4,699	100.0	4,981 (19)	100.0	257	100.0
Members or shareholders resident locally[f]	279	97.2	9	100.0	36	97.3	198	98.0	70	95.9	51	94.4	31	96.9
Shares held locally[f]	1,477	96.4	14	100.0	229	100.0			4,349	92.6	4,650	93.0	225	87.5

287

Appendix 1a (cont.)

	Cowdenbeath		Dumbarton				Dundee Football and Athletic Club						Dundee Hibernian		East Fife	
Members or shareholders[b]	S/h Public		Members		S/h Public		Dundee S/h Private		S/h Private		S/h Private		S/h Private		S/h Public	
Public or private company / Size of share / Year[c] / Nominal capital	5s. 1905		1914		£1 1914 £1,000		£1 1897 ?		£1 1900–2 £1,000		£1 1912 £1,000		£1 1909 £1,000		£1 1911 ?	
	No.	%[d]	No.	%	No.	%	No.	%	No.	%	No.	%	No.	%	No.	%
Members or shareholders by occupational groups[e]																
A	—	—	8	3.6	5	8.5	—	—	—	—	—	—	—	—	—	—
B	—	—	8	3.6	5	8.5	—	—	—	—	—	—	—	—	9	12.2
C	1	2.1	6	2.7	5	8.5	1	5.0	2	10.5	4	17.4	—	—	3	4.1
D	6	12.8	7	3.1	8	13.6	2	10.0	—	—	1	4.3	2	13.3	16	21.6
E	13	27.7	5	2.2	3	5.1	7	35.0	5	26.3	4	17.4	1	6.7	9	12.2
F	—	—	15	6.7	4	6.8	—	—	1	5.3	4	17.4	8	53.3	3	4.1
G	—	—	2	0.9	2	3.4	4	20.0	1	5.3	—	—	—	—	7	9.5
H	—	—	—	—	—	—	—	—	1	5.3	5	21.7	2	13.3	1	1.4
I	24	51.1	155	69.2	27	45.8	4	20.0	8	42.1	—	—	—	—	20	27.0
J	3	6.4	12	5.4	—	—	2	10.0	1	5.3	2	8.7	1	6.7	3	4.1
K	—	—	6	1.7	—	—	—	—	—	—	2	8.7	1	6.7	3	4.1
L Total traced	47	100.0	224	100.0	59	100.0	20	100.0	19	100.0	23	100.0	15	100.0	74	100.0
	20		98		32		103		605		420		1,000		1	
Shareholdings by occupational groups[e]																
A	—	—			50	10.7	—	—	—	—	—	—	—	—	—	—
B	—	—			30	6.5	—	—	—	—	—	—	—	—	60	6.0
C	4	0.7			41	8.7	1	1.0	50	8.3	55	13.1	—	—	24	2.4
D	244	42.1			75	16.0	21	20.4	—	—	10	2.4	40	4.0	658	66.1
E	180	31.0			30	6.4	65	63.1	250	41.3	70	16.7	20	2.0	55	5.5
F	—	—			30	6.4	—	—	25	4.1	90	21.4	880	88.0	24	2.4
G	—	—			7	1.5	9	8.7	25	4.1	25	6.0	—	—	86	8.6
H	—	—			—	—	—	—	15	2.5	90	21.4	10	1.0	10	1.0
I	132	22.8			206	43.9	4	3.9	190	31.4	35	8.3	—	—	64	6.4
J	20	3.4			—	—	3	2.9	50	8.3	45	10.7	20	2.0	9	0.9
K	—	—			—	—	—	—	—	—	—	—	30	3.0	6	0.6
L Total traced	580	100.0			469	100.0	103	100.0	605	100.0	420	100.0	1,000	100.0	996	100.0
	20				212		20		19		23		15		4	
Members or shareholders resident locally[f]	67	100.0	321	99.7	89	97.8	20	100.0	19	100.0	23	100.0	15	100.0	72	97.3
Shares held locally[f]	600	100.0			672	98.7	103	100.0	605	100.0	420	100.0	1,000	100.0	980	98.0

Table: Members or shareholders and shareholdings by occupational groups in Scottish football clubs.

	East Stirlingshire[b] S/h Public 5s. 1910 £750 No.	%[d]	Falkirk S/h Public 10s. 1905–6 £3,000 No.	%	Hamilton Academicals Members 1903 No.	%	Hamilton Academicals S/h Public £1 1903 ? No.	%	Heart of Midlothian Members 1903 No.	%	Heart of Midlothian[i] S/h Public £1 1905 £5,000 No.	%	Hibernian S/h Private £1 1905 £2,000 No.	%	Kilmarnock Members 1906 No.	%
Members or shareholders by occupational groups[c]																
A	—	—	3	2.6	—	—	—	—	—	—	—	—	—	—	—	2.9
B	—	—	4	3.4	1	1.4	3	4.5	5	1.3	20	2.3	—	—	7	1.3
C	4	2.9	6	5.2	2	2.8	1	1.5	5	1.3	34	7.9	—	—	3	4.2
D	10	7.3	14	12.1	2	2.8	21	31.8	8	2.1	38	8.9	2	22.2	10	9.2
E	12	8.8	18	15.5	3	4.2	15	22.7	14	3.6	22	5.1	—	—	22	5.0
F	3	2.2	4	3.4	—	1.4	1	1.5	12	3.1	10	2.3	—	—	12	11.7
G	20	14.5	16	13.8	10	14.1	7	10.6	38	9.9	62	14.5	2	22.2	18	2.1
H	5	3.6	3	2.6	2	2.8	—	—	5	1.3	4	0.9	4	44.4	5	51.5
I	76	55.5	43	37.1	45	63.4	17	25.8	230	59.7	178	41.5	1	11.1	123	9.2
J	6	4.3	5	4.3	4	5.6	—	—	64	16.6	62	14.5	—	—	22	2.9
K	1	0.7	—	—	1	1.4	1	1.5	4	1.0	9	2.1	—	—	7	
Total traced L	137	100.0	116	100.0	71	100.0	66	100.0	385	100.0	429	100.0	9	100.0	239	100.0
	1		2[j]		116		9		13		19		—		99	
Shareholdings by occupational groups[c]																
A	—	—	24	1.5			—	—			—	—	—	—		
B	—	—	50	3.1			45	6.1			160	8.2	—	—		
C	46	3.3	75	4.6			5	0.7			206	10.5	—	—		
D	539	38.5	460	28.3			238	32.5			404	20.6	201	22.2		
E	121	8.6	380	23.4			160	21.8			214	10.9	—	—		
F	18	1.3	50	3.1			5	0.7			54	2.8	—	—		
G	112	8.0	283	17.4			92	12.6			161	8.2	202	22.3		
H	58	4.1	6	0.4			—	—			13	0.7	404	44.5		
I	473	33.8	271	16.7			183	25.0			562	28.7	100	11.0		
J	29	2.1	24	1.5			—	—			159	8.1	—	—		
K	4	0.3	—	—			5	0.7			28	1.4	—	—		
Total traced L	1,400	100.0	1,623	100.0			733	100.0			1,961	100.0	907[k]	100.0		
	1		21				73				281[l]		—			
Members or shareholders resident locally[f]	137	99.3	118	100.0	187	100.0	75	100.0	396	99.5	444	99.1	9	100.0	237	99.1
Shares held locally[f]	1,396	99.7	1,644	100.0			806	100.0			2,228	99.4	907	100.0		

Appendix 1a (cont.)

	Motherwell				Partick Thistle						Rangers				St Bernards	
Members or shareholders[b]	Members		S/h		Members		S/h		S/h		Members		S/h		S/h	
Public or private company			Public				Public		Public				Public		Private	
Size of share			£1				£1		£1				£1		£1	
Year[c]	1904		1904		1903		1903		1909–11		1899		1899–1900		1908–9	
Nominal capital			£3,000				?		3,350[m]				£12,000		£1,000	
	No.	%[d]	No.	%	No.	%	No.	%	No.	%	No.	%	No.	%	No.	%
Members or shareholders by occupational groups[e]																
A	2	2.1	1	1.2	—	—	—	—	—	—	2	0.3	1	0.3	—	—
B	2	2.1	2	2.4	6	3.5	2	3.2	1	1.6	22	3.7	9	3.0	1	8.3
C	1	1.0	9	10.8	9	5.3	3	4.8	2	3.2	40	6.8	33	10.8	—	—
D	—	—	6	7.2	16	9.4	27	43.5	31	50.0	23	3.9	28	9.2	5	41.7
E	—	—	4	4.8	15	8.8	8	12.9	5	8.1	83	14.0	28	12.5	—	—
F	1	1.0	5	6.0	5	2.9	3	4.8	4	6.5	11	1.9	12	3.9	3	25.0
G	6	6.2	1	1.2	26	15.3	2	3.2	9	14.5	49	25.2	55	18.0	3	25.0
H	—	—	—	—	2	1.2	3	4.8	—	—	15	2.5	9	3.0	—	—
I	58	59.8	38	45.8	80	47.1	13	21.0	7	11.3	207	35.0	96	31.0	—	—
J	25	25.8	17	20.1	6	3.5	1	1.6	2	3.2	34	5.7	21	6.9	—	—
K	2	2.1	—	—	5	2.9	—	—	—	—	6	1.0	3	1.0	—	—
Total traced L	97	100.0	83	100.0	170	100.0	62	100.0	62	100.0	592	100.0	305	100.0	12	100.0
	343		1		12				?		8		20			
Shareholdings by occupational groups[e]																
A			—	—	—	—	—	—	100	3.0			200	2.4	—	—
B			10	1.6	20	2.5	10	0.3	10	0.3			376	4.5	10	1.7
C			22	3.5	15	1.9	150	4.5	150	4.5			1,100	13.1	—	—
D			205	33.0	457	58.2	2,525	75.4	2,525	75.4			1,090	13.0	345	57.5
E			107	17.2	106	13.5	187	5.6	187	5.6			1,580	18.8	—	—
F			34	5.5	25	3.2	110	3.3	110	3.3			355	4.2	115	19.2
G			9	1.4	20	2.5	98	2.9	98	2.9			1,014	12.1	130	21.7
H			5	0.8	30	3.8	—	—	—	—			170	2.0	—	—
I			168	27.1	107	13.6	130	3.9	130	3.9			2,130	25.4	—	—
J			61	9.8	5	0.6	40	1.2	40	1.2			330	3.9	—	—
K			—	—	—	—	—	—	—	—			45	0.5	—	—
Total traced L			621	100.0	785	100.0	3,350[m]	100.0	3,350	100.0			8,390	100.0	600	100.0
			5										610			
Members or shareholders resident locally[f]	440	100.0	84	100.0	182	100.0	62	100.0	62	100.0	587	97.8	316	97.2	12	100.0
Shares held locally[f]			626	100.0			785	100.0	3,350	100.0			8,849	98.3	600	100.0

		St Johnstone Members		St Johnstone S/h		St Mirren Members		St Mirren S/h	
Members or shareholders[b]		Members		S/h		Members		S/h	
Public or private company		Public		Public				Public	
Size of share				5s.				10s.	
Year[c]		1910		1910–11		1905		1905	
Nominal capital				£750				£4,000	
		No.	%[d]	No.	%	No.	%	No.	%
Members or shareholders by occupational groups[e]	A	1	0.7	—	—	1	0.5	1	0.3
	B	3	2.1	13	13.8	11	5.1	11	3.1
	C	—	—	—	—	5	2.3	10	2.9
	D	2	1.4	5	5.3	10	4.7	27	7.7
	E	4	2.8	17	18.1	17	7.9	44	12.6
	F	3	2.1	8	8.5	11	5.1	17	4.9
	G	12	8.4	9	9.6	38	17.8	61	17.4
	H	4	2.8	1	1.1	6	2.8	6	1.7
	I	71	49.7	29	30.9	100	46.7	139	39.7
	J	30	21.0	10	10.6	10	4.7	27	7.7
	K	13	9.1	2	2.1	5	2.3	7	1.0
Total traced		143	100.0	94	100.0	214	100.0	350	100.0
	L	—		1		240[m]		29	
Shareholdings by occupational groups[e]	A			—	—			15	0.6
	B			167	17.8			92	3.9
	C			—	—			64	2.7
	D			215	23.0			406	17.1
	E			227	24.3			466	19.6
	F			79	8.4			202	8.5
	G			63	6.7			284	12.0
	H			8	0.9			21	0.9
	I			147	15.7			669	28.2
	J			25	2.7			123	5.2
	K			5	0.5			30	1.3
Total traced				936	100.0			2,372	100.0
	L			2				66	
Members or shareholders resident locally[f]		141	98.6	94	98.9		100.0[o]	376	99.2
Shares held locally[f]				918	97.9			2,430	98.6

[a] The analysis was done only for clubs which adopted company status before 1915. Unfortunately renovation and staff problems rendered the Companies Registry somewhat inefficient at the time of my visits and Kilmarnock's shareholders' register could not be found.

[b] The lists of shareholders and shareholdings exclude members except where they purchased shares in addition to those offered specifically to members.

[c] The members' lists refer to the year in which company status was adopted. The shareholders' lists cover the year or years in which the bulk of shares were taken up; a second list refers to a fresh issue of shares.

[d] The percentage for all clubs is of the totals traced, in order to facilitate comparisons between clubs.

[e] Occupation categories are as follows: A. Aristocracy and gentry; B. Upper professional; C. Lower professional; D. Proprietors and employers associated with the drink trade; E. Other proprietors and employers; F. Managers and higher administration; G. Clerical; H. Foremen, supervisors and inspectors; I. Skilled manual; J. Semi-skilled manual; K. Unskilled manual; L. Untraced or unspecified.

[f] Within 25 miles of the ground.

[g] Dundee Football and Athletic Club was dissolved in 1898 and resurrected two years later as Dundee.

[h] Includes 25 shares from previous issue which were not fully paid up because of the death of the subscriber.

[i] The initial Heart of Midlothian Company was created in 1903 but dissolved in 1905 and a second company established.

[j] Includes 20 shares held by Stirlingshire Football Association.

[k] Only 7 shares were issued for cash, the rest were issued for the rights of the allottees as leasees of Easter Road, the Hibernian's ground.

[l] Includes 100 shares held by the Edinburgh and District Tramway Company.

[m] Includes 350 shares of the previous issue on which the subscribers defaulted.

[n] Of the 554 members 405 took up the shares offered to them; of these 191 did not have an occupation specified in the shareholders' register. The remaining 149 members could not be traced at all.

[o] All the 405 traced members were local.

APPENDIX 1b An occupational and spatial analysis of shareholders in some Scottish sports companies

	Hamilton Park Racecourse 1888 £10,000 £100		Lanark Racecourse 1908–12 ? £5		Ayr Racecourse Syndicate 1913[b] £7,000 £5		Glasgow Real Ice-Skating Palace 1895–6 £20,000 £1		Edinburgh Ice Rink 1911–13 £22,000 £1		Edinburgh Lawn Tennis Co. 1877 £2,800 £25	
Year[a] / Nominal capital / Size of share	No.	%[c]	No.	%	No.	%	No.	%	No.	%	No.	%
Shareholders by occupational groups[d]												
A	3	8.3	17	73.9	16	88.9	2	2.3	7	4.3	—	—
B	2	5.6	3	13.0	—	—	21	12.7	31	19.1	24	88.9
C	7	19.4	—	—	—	—	16	9.6	3	1.9	—	—
D	10	27.8	1	4.3	—	—	8	4.8	9	5.6	1	3.7
E	13	36.1	2	8.7	2	11.1	51	30.7	84	51.9	2	7.4
F	—	—	—	—	—	—	11	6.6	13	8.0	—	—
G	1	2.8	—	—	—	—	33	19.9	6	3.7	—	—
H	—	—	—	—	—	—	2	1.2	2	1.2	—	—
I	—	—	—	—	—	—	20	12.0	7	4.3	—	—
J	—	—	—	—	—	—	2	1.2	—	—	—	—
K	—	—	—	—	—	—	—	—	—	—	—	—
Total traced L	36	100.0	23	100.0	18	100.0	166	100.0	162	100.0	27	100.0
(not traced)	3		3		—		86		79		3	
Shareholdings by occupational groups[d]												
A	8	8.7	675	76.1	6,222	88.9	400	5.0	825	5.0	—	—
B	4	4.3	61	6.9	—	—	1,585	20.0	4,583	27.6	72	85.7
C	16	17.4	—	—	—	—	651	8.2	80	0.5	—	—
D	28	30.4	100	11.3	—	—	695	8.8	540	3.2	2	2.4
E	35	38.0	50	5.6	778	11.1	2,845	35.8	9,294	55.9	10	11.9
F	—	—	—	—	—	—	380	4.8	940	5.7	—	—
G	1	1.1	—	—	—	—	442	5.6	113	0.7	—	—
H	—	—	—	—	—	—	2	0.0	110	0.7	—	—
I	—	—	—	—	—	—	819	10.3	147	0.9	—	—
J	—	—	—	—	—	—	120	1.5	—	—	—	—
K	—	—	—	—	—	—	—	—	—	—	—	—
Total traced L	92	100.0	886	100.0	7,000	100.0	7,939	100.0	16,612	100.0	84	100.0
(not traced)	6		45		—		3,683[c]		3,368		7	
Shareholders resident locally[f]	24	61.5	21	80.8	14	77.8	237	94.0	166	68.9	30	100.0
Shares held locally[f]	55	56.1	835	89.7	5,444	77.8	8,798	75.7	13,771	68.9	91	100.0

	Glasgow Swimming Baths 1874[g] £2,500 £5		Dundee Athletic Grounds 1891–2 £1,000 10s.		Aberdeen Skating, Curling and Yachting Co. 1897 £10,000 £1		Aberdeen Cycling and Athletic Association 1889 £1,000 £1		Glasgow Indoor Bowling and Recreation Co. 1913 £2,500 10s.		Edinburgh Cycling Academy 1897 £5,000 £1	
Year[a] / Nominal capital / Size of share	No.	%[c]	No.	%	No.	%	No.	%	No.	%	No.	%
Shareholders by occupational groups[d]												
A	23	7.0	1	0.7	1	2.6	—	—	1	5.9	—	—
B	37	11.2	3	2.0	4	10.5	1	0.7	1	5.9	3	10.7
C	30	9.1	9	6.1	9	23.7	14	9.3	2	11.8	4	14.3
D	13	4.0	8	5.4	—	—	2	1.3	2	11.8	—	—
E	115	35.0	26	17.6	6	15.8	19	12.7	4	23.5	11	39.3
F	6	1.8	2	1.4	3	7.9	4	2.7	—	—	2	7.1
G	53	16.1	49	33.1	2	5.3	16	10.7	4	23.5	4	14.3
H	—	0.7	1	0.7	—	—	2	1.3	—	—	—	—
I	48	14.6	37	25.0	5	13.2	63	42.0	2	11.8	4	14.3
J	4	1.2	10	6.8	4	10.5	19	12.7	1	5.9	—	—
K	—	—	2	1.4	4	10.5	10	6.7	—	—	—	—
Total traced L	329 / 7	100.0	148 / 8	100.0	38 / —	100.0	150 / 2	100.0	17 / 4	100.0	28 / 2	100.0
Shareholdings by occupational groups[d]												
A	61	9.1	2	0.2	25	2.1	—	—	50	6.3	—	—
B	103	15.3	9	1.1	68	5.7	10	1.3	50	6.3	60	3.2
C	51	7.6	106	12.4	325	27.2	80	10.4	45	5.6	255	13.7
D	30	4.5	40	4.7	—	—	7	0.9	70	8.8	—	—
E	190	28.2	342	40.0	215	18.0	128	16.6	275	34.4	1,220	65.6
F	14	2.1	7	0.8	155	12.9	25	3.2	—	—	60	3.2
G	69	10.2	166	19.4	9	0.8	81	10.5	175	21.9	60	3.2
H	—	—	2	0.2	—	—	25	3.2	—	—	—	—
I	143	21.2	137	16.0	215	18.0	247	32.0	110	13.8	205	11.0
J	13	1.9	35	4.1	65	5.4	79	10.2	25	3.1	—	—
K	—	—	8	0.9	120	10.0	90	11.7	—	—	—	—
Total traced L	674 / 126[b]	100.0	854 / 32	100.0	1,197 / —	100.0	772 / 12	100.0	800 / 350[i]	100.0	1,860 / 100	100.0
Shareholders resident locally[f]	329	97.9	156	100.0	37	97.4	150	98.7	19	90.5	30	100.0
Shares held locally[f]	791	98.9	886	100.0	1,172	97.9	769	98.1	1,080	93.9	1,960	100.0

Appendix 1b (cont.)

[a] All analysis is based on the shareholders in the year or years in which the bulk of the shares were taken up. The year indicated is that in which the shares were first issued.

[b] For some years prior to the incorporation of the Syndicate a body of private individuals had subleased Ayr racecourse from the Western Meeting Club. At the time of incorporation a sum of £6,787 17s. 10d. stood to their credit. This sum was transferred to the credit of the Syndicate and the 7,000 shares issued to the previous promoters, who all became members of the Syndicate. The difference of £112 2s. 2d. represented goodwill.

[c] The percentage is of the totals traced, in order to facilitate comparisons.

[d] Occupational categories are as follows: A. Aristocracy and gentry; B. Upper professional; C. Lower professional; D. Proprietors and employers associated with the drink trade; E. Other proprietors and employers; F. Managers and higher administration; G. Clerical; H. Foremen, supervisors and inspectors; I. Skilled manual; J. Semi-skilled manual; K. Unskilled manual; L. Untraced or unspecified.

[e] Includes 1,500 shares held by the National Ice Producing Company of London.

[f] Within 25 miles of course, ground, rink, or headquarters of the concern.

[g] Although shares were issued from 1870 the early registers did not give occupations, so the first year of more complete information was taken.

[h] Includes 118 shares held by the Arlington Swimming Club, who frequently leased the baths.

[i] Held by four women with no other information given.

APPENDIX 1c An occupational and spatial analysis of shareholders of English soccer clubs before 1915

	Aston Villa 1896 £10,000 £5		Blackburn Rovers 1897 £8,000 £1		Blackpool 1896 £5,000 £1		Bolton Wanderers 1895 £4,000 £1		Bristol City 1897 £2,500 £1		Bradford City 1908 £7,000 £1		Burnley 1898 £4,000 £1	
Year[a] / Nominal capital / Size of share	No.	%[b]	No.	%	No.	%	No.	%	No.	%	No.	%	No.	%
Shareholders by occupational groups[c]														
A	15	2.3	2	2.0	4	5.7	1	0.5	5	2.6	2	0.4	—	—
B	39	6.1	2	2.0	1	1.4	11	5.5	13	6.8	14	2.9	14	9.1
C	56	8.8	6	6.1	2	2.9	6	3.0	2	1.0	14	2.9	8	5.2
D	37	5.8	16	16.3	12	17.1	22	11.1	14	7.3	19	3.9	12	7.8
E	165	25.8	22	22.4	18	25.7	42	21.1	20	10.4	67	13.8	37	24.0
F	47	7.4	10	10.2	7	10.0	12	6.0	5	2.6	15	3.1	10	6.5
G	114	17.8	5	5.1	3	4.3	22	11.1	27	14.1	94	19.4	16	10.4
H	10	1.6	8	8.2	—	—	6	3.0	6	3.1	14	2.9	5	3.2
I	135	21.1	22	22.4	18	25.7	65	32.7	80	41.7	179	36.9	41	26.6
J	18	2.8	5	5.1	5	7.1	9	4.5	8	4.2	29	6.0	8	5.2
K	3	0.5	—	—	—	—	3	1.5	12	6.3	38	7.8	3	1.9
L Total traced	639	100.0	98	100.0	70	100.0	199	100.0	192	100.0	485	100.0	145	100.0
	45		1		1		12		56		28		3	
Shareholdings by occupational groups[c]														
A	90	6.1	26	2.3	227	20.7	25	0.8	28	6.7	20	0.6	—	—
B	103	7.0	35	3.1	100	9.1	171	5.7	33	7.9	240	7.6	112	10.9
C	87	5.9	29	2.6	10	0.9	130	4.3	6	1.4	97	3.1	20	1.9
D	205	13.9	287	25.3	422	38.5	751	25.0	104	24.8	577	18.2	192	18.6
E	387	26.2	337	29.7	128	11.7	1,096	36.5	65	15.5	1,367	43.1	312	30.2
F	86	5.8	185	16.3	107	9.8	111	3.7	14	3.3	70	2.2	64	6.2
G	269	18.2	30	2.6	8	0.7	186	6.2	40	9.5	180	5.7	94	9.1
H	18	1.2	54	4.8	—	—	14	0.5	8	1.9	25	0.8	55	5.3
I	197	13.3	130	11.4	81	7.4	440	14.7	100	23.9	480	15.1	154	14.9
J	30	2.0	23	2.0	14	1.3	60	2.0	8	1.9	77	2.4	26	2.5
K	4	0.3	—	—	—	—	15	0.5	13	3.1	42	1.3	3	0.3
L Total traced	1,476	100.0	1,136	100.0	1,097	100.0	2,999	100.0	419	100.0	3,175	100.0	1,032	100.0
	259[d]		10		5		91		70		444		9	
Shareholders resident locally[e]	664	97.1	96	97.0	692	97.2	205	97.2	247	99.6	498	97.1	157	100.0
Shares held locally[e]	1,649	95.0	1,121	97.8	1,087	98.6	3,024	97.9	483	98.7	3,360	92.8	1,041	100.0

295

Appendix 1c (cont.)

		Bury 1897 £5,000 £1		Derby 1896 £5,000 £1		Eastville Rovers[f] 1897 £1,500 £1		Everton 1892 £2,500 £1		Fulham 1904 £7,500 10s.		Grimsby Town 1891 £1,500 £1		Huddersfield Town 1912[g] £10,000 £1		Liverpool 1893 £15,000 £1		Manchester City 1894 £2,000 £1	
Year[a] / Nominal capital / Size of share		No.	%[b]	No.	%	No.	%	No.	%	No.	%	No.	%	No.	%	No.	%	No.	%
Shareholders by occupational groups[c]	A	1	0.4	6	3.8	—	—	4	0.9	21	6.9	1	0.9	2	5.1	—	—	—	—
	B	10	4.3	33	20.9	2	4.8	23	5.1	9	3.0	2	1.9	2	5.1	5	11.4	1	0.5
	C	7	3.0	10	6.3	6	14.3	8	1.8	19	6.2	6	5.7	1	2.6	6	13.6	9	4.2
	D	24	10.3	8	5.1	5	11.9	19	4.2	8	2.6	4	3.8	2	5.1	2	4.5	19	9.0
	E	35	15.0	25	15.8	9	21.4	54	12.0	42	13.8	36	34.0	17	43.6	4	9.1	28	13.2
	F	16	6.9	18	11.4	2	4.8	32	7.1	17	5.6	8	7.5	3	7.7	10	22.7	9	4.2
	G	35	15.0	25	15.8	2	4.8	136	30.2	41	13.4	11	10.4	4	10.3	12	27.3	22	10.4
	H	3	1.3	1	0.6	3	7.1	7	1.6	4	1.3	—	—	—	—	3	6.8	3	1.4
	I	75	32.2	27	17.1	8	19.0	126	28.0	115	37.7	25	23.6	8	20.5	2	4.5	78	36.8
	J	23	9.9	5	3.2	4	9.5	35	7.8	24	7.9	3	2.8	—	—	—	—	27	12.7
	K	4	1.7	—	—	1	2.4	6	1.3	5	1.6	10	9.4	—	—	—	—	16	7.5
Total traced	L	233	100.0	158	100.0	42	100.0	450	100.0	305	100.0	106	100.0	39	100.0	44	100.0	212	100.0
		23		33		24		21		7		4		1		2		1	
Shareholdings by occupational groups[c]	A	5	0.3	90	7.4	—	—	37	1.7	313	8.5	5	1.1	56	5.1	—	—	—	—
	B	93	6.0	371	30.4	30	4.0	199	9.1	279	7.6	12	2.7	31	2.8	138	20.5	5	1.0
	C	15	1.0	55	4.5	142	19.0	39	1.8	128	3.5	15	3.3	5	0.5	36	5.3	26	5.3
	D	312	20.3	75	6.1	243	32.5	215	9.8	175	4.8	20	4.4	51	4.6	200	29.7	157	32.0
	E	387	25.1	141	11.5	233	31.1	249	11.3	1,197	32.6	306	67.8	800	72.2	24	3.6	58	11.8
	F	154	10.0	107	8.8	21	2.8	191	8.7	247	6.7	11	2.4	52	4.7	73	10.8	33	6.7
	G	110	7.1	129	10.6	17	2.3	555	25.3	228	6.2	21	4.7	13	1.2	67	10.0	28	5.7
	H	15	1.0	5	0.4	12	1.6	46	2.1	16	0.4	—	—	—	—	113	16.8	5	1.0
	I	346	22.5	223	18.3	28	3.7	499	22.7	947	25.8	48	10.6	100	9.0	22	3.3	114	23.2
	J	91	5.9	25	2.0	21	2.8	149	6.8	131	3.6	3	0.7	—	—	—	—	46	9.4
	K	12	0.8	—	—	1	0.1	18	0.8	9	0.2	10	2.2	—	—	—	—	18	3.7
Total traced	L	1,540	100.0	1,221	100.0	748	100.0	2,197	100.0	3,670	100.0	451	100.0	1,108	100.0	673	100.0	490	100.0
		116		272		201		99		40		14		5		125		5	
Shareholders resident locally[e]		256	100.0	181	94.8	63	95.5	461	97.8	310	99.1	110	100.0	40	100.0	46	100.0	208	97.7
Shares held locally[e]		1,656	100.0	1,372	91.9	838	88.3	2,230	97.1	3,600	97.0	465	100.0	1,113	100.0	798	100.0	458	92.4

296

	Middlesbrough 1892 £2,000		Newcastle East End[f] 1890 £1,000		Oldham Athletic 1906 £2,000		Plymouth 1910 £1,000		Portsmouth 1912 £10,000				Preston North End 1893 £5,000		Queen's Park Rangers 1898 £5,000		Reading 1898 £6,000	
Size of share	£1		10s.		10s.		5s.		8s.		£1		£1		10s.		10s.	
	No.	%[b]	No.	%	No.	%	No.	%	No.	%	No.	%	No.	%	No.	%	No.	%
Shareholders by occupational groups[c]																		
A	1	0.3					22	13.2	12	10.3	9	7.5	9	2.3	14	6.4	10	5.3
B	15	4.3	2	1.9	7	5.2	11	6.6	14	12.0	17	14.2	22	5.7	3	1.4	5	2.7
C	24	6.9	2	1.9			3	1.8	4	3.4	7	5.8	15	3.9	5	2.3	6	3.2
D	6	1.7	8	7.7	9	6.7	29	17.4	10	8.5	21	17.5	40	10.4	8	3.6	6	3.2
E	37	10.7	24	23.1	17	12.7	26	15.6	22	18.8	34	28.3	78	20.3	21	9.5	25	13.3
F	12	3.5	7	6.7	11	8.2	22	13.2	6	5.1	5	4.2	26	6.8	3	1.4	11	5.9
G	45	13.0	13	12.5	12	9.0	13	7.8	10	8.5	3	2.5	38	9.9	83	37.7	20	10.6
H	11	3.2	3	2.9	6	4.5	3	1.8	1	0.9	1	0.8	17	4.4	2	0.9	1	0.5
I	147	42.5	39	37.5	50	37.3	32	19.2	32	27.3	19	15.8	118	30.6	67	30.5	60	31.9
J	33	9.5	5	4.8	12	9.0	5	3.0	6	5.1	4	3.3	15	3.9	10	4.5	31	16.5
K	15	4.3	1	1.0	10	7.5	1	0.6					7	1.8	4	1.8	13	6.9
L Total traced	346	100.0	104	100.0	134	100.0	167	100.0	117	100.0	120	100.0	385	100.0	220	100.0	188	100.0
(untraced)	4		17		4		26[b]		49		60		4		10		7	
Shareholdings by occupational groups[c]																		
A	2	0.3					335	24.2	425	23.8	200	6.1	76	3.9	181	10.2	294	14.6
B	44	7.0	10	3.0	71	5.5	79	5.7	444	24.9	360	11.0	253	13.0	155	8.8	70	3.5
C	38	6.0	2	0.6			7	0.5	17	1.0	360	11.0	47	2.4	41	2.3	35	1.7
D	26	4.1	47	13.9	207	15.9	358	25.9	180	10.1	800	24.4	422	21.7	115	6.5	51	2.5
E	95	15.0	82	24.3	232	17.9	192	13.9	256	14.3	760	23.2	585	30.1	319	18.0	870	43.1
F	24	3.8	38	11.2	216	16.6	150	10.8	47	2.6	100	3.0	106	5.5	16	0.9	154	7.6
G	71	11.2	42	12.4	105	8.1	74	5.3	38	2.1	160	4.9	114	5.9	483	27.3	70	3.5
H	24	3.8	11	3.3	55	4.2	53	3.8	1	0.1	20	0.6	36	1.9	25	1.4	2	0.1
I	237	37.4	97	28.7	366	28.2	120	8.7	313	17.5	380	11.6	262	13.5	357	20.2	151	7.5
J	54	8.5	7	2.1	29	2.2	15	1.1	63	3.5	140	4.3	27	1.4	69	3.9	289	14.3
K	18	2.8	2	0.6	17	1.3	1	0.1					16	0.8	9	0.5	33	1.6
L Total traced	633	100.0	338	100.0	1,298	100.0	1,384	100.0	1,784	100.0	3,280	100.0	1,944	100.0	1,770	100.0	2,019	100.0
(untraced)	17		38		27		167		561		1,580		8		38		8	
Shareholders resident locally[d]	342	97.7	121	100.0	137	99.3	186	96.4	162	97.6	176	97.8	369	94.9	225	97.8	193	99.0
Shares held locally[e]	635	97.6	376	100.0	1,215	92.5	1,311	85.1	2,289	97.6	4,780	98.4	1,785	91.4	1,770	97.9	2,023	99.8

Appendix 1c (cont.)

	Sheffield United 1899 £20,000				Small Heath 1889 £500		Southampton 1897 £5,000		Stoke 1908 £2,000		Tottenham Hotspur 1898 £8,000		Wednesday[f] 1899 £7,000				West Bromwich Albion 1893 £1,500	
Size of share	£20		£1		10s.		£1		£1		£1		£5		£10		£1	
	No.	%[b]	No.	%	No.	%	No.	%	No.	%	No.	%	No.	%	No.	%	No.	%
Shareholders by occupational groups[c]																		
A	41	12.8	8	7.9	—	—	3	2.4	10	4.7	13	3.1	—	—	4	2.1	9	18.8
B	54	16.9	22	21.8	2	4.8	11	8.7	10	4.7	13	3.1	8	17.4	13	6.8	4	8.3
C	13	4.1	4	4.0	1	2.4	5	3.9	10	4.7	35	8.4	3	6.5	3	1.6	5	10.4
D	22	6.9	12	11.9	3	7.1	12	9.4	33	15.6	21	5.1	1	2.2	15	7.9	17	35.4
E	124	38.9	34	33.7	9	21.4	25	19.7	19	9.0	68	16.4	17	37.0	50	26.2	4	8.3
F	30	9.4	7	6.9	2	4.8	13	10.2	39	18.4	25	6.0	4	8.7	19	9.9	2	4.2
G	16	5.0	5	5.0	8	19.0	17	13.4	4	1.9	89	21.4	3	6.5	13	6.8	—	—
H	—	—	—	—	1	2.4	5	3.9	52	24.5	11	2.7	—	—	2	1.0	—	—
I	18	5.6	9	8.9	14	33.3	27	21.3	28	13.2	107	25.8	10	21.7	64	33.5	7	14.6
J	1	0.3	—	—	2	4.8	7	5.5	7	3.3	29	7.0	—	—	7	3.7	—	—
K	—	—	—	—	—	—	2	1.6	—	—	4	1.0	—	—	1	0.5	—	—
Total traced L	319	100.0	101	100.0	42	100.0	127	100.0	212	100.0	415	100.0	46	100.0	191	100.0	48	100.0
(untraced)	61		6		—		1		25		66		3		5		3	
Shareholdings by occupational groups[c]																		
A	48	13.4	101	14.5	—	—	35	6.1	37	4.0	115	5.7	—	—	6	0.9	172	29.0
B	56	15.6	77	11.0	21	9.6	58	10.1	16	1.7	50	2.5	8	17.0	69	10.9	25	4.2
C	13	3.6	19	2.7	2	0.9	9	1.6	188	20.2	60	3.0	3	6.4	14	2.2	70	11.8
D	22	6.1	133	19.1	21	9.6	147	25.7	150	16.1	198	9.8	1	2.1	67	10.6	203	34.2
E	150	41.9	251	36.0	94	43.1	36	6.3	315	33.8	588	29.2	18	38.3	217	34.2	25	4.2
F	31	8.7	26	3.7	16	7.3	72	12.6	81	8.7	107	5.3	4	8.5	35	5.5	3	0.5
G	19	5.3	24	3.4	27	12.4	64	11.2	8	0.9	502	25.0	3	6.4	27	4.3	—	—
H	—	—	—	—	5	2.3	19	3.3	79	8.5	13	0.6	—	—	6	0.9	—	—
I	18	5.0	69	9.9	30	13.8	88	15.4	51	5.5	261	13.0	10	21.3	108	17.0	95	16.0
J	1	0.3	—	—	2	0.9	41	7.2	7	0.8	112	5.6	—	—	84	13.2	—	—
K	—	—	—	—	—	—	2	0.4	—	—	5	0.2	—	—	2	0.3	—	—
Total traced L	358	100.0	698	100.0	218	100.0	571	100.0	932	100.0	2,011	100.0	47	100.0	635	100.0	593	100.0
(untraced)	70		22		—		1		95		127		3		9		15	
Shareholders resident locally[e]	363	95.5	105	98.1	40	95.2	123	96.1	237	100.0	479	99.6	48	98.0	192	98.0	50	98.0
Shares held locally[e]	400	93.5	700	97.2	216	99.1	566	99.0	1,027	100.0	2,136	99.9	49	98.0	633	98.3	588	96.7

Year[a]		West Ham 1900		Woolwich Arsenal[f] 1910	
Nominal capital		£2,000		£7,000	
Size of share		10s.		£1	
		No.	%[b]	No.	%
Shareholders by occupational groups[c]	A	1[i]	0.7	2	2.2
	B	4	2.8	8	9.0
	C	3	2.1	5	5.6
	D	8	5.6	12	13.5
	E	20	14.0	19	21.3
	F	10	7.0	8	9.0
	G	17	11.9	6	6.7
	H	2	1.4	—	—
	I	45	31.5	17	19.1
	J	16	11.2	9	10.1
	K	17	11.9	3	3.4
Total traced		143	100.0	89	100.0
	L	17		40	
Shareholdings by occupational groups[c]	A	600	42.8	7	0.9
	B	57	4.1	57	6.3
	C	6	0.4	7	0.8
	D	63	4.5	96	10.6
	E	224	16.0	551	60.6
	F	100	7.1	44	4.8
	G	64	4.6	11	1.2
	H	22	1.6	—	—
	I	191	13.6	83	9.1
	J	50	3.6	50	5.5
	K	25	1.8	3	0.3
Total traced		1,402	100.0	909	100.0
	L	40		515[j]	
Shareholders resident locally[e]		156	97.5	118	91.5
Shares held locally[e]		1,411	97.9	1,289	90.5

[a] All analysis is based on the shareholders in the year or years in which the bulk of shares were taken up. The year indicated is that in which the shares were first issued.
[b] The percentage is of the totals traced, in order to facilitate comparisons.
[c] Occupation categories are as follows: A. Aristocracy and gentry; B. Upper professional; C. Lower professional; D. Proprietors and employers associated with the drink trade; E. Other proprietors and employers; F. Managers and higher administration; G. Clerical; H. Foremen, supervisors and inspectors; I. Skilled manual; J. Semi-skilled manual; K. Unskilled manual; L. Untraced or unspecified.
[d] Includes 50 shares held by the Birmingham and Aston Tramway Company.
[e] Defined as within 25 miles of the ground.
[f] Eastville Rovers became Bristol Rovers in 1899; Newcastle East End became Newcastle United in 1892; Small Heath became Birmingham in 1905; Wednesday became Sheffield Wednesday in 1929; and Woolwich Arsenal became Arsenal in 1913.
[g] The Huddersfield club of 1908 was reconstituted in 1912. Pre-existing shareholders could not be distinguished.
[h] One whole sheet with occupations was missing from the Plymouth material.
[i] Although this shareholder, A. F. Hills, was actually the owner of the Thames Iron Works he designated himself as a gentleman. He had inherited the business from his father and had joined the board after an education at Harrow and Oxford. See C. P. Korr, 'West Ham United Football Club and the beginnings of professional football in East London, 1895–1914', *Journal of Contemporary History*, XIII, 1978, p. 215.
[j] Includes two shares held by Glasgow Rangers F. C. and Fulham F. C.

APPENDIX 1d An occupational and spatial analysis of shareholders of some English sports companies before 1915

	Leeds Cricket, Football and Athletic Club 1889 £25,000 £1		Rochdale Hornets 1906 ? 10s.		Warwickshire Cricket Ground 1886 £3,000 £10		Hampshire County Cricket Ground 1894 £8,000 £5		Haydock Park Racecourse 1898 £34,000 £50		Newbury Racecourse 1905 £80,000 £50	
Year[a] / Nominal capital / Size of share	No.	%[b]	No.	%	No.	%	No.	%	No.	%	No.	%
Shareholders by occupational groups[c]												
A	7	2.5	1	0.7	4	20.0	11	16.4	19	26.3	22	38.7
B	49	17.6	10	6.8	7	35.0	25	37.3	3	4.2	9	15.0
C	6	2.2	7	4.8	1	5.0	8	11.9	19	26.3	11	18.3
D	10	3.6	9	6.2	—	—	2	3.0	11	15.3	5	8.3
E	68	24.4	49	33.6	7	35.0	13	19.4	15	20.8	12	20.0
F	28	10.0	12	8.2	—	—	1	1.5	2	2.8	1	1.7
G	52	18.6	12	8.2	1	5.0	5	7.5	3	4.2	—	—
H	1	0.4	1	0.7	—	—	—	—	—	—	—	—
I	47	16.8	43	29.9	—	—	2	3.0	—	—	—	—
J	9	3.2	1	0.7	—	—	—	—	—	—	—	—
K	2	0.7	1	0.7	—	—	—	—	—	—	—	—
Total traced L	279	100.0	146	100.0	20	100.0	67	100.0	72	100.0	60	100.0
	49		—		7		10		2			
Shareholdings by occupational groups[c]												
A	555	5.3	10	0.9	9	13.4	214	29.4	178	30.8	567	48.0
B	4,257	40.9	131	11.4	27	40.3	346	47.5	13	2.3	217	18.4
C	96	0.9	60	5.2	3	4.5	85	11.7	155	26.9	126	10.7
D	925	8.9	117	10.2	—	—	6	0.8	83	14.4	172	14.6
E	2,176	20.9	499	43.5	27	40.3	44	6.0	100	17.3	95	8.0
F	720	6.9	74	6.5	—	—	5	0.7	33	5.7	2	0.2
G	452	4.3	98	8.5	1	1.5	27	3.7	15	2.6	—	—
H	5	—	10	0.9	—	—	—	—	—	—	—	—
I	1,102	10.6	139	12.1	—	—	3	0.4	—	—	—	—
J	96	0.9	5	0.4	—	—	—	—	—	—	—	—
K	35	0.3	4	0.3	—	—	—	—	—	—	—	—

	L											
Total traced	10,419	100.0	1,147	100.0	67	100.0	728	100.0	577	100.0	1,181	100.0
	3,324		—		—		39		70		22	
Shareholders resident locally[d]	301	91.8	140	95.9	14	70.0	64	86.5	33	40.2	12	19.4
Shares held locally[d]	11,051	80.4	1,107	96.5	56	83.6	524	68.3	190	29.4	257	19.7

[a] All analysis is based on the shareholders in the year or years in which the bulk of shares were taken up. The year indicated is that in which the shares were first issued.

[b] The percentage is of the totals traced, in order to facilitate comparisons.

[c] Occupation categories are as follows: A. Aristocracy and gentry; B. Upper professional; C. Lower professional; D. Proprietors and employers associated with the drink trade; E. Other proprietors and employers; F. Managers and higher administration; G. Clerical; H. Foremen, supervisors and inspectors; I. Skilled manual; J. Semi-skilled manual; K. Unskilled manual; L. Untraced or unspecified.

[d] Defined as being within 25 miles of the ground or course.

Appendix 2: Regulations defining amateurism and professionalism in British sports

APPENDIX 2a

Extract from National Hunt Rules

1. Persons who have never ridden for hire, and who are not otherwise disqualified under these rules need no qualification to ride in steeplechases or hurdle races unless the conditions of any such steeplechase or hurdle race require a particular qualification.

2. Qualified riders under these rules are persons who have never ridden for hire, and who are qualified either: (a) as Gentlemen, (b) as Farmers, (c) by Election, (d) as Yeomen when riding at their own regimental meetings.

(a) Riders qualified as gentlemen must be members of the National Hunt Committee, the Irish National Hunt Steeple Chase Committee, or of one of the following Clubs: The Jockey Club, Turf Club of Ireland, Croxton Park, Bibury, Southdown and Ludlow Race Clubs, the New Rooms at Newmarket, the Jockey Clubs of Paris, Berlin, and Vienna, the Army and Navy, Junior Army and Navy, Arthur's, Turf, Boodle's, Brook's, Carlton, Junior Carlton, Guards', Pratt's, Travellers', United Service, White's, the Conservative, the Oxford and Cambridge, the Naval and Military, the Oriental, the Badminton, the Devonshire, the New University, the Windham, the St James's or the United University Club, the Kildare Street, Sackville Street, Hibernian United Services or Stephen's Green Clubs, in Dublin, the Western Meeting (Ayr), or the New Club, Edinburgh; or that they be officers on full pay in the Army or Navy, or persons holding commissions under the Crown, or bearing titles in their own right or by courtesy.

(b) Riders qualified as farmers must be now farming at least 100 acres of land, and their sons if following the same occupation, and for the purposes of this rule a 'farmer' shall be understood to mean one who resides permanently on his farm, working it himself, and deriving therefrom his principal and ostensible means of subsistence.

(c) Persons not qualified as 'gentleman riders' or 'farmers', who are desirous of becoming 'qualified riders', must send their names in for election, with the names of their proposer and seconder, who must be members of the National Hunt Committee, to the Registry Office for publication in at least one 'Calendar' before the day of election. The names of persons elected must be submitted annually to the Committee at the general meeting on the second

Monday in December for re-election. Should any qualified rider subsequently ride for hire or appear in the Forfeit List, or be reported by the Committee of the Subscription Rooms at Newmarket or at Tattersall's as being a defaulter for bets lost on horse-racing, he will lose his qualification, and if a qualified rider by election his name will be erased from the list of qualified riders.

Source: Earl of Suffolk, H. Peek and F. G. Aflalo (eds.), *The Encyclopaedia of Sport*, London, 1900, III, p. 240.

APPENDIX 2b

Extract from the Constitution of the Amateur Rowing Association (as revised 23 April 1894)

No person shall be considered an amateur oarsman, sculler, or coxswain:

1 Who has ever rowed or steered in any race for a stake, money or entrance-fee. (This clause is not to be construed as disqualifying any otherwise duly qualified amateur who previously to April 23rd, 1894, has rowed or steered for a stake, money or entrance-fee in a race confined to members of any one club, school, college, or university.)

2 Who has ever knowingly rowed or steered with or against a professional for any prize.

3 Who has ever taught, pursued, or assisted in the practice of athletic exercises of any kind for profit.

4 Who has ever been employed in or about boats, or in manual labour, for money or wages.

5 Who is or has been by trade or employment for wages a mechanic, artisan or labourer, or engaged in any menial duty.

6 Who is disqualified as an amateur in any other branch of sport.

Source: R. C. Lehmann, *Rowing*, London, 1898, pp. 316–17.

APPENDIX 2c

Extract from the Laws of the Amateur Athletic Association

1 All competitions must be limited to amateurs. This law does not interfere with the right of any club to refuse an entry to its own sports.

As to the Qualification of Competitors

An amateur is one who has never competed for a money prize or staked bet, or with or against a professional for any prize, or who has never taught, pursued, or assisted in the practice of athletic exercise as a means of obtaining a livelihood.

The following exceptions shall be made to this Law, viz:

(a) Amateur athletes shall not lose their amateur status by competing with or against professional football players in ordinary club matches for which no prizes are given, or in cup competitions permitted by the National Football Associations or Rugby Unions of England, Ireland, Scotland or Wales, providing that such competitions or matches form no part of, nor have connection with, any athletic meeting.

(b) Competitions at arms between volunteers and regulars shall not be considered as coming within the scope of the A. A. A. laws.

(c) Competitors in Officers' Races at Naval and Military Athletic Meetings (such races being for officers only, and for which money prizes are not given) shall be exempt from any of the laws of the A. A. A. disqualifying runners for competing at mixed meetings.

(d) The 'Championship of the Army' Race at the Aldershot Sports shall be exempted from the effect of this law.

(e) No person must be allowed to compete while under a sentence of suspension passed by the A. A. A., National Cyclists' Union, Amateur Swimming Association, Amateur Gymnastic Association, Scottish A. A. A. or Irish A. A. A.

(f) No one shall be allowed to compete at any meeting held under the laws of the A. A. A. as 'unattached' for more than one season.

(g) A paid handicapper is not a professional.

(h) A competitor who asks for and/or receives expenses ceases to be an amateur.

As to Prizes

2 No 'value' prize (*i.e.* a cheque on a tradesman) must be offered.

3 No prize must be offered in a handicap of greater value than £10. 10s.

4 Every prize of the value of £5 or upwards must be engraved (when practicable) with the name and date of the meeting.

5 All prizes shall be of the full advertised value, that is, without discount, and must be publicly presented on the grounds on the day of the sports.

6 In no case must a prize and money be offered as alternatives.

Source: Earl of Suffolk, H. Peek and F. G. Aflalo (eds.), *The Encyclopaedia of Sport*, London, 1900, I, p. 62.

APPENDIX 2d

Recommendations of F. A. Sub-Committee on Professionalism

The full report and recommendation of the sub-Committee, as adopted, were these:

No player can be termed an amateur who receives any remuneration or consideration above his necessary hotel and travelling expenses, but under certain conditions professionals, viz. players receiving for playing more than those expenses, may be allowed to take part in all cup, county and inter-association matches, the qualification for their so playing being in each case as follows:

1 *In Cup Matches*: Birth or residence for two years last past within six miles of the ground or headquarters of the Club for which they play.

2 *In County Matches*: As defined in Rule 11, viz., those recognized by the leading county cricket clubs.

3 *In Inter-Association Matches*: Bona fide membership for two years last past of some Club belonging to one of the competing Associations.

n.b. The question in the case of international matches must be left to the decision of the competing nationalities.

This sub-Committee, while they do not wish to debar professionals from serving on their club committees, consider that no professional should be allowed to serve on any association committees, or to represent his own or any other club at any meeting of the Football Association; and further, that no professional should be permitted to play for more than one club in any one season without special permission of the Committee of The Football Association.

Source: G. Green, *The History of the Football Association*, London, 1953, pp. 107–8.

APPENDIX 2e

Extract from the Constitution and Rules of the Scottish Football Association

A player shall not receive any remuneration whatever, either directly or indirectly over and above his actual expenses, which shall be his travelling and hotel expenses, and not more than one day's wage in any week for lost time. A day's wage in any case shall not exceed 5s. But players must not be paid for more than the *actual* time lost. Lost time can be paid to players off work through injuries sustained while playing, provided a medical certificate be obtained for production, in case Committee should desire it. Club committees shall satisfy themselves as far as practicable, that players have actually expended, or lost through absence from work, money to the extent asked for, before payment is made. Players found guilty of professionalism shall be suspended for such time as the Committee may deem expedient. Clubs found guilty of *knowingly* securing the services of any player under such circumstances, or of admitting any player to their membership during his term of suspension, shall be liable to suspension from the Association.

(a) A member of any club belonging to this Association can protest against any player on the ground of professionalism. Said protest to be accompanied by a deposit of one guinea.

(b) Any club inducing a player, by promises of remuneration, to leave his club, shall be declared guilty of professionalism, and shall be liable to suspension from this Association. (Definition of remuneration: any club offering a player money or gifts to induce him to leave his club. Clubs are permitted to provide uniforms and bags to players).

(c) Any club playing a match with a club under the jurisdiction of this Association, which has been declared guilty of professionalism, shall be liable to be declared professional, and suspended from this Association.

(d) The names of clubs and players declared professional shall be posted in the Association Rooms and intimated to the various clubs at periods not exceeding three months.

(e) No player under the jurisdiction of this Association can play with any club or players under the jurisdiction of any other Association without permission.

(f) Any registered professional who has played under the jurisdiction of another Association shall be suspended for a period of not less than one year.

(g) The financial transactions shall be entered in the club-book in detail.

(h) Clubs cannot pay expenses of 4-a-side, 5-a-side, or any number of players less than eleven in teams competing for prizes at amateur sports or tournaments.

(i) Money presents are admissable [*sic*] on occasion of marriage.

(j)   Clubs cannot play paid groundsmen.
(k)   Benefit matches can be sanctioned for players in ill health, provided a medical certificate be produced.
(l)   Any player engaging in a football contest at an athletic meeting for a money prize, shall be held guilty of professionalism.
(m) Suspended clubs cannot play any recognised club during their term of suspension.
(n)   Members of suspended clubs, who have not been declared professionals, can play for any other club.

Clubs must produce their books and documents for inspection at any time the committee may desire.

Source: Scottish Football Annual 1892/93, pp. 21–2.

APPENDIX 2f

Extract from the Rugby Football Union's Rules as to Professionalism

1. Professionalism is illegal.
2. Acts of professionalism are:

By an individual:
(a)   Asking, receiving, or relying on a promise, direct or implied, to receive any money consideration whatever, actual or prospective, any employment or advancement, any establishment in business, or any compensation whatever for playing football or rendering any service to a football organisation; training or loss of time connected therewith; time lost in playing football, or in travelling in connection with football; expenses in excess of the amount actually disbursed on account of reasonable hotel or travelling expenses.
(b)   Transferring his services from one club to another in opposition to rule 6.
(c)   Playing for a club while receiving, or after having received, from such club any consideration whatever for acting as secretary, treasurer, or in any other office, or for doing, or for having done any work or labour about the club's ground or in connection with the club's affairs.
(d)   Remaining on tour at his club's expense longer than is reasonable.
(e)   Giving or receiving any money testimonial, or giving or receiving any other testimonial, except under the authority of this union.
(f)   Receiving any medal or other prize for any competition, except under the authority of this union.
(g)   Playing on any ground where gate money is taken during the close season: in any match or contest where it is previously agreed that less than fifteen players on each side shall take part.
(h)   Knowingly playing with or against any expelled or suspended player or club.
(i)   Refusing to give evidence or otherwise assist in carrying out these rules when requested by this union to do so.
(j)   Being registered as or declared a professional, or suspended by any national union, or by the Football Association.
(k)   Playing within eight days of any accident for which he has claimed or received insurance compensation, if insured under these rules.

(l) Playing in any benefit match connected directly or indirectly with football.

(m) Knowingly playing or acting as referee or touch-judge on the ground of an expelled or suspended club.

By a club or other organisation:

(a) Paying or promising payment, or giving, offering, or promising any inducement as to employment, advancement, or establishment in business, or any compensation whatever, to any player for playing for that club, training, or for travelling expenses to or from any training resort, or for loss of time in connection with training, loss of time while playing or travelling in connection with football, hotel or travelling expenses in excess of the sum actually and reasonably disbursed.

(b) Receiving as a member a member of another club in opposition to rule 6.

(c) Receiving or continuing as a member anyone it may pay or have paid for either regular or occasional services.

(d) Paying for any of its teams, players, officials, or members on tour longer than a reasonable time, or paying for more than a reasonable number.

(e) Giving from its funds, subscribing, or playing a match for any testimonial.

(f) Giving any medal or other prize for any competition except under the authority of this union.

(g) Taking gate money at any ground during the close season, at any match or contest where it is previously agreed that less than fifteen players on each side shall take part.

(h) Knowingly playing or allowing its members to play with or against any expelled or suspended player or club.

(i) Refusing to produce its books or documents, or to allow its officials or members to give evidence, or to assist in carrying out these rules when requested by the union to do so.

(j) Knowingly playing or admitting as a member without the consent of the union any member of an expelled or suspended club, or any expelled or suspended player, or any person registered as a declared professional, or suspended by any National Rugby Union, or by the Football Association.

(k) Knowingly allowing a player to play in its matches within eight days of any accident for which he has received or claimed insurance compensation if insured under these rules.

(l) Playing or allowing its ground to be used for any benefit match connected directly or indirectly with football.

(m) Knowingly allowing its members or teams to play on the ground of any expelled or suspended club.

(n) Refusing to pay within one month any costs or expenses ordered by this union for inquiries held under these rules.

Source: A. Budd *et al.*, *Football*, London, 1900, pp. 84–5.

Notes

1 Is money the root of all evil?

1 W. J. Murray, *The Old Firm*, Edinburgh, 1984, p. 81.
2 *Glasgow Herald*, 19 April 1909; Minutes of Scottish Football Association, 19 April, 7 June 1909.
3 For justification of this generalisation, readers need only sample the popular press (though the electronic media are by no means blameless), particularly after a sports scandal has surfaced.
4 Again the popular press provides sufficient documentation, though, for a detailed example, see the views of sports commentator and ex-Olympic coach, Ron Pickering, as expressed in his 1985 address to the Central Council of Physical Recreation, in which he attributed much that was wrong with modern sport to 'market forces' (*Daily Express*, 22 November 1985).
5 *Yorkshire C. C. C. Year Books*; C. Richardson, *The English Turf*, London, 1901, p. 213; H. MacFarlane, 'Football of yesterday and today: a comparison', *Monthly Review*, XXV, 1906, p. 129; A. Mason, *Association Football and English Society, 1863–1915*, Brighton, 1980, p. 168; Murray, *Old Firm*, p. 36.
6 Prospectus of Newbury Racecourse Company 1905; J. J. Bentley, 'Is football a business?', *World's Work*, 1912, p. 384.
7 Bentley, 'Football', p. 384; W. Vamplew, *The Turf*, London, 1976, p. 96.
8 T. A. Cook, *A History of the English Turf*, London, 1905, pp. xxi–xxii; D. Craig, *Horse-Racing*, London, 1982, p. 55.
9 *Yorkshire C. C. C. Year Book 1905*, pp. 17–18; see also Table 13.11.
10 J. Welcome, *Fred Archer*, London, 1967, p. 88.
11 Mason, *Association Football*, p. 46.
12 See chapter 9.
13 See chapter 15.
14 'Doping', *Badminton Magazine*, XLII, 1913, p. 88.
15 'Association football: a retrospect and lament', *Saturday Review*, 3 March 1900.
16 J. H. Morrison, 'The rise of Newcastle United', in *The Book of Football*, London, 1906, p. 27.
17 J. Hutchinson, 'Some aspects of football crowds before 1914', in *Society for Study of Labour History Conference*, University of Sussex, 1975, p. 11.

18 W. Vamplew, 'Unsporting behaviour: the control of football and horse-racing crowds in England, 1875–1914', in J. H. Goldstein (ed.), *Sports Violence*, New York, 1983, pp. 21–32.

19 See chapter 18.

20 H. Gordon, 'Cricket', in *Victoria County History of Sussex*, II, London, 1907, p. 468.

21 Vamplew, *The Turf*, pp. 89–91.

22 A. Maley, *The Story of Celtic*, Glasgow, 1939, p. 28.

23 E. Midwinter, *W. G. Grace*, London, 1981, pp. 155–6.

24 *Scotsman*, 5 January 1979. See also P. Lovesey, *The Official Centenary History of the Amateur Athletic Association*, London, 1979, pp. 44–6.

25 D. Birley, *The Willow Wand*, London, 1979, pp. 29–37; P. Murphy, *Tiger Smith*, Newton Abbot, 1981, p. 12.

26 G. Williams, 'How amateur was my valley: professional sport and national identity in Wales 1890–1914', *British Journal of Sports History*, II, 1985, p. 262.

27 See, for example, E. H. D. Sewell, 'Rugby football', *Fortnightly Review*, XCII, 1912, p. 755.

28 'Memorable Olympic boilovers', *Sport Magazine*, November 1956, pp. 15–16; G. R. Matthews, 'The controversial Olympic Games of 1908 as viewed by the New York Times and The Times of London', *Journal of Sport History*, VII, 1980, pp. 40–53.

29 W. J. Ford, 'Thoughts on spectators', *Badminton Magazine*, XIII, 1899, p. 529; *Spectator*, 11 July 1896.

30 Sirius, 'Football', *Gentleman's Magazine*, X, 1873, p. 388; 'Football accidents', *Saturday Review*, 10 December 1892.

31 R. P. P. Rowe and C. M. Pitman, *Rowing*, London, 1898, p. 149.

32 For a useful survey of the values espoused, see J. R. Mallea, 'The Victorian sporting legacy', *McGill Journal*, X, 1975, pp. 184–96. That these ideals were essentially middle class is demonstrated by J. Maguire, 'Images of manliness and competing ways of living in late Victorian and Edwardian Britain', *British Journal of Sports History*, III, 1986, pp. 265–87.

33 *Scottish Athletic Journal*, 24 November 1882; W. H. B. Court, *British Economic History, 1870–1914*, Cambridge, 1965, pp. 123–4; P. M. Young, *Manchester United*, London, 1960, p. 36.

34 Minutes of Lancashire C. C. C., 27 September 1892; D. Frith, *The Slow Men*, London, 1985, p. 51.

35 Minutes of Scottish Football Association, 11 February 1913.

36 Vamplew, *The Turf*, p. 164.

37 See chapters 9 and 13.

38 Minutes of Northern Rugby Football Union Committee, 8 May 1902.

2 Comments on the state of play: economic historians and sports history

1 J. Fairgrieve, *Away wi' the Goalie*, London, 1977, p. 121.

2 W. A. Baille-Grohman, 'The shortcomings of our sporting literature', *Fortnightly Review*, LXII, 1902, p. 233.

3 A. Mason, *Association Football and English Society, 1863–1915*, Brighton, 1980, p. 1.

4 W. F. Mandle, 'The professional cricketer in England in the nineteenth century', *Labour History*, XXIII, 1972, pp. 1–3; W. Vamplew, *The Turf*, London, 1976, p. 146.

5 A. Guttmann, 'Recent work in European sport history', *Journal of Sport History*, X, 1983, pp. 35–52; W. J. Baker, 'The state of British sport history', *ibid.*, pp. 53–66; M. L. Adelman, 'Academicians and American athletics: a decade of progress', *ibid.*, pp. 80–106.

6 *Economic History Review*, XXXVI, 1983, pp. 586–625. It is salutary for economic historians to note that, in an American Historical Association study which ranked journals according to the ratio of articles published to citations of those articles in other journals, the *Journal of Sport History* was in seventh place, ahead of both the *Economic History Review* and the *Journal of Economic History* (American Historical Association, *Newsletter*, XXIII, 1985, pp. 12–13). There are signs of change in the profession. Slightly more articles are being listed in the *Economic History Review* bibliographic survey: 13 for 1983, 8 for 1984 and 13 again for 1985 (*Economic History Review*, XXXVII, 1984, pp. 563–608; XXXVIII, 1985, pp. 597–636; XXXIX, 1986, pp. 612–51).

7 Ironically even in an article by D. C. Coleman entitled 'Gentlemen and players', *Economic History Review*, XXVI, 1973, pp. 92–116.

8 W. F. Mandle, 'Sports history', in G. Osborne and W. F. Mandle (eds.), *New History: Studying Australia Today*, Sydney, 1982, p. 83.

9 A. H. Cole, 'Perspectives on leisure time business', *Explorations in Entrepreneurial History*, I, 1963–4, Supplement, p. 1.

10 For a review of the literature, see J. Cairns, N. Jennett and P. J. Sloane, 'The economics of professional team sports: a survey of theory and evidence', *Department of Political Economy Discussion Paper 84–06*, University of Aberdeen, 1984, pp. 15–25.

11 Quoted in J. A. Mangan, 'Athletics: a case study of the evolution of an educational ideology', in B. Simon and I. Bradley (eds.), *The Victorian Public School*, Dublin, 1975, p. 158.

12 W. C. Neale, 'The peculiar economics of professional sport', *Quarterly Journal of Economics*, LXXVIII, 1964, p. 2.

13 Cairns *et al.*, 'Economics of team sports', pp. 5–14.

14 On the cost of pheasants, see R. Carr, 'Country sports', in G. E. Mingay (ed.), *The Victorian Countryside*, II, London, 1981, p. 482. On horse owners and club directors, see chapters 8–10.

15 D. Birley, *The Willow Wand*, London, 1979.

16 Two examples will suffice. Steven Tischler, in his undoubted major contribution to sports history, *Footballers and Businessmen*, New York, 1981, appears to accept balance sheet figures at face value when he notes that some clubs exhibited only 'modest' profits, but he confuses *net* with *gross* profit figures and does not consider how much undistributed profit was ploughed back into facilities and transfer fees. He argues that profits were the prime motive in English League football, but fails to identify how the policies of a profit-seeking directorate would have differed from those pursued by boards

who put premierships before profits. In a very different work, Foundation Dams of the American Quarterhorse, Norman, 1982, one of the most esoteric pieces of feminist literature ever published – basically the life histories of eight hundred or so quarterhorse dams – Robert Denhardt implicitly suggests that the economic rationality of breeders has done much to improve the quality of the breed. One can question, however, the weighting of the variables entering into their calculations in that, for a long time, conformation was regarded as being as important as performance.

17 For a recent stimulating discussion, see S. Hardy, 'Entrepreneurs, organisations, and the sport marketplace: subjects in search of historians', *Journal of Sport History*, XIII, 1986, pp. 14–33.

18 Vamplew, *The Turf*, p. 194; H. Cunningham, *The Volunteer Force*, London, 1975, p. 2.

19 Quoted in J. H. Clapham, 'Economic history as a discipline', in E. R. A. Seligman (ed.), *Encyclopaedia of the Social Sciences*, New York, 1963, V, p. 328.

3 Popular recreation before the Industrial Revolution

1 Although, for ease of explanation, this chapter adopts a relatively static approach, it is not assumed that recreational activity remained unchanged throughout the centuries preceding industrialisation. A reading of R. W. Malcolmson, *Popular Recreations in English Society, 1700–1850*, Cambridge, 1973, and D. Brailsford, *Sport and Society*, London, 1967, clearly shows that this was not the case. It is also appreciated that pre-industrialised Britain was not an entity and that much of this chapter is most applicable to England: even so, readers will be aware of local variations in recreational practices attributable to economic, geographic and religious diversity.

2 T. S. Ashton, *Economic Fluctuations in England, 1700–1800*, Oxford, 1959, pp. 3–10; I. Blanchard, 'Labour productivity and work psychology in the English mining industry, 1400–1600', *Economic History Review*, XXXI, 1978, pp. 2–3; D. C. Coleman, *The Economy of England, 1450–1750*, Oxford, 1977, p. 71; B. A. Holderness, *Pre-Industrial England*, London, 1976, pp. 2–4.

3 D. C. Coleman, 'Labour in the English economy of the seventeenth century', *Economic History Review*, VIII, 1955–6, p. 290; J. Mokyr, 'Demand versus supply in the Industrial Revolution', *Journal of Economic History*, XXXVI, 1977, p. 63; E. P. Thompson, 'Time, work-discipline and industrial capitalism', *Past and Present*, XXXVIII, 1967, p. 71.

4 Thompson, 'Time', pp. 59–60.

5 H. Freudenberger and G. Cummins, 'Health, work and leisure before the Industrial Revolution', *Explorations in Economic History*, XIII, 1976, pp. 1–12. How short they believed the working week to be is unclear. At one stage they argue that averaged over the year it 'may have been in the vicinity of 30 hours' (p. 1). Later, however, they state that 'at the outside the average work week would have been about 58 hours, a figure that is obtained by assuming a 12 hour day and deducting Sundays and official holidays' (p. 6). Whether climate, illness and voluntary time off could account for almost a 50%

reduction is not discussed. Theoretically energy scarcity could have led to a
different work–leisure pattern to that envisaged by Freudenberger and
Cummins, in that time could have been used as a partial substitute for energy:
the option of regulating the pace and physical effort of work was open to
task-work labourers and independent farmers and craftsmen. Empirical
testing of either pattern awaits better data.

6 W. H. Hoskins, 'Harvest fluctuations in English economic history 1480–
1619', *Agricultural History Review*, XI, 1964, pp. 28–46; W. H. Hoskins,
'Harvest fluctuations in English economic history 1620–1759', *Agricultural
History Review*, XVI, 1968, pp. 15–31. See also A. B. Appleby, *Famine in
Tudor and Stuart England*, Stanford, 1978; and R. B. Outhwaite, 'Food crises
in early modern England: patterns of public response', in *Economic Fluc-
tuations and Policy Responses in Pre-Industrial Europe*, Theme B7 Seventh
International Economic History Congress, Edinburgh, 1978, pp. 367–74.

7 Coleman, *Economy of England*, p. 17; Holderness, *Pre-Industrial England*,
pp. 12–13.

8 Thompson, 'Time', p. 71. Students may appreciate this point most easily. How
more intense does work become as essay deadlines approach, or even pass?

9 This was commented upon by many contemporary writers with respect to
agricultural *and* industrial workers (both rural and urban). See Coleman,
Economy of England, pp. 290–1; and P. Mathias, *The Transformation of
England*, London, 1979, p. 149.

10 Blanchard, 'Labour productivity', pp. 1–24.

11 Blanchard, 'Labour productivity', p. 5.

12 Blanchard, 'Labour productivity', p. 10.

13 J. Thirsk, *Economic Policy and Projects*, Oxford, 1978.

14 This is not just for domestically produced goods. R. Davis, 'English foreign
trade, 1660–1700', *Economic History Review*, VII, 1954, pp. 150–66, has
shown that, in the late seventeenth century, retained imports of tobacco,
sugar, calicoes, tea, coffee and porcelain all increased.

15 Thirsk, *Economic Policy*, p. 175. See also M. Spufford, *The Great Reclothing
of Rural England*, London, 1984.

16 If the existence of the backward sloping supply curve of labour is admitted,
then it has to be considered why there is no evidence of employers reducing
wages when they wished to increase output. (Mathias, *Transformation*,
p. 161). The answer may be that wages were not high in absolute terms and
any increase in hours to be worked might have been regarded as excessive in
terms of the energy required and the ability to purchase the requisite energy.
When real wages fell it had more to do with an oversupply of labour and/or a
rise in the price of food, both products of population expansion in an age when
labour productivity per unit of time worked was difficult to increase. A fall in
real wages which was attributable to a rise in population might have seen a rise
in the aggregate amount of labour offered but not necessarily an increased
individual supply.

17 In addition to specific references the general sources on which this section has
been based include Brailsford, *Sport and Society*; C. Hole, *English Sports and
Pastimes*, London, 1949; Malcolmson, *Popular Recreations*; J. Strutt, *The

Sports and Pastimes of the People of England, London, 1834; and volumes of the *Victoria County Histories*.

18 Malcolmson, *Popular Recreations*, p. 18; E. P. Thompson, 'Patrician society, plebeian culture', *Journal of Social History*, v, 1972, p. 392.

19 Coleman, *Economy of England*, p. 20. By way of contrast the 1970 figure was 328.

20 E. A. Wrigley, 'A simple model of London's importance in changing English society and economy, 1650–1750', *Past and Present*, XXXVII, 1967, p. 50.

21 Brailsford, *Sport and Society*, pp. 215–17; D. Brailsford, 'Sporting days in eighteenth-century England', *Journal of Sport History*, IX, 1982, pp. 41–54. Nevertheless there is no indication of regularly organised spectator sport.

22 P. Laslett, *The World We Have Lost*, London, 1973, pp. 57–8.

23 C. Brookes, *English Cricket*, Newton Abbot, 1978, pp. 34–44; Malcolmson, *Popular Recreations*, pp. 34–51.

24 Attempts by an elite to reserve certain sports activities for their exclusive participation have a long history, perhaps as long as that of English sport itself (T. S. Henricks, 'Sport and social hierarchy in medieval England', *Journal of Sport History*, IX, 1982, pp. 20–37).

25 D. Hay, 'Poaching and the game laws on Cannock Chase', in D. Hay, P. Linebaugh and E. P. Thompson (eds.), *Albion's Fatal Tree*, London, 1975, p. 189. For a fuller discussion, see P. B. Munsche, *The English Game Laws, 1671–1831*, Cambridge, 1981.

26 Quoted in Hay, 'Poaching', p. 191.

27 On the recreational role of the alehouse, see K. Wrightson, 'Alehouses, order and reformation in rural England, 1590–1660', in E. and S. Yeo (eds.), *Popular Culture and Class Conflict, 1590–1914*, Brighton, 1981, pp. 1–27; and Malcolmson, *Popular Recreations*, pp. 72–3.

28 C. Hill, *Society and Puritanism in Pre-Revolutionary England*, London, 1964, p. 192; Malcolmson, *Popular Recreations*, pp. 9, 31; W. Hone, *The Everyday Book*, London, 1830, II, pp. 676–8.

29 Wrightson, 'Alehouses', p. 5.

30 Wrightson, 'Alehouses', p. 26; Thompson, 'Time', p. 61.

31 Coleman, 'Labour', pp. 283–4.

32 F. P. Magoun, 'Football in medieval England and in middle-English literature', *American Historical Review*, XXXV, 1929, pp. 33–45; F. P. Magoun, 'Scottish popular football, 1424–1815', *American Historical Review*, XXXVII, 1931, pp. 1–13; W. A. Dutt, 'The last camping match', *Badminton Magazine*, IX, 1899, pp. 91–6.

33 P. H. Ditchfield, 'Sport ancient and modern', in *Victoria County History of Berkshire*, II, London, 1907, pp. 313–15.

34 Brailsford, *Sport and Society*, pp. 80–3.

35 F. Bonnett, 'Old-time sports', in *Victoria County History of Nottinghamshire*, III, London, 1910, p. 411.

36 Wrightson, 'Alehouses', p. 2.

37 Malcolmson, *Popular Recreations*, pp. 72–3; Laslett, *World We Have Lost*, p. 139.

38 Malcolmson, *Popular Recreations*, pp. 20–3. For hiring fairs, see Hone, *Everyday Book*, III, pp. 174–7, 202–5.

39 Hay, 'Poaching', pp. 201–2.

40 Malcolmson, *Popular Recreations*, p. 78.

41 Hone, *Everyday Book*, I, pp. 567, 1349; III, p. 850.

42 Malcolmson, *Popular Recreations*, p. 81.

43 Malcolmson, *Popular Recreations*, pp. 39–40.

44 Laslett, *World We Have Lost*, p. 206.

45 Many of the Plough Monday events, May celebrations and harvest feasts which became sanctified by the Church were pagan in origin and associated with fertility rites. They had become ritualised long before the Church became associated with them.

46 Coleman, 'Labour', pp. 290–1.

47 The *Oxford English Dictionary*, Oxford, 1961, cites the first *written* reference as in the *Scots Magazine* of 1753.

48 J. K. Rühl, 'Religion and amusements in sixteenth- and seventeenth-century England: "time might be better bestowed, and besides wee see sin acted"', *British Journal of Sports History*, I, 1984, pp. 125–65; D. Brailsford, 'Puritanism and sport in seventeenth-century England', *Stadion*, I, 1975, pp. 316–30; J. T. Jable, 'The English Puritans: suppressors of sport and amusement?', *Canadian Journal of History of Sport and Physical Education*, VII, 1978, pp. 33–40; N. L. Struna, 'The declaration of sports reconsidered', *Canadian Journal of History of Sport*, XIV, 1983, pp. 44–68.

49 Malcolmson, *Popular Recreations*, p. 9.

50 Malcolmson, *Popular Recreations*, pp. 5–14; Brailsford, *Sport and Society*, pp. 122–57; I. Bradley, 'The English Sunday', *History Today*, XXII, 1972, pp. 355–8; Hill, *Society and Puritanism*, pp. 145–218.

4 Sporting activities and economic change, 1750–1830

1 Again for analytical purposes the period is partially being treated as a whole, though in fact the pace and timing of economic change, and hence the developments in work and leisure, would vary extensively over the nation and between employments and employers.

2 J. S. Cohen, 'The achievements of economic history: the Marxist school', *Journal of Economic History*, XXXVIII, 1978, pp. 52–3; J. S. Lyons, 'The Lancashire cotton industry and the introduction of the powerloom, 1815–1850', *Journal of Economic History*, XXXVIII, 1978, p. 284.

3 Increased capitalisation within mining was making similar demands for a more specialised, permanent and disciplined labour force (J. G. Rule, 'Some social aspects of the Industrial Revolution in Cornwall', in R. Burt (ed.), *Industry and Society in the South West*, Exeter, 1970, pp. 71–106).

4 Later research has only slightly modified the views presented in the seminal article by S. Pollard, 'Factory discipline in the Industrial Revolution', *Economic History Review*, XV, 1963–4, pp. 254–71.

5 H. Pelling, *A History of British Trade Unionism*, London, 1977, pp. 13–32; S. Pollard, 'Labour in Great Britain', in P. Mathias and M. M. Postan (eds.),

Cambridge Economic History of Europe, VII, Cambridge, 1978, part 1, p. 154.

6 P. Mathias, *The Transformation of England*, London, 1979, p. 149. It can be suggested that becoming wage-dependent might have given work an even greater disutility to the previously self-employed.

7 Increased wage rates which caused one individual to reduce the volume of labour offered could of course be sufficient to attract another into the labour market. As Mathias (*Transformation*, p. 164) puts it: 'one man's leisure preference proved to be another man's employment opportunity'.

8 Mathias, *Transformation*, pp. 162–3; D. E. C. Eversley, 'The home market and economic growth in England, 1750–1780', in E. L. Jones and G. E. Mingay (eds.), *Land, Labour and Population in the Industrial Revolution*, London, 1967, pp. 206–59; N. McKendrick, 'Home demand and economic growth', in N. McKendrick (ed.), *Historical Perspectives*, London, 1974, pp. 152–210; W. A. Cole, 'Factors in demand 1700–80', in R. Floud and D. McCloskey (eds.), *The Economic History of Britain since 1700*, I, Cambridge, 1981, pp. 36–65.

9 H. Perkin, *The Origins of Modern English Society, 1780–1880*, London, 1972, p. 277.

10 A. W. Coats, 'The classical economists and the labourer', in A. W. Coats (ed.), *The Classical Economists and Economic Policy*, London, 1971, p. 149.

11 D. Brailsford, 'Religion and sport in eighteenth-century England: "for the encouragement of piety and virtue, and for the preventing or punishing of vice, profanement and immorality"', *British Journal of Sports History*, I, 1984, pp. 166–83.

12 E. P. Thompson, *The Making of the English Working Class*, London, 1963, p. 442.

13 R. W. Malcolmson, *Popular Recreations in English Society, 1700–1850*, Cambridge, 1973, pp. 106–7; J. G. Rule, 'Methodism, popular beliefs and village culture in Cornwall, 1800–50', in R. D. Storch (ed.), *Popular Culture and Custom in Nineteenth-Century England*, London, 1982, pp. 48–70; B. Harrison, 'Religion and recreation in nineteenth-century England', *Past and Present*, XXXVIII, 1967, 98–125; B. Harrison, 'Animals and the state in nineteenth-century England', *English Historical Review*, LXXXVIII, 1973, pp. 786–820; I. Bradley, 'The English Sunday', *History Today*, XXII, 1972, pp. 358–63; S. K. Phillips, 'Primitive Methodist confrontation with popular sports: case study of early nineteenth-century Staffordshire', in R. Cashman and M. McKernan (eds.), *Sport: Money, Morality and the Media*, Sydney, 1981, pp. 289–303.

14 H. Cunningham, 'The metropolitan fairs: a case study in the social control of leisure', in A. P. Donajgrodzki (ed.), *Social Control in Nineteenth-Century Britain*, London, 1977, pp. 163–5; W. Hone, *The Everyday Book*, London, 1830, I, pp. 436, 441, 1168–1252; R. D. Storch, '"Please to remember the fifth of November": conflict, solidarity and public order in southern England, 1815–1900', in R. D. Storch (ed.), *Popular Culture*, pp. 72–3.

15 C. Elmsley, *British Society and the French Wars, 1793–1815*, London, 1980; S. Tischler, *Footballers and Businessmen*, New York, 1981, p. 13.

16 P. McCann (ed.), *Popular Education and Socialization in the Nineteenth Century*, London, 1977, especially the chapters by McCann and Goldstrom; D. A. Reid, 'The decline of St Monday 1766–1876', *Past and Present*, LXXI, 1976, p. 94; M. Sanderson, *Education, Economic Changes and Society in England, 1780–1870*, London, 1983, pp. 10–16.

17 A. J. Field, 'Occupational structure, dissent and educational commitment: Lancashire, 1841', *Research in Economic History*, IV, 1979, pp. 262–3; M. Sanderson, 'Education and the factory in industrial Lancashire 1780–1840', *Economic History Review*, XX, 1967, pp. 273–4.

18 E. L. Jones, 'Agriculture, 1700–80', in R. Floud and D. McCloskey (eds.), *The Economic History of Britain since 1700*, I, Cambridge, 1981, pp. 66–86.

19 M. Turner, 'Agricultural productivity in England in the eighteenth century: evidence from crop yields', *Economic History Review*, XXXV, 1982, pp. 489–510.

20 R. W. Fogel *et al.*, 'The economics of mortality in North America, 1650–1910: a description of a research project', *Historical Methods*, XI, 1978, p. 84.

21 R. Floud and K. W. Wachter, 'Poverty and physical stature: evidence on the standard of living of London boys 1770–1870', *Social Science History*, VI, 1982, pp. 422–52.

22 A. B. Appleby, 'Grain prices and subsistence crises in England and France, 1590–1740', *Journal of Economic History*, XXXIX, 1979, pp. 864–87.

23 Figures are in 1851–60 prices. See C. H. Feinstein, 'Capital formation in Great Britain' in P. Mathias and M. M. Postan (eds.), *Cambridge Economic History of Europe*, VII, Cambridge, 1978, part 1, p. 40. There are too many difficulties in defining and calculating agricultural capital formation for these figures to be regarded as accurate.

24 M. E. Turner, *Enclosures in Britain, 1750–1830*, London, 1984, pp. 64–81.

25 R. W. Malcolmson, 'Leisure', in G. E. Mingay (ed.), *The Victorian Countryside*, London, 1981, p. 604.

26 A. Howkins, *Whitsun in Nineteenth-Century Oxfordshire*, History Workshop Pamphlet No. 8, Oxford, 1973, pp. 1–2.

27 Malcolmson, *Popular Recreations*, p. 16.

28 J. H. Plumb, *The Commercialisation of Leisure in Eighteenth-Century England*, Reading, 1974, supports his case that leisure was becoming increasingly commercialised by listing an array of activities which involved consumer expenditure, but he does not show that these were organised regularly or that they were available to the mass of the population. Similarly, D. Brailsford's otherwise excellent 'Sporting days in eighteenth-century England', *Journal of Sport History*, IX, 1982, pp. 41–54, fails to note that, although commercialised sport was organised, it was not organised regularly. His sources on pugilism and cricket list less than five fights and just over nine matches a year. Horse-racing was more common – 1787 saw 61 meetings and 154 race days in just three months – but there was rarely more than one meeting per annum in the same place.

29 J. Myerscough, 'The recent history of the use of leisure time', in I. Appleton (ed.), *Leisure Research and Policy*, Edinburgh, 1974, pp. 3, 6.

30 Rule, 'Social aspects', pp. 77–8.

31 M. A. Bienefeld, *Working Hours in British Industry*, London, 1972, p. 39.

32 H. Freudenberger and G. Cummins, 'Health, work and leisure before the Industrial Revolution', *Explorations in Economic History*, XIII, 1976, p. 6. However, this increase is perhaps exaggerated. N. L. Tranter, 'The labour supply 1780–1860', in R. Floud and D. McCloskey (eds.), *The Economic History of Britain since 1700*, I, Cambridge, 1981, p. 220.

33 One survey has the sports under successful attack from the second half of the eighteenth century to beyond 1835 (W. J. Baker, 'The leisure revolution in Victorian England: a review of the recent literature', *Journal of Sport History*, VI, 1979, pp. 76–87).

34 *The Sporting Repository*, London, 1822; P. Egan, *Book of Sports*, London, 1832; Hone, *Everyday Book*. These sources are supplemented by reference to contemporary evidence in the *Victoria County Histories*. More local studies are required to help date the decline of particular sports and to assess whether or not this was associated with industrialisation and/or urbanisation.

35 Malcolmson, *Popular Recreations*, pp. 123–6; J. Ford, *Prizefighting*, Newton Abbot, 1971, pp. 96–9.

36 For a survey of current views, see Sanderson, *Education*, pp. 9–16.

37 See, for example, P. McCann, 'Popular education, socialization and social control: Spitalfields 1812–1824', in McCann (ed.), *Popular Education*, pp. 1–40.

38 The most recent evidence has been supplied by C. K. Harley, 'British industrialisation before 1841: evidence of slower growth during the Industrial Revolution', *Journal of Economic History*, XLII, 1982, pp. 267–90; J. G. Williamson, 'Why was British growth so slow during the Industrial Revolution?', *Journal of Economic History*, XLIV, 1984, pp. 687–712; N. F. R. Crafts, *British Economic Growth during the Industrial Revolution*, Oxford, 1985.

39 C. H. Lee, *British Regional Employment Statistics, 1841–1971*, Cambridge, 1979, pp. 3–6.

40 Myerscough, 'Use of leisure', p. 4.

41 J. Saville, *Rural Depopulation in England and Wales, 1851–1951*, London, 1957, p. 61.

42 Figures in 1851–60 prices (Feinstein, 'Capital', pp. 40–1).

43 Reid, 'St Monday', pp. 76–101; L. D. Schwarz, 'The standard of living in the long run: London, 1700–1860', *Economic History Review*, XXXVIII, 1985, p. 24.

44 E. Hopkins, 'Working hours and conditions during the Industrial Revolution: a re-appraisal', *Economic History Review*, XXXV, 1982, p. 53.

45 G. Hueckel, 'Agriculture during industrialisation', in R. Floud and D. McCloskey (eds.), *The Economic History of Britain since 1700*, I, Cambridge, 1981, p. 185.

46 Malcolmson, 'Leisure', pp. 606–7.

47 Malcolmson, 'Leisure', pp. 605–6.

48 D. Brailsford, 'The locations of eighteenth-century spectator sport', in J. Bale and C. Jenkins (eds.), *Geographical Perspectives on Sport*, Birmingham, 1983, pp. 27–62. Plumb, *Commercialisation of Leisure*, p. 10, argues that

eighteenth-century racing had a paying public but cites no evidence. Possibly he has confused spending to see the races with spending at the races. Most spectators wanted more than a view of the horses, a fact appreciated by the leasees of the gambling booths, beer tents and food stalls.

49 Brailsford, 'Sporting days', pp. 45, 49. The Artillery ground continued under new management but with what financial success is undocumented.

50 Hone, *Everyday Book*, II, p. 1561; J. C. Whyte, *History of the British Turf*, London, 1840, pp. 274–7.

51 For a bibliography of the debate, see P. H. Lindhert and J. G. Williamson, 'English workers' living standards during the Industrial Revolution: a new look', *Economic History Review*, XXXVI, 1983, n. 1.

52 Lindhert and Williamson, 'Living standards', p. 11.

5 The precursors of commercialised sport, 1830–75

1 R. D. Storch, 'Introduction: persistence and change in nineteenth-century popular culture', in R. D. Storch (ed.), *Popular Culture and Custom in Nineteenth-Century England*, London, 1982, p. 14.

2 A. Delves, 'Popular recreation and social conflict in Derby, 1800–1850', in E. and S. Yeo (eds.), *Popular Culture and Class Conflict, 1590–1914*, Brighton, 1981, p. 97; R. D. Storch, 'The plague of the blue locusts: police reform and popular resistance in northern England, 1840–1857', *International Review of Social History*, XX, 1975, pp. 61–90.

3 H. Cunningham, 'The metropolitan fairs: a case study in the social control of leisure', in A. P. Donajgrodzki (ed.), *Social Control in Nineteenth-Century Britain*, London, 1977, pp. 163–84; Delves, 'Popular recreation', pp. 89–127; R. D. Storch, 'The policeman as domestic missionary: urban discipline and popular culture in northern England, 1850–1880', *Journal of Social History*, IX, 1976, pp. 481–509; R. D. Storch, '"Please to remember the fifth of November": conflict, solidarity and public order in southern England, 1815–1900', in Storch (ed.), *Popular Culture*, pp. 71–99; J. K. Walton and R. Poole, 'The Lancashire wakes in the nineteenth century', in Storch (ed.), *Popular Culture*, pp. 100–24; D. A. Reid, 'Interpreting the festival calendar: wakes and fairs as carnivals', in Storch (ed.), *Popular Culture*, pp. 125–53.

4 B. Harrison, 'Animals and the state in nineteenth-century England', *English Historical Review*, LXXXVIII, 1973, p. 792.

5 B. Harrison, 'Religion and recreation in nineteenth-century England', *Past and Present*, XXXVIII, 1967, pp. 103–5.

6 B. Harrison, *Drink and the Victorians*, Pittsburgh, 1971.

7 T. S. Ashton, *An Economic History of England*, London, 1959, p. 217.

8 H. McLeod, *Religion and the Working Class in Nineteenth-Century Britain*, London, 1984, p. 57.

9 Delves, 'Popular recreation', p. 99; J. Rule, 'Methodism, popular beliefs and village culture in Cornwall, 1800–50', in Storch (ed.), *Popular Culture*, pp. 55–7.

10 A. Howkins, 'The taming of Whitsun: the changing face of a nineteenth-century rural holiday', in Yeo and Yeo (eds.), *Popular Culture*, p. 194.

11 Delves, 'Popular recreation', pp. 100–1.

12 Delves, 'Popular recreation', pp. 96–8; Walton and Poole, 'Lancashire wakes', p. 106; Rule, 'Methodism', p. 55; R. D. Storch, 'The problem of working-class leisure: some roots of middle-class moral reform in the industrial north, 1825–50', in Donajgrodzki (ed.), *Social Control*, p. 145.
13 W. Vamplew, *The Turf*, London, 1976, p. 203; J. Benson, *The Penny Capitalists*, Dublin, 1983, p. 70.
14 See, for example, Reid, 'Interpreting the festival', p. 132; or Storch, 'Introduction', pp. 5–6. There is a danger that a myth is perhaps being created. There seems to be no dark side to these working-class leaders. Surely they cannot all have been abstemious, chapel-going and non-promiscuous?
15 Delves, 'Popular recreation', pp. 104–5.
16 G. Stedman Jones, 'Working-class culture and working-class politics in London 1870–1900: notes on the remaking of a working class', *Journal of Social History*, VIII, 1975, p. 471.
17 A. Lloyd, *The Great Prize Fight*, London, 1977; K. Chesney, *The Victorian Underworld*, London, 1979, p. 328.
18 C. Brookes, *English Cricket*, Newton Abbot, 1978, pp. 101–17.
19 C. Richardson, *The English Turf*, London, 1901, p. 156; Vamplew, *The Turf*, pp. 32–3; D. A. Reid, '"To boldly go where no worker had gone before": railway excursions from Birmingham 1846–1876', paper presented at the Eighth International Economic History Congress, Budapest, 1982; J. Crump, '"The great carnival of the year": the Leicester races in the 19th century', *Transactions of the Leicestershire Historical and Archaeological Society*, LVIII, 1982–3, p. 63.
20 E. P. Hobsbawm, *Industry and Empire*, London, 1968, p. 74; S. Pollard, 'Labour in Great Britain', in P. Mathias and M. M. Postan (eds.), *Cambridge Economic History of Europe*, VII, Cambridge, 1978, part 1, p. 161.
21 Calculated from data in B. R. Mitchell and P. Deane, *Abstract of British Historical Statistics*, Cambridge, 1962, p. 543.
22 E. P. Thompson, *The Making of the English Working Class*, London, 1963, pp. 90–1; Pollard, 'Labour', p. 156.
23 E. Hopkins, 'Working hours and conditions during the Industrial Revolution: a re-appraisal', *Economic History Review*, XXXV, 1982, pp. 55, 63.
24 C. H. Feinstein, 'Capital formation in Great Britain', in Mathias and Postan (eds.), *Cambridge Economic History*, p. 40; D. A. Reid, 'The decline of St Monday, 1776–1876', *Past and Present*, LXXI, 1976, p. 95.
25 Pollard, 'Labour', p. 158.
26 Pollard, 'Labour', p. 174; Reid, 'St Monday', p. 87.
27 Here the moral revolution had perhaps backfired on some of its supporters, for if animals were to be protected then why not children and women. Once *laissez-faire* had been breached for these workers there was a precedent for others to attempt to follow.
28 Pollard, 'Labour', p. 173. See also M. A. Bienefeld, *Working Hours in British Industry*, London, 1972, pp. 82–106.
29 W. H. Fraser, *The Coming of the Mass Market, 1850–1914*, London, 1981, p. 79; J. K. Walton, 'The demand for working-class seaside holidays in Victorian England', *Economic History Review*, XXXIV, 1981, p. 252.
30 There were also geographical variations (Reid, 'St Monday', p. 86).

31 Reid, 'St Monday', p. 101. In Nottingham it replaced the Goose Fair and race-day holidays (R. A. Church, *Economic and Social Change in a Midland Town*, London, 1966, p. 375).

32 M. B. Smith, 'The Growth and Development of Popular Entertainment and Pastimes in the Lancashire Cotton Towns 1830–1870', M. Litt., University of Lancaster, 1970, pp. 136–46; Walton and Poole, 'Lancashire wakes', p. 103; Delves, 'Popular recreation', p. 121 n. 44; M. Huggins, '"Mingled pleasure and speculation": the survival of the enclosed racecourses on Teesside, 1855–1902', *British Journal of Sports History*, III, 1986, p. 163.

33 J. R. Ross, 'Pedestrianism and Athletics in England and Australia in the Nineteenth Century: A Case Study in the Development of Sport', B. H. M. S. (Hons.), University of Queensland, 1985, p. 22; see also the surveys of 'Sport ancient and modern' in the *Victoria County Histories*.

34 Storch, 'Introduction', p. 10; A. Metcalfe, 'Organized sport in the mining communities of south Northumberland, 1800–1889', *Victorian Studies*, XXV, 1981–2, pp. 480–2.

35 P. Bailey, 'Custom, capital and culture in the Victorian music hall', in Storch (ed.), *Popular Culture*, pp. 181–6; Delves, 'Popular recreation', pp. 114, 126 n. 112; Reid, 'Interpreting the festival', pp. 140–1; H. Cunningham, *Leisure in the Industrial Revolution*, London, 1980, pp. 28–38; Reid, 'To boldly go'; M. Smith, 'Victorian music hall entertainment in the Lancashire cotton towns', *Local Historian*, 1968–71, pp. 379–86.

36 Calculated from data in the *Racing Calendar*.

37 Reid, 'To boldly go'.

38 Reid, 'St Monday', pp. 100–1; Pollard, 'Labour', p. 173.

6 The rise of professional gate-money sport, 1875–1914

1 T. Gourvish, 'The standard of living, 1890–1914', in A. O'Day (ed.), *The Edwardian Age*, London, 1979, p. 22; E. H. Phelps-Brown and M. Browne, *A Century of Pay*, London, 1968, pp. 444–5.

2 If 1890–9 is indexed at 100 then 1900–13 is 100 (Kuczynski), 102 (Bowley), or 103 (Phelps-Brown and Brown). Calculated from data in Gourvish, 'Standard of living', p. 22.

3 Gourvish, 'Standard of living', pp. 16–19.

4 Gourvish, 'Standard of living', pp. 19–21; E. H. Hunt, *Regional Wage Variation in Britain, 1850–1914*, Oxford, 1973, p. 357; W. H. Fraser, *The Coming of the Mass Market, 1850–1914*, London, 1981, pp. 14–26.

5 Gourvish, 'Standard of living', pp. 22–8; E. Roberts, 'Working-class standards of living in Barrow and Lancaster, 1890–1914', *Economic History Review*, XXX, 1977, pp. 306–21.

6 J. Walvin, *Leisure and Society, 1830–1950*, London, 1978, pp. 86–7; A. Mason, *Association Football and English Society, 1863–1915*, Brighton, 1980, pp. 12–15. On muscular Christianity in general, see J. A. Mangan, *Athleticism in the Victorian and Edwardian Public School*, Cambridge, 1981; and N. Vance, *The Sinews of the Spirit*, Cambridge, 1981. Cricket became their special game, as documented in P. Scott, 'Cricket and the religious world

in the Victorian period', *Church Quarterly*, III, 1970, pp. 134–44; and K. Sandiford, 'Cricket and the Victorian society', *Journal of Social History*, XVII, 1983, pp. 305–7.

7 Walvin, *Leisure and Society*, p. 87; Mason, *Association Football*, p. 26; R. Rees, 'The Development of Physical Recreation in Liverpool during the Nineteenth Century', M. A., University of Liverpool, 1968, p. 69.

8 In the period 1876–84 about 10% of both football and cricket teams around Birmingham had works names and 27 of the 227 cricket teams in Liverpool in 1885 have also been identified as works sides (D. D. Molyneux, 'The Development of Physical Recreation in the Birmingham District from 1871 to 1892', M. A., University of Birmingham, 1957, p. 41, Rees, 'Physical Recreation in Liverpool', p. 69). The motivations suggested here are speculative. It has been argued elsewhere that national social welfare policies served the interests of employers by increasing the efficiency of the labour force (J. R. Hay, 'Employers and social policy in Britain: the evolution of welfare legislation, 1905–14', *Social History*, IV, 1977, pp. 435–55). Perhaps this was a lesson learned through works teams, bands, outings, etc.

9 T. C. Barker, *The Glassmakers*, London, 1977, p. 93. This conclusion on chronology is based on a survey of 33 business histories which contained references to recreation.

10 C. Ó Gráda, 'Agricultural decline', in R. Floud and D. McCloskey (eds.), *The Economic History of Britain since 1700*, II, Cambridge, 1981, pp. 175–97.

11 Molyneux, 'Physical Recreation in Birmingham'; Rees, 'Physical Recreation in Liverpool'; E. H. Roberts, 'A Study of the Growth of the Provision of Public Facilities for Leisure Time Occupations by Local Authorities of Merseyside', M. A., University of Liverpool, 1933. The availability of recreational space in general should not be exaggerated. Much was dependent on the local authorities and attitudes towards municipal provision of such facilities varied considerably. See W. Bessant, 'The amusements of the people', *Contemporary Review*, XLV, 1884, pp. 342–8; C. Charrington, 'Communal recreation', *Contemporary Review*, LXXIX, 1901, pp. 839–41; A. Giddens, 'Sport and Society in Contemporary England', M. A., University of London, 1961, pp. 67–9; and P. Bilsborough, 'The Development of Sport in Glasgow, 1850–1914', M. Litt., University of Stirling, 1983, pp. 158–80.

12 Molyneux, 'Physical Recreation in Birmingham', pp. 26–7; Rees, 'Physical Recreation in Liverpool', p. 69; B. R. Mitchell and P. Deane, *Abstract of British Historical Statistics*, Cambridge, 1962, pp. 6, 24–5.

13 G. Green, *The History of the Football Association*, London, 1953, pp. 251, 261. J. J. Bentley, 'Is football a business?', *World's Work*, 1912, p. 383, suggests 750,000 in 1912.

14 Perhaps they were too old, too tired or too unfit. Many industrial workers were in fact deemed too unfit to be allowed to fight in the 1914–18 war (J. M. Winter, 'Britain's "lost generation" of the First World War', *Population Studies*, XXXI, 1977, p. 449).

15 A. E. Dingle, 'Drink and working-class living standards in Britain, 1870–1914', *Economic History Review*, XXV, 1972, pp. 615–16.

16 See, for example, C. Booth, *Life and Labour of the People*, London, 1889; and

B. S. Rowntree, *Poverty*, London, 1901. Rowntree found that 28% of all wage earners in York were in 'secondary poverty' due to nutritionally unwise allocation of income which, if better spent, would have provided for 'merely physical efficiency' (p. 140). See also D. J. Oddy, 'Working-class diets in late nineteenth-century Britain', *Economic History Review*, XXIII, 1970, p. 322.

17 Fraser, *Mass Market*, pp. 3–6.

18 J. Saville, *Rural Depopulation in England and Wales, 1851–1951*, London, 1957, p. 61. It is worth noting that all but two of the original Football League clubs came from towns of over 80,000 inhabitants (R. Holt, 'Working-class football and the city: the problem of continuity', *British Journal of Sports History*, III, 1986, p. 11).

19 D. A. Reid, 'The decline of St Monday, 1776–1876', *Past and Present*, LXXI, 1976, pp. 76–101; E. Hopkins, 'Working hours and conditions during the Industrial Revolution: a re-appraisal', *Economic History Review*, XXXV, 1982, pp. 52–66; H. Cunningham, 'Leisure', in J. Benson (ed.), *The Working Class in England, 1875–1914*, London, 1985, p. 135. See also M. W. Bienefeld, *Working Hours in British Industry*, London, 1972, pp. 106–44.

20 J. E. Handley, *The Celtic Story*, London, 1960, p. 33. J. R. Lowerson, 'Sport and the Victorian Sunday: the beginnings of middle-class apostasy', *British Journal of Sports History*, I, 1984, pp. 202–20.

21 Figures derived from *Wisden Cricketers' Almanack 1911*; *Racing Calendar, 1910*; Annual Report of Scottish Football Association 1909/10; and Football Association, Circular on Financial Arrangements between Clubs and Players, 10 January 1910.

22 This is true of all sections of the entertainment industry (Cunningham, 'Leisure', p. 141).

23 One estimate is of 10,000 people employed in connection with racing (T. Longueville, 'Racing and its fascination', *New Review*, VI, 1892, p. 741).

24 See, for example, A. E. Harrison, 'The competitiveness of the British cycle industry, 1890–1914', *Economic History Review*, XXII, 1969, p. 287.

25 H. Leach, 'The golfer and his millions', *Fry's Magazine*, VI, p. 422ff, cited in J. R. Lowerson, 'Joint stock companies, capital formation and suburban leisure in England 1880–1914', in W. Vamplew (ed.), *The Economic History of Leisure: Papers Presented at the Eighth International Economic History Congress*, Budapest, 1982, p. 61.

26 'Cycling for health and pleasure', *Chamber's Journal*, LXXII, 1895, p. 529. See also 'The cycle and the trade of the Midlands', *Chamber's Journal*, LXXIV, 1897, pp. 459–61.

27 W. Shillcock, 'The ball and the boot – how they are made', in *The Book of Football*, London, 1906, p. 86.

28 J. R. Lowerson, 'English middle-class sport, 1880–1914', in J. R. Cox (ed.), *Aspects of the Social History of Nineteenth-Century Sport*, Liverpool, 1982, pp. 15–16.

29 Shillcock, 'Ball and boot', p. 86.

30 It has been argued that capacity should be the measure (C. Gratton and P. Taylor, *Sport and Recreation: An Economic Analysis*, London, 1985, p. 243).

However, this is surely investment, with crowd size showing how effectively that capital formation has been utilised. Gratton and Taylor also argue that crowd size is solely a demand-side measure, but the equilibrium point is determined by both supply and demand in that the quality of the game is a supply-side influence on demand.

31 'In and about Newmarket', *Strand Magazine*, II, 1891, p. 171; Select Committee on Betting, *British Parliamentary Papers 1902*, V, p. viii.

32 W. C. Neale, 'The peculiar economics of professional sport', *Quarterly Journal of Economics*, LXXVIII, 1964, p. 3. On the importance of this benefit, see S. Tischler, *Footballers and Businessmen*, New York, 1981, p. 79.

33 Mason, *Association Football*, pp. 187–95; W. Vamplew, *The Turf*, London, 1986, p. 220.

34 Mason, *Association Football*, pp. 190–2. On the Birmingham sporting press, see Molyneux, 'Physical Recreation in Birmingham', pp. 101–5.

35 C. Richardson, *The English Turf*, London, 1901, p. 213.

36 Shareholders' Register of Haydock Park Racecourse Company, 1898; Prospectus of Newbury Racecourse Company, 1905.

37 Richardson, *English Turf*, p. 197; J. Rickman, *Homes of Sport: Racing*, London, 1952, p. 30. G. H. Verrall, 'The financial aspect of racing from another point of view', *Badminton Magazine*, XXIII, 1906, pp. 508–9.

38 Richardson, *English Turf*, pp. 149–55; H. A. Bryden and E. D. Cuming, 'Racing', in *Victoria County History of Sussex*, II, London, 1907, p. 455. Their situation was aggravated by a Jockey Club rule of 1877 which required race committees to provide a minimum of 300 sovereigns added money for each day of racing.

39 Earl of Suffolk, *Racing and Steeplechasing*, London, 1886, p. 211.

40 Vigilant, 'Recollections of Epsom and the Derby', *English Illustrated Magazine*, 1891–2, p. 656; L. H. Curzon, *The Blue Riband of the Turf*, London, 1890, p. 19.

41 Richardson, *English Turf*, p. 74.

42 Earl of Suffolk, *Racing*, pp. 74–5.

43 K. A. P. Sandiford, 'English cricket crowds during the Victorian age', *Journal of Sport History*, IX, 1982, pp. 5–22.

44 J. Kay, *Cricket in the Leagues*, London, 1972; R. Genders, *League Cricket in England*, London, 1952.

45 Sandiford, 'Cricket crowds', pp. 6–7.

46 P. F. Warner, 'The coming cricket season', *Badminton Magazine*, XXXVI, 1913, p. 502.

47 W. McGregor, 'The League and the League system', in *The Book of Football*, p. 171.

48 McGregor, 'The League', p. 171. See also his letter quoted in C. E. Sutcliffe, J. A. Brierley and F. Howarth, *The Story of the Football League, 1888–1938*, Preston, 1939, p. 2.

49 R. M. Connell, 'The Scottish Football League and its history', in *The Book of Football*, p. 266.

50 See chapter 12.

51 In 1909 the F. A. estimated that around one million people watched soccer in

England every Saturday, of which about a quarter were at Football League games (Green, *Football Association*, p. 253).

52 Mason, *Association Football*, p. 138; Tischler, *Footballers and Businessmen*, p. 50.
53 Mason, *Association Football*, p. 138; Tischler, *Footballers and Businessmen*, p. 46.
54 Tischler, *Footballers and Businessmen*, pp. 57–8.
55 Calculations based on H. MacFarlane, 'Football of yesterday and today: a comparison', *Monthly Review*, xxv, 1906, p. 129; Mason, *Association Football*, p. 143.
56 Calculated from data in Tischler, *Footballers and Businessmen*, pp. 84–5. League position should not have unduly influenced the figures as the range was from first to seventeenth with a mean of ninth in a league of 20 teams. Profit levels are discussed in more detail in chapter 8.
57 Football Association, Manchester United: Report of Commission, 30 September 1910; C. Francis, *History of the Blackburn Rovers Football Club, 1875–1925*, Blackburn, 1925, p. 196; T. Keates, *History of the Everton Football Club, 1878/79–1928/29*, Liverpool, 1929, p. 129.
58 Mason, *Association Football*, p. 55   n. 78.
59 Mason, *Association Football*, p. 138.
60 W. J. Murray, *The Old Firm*, Edinburgh, 1984, pp. 36, 55.
61 Hampden Park, home of Queen's Park, actually held a 105,000 crowd in 1906 for a Scotland versus England game (Annual Report of Scottish Football Association 1905/06).
62 For some speculations on this, see P. J. Doyle, 'Some problems for the regional historian of rugby league', *Journal of Local Studies*, i, 1980, pp. 9–11.
63 What follows is based on T. Delaney, *The Roots of Rugby League*, Keighley, 1984; J. H. Smith, 'The history of the Northern Union', in *The Book of Football*, pp. 274–7; K. Macklin, *The History of Rugby League Football*, London, 1962; E. Dunning and K. Sheard, *Barbarians, Gentlemen and Players*, Oxford, 1979; and Minutes of the Northern Rugby Football Union.
64 *Bradford Observer*, 30 July 1895; 30 April, 28 August 1896.
65 Smith, 'Northern Union', p. 277.
66 Smith, 'Northern Union', p. 277.
67 Vamplew, *The Turf*, pp. 131–7; Huggins, 'Mingled pleasure', pp. 162–5.
68 Mason, *Association Football*, p. 150; Tischler, *Footballers and Businessmen*, p. 123; J. Hutchinson, 'Some aspects of football crowds before 1914', in *Society for Study of Labour History Conference*, University of Sussex, 1975, pp. 7–9.
69 W. McGregor, 'Characteristics of the crowd', in B. O. Corbett *et al.*, *Football*, London, 1907, p. 19.
70 W. F. Mandle, 'Games people played: cricket and football in England and Victoria in the late nineteenth century', *Historical Studies*, xv, 1973, p. 515.
71 Cited in S. Meacham, *A Life Apart*, London, 1977, p. 167.
72 Sandiford, 'Cricket crowds', p. 17.
73 A. J. Lee, *The Origins of the Popular Press in England, 1855–1914*, Towata, 1976.

74 P. Bailey, 'Custom, capital and culture in the Victorian music hall', in R. D. Storch (ed.), *Popular Culture and Custom in Nineteenth-Century England*, London, 1982, p. 187; Fraser, *Mass Market*, pp. 217–19.

75 J. K. Walton, *The English Seaside Resort*, Leicester, 1983; Fraser, *Mass Market*, pp. 223–4; J. Lowerson and J. Myerscough, *Time to Spare in Victorian England*, Hassocks, 1977, pp. 23–46.

76 Dingle, 'Drink', pp. 617–18; Fraser, *Mass Market*, pp. 110–46.

77 Dingle, 'Drink', p. 615.

78 Mason, *Association Football*, p. 187.

79 D. A. Reid, '"To boldly go where no worker had gone before": railway excursions from Birmingham 1846–1876', paper presented at the Eighth International Economic History Congress, Budapest, 1982; Fraser, *Mass Market*, p. 222.

80 Bailey, 'Victorian music hall', p. 186.

81 *Hansard*, CCXXXVII, 29 January 1878; CCXL, 13 June 1878; CCXLIII, 14 February 1879.

82 J. Porter and E. Moorehouse, *John Porter of Kingsclere*, London, 1919, pp. 444–7.

83 J. Myerscough, 'The recent history of the use of leisure time', in I. Appleton (ed.), *Leisure Research and Policy*, Edinburgh, 1974, p. 13.

84 J. K. Walton, 'The demand for working-class seaside holidays in Victorian England', *Economic History Review*, XXXIV, 1981, p. 252.

85 R. W. Malcolmson, 'Leisure', in G. E. Mingay (ed.), *The Victorian Country-side*, II, London, 1981, pp. 612–13; Fraser, *Mass Market*, p. 14; A. Howkins, *Whitsun in Nineteenth-Century Oxfordshire*, History Workshop Pamphlet No. 8, Oxford, 1973.

86 Dingle, 'Drink', p. 609; Myerscough 'Use of leisure', p. 13; P. Payne, 'The emergence of the large-scale company in Great Britain, 1870–1914', *Economic History Review*, XX, 1967, pp. 539–40.

87 Fraser, *Mass Market*, pp. 76, 209–10.

88 T. G. Ashplant, 'London working men's clubs, 1875–1914', in E. and S. Yeo (eds.), *Popular Culture and Class Conflict, 1590–1914*, Brighton, 1981, pp. 241–70; J. Taylor, *From Self-Help to Glamour: The Working Man's Club, 1860–1972*, History Workshop Pamphlet No. 7, Oxford, 1972.

89 J. Benson, *The Penny Capitalists*, Dublin, 1983, p. 70; Vamplew, *The Turf*, p. 223.

90 Mason, *Association Football*, pp. 181–6.

91 Benson, *Penny Capitalists*, p. 72.

92 H. J. Perkins, 'The "social tone" of Victorian seaside resorts in the north-west', *Northern History*, II, 1975, p. 193.

93 Minutes of Leicestershire C. C. C., 9 March 1897; H. Gordon, 'Cricket twenty years ago and now', *Badminton Magazine*, XIV, 1902, p. 613; Minutes of Essex C. C. C., 11 September 1895.

94 McGregor, 'Characteristics of the crowd', pp. 23–4.

95 McGregor, 'Characteristics of the crowd', p. 23.

96 Mason, *Association Football*, pp. 176–9.

97 Vamplew, *The Turf*, p. 43.

98 Mason, *Association Football*, p. 180; Tischler, *Footballers and Business-men*, p. 129; Bentley, 'Football', p. 393; E. Needham, *Association Football*, London, 1900, p. 7; Minutes of Scottish Football Association, 12 January 1909.

99 J. K. Walton, 'Residential amenity, respectable morality and the rise of the entertainment industry: the case of Blackpool 1860–1914', *Literature and History*, I, 1975, pp. 62–78; Perkins, 'Victorian seaside resorts', pp. 180–94; Bailey, 'Victorian music hall', pp. 196–8; D. Dixon, '"Class law": the Street Betting Act of 1906', *International Journal of the Sociology of Law*, VIII, 1980, pp. 101–28; Cunningham, 'Leisure', pp. 138–9; R. McKibben, 'Working-class gambling in Britain 1880–1939', *Past and Present*, LXXXII, 1979, pp. 147–78.

100 See chapters 17 and 18.

8 Profits or premierships?

1 H. Smart, 'The present state of the turf', *Fortnightly Review*, XXXVIII, 1885, p. 534; *Scottish Sport*, 14 May 1894.

2 W. E. Hodgson, 'The degradation of British sport', *National Review*, XVII, 1891, p. 787; W. McGregor, 'The £ s. d. of football', in *The Book of Football*, London, 1906, p. 60.

3 Fry is quoted in D. Birley, *The Willow Wand*, London, 1979, p. 5; R. D. Walker, 'Lord's up to date', *Badminton Magazine*, X, 1900, p. 325.

4 For North American studies, see R. G. Noll, 'Alternatives in sports policy', in R. G. Noll (ed.), *Government and the Sports Business*, Washington, 1974, p. 415; J. C. H. Jones, 'The economics of the national hockey league', *Canadian Journal of Economics*, II, 1969, pp. 1–21; H. G. Demmert, *The Economics of Professional Team Sports*, Lexington, 1973; and G. W. Skully, 'Pay and performance in major league baseball', *American Economic Review*, LXIV, 1974, pp. 915–30. L. E. Davis, 'Self-regulation in baseball, 1909–71', in Noll (ed.), *Government and Sports*, accepts general profit-maximisation but suggests that a minority of owners were not particularly profit-motivated. M. El Hodiri and J. Quirk, in 'An economic model of a professional sports league', *Journal of Political Economy*, LXXIX, 1971, pp. 1302–19, whilst acknowledging that owners are not always motivated solely by profits, found that the evidence supported their hypotheses based on profit-maximisation. D. S. Davenport, 'Collusive competition in major league baseball: its theory and institutional development', *American Economist*, XIII, 1969, p. 8, suggests that owners of baseball teams are frequently 'just as interested' in winning championships as in making profits. On Britain, see N. C. Wiseman, 'The economics of football', *Lloyds Bank Review 1977*, p. 30; and J. A. Schofield, 'The development of first-class cricket in England: an economic analysis', *Journal of Industrial Economics*, XXX, 1982, p. 339. For a survey of the literature, see P. J. Sloane, *Sport in the Market*, Hobart Paper No. 85, London, 1980; J. Cairns, 'Economic analysis of league sports: a critical review of the literature', *Department of Political Economy Discussion Paper 83–01*, University of Aberdeen, 1983; and J. Cairns, N. Jennett and P. J. Sloane, 'The economics of professional team sports: a survey of theory and evidence',

Department of Political Economy Discussion Paper 84–06, University of Aberdeen, 1984.

5 P. J. Sloane pioneered the concept theoretically in 'The economics of professional football: the football club as a utility maximiser', *Scottish Journal of Political Economy*, XVIII, 1971, pp. 121–46, but the idea had been broached before; see P. E. P., 'English professional football', *Planning*, XXII, No. 496, 1966.

6 This has become almost an article of faith in the economics of sport literature. See, for example, Jones, 'Economics of hockey league', p. 3; Davenport, 'Collusive competition', p. 7; B. Dabscheck, 'The wage determination process for sportsmen', *Economic Record*, LI, 1975, p. 53; S. Rottenberg, 'The baseball players' labor market', *Journal of Political Economy*, LXIV, 1956, p. 51; W. C. Neale, 'The peculiar economics of professional sport', *Quarterly Journal of Economics*, LXXVIII, 1964, p. 2; R. G. Noll, 'Attendance and price setting', in R. G. Noll (ed.), *Government and the Sports Business*, Washington, 1974, p. 156; Sloane, *Sport in the Market*, p. 25; and Wiseman, 'Economics of football', p. 36. Yet it is faith rather than established fact. Empirical testing of the hypothesis has proved inconclusive in that, while not dismissing the influence of the uncertainty of outcome, it has not supported the idea that such unpredictability is the most important influence on demand. For reviews, see Cairns, 'Economic analysis', pp. 10–21; and Cairns *et al.*, 'Economics of team sports', pp. 15–25. Data deficiencies have meant that no comprehensive tests of the hypothesis have been made in a historical context. Nevertheless, even if mistaken in its emphasis, the belief that uncertainty is so important could influence club and league behaviour.

7 C. Gratton and P. Taylor, *Sport and Recreation: An Economic Analysis*, London, 1985, p. 243. In team sports, for any given *home* match most costs can be regarded as fixed. All capital expenditure has already been incurred; players' wages have been decided beforehand, often at the start of the season; and groundstaff, administrators and clerks have to be employed anyway. Possibly the only short-run variable cost would be stewards and police, and frequently the former might be volunteers. In horse-racing capital costs were probably a much larger proportion of outlays, given both the lower intensity of use of most racecourses as compared to most cricket and football grounds and the higher establishment costs.

8 I owe the phrase, but not this specific interpretation, to O. Covick, 'Sporting equality in professional team sports leagues and labour market controls: what is the relationship?', *Sporting Traditions*, II, 1985–6, p. 66.

9 Knockout competitions are somewhat different in that the end of the tournament brings together the unbeaten teams, whereas end-of-season league games, even those involving leading clubs, may have no bearing whatsoever on the championship. There is also a quality aspect to any individual game in that a close contest between teams at the top of the league is likely to attract a larger crowd than an equally close game at the foot of the table.

10 Cairns, 'Economic analysis', p. 24.

11 This would not, of course, necessarily apply at the league level. Joint maximisation of profits might still require uncertain results.

12 Dabscheck, 'Wage determination', pp. 52–64.

13 No reason was given for the choice of time period. Possibly a few seasons are necessary to fully integrate a group of players into a team; contracts lasting more than one season would also bind players to the club while this integration occurred.

14 *Athletic News*, 18 March 1889; McGregor, '£ s. d.', p. 61.

15 Annual Report of Plymouth Argyle F. C. 1912/13.

16 It should be noted that 'scarcely two clubs adopt the same way of keeping their accounts' (McGregor, '£ s. d.', p. 60) and that thus little reliance can be placed on financial data cited in the literature; even the original accounts have to be adjusted in the light of modern accounting procedures.

17 Calculated from Annual Financial Statements of Heart of Midlothian F. C.

18 Calculated from data in McGregor, '£ s. d.', p. 61; S. Tischler, *Footballers and Businessmen*, New York, 1981, p. 84; and Football League Circular, 30 September 1914.

19 Of the 90 English and 30 Scottish clubs whose record home crowds could be traced in M. Golesworthy (ed.), *The Encyclopaedia of Association Football*, Newton Abbot, 1977, 63 and 24 respectively had them at cup ties.

20 Annual Reports of Scottish Football Association 1903/04, 1904/05.

21 Annual Financial Statement of Heart of Midlothian F. C. 1906/07.

22 J. J. Bentley, 'Is football a business?', *World's Work*, 1912, p. 393.

23 In successive seasons from 1911/12 average English first-division Saturday gates were £563, £647 and £735 compared to second-division gates of £250, £275 and £306 (Football League Circular, 30 September 1914).

24 Minutes of Sheffield Wednesday F. C., 19 September 1887.

25 Minutes of Sheffield Wednesday F. C., 13 April, 22 April 1901.

26 Annual Report of East Stirlingshire F. C. 1911/12; Prospectus of Birmingham F. C. 1906.

27 Minutes of Sheffield Wednesday F. C., *passim*; Tischler, *Footballers and Businessmen*, p. 58; A. Mason, *Association Football and English Society, 1863–1915*, Brighton, 1980, p. 149; Annual Report of Southampton F. C. 1907/08; Annual Report of Tottenham Hotspur F. C. 1908/09.

28 Minutes of the Football League Management Committee, 28 March 1890; *Athletic Journal*, 13 May 1890. Until 1895/96 the Football League second division was allowed to charge only 4d. (*Rules of the Football League 1895/96*, Preston, 1895).

29 *Athletic News*, 1 May 1899.

30 P. M. Young, *A History of British Football*, London, 1969, p. 164.

31 The rationale behind this is unknown but it was in vogue by 1888 and did not cease until 1918. See *Scottish Sport*, 6 November 1888; and R. Crampsey, *The Scottish Footballer*, Edinburgh, 1978, p. 19.

32 Between 1894 and 1899 the proportion of Celtic's income coming from athletic sports and cycling ranged from 3.8% to 11.3%. For Rangers the figures were 3.0% to 10.3% (P. Bilsborough, 'The Development of Sport in Glasgow, 1850–1914', M. Litt., University of Stirling, 1983, p. 362). Interestingly Celtic and Rangers came to an agreement that neither would let their grounds for less than the total stand drawings (J. E. Handley, *The Celtic Story*, London, 1960, p. 43).

33 *Scottish Football Annual 1888/89*, p. 35.

34 *Scottish Sport*, 2 June 1891.

35 Handley, *Celtic Story*, p. 30; *Scottish Sport*, 19 June 1891.

36 C. E. Sutcliffe, J. A. Brierley and F. Howarth, *The Story of the Football League, 1888–1938*, Preston, 1939, pp. 118–19.

37 W. I. Bassett, 'Big transfers and the transfer system', in *The Book of Football*, p. 162. However, J. A. H. Catton, *The Real Football*, London, 1900, p. 101, is less supportive.

38 W. J. Murray, *The Old Firm*, Edinburgh, 1984, *passim*.

39 Minutes of Football League, 18 May 1910; *The Book of Football*, *passim*.

40 Minutes of Sheffield Wednesday F. C., 6 February 1888; 13 December 1899; 22 September, 9 November 1909.

41 See, for example, W. McGregor, 'Birmingham (late Small Heath) F. C.', in *The Book of Football*, p. 120.

42 Minutes of Football Association, 29 May 1896.

43 Bentley, 'Football', p. 384; Minutes of Sheffield Wednesday F. C., 23 January 1913. The *Athletic News*, 6 September 1909, maintained that 'no-one who is out for a business return would look at football shares' but *rentier* returns might be another issue. Consols averaged 3% for most of the 1890s but reached 5% in October 1899 and hovered near 4% in the first decade of the twentieth century (B. R. Mitchell and P. Deane, *Abstract of British Historical Statistics*, Cambridge, 1962, p. 450).

44 Handley, *Celtic Story*, pp. 13–15. There was in fact a revolt by many Celtic shareholders on one occasion when dividends were declared in preference to donations to charity (G. McNee, *The Story of Celtic*, London, 1978, pp. 94–5).

45 Annual Report of Scottish Football Association 1894/95; Bentley, 'Football', p. 390.

46 At their 1895 annual general meeting Everton specifically set up a reserve fund so that 'should adverse circumstances arise in the immediate future they had something to fall back upon without calling upon the shareholders or members for their support'. Quoted in P. M. Young, *Football on Merseyside*, London, 1964, p. 56.

47 Calculated from Annual Financial Statements of West Bromwich Albion F. C. and Burnley F. C.

48 Quoted in H. Gordon, 'Is first class cricket losing its popularity?', *Badminton Magazine*, XXI, 1905, p. 328.

49 Quoted in H. Gordon, 'The coming cricket season', *Badminton Magazine*, XXIV, 1907, p. 454; Minutes of Leicestershire C. C. C., 16 October 1895.

50 *Wisden* editorial, cited in L. Duckworth, *The Story of Warwickshire Cricket*, London, 1974, p. 121.

51 *Wisden Cricketers' Almanack 1911*, p. 86.

52 The low figure for Yorkshire is due to that county's dominance of first and second positions; those for Leicestershire and Derbyshire are attributable to a similar lack of variation at the other end of the table.

53 H. Gordon, 'Cricket problems of today', *Badminton Magazine*, XIX, 1904, p. 195.

54 Minutes of Leicestershire C. C. C., 5 March 1902; 26 June 1905; 30 October 1907.
55 Minutes of Lancashire C. C. C., 11 December 1906; Minutes of Essex C. C. C., 29 November 1910.
56 Minutes of Leicestershire C. C. C., 23 October 1907; 1 June 1910; 14 February 1912; *Wisden Cricketers' Almanack 1911*, p. 28.
57 Minutes of Leicestershire C. C. C., 9 March 1898; Minutes of Lancashire C. C. C., 18 May 1906.
58 Minutes of Leicestershire C. C. C., 21 March 1906; 20 November 1912.
59 Duckworth, *Warwickshire Cricket*, p. 100.
60 K. A. P. Sandiford, 'English cricket crowds during the Victorian age', *Journal of Sport History*, IX, 1982, pp. 16–17.
61 *Yorkshire C. C. C. Year Book, 1913*.
62 *Leicester Daily Mercury*, 25 November 1909.
63 Duckworth, *Warwickshire Cricket*, p. 98.
64 Annual Reports of Essex C. C. C. 1893, 1905, 1910.
65 Duckworth, *Warwickshire Cricket*, pp. 68–72. D. D. Molyneux, 'The Development of Physical Recreation in the Birmingham District from 1871 to 1892', M. A., University of Birmingham, 1957, p. 91, says that Warwickshire had earlier conceded two contracts of over a year in 1893.
66 See chapter 13.
67 Calculated from data in *Wisden Cricketers' Almanack*.
68 *Yorkshire C. C. C. Year Book 1906*.
69 *Wisden Cricketers' Almanack 1906*, p. 69.
70 *Yorkshire C. C. C. Year Book 1895; 1897; 1904*.
71 *Leicester Daily Mercury*, 25 November 1909.
72 Gordon, 'Is cricket losing popularity', p. 329; Duckworth, *Warwickshire Cricket*, p. 98.
73 Surrey did very well out of the lucrative market for F. A. Cup finals which, thanks to their enterprising secretary Charles Alcock, were held at the Oval every year from 1872 to 1892 with the solitary exception of 1873. That Alcock was also secretary of the Football Association did not pass unnoticed (F. O'C. Slingo to president, Sheffield F. C., 30 May 1884, Minutes of Sheffield Wednesday F. C.).
74 Annual Report of Essex C. C. C., April 1900.
75 P. F. Warner, 'The end of the cricket season', *Badminton Magazine*, XXXV, 1912, p. 398.
76 Minutes of Essex C. C. C., 16 June 1890.
77 Quoted in Duckworth, *Warwickshire Cricket*, p. 19.
78 Annual Reports of Hampshire Cricket Ground Company and Warwickshire Cricket Ground Company.
79 *Wisden Cricketers' Almanack 1889*, p. xxxiii.
80 Minutes of Lancashire C. C. C., 11 December 1906. See also R. Genders, *Worcestershire County Cricket*, London, 1952, p. 16.
81 Annual Report of Surrey C. C. C. 1897.
82 Annual Financial Statement of Essex C. C. C., 31 December 1895; Duckworth, *Warwickshire Cricket*, p. 80.

83 P. C. W. Trevor, 'Then and now – cricket', *Badminton Magazine*, XXXVI, 1913, p. 647.
84 Minutes of Lancashire C. C. C., 12 September 1913.
85 Minutes of Leicestershire C. C. C., 21 March 1906; 20 October 1907.
86 Minutes of Leicestershire C. C. C., 25 March 1899.
87 Minutes of Leicestershire C. C. C., 5 March 1902; 15 March 1905; 30 October 1907; 24 November 1909; 20 November 1912.
88 Minutes of Leicestershire C. C. C., 2 October 1907.
89 Minutes of Leicestershire C. C. C., 4 March 1901.
90 Annual Report of Essex C. C. C. 1911.
91 Minutes of Lancashire C. C. C., 30 January, 15 December 1889; 14 December 1900; 19 November 1901.
92 J. A. H. Catton, 'Competitive county cricket', *Badminton Magazine*, XXXIV, 1912, p. 539. See also W. F. Mandle, 'Games people played: cricket and football in England and Victoria in the late nineteenth century', *Historical Studies*, XV, 1973, p. 514.
93 W. T. Taylor, 'History of Derbyshire cricket', *Wisden Cricketers' Almanack* 1953, p. 104; *Cricket*, 9 September 1886; 9 June 1887; 16 April 1891; 18 April 1895; 2 May 1896; 14 April 1898; 25 April 1901; *Cricket Field*, 29 October, 31 December 1892; 25 February 1893; 4 May 1895.
94 *Cricket*, 31 October 1889; 9 May 1895; *Cricket Field*, 28 January, 29 April 1893; Minutes of Essex C. C. C., 9 August 1892; 31 January 1893; 10 November 1908; 3 December 1912.
95 H. S. Altham, *Hampshire County Cricket*, London, 1958, p. 52; *Cricket*, 24 November 1887; 21 December 1899; 20 December 1900.
96 Annual Report of Leicestershire C. C. C. 1901.
97 J. D. Coldham, *Northamptonshire Cricket*, London, 1959, pp. 35–56.
98 *Athletic News*, 28 July 1885; 17 May 1887; also information supplied by Derek Deadman, University of Leicester.
99 Duckworth, *Warwickshire Cricket*, p. 84.
100 *Cricket*, 26 March, 26 November 1891; 28 November 1901; *Cricket Field*, 2 March 1895; also information supplied by Derek Deadman.
101 Minutes of Leicestershire C. C. C., 23 March 1910.
102 Minutes of Leicestershire C. C. C., 18 March 1903.
103 H. Gordon, 'Cricket twenty years ago and now', *Badminton Magazine*, XIV, 1902, p. 620; H. Gordon, 'The real meaning of this cricket season', *Fortnightly Review*, XCI, 1912, p. 1143.
104 For a useful collection of such beliefs, see D. Lemmon, *The Wisden Book of Cricket Quotations*, London, 1982, especially those by Lord Harris (p. 509), A. E. Knight (pp. 463, 540), Andrew Lang (p. 529), Edward Lefroy (p. 589), Bishop Henry Montgomery (p. 587), Sir Henry Newbolt (p. 586), and James Pycroft (pp. 553, 556). See also K. A. P. Sandiford, 'Cricket and the Victorians: a historiographical essay', *Historical Reflections*, IX, 1982, pp. 421–36.
105 Warwickshire actually appealed for financial support from those who were 'naturally anxious as Englishmen for the advancement of the purest and noblest of our national sports'. Quoted in Molyneux, 'Physical Recreation in Birmingham', p. 98.

106 Views of Rowland Hill, president of the English R. F. U. (*Bradford Observer*, 24 August 1896) and R. Westray, president of the Cumberland R. F. U. (*Bradford Observer*, 29 May 1896).

107 *Bradford Observer*, 14 March 1896.

108 *Bradford Observer*, 28 March 1896.

109 Annual Report of the Northern Rugby Football League 1909/10.

110 *Bloodstock Breeders Review*, IV, 1914, p. 282.

111 C. Richardson, *The English Turf*, London, 1901, p. 175.

112 Richardson, *English Turf*, p. 176.

113 C. Richardson, *Racing at Home and Abroad*, London, 1923, I, p. 262.

114 Richardson, *English Turf*, p. 176.

115 C. J. Cawthorne and R. S. Herod, *Royal Ascot*, London, 1900, p. 58; R. Onslow, *The Heath and the Turf*, London, 1971, p. 41; entry in Minute Book of York Race Committee, quoted in Notes for York Race Committee, p. 5.

116 J. Crump, '"The great carnival of the year": the Leicester races in the 19th century', *Transactions of the Leicestershire Historical and Archaeological Society*, LVIII, 1982–3, p. 59.

117 Smart, 'Present state of the turf', *Fortnightly Review*, XXXVIII, 1885, p. 542. See also Whiz, 'Newmarket', *Gentleman's Magazine*, VII, 1871, p. 317.

118 F. Bonnett, 'Racing', in *Victoria County History of Nottinghamshire*, II, London, 1910, p. 397.

119 See G. Plumptre, *The Fast Set*, London, 1985.

120 'Notes', *Badminton Magazine*, V, 1897, p. 745.

121 Plumptre, *Fast Set*, p. 32; R. Cecil, *Life in Edwardian England*, London, 1972, p. 9.

122 G. H. Strutfield, 'Racing in 1890', *Nineteenth Century*, XXVII, 1890, p. 925; W. Day, 'Our national pastime', *Fortnightly Review*, XLVI, 1888, p. 387; E. T. Sachs, 'Modern racing and the Derby', in F. G. Aflalo (ed.), *The Sports of the World*, London, n.d., II, p. 298.

123 Sachs, 'Modern racing', p. 298.

124 Strutfield, 'Racing in 1890', p. 925.

125 Calculated from data in the *Racing Calendar* and *Ruffs Guide to the Turf*.

126 'Racing', *Saturday Review*, 20 July 1888.

127 Richardson, *English Turf*, p. 274; 'Owners and owning', *Badminton Magazine*, XVII, 1903, p. 313.

128 'The turf: its frauds and chicaneries', *Contemporary Review*, XXII, 1873, p. 36; L. H. Curzon, 'The horse as an instrument of gambling', *Contemporary Review*, XXX, 1877, p. 378; 'Modern horse-racing', *Edinburgh Review*, CLI, 1880, p. 432.

129 Smart, 'Present state of the turf', p. 542; 'The racing season', *Saturday Review*, 5 April 1884.

130 Based on data (with allowance for capital depreciation, forfeits and entries) in Lord Hamilton, 'The financial aspects of racing', *Badminton Magazine*, XXIII, 1906, p. 253; and *Bloodstock Breeders Review*, passim.

131 *Ruffs Guide to the Turf*, passim.

132 Calculated from data in *Ruffs Guide to the Turf*.

133 *Bloodstock Breeders Review*, VII, 1918, pp. 18–19.

134 G. H. Verrall, 'The financial aspect of racing from another point of view', *Badminton Magazine*, XXIII, 1906, p. 504.

135 A. E. T. Watson, 'Racing in 1896', *Badminton Magazine*, III, 1896, p. 687.

136 Earl of Suffolk, *Racing and Steeplechasing*, London, 1886, p. 157.

137 W. Day, *The Racehorse in Training*, London, 1880, p. 243.

138 A. E. T. Watson, *The Turf*, London, 1898, p. 153.

139 R. Black, *Horse-Racing in England*, London, 1893, p. 269.

140 A. E. T. Watson, 'Racing', in Earl of Suffolk, H. Peek and F. G. Aflalo (eds.), *The Encyclopaedia of Sport*, London, 1900, p. 179.

141 *Bloodstock Breeders Review*, I, 1912, pp. 37–40; J. B. Robertson, 'The figure system', *Badminton Magazine*, XXXVI, 1913, pp. 282–90.

142 It has recently been demonstrated that in the 1970s there was a very weak correlation between pedigree/auction price and racecourse performance (S. Macken, 'Economic Aspects of Bloodstock Investment in Britain', Ph. D., University of Cambridge, 1986).

143 Calculated from data in Richardson, *English Turf*, pp. 273, 276.

144 F. G. Aflalo, 'The sportsman's library', *Fortnightly Review*, LXX, 1901, p. 1043; M. McKenzie, 'Training: its bearing on health', *New Review*, V, 1891, pp. 454–5.

145 'English field sports', *Bentley's Quarterly Review*, III, 1859, p. 281.

146 Select Committee on Horses, *British Parliamentary Papers 1873*, XIV, q. 3846.

147 Day, 'Our national pastime', p. 381; Richardson, *English Turf*, p. 5.

148 Calculated from data in Curzon, 'Horse as an instrument', p. 378; Strutfield, 'Racing in 1890', pp. 427–34; *Ruffs Guide to the Turf, passim*.

149 Calculated from data in *Ruffs Guide to the Turf, passim*.; Lord Durham, 'Turf reform', *New Review*, II, 1890, p. 279.

150 C. Leicester, *Bloodstock Breeding*, London, 1959, p. 27; J. B. Robertson, 'The principles of heredity applied to the racehorse', in Earl of Harewood (ed.), *Flat Racing*, London, 1940, p. 105; *Bloodstock Breeders Review*, VI, 1917, pp. 109–10.

151 Calculated from data in *Ruffs Guide to the Turf*. The number of mares will be understated as it is based on yearlings offered for sale at auction and thus excludes those mares whose produce was sold privately or retained by the owner-breeder.

152 George Bryatt to W. J. Scott, 24 July 1843. Bowes Papers D/St. Box 162, Durham County Record Office.

153 D. Craig, *Horse-Racing*, London, 1982, p. 55.

154 *Bloodstock Breeders Review*, V, 1913, pp. 209–21; Richardson, *English Turf*, p. 5; Richardson, *Racing at Home and Abroad*, p. 169.

9 All for one and one for all

1 What follows is based on ideas gleaned from the literature on sports cartels cited in notes 4–6 of chapter 8; and, additionally, P. J. Sloane, 'Restriction of competition in professional team sports', *Bulletin of Economic Research*,

XXVIII, 1976, pp. 3–22; G. Daly and W. J. Moore, 'Externalities, property rights and the allocation of resources in major league baseball', *Economic Inquiry*, XIX, 1981, pp. 77–95; and J. W. Hunt and K. A. Lewis, 'Dominance, recontracting and the reserve clause: major league baseball', *American Economic Review*, LXVI, 1976, pp. 936–43.

2 For more detail on the Jockey Club, see W. Vamplew, *The Turf*, London, 1976, pp. 77–109; and R. Mortimer, *The Jockey Club*, London, 1958.

3 Lord Cadogan, 'The state of the turf', *Fortnightly Review*, XXXVII, 1885, p. 106; R. F. Mersey Thompson, 'Ethics of horse-racing', *National Review*, XXXIII, 1899, p. 606.

4 Vamplew, *The Turf*, pp. 110–29.

5 Vamplew, *The Turf*, pp. 187–9.

6 The Sportsman, *British Sports and Pastimes: Racing*, London, 1920, pp. 174, 182–3.

7 Vamplew, *The Turf*, pp. 49–61.

8 Mortimer, *Jockey Club*, pp. 138–43; T. H. Browne, *A History of the English Turf, 1904–1930*, London, 1931, I, pp. 91–2.

9 *Bloodstock Breeders Review*, II, 1913, p. 129.

10 R. Webber, *The Phoenix History of Cricket*, London, 1960, pp. 15, 48–9, 59; J. A. Schofield, 'The development of first-class cricket in England: an economic analysis', *Journal of Industrial Economics*, XXX, 1982, p. 338.

11 M. Golesworthy (ed.), *The Encyclopaedia of Cricket*, London, 1964, p. 163.

12 *Wisden Cricketers' Almanack 1887*, p. 308.

13 *Wisden Cricketers' Almanack 1906*, p. xxvi.

14 *Wisden Cricketers' Almanack 1906*, p. xxvii.

15 R. H. Lyttelton, 'Cricket', *Badminton Magazine*, III, 1896, p. 232; H. Gordon, 'A cricket problem', *Badminton Magazine*, XXII, 1906, pp. 529–37.

16 Lyttelton, 'Cricket', p. 232.

17 Nor did Kent, who provided 9.9% of international players between 1905 and 1914.

18 This clause allowed the entry of Derbyshire, Essex, Hampshire, Leicestershire and Warwickshire for the 1895 season. Two later entrants appear to have come in via the side door. In 1899 the M. C. C. accepted a recommendation from the county secretaries that in view of the visit of the Australians, the number of qualifying fixtures should be reduced to six. Worcestershire, who had been seeking admission to the championship for several seasons, managed to secure this number. Northamptonshire took advantage of a similar provision in 1905.

19 Occasionally this produced a peculiar form of championship. In 1911 neither Kent (second) nor Middlesex (third) played the champion county Warwickshire.

20 Minutes of Lancashire C. C. C., 7 April 1911; Minutes of Essex C. C. C., 21 April 1910; Minutes of Leicestershire C. C. C., 8 October 1890; 2 February 1910.

21 Neville Cardus, music critic and cricket mythologist, has a lot to answer for.

He created the concept of the 'golden age' of English cricket in the two decades before 1914 when great players, especially batsmen, had 'style'. He never ·mentioned the abundance of boring draws.

22 *Wisden Cricketers' Almanack 1902*, p. xxii; *1905*, p. lxxviii; F. Lyttelton, 'More about the cricket problem', *Badminton Magazine*, XI, 1900, pp. 647–53. The growing superiority was reflected in the first-class averages. At five-year intervals from 1895 the average of the batter ranked twenty-fifth was 26.3, 36.3 and 38.6 and of the fiftieth 21.8, 31.7 and 33.1. For bowlers the corresponding figures were, for the twenty-fifth, 15.1, 21.8 and 21.8 and, for the fiftieth, 20.7, 25.3 and 24.4.

23 *Wisden Cricketers' Almanack 1905*, p. lxxviii. In 1909 the averages for batters ranked twenty-fifth and fiftieth had fallen to 31.9 and 28.3, and those for similarly ranked bowlers to 19.0 and 21.3.

24 *Wisden Cricketers' Almanack 1902*, pp. 269–81; *1904*, p. 251.

25 E. H. D. Sewell, 'The past cricket season', *Fortnightly Review*, LXXXVIII, 1910, pp. 539–40. Tarpaulins had long been used to protect pitches *before* the start of matches.

26 H. Gordon, 'Cricket problems of today', *Badminton Magazine*, XIX, 1904, p. 194.

27 Minutes of Leicestershire C. C. C., 12 May 1909; Minutes of Lancashire C. C. C., 4 June 1909.

28 A brief history of the various points systems used in county cricket can be found in *Wisden Cricketers' Almanack 1912*, p. 150.

29 H. Gordon, 'County cricket', *Badminton Magazine*, XVI, 1903, p. 620. Only five teams entered and two of those withdrew; one match was played, in which Kent beat Sussex (Webber, *Phoenix History*, p. 49).

30 Webber, *Phoenix History*, p. 89; Minutes of Leicestershire C. C. C., 16 December 1903.

31 Gordon, 'Cricket problems', p. 196.

32 Minutes of Leicestershire C. C. C., 8 June 1893; 14 July 1896; 18 September 1901; 21 November 1906; Minutes of Lancashire C. C. C., 12 May 1913.

33 Based on a survey of Minutes and Annual Reports of Essex C. C. C., Leicestershire C. C. C., Lancashire C. C. C., Surrey C. C. C., Worcestershire C. C. C., Kent C. C. C. and Warwickshire C. C. C.

34 *Wisden Cricketers' Almanack 1911*, p. 180. That the earnings in the Lancashire leagues were not insubstantial can be inferred from the refusal of Cook of Burnley to join Lancashire in 1907 despite an offer of £100 per annum, a guarantee of at least eight county games a year and a £1,000 benefit after ten years' service (Minutes of Lancashire C. C. C., 17 August 1907).

35 Minutes of Leicestershire C. C. C., *passim.*; Minutes of Essex C. C. C., *passim.*

36 Minutes of Lancashire C. C. C., 8 April 1904.

37 Webber, *Phoenix History*, p. 77.

38 In 1899 tests were held at Trent Bridge, Lord's, Headingley, Old Trafford and the Oval. These continued to be the test venues except in 1902, when Edgbaston and Bramall Lane replaced Trent Bridge and Headingley, and in 1909, when Edgbaston again replaced Trent Bridge.

39 Minutes of Lancashire C. C. C., 11 February 1890 (to Essex); 11 January 1898 (to Somerset); 4 March 1901 (to Leicestershire).
40 Webber, *Phoenix History*, pp. 71–2.
41 Hence, although relationships were occasionally strained, the county club took pains to develop harmonious working arrangements with the leagues and their constituent clubs regarding the use of league players in county games (Minutes of Lancashire C. C. C., 11 December 1903; 13 April 1910; 5 December 1913; 11 December 1914).
42 Minutes of Football League, 22 March 1888.
43 W. McGregor, 'The League and the League system', in *The Book of Football*, London, 1906, p. 171.
44 Minutes of Football League, 17 April 1888.
45 G. Green, *The History of the Football Association*, London, 1953, p. 396.
46 Readers are advised to consult Green, *Football Association*; and C. E. Sutcliffe, J. A. Brierley and F. Howarth, *The Story of the Football League, 1888–1938*, Preston, 1939.
47 McGregor, 'The League', p. 174.
48 J. J. Bentley, 'Is football a business?', *World's Work*, 1912, p. 390.
49 *Athletic News*, 5 February 1900.
50 What follows is based on Sutcliffe *et al.*, *Football League*.
51 J. H. Morrison, 'The rise of Newcastle United', in *The Book of Football*, p. 27.
52 Minutes of Football League, 24 May 1897.
53 Quoted in S. Tischler, *Footballers and Businessmen*, New York, 1981, p. 82.
54 Minutes of Football League, 22 March, 17 April 1888.
55 Minutes of Football League, 1 December, 15 December 1893.
56 *Athletic News*, 6 May 1895.
57 Sutcliffe *et al.*, *Football League*, p. 115.
58 Sutcliffe *et al.*, *Football League*, p. 116.
59 Green, *Football Association*, pp. 409, 419; *Athletic News*, 1 June 1908.
60 D. D. Molyneux, 'The Development of Physical Recreation in the Birmingham District from 1871 to 1892', M. A., University of Birmingham, 1957, p. 282.
61 Minutes of Football League, 1 July 1892; 12 November 1893.
62 Minutes of Football League, 19 May 1896; 24 May 1897.
63 C. W. Alcock, *Association Football*, London, 1906, p. 74.
64 *Athletic News*, 1 June, 24 October 1908; P. M. Young, *The Wolves*, London, 1959, p. 79.
65 See chapter 13.
66 *Athletic News*, 2 January 1910.
67 *Athletic News*, 1 June 1908.
68 Calculated from data in Sutcliffe *et al.*, *Football League*.
69 Sutcliffe *et al.*, *Football League*, p. 9.
70 Minutes of Football League, 18 September 1891.
71 Minutes of Football League, 29 May, 5 November 1897.
72 Minutes of Football League, 5 December 1890.
73 Minutes of Football League, 12 January 1891.
74 Minutes of Football League, 3 July 1891; 30 May 1896.

75 A. Davis, 'The Southern League: its rise and progress', in *The Book of Football*, pp. 284–6.
76 Minutes of Football League, 24 May 1897; Sutcliffe *et al.*, *Football League*, p. 80.
77 For election figures, see Sutcliffe *et al.*, *Football League*, pp. 108–12.
78 Annual Report of Football League 1900/01; Minutes of Football League, 30 April 1909; Minutes of Sheffield Wednesday F. C., 1 March 1909.
79 Minutes of Football League, 29 June 1908.
80 Minutes of Football League, 16 March 1909.
81 *Athletic News*, 1 June 1908.
82 Minutes of Football League, 22 March, 17 April 1888; 28 March 1890; 4 May 1891; 31 May 1908.
83 Minutes of Football League, 17 June 1888; 29 May 1891; 29 May 1908.
84 Minutes of Football League, 4 May 1891.
85 Minutes of Football League, 1 March 1913.
86 *Athletic News*, 25 September 1899.
87 A. Mason, *Association Football and English Society, 1863–1915*, Brighton, 1980, p. 47.
88 F. A. Circular quoted in Green, *Football Association*, p. 407.
89 W. I. Bassett, 'Big transfers and the transfer system', in *The Book of Football*, p. 162.
90 Minutes of Football League, 7 October 1914.
91 Annual Report of Scottish Football Association 1911/12.
92 G. Green, *The Official History of the F. A. Cup*, London, 1960, pp. 40–1.
93 R. M. Connell, 'The association game in Scotland', in *The Book of Football*, p. 269.
94 Next season they finished eighth in the second division and left the League altogether.
95 *Scottish Sport*, 2 May 1890.
96 *Scottish Sport*, 26 May 1893.
97 What follows is based on J. R. Mackay, *The Hibees*, Edinburgh, 1985, and information supplied by Peter Bilsborough, University of Stirling.
98 By-laws Northern Rugby Football League, 5 February 1901.
99 By-laws Northern Rugby Football League, 5 February 1901.
100 Minutes of Northern Rugby Football Union, 7 November 1899.
101 K. Macklin, *The History of Rugby League Football*, London, 1962, p. 58.
102 Minutes of Northern Rugby Football Union, 30 May 1907; 2 September 1908.
103 *Bradford Observer*, 14 August 1906.
104 Four clubs in fact had 64.9% of all selections. Hunslet (31 caps) actually had more than Huddersfield (24) but surprisingly were ranked only seventh in terms of winning percentages.
105 T. Delaney, *The Roots of Rugby League*, Keighley, 1984, pp. 106–7.
106 J. H. Smith, 'The history of the Northern Union', in *The Book of Football*, p. 275.
107 Macklin, *Rugby League*, p. 37.
108 Minutes of Northern Rugby Football League, 25 June 1907; 28 June 1911.

109 Macklin, *Rugby League*, p. 34.
110 Minutes of Northern Rugby Football League, 25 June 1907.
111 E. H. D. Sewell, 'Rugby football', *Fortnightly Review*, LXXXV, 1909, p. 978; *Bradford Observer*, 28 August 1906; A. Budd, 'The Northern Union', in A. Budd, C. B. Fry, B. F. Robinson and T. A. Cook, *Football*, London, 1897, pp. 33–5.
112 Annual Report of the Northern Rugby Football Union 1906/07.
113 It is not clear from the available records whether or not any pooling arrangements operated at the league level.
114 Minutes of Northern Rugby Football League, 1 June, 14 June 1908.
115 Minutes of Northern Rugby Football League, 9 February 1909.
116 Actually Liverpool drew a match with Bramley but had the point taken away when they refused to fulfil the return fixture.
117 *Bradford Observer*, 27 August 1896.
118 Minutes of Northern Rugby Football Union, 14 August 1908.
119 Annual Report of Northern Rugby Football Union 1911/12.
120 P. C. W. Trevor, 'The future of cricket', *Fortnightly Review*, XC, 1911, p. 533.

10 Paying the piper: shareholders and directors

1 Although no county cricket club adopted company status, the names of committee members are relatively easy to obtain. Unfortunately occupations are seldom given and limitations of time, money and geography prevented this study from being expanded to explore their social and economic background. It would be interesting to test the view that 'usually they consist of between twenty and thirty members, half being county magnates who give valuable patronage. Of the other half some six to eight are leading amateurs, past and present, and the rest are enthusiasts, more or less useful' (H. Gordon, 'From colts match to test match', *Badminton Magazine*, XVIII, 1904, p. 659).
2 Most social theorists, whilst acknowledging that occupation by itself is an imperfect indicator of social classification, have accepted that it is a reasonable proxy, particularly if the social groupings are not too narrow. The general issues are discussed in W. A. Armstrong, 'The use of information about occupation', in E. A. Wrigley (ed.), *Nineteenth-Century Society*, Cambridge, 1972, pp. 191–310.
3 Occupations were allocated to these categories utilising G. Routh, *Occupations and Pay in Great Britain, 1906–60*, London, 1965, appendix A.
4 For English clubs these totalled 1.5% of shareholders and 2.2% of shareholdings; for Scottish clubs the proportions were 1.3% of members, 2.7% of shareholders and 3.4% of shareholdings.
5 Celtic fans, no doubt, will have a different interpretation for the Rangers' shareholder who styled himself as a 'comedian'!
6 On this problem, see C. H. Lee, *British Regional Employment Statistics, 1841–1971*, Cambridge, 1979, pp. 3–29.
7 D. D. Molyneux, 'The Development of Physical Recreation in the Birmingham District from 1871 to 1892', M. A., University of Birmingham, 1957, pp. 20–4.

8 When all clubs are considered, including those for which membership figures were unavailable, the proportion is 47.3%.

9 Correlation tests were run between occupational group shareholders and county/city occupational structures as revealed in the 1911 Census of Scotland. Results ranged between −0.23 to +0.37, which suggests no strong relationship.

10 As there was no way of identifying a random sample of sports companies short of the daunting task of ploughing through all company registrations before 1915, a second-best solution was adopted in that the index was searched for company titles beginning with the name of a major Scottish city.

11 It may be significant that of the four Scottish clubs traced whose prospectus suggested the possibility of dividends Ayr, Hamilton and Partick Thistle had relatively low working-class participation. Similarly the working-class involvement in Woolwich Arsenal, who also promised dividends, was less than the English average. The one Scottish exception was Motherwell and this may be explicable in terms of an exceptionally high initial working-class membership.

12 A. Mason, *Association Football and English Society, 1863–1915*, Brighton, 1980, p. 23.

13 Interestingly an analysis of licences to sell drink suggests that less were held per capita in Scotland than in England (G. B. Wilson, *Alcohol and the Nation*, London, 1940). Clearly this is an area for further research.

14 Even the company records are incomplete as not all clubs filed details of changes in their directorates.

15 I am grateful to John Hutchinson for access to his research findings.

16 Mason, *Association Football*, p. 43; S. Tischler, *Footballers and Businessmen*, New York, 1981, pp. 72, 76.

17 In addition to the clubs cited in Table 10.4, directors of Chelsea needed 100 shares, Sunderland 50 shares and Arsenal 25 shares (Tischler, *Footballers and Businessmen*, p. 75).

18 Tischler, *Footballers and Businessmen*, p. 74.

19 J. Moynihan, *The Chelsea Story*, London, 1982, p. 108; D. Hodgson, *The Liverpool Story*, London, 1978, pp. 9–10; D. Hodgson, *The Manchester United Story*, London, 1977, pp. 21–2.

20 Tischler, *Footballers and Businessmen*, p. 74.

21 C. P. Korr, 'The men at the top: the board of directors of the West Ham United Football Club', in W. Vamplew, *The Economic History of Leisure: Papers presented at the Eighth International Economic History Congress*, Budapest, 1982, p. 4.

22 Nothing is known about voting procedures in the boardroom.

23 Loans were made. The West Ham directors lent the club more than £3,000 prior to the 1904 season (C. P. Korr, 'West Ham United Football Club and the beginnings of professional football in east London, 1895–1914', *Journal of Contemporary History*, XIII, 1978, p. 276). Several articles in *The Book of Football*, London, 1906, pp. 82, 88, 146, 272, 292, also imply that clubs were assisted financially by some of their directors. See also Football Association, Report of Commission on Manchester United, 30 September 1910.

24 Financial statements prior to 1906 were not available from company files.

Some synopses of earlier accounts appear in the *Athletic News* and this promises to be a fruitful future line of inquiry which will enable concurrent shareholders' registers and company accounts to be compared. Later registers also remain to be examined.

25 J. E. Handley, *The Celtic Story*, London, 1960, p. 77.

26 W. McGregor, 'The £ s. d. of football', in *The Book of Football*, p. 60.

27 Hutchinson has shown that many Hearts' contracts went to committeemen and directors, but after an acrimonious dispute in 1907 it was resolved that 'no member of the Board do any work connected with the club in the future' (Minutes of Heart of Midlothian F. C., 27 April 1907).

28 McGregor, '£ s. d.', p. 60.

29 J. J. Bentley, quoted in Mason, *Association Football*, p. 48.

30 S. Wagg, *The Football World*, Brighton, 1984, p. 5; Mason, *Association Football*, p. 48.

11 Winning at any cost?

1 Minutes of Football League, 11 March 1898; H. Gordon, 'The past cricket season', *Badminton Magazine*, xv, 1902, p. 402.

2 For football, see Table 8.3. Racecourses were the most highly capitalised enterprises, but both those for which data was obtained, Haydock Park and Newbury, had tangible assets ratios of only 1.11.

3 W. Nicholson, *Micro-Economic Theory*, Hinsdale, 1978, pp. 381–3. For some comments on the period studied, see P. L. Payne, 'The emergence of the large-scale company in Great Britain, 1870–1914', *Economic History Review*, xx, 1967, pp. 519–42.

4 K. A. P. Sandiford, 'Cricket and the Victorian society', *Journal of Social History*, xvii, 1983, p. 309.

5 Quoted in E. H. D. Sewell, 'Has public interest in first class cricket declined', *Badminton Magazine*, xxxvii, 1913, p. 188.

6 Unfortunately results are to hand only prior to the season 1899/1900, but in that first nine years of the Scottish Football League the following clubs all won major regional trophies while their League performance was moderate: St Mirren (30.6), St Bernards (38.9), Dundee (38.9), Dumbarton (18.5) and Abercorn (38.6). Figures in parentheses indicate the winning percentage in the Scottish League in the season in which they won their trophy.

7 J. A. H. Catton, 'Competitive county cricket', *Badminton Magazine*, xxxiv, 1912, p. 539.

8 'Test match cricket of 1912', *Blackwoods Magazine*, cxcii, 1912, p. 847; H. Gordon, 'The real meaning of this cricket season', *Fortnightly Review*, xci, 1912, p. 1144.

9 More research is needed on the degree to which a club, or even a sport, lay in the voluntary rather than the commercial sector. To what extent were cricket and soccer clubs, or race meetings, regarded historically as quasi-public goods either at national or local level? Modern studies have suggested that support for a team is greater than the numbers who pay at the gate or take out membership and that such external benefits to free riders have been financed

by those who see sport and sports clubs as having an important community role. See, for example, C. Gratton and B. Lisewski, 'The economics of sport in Britain: a case of market failure', *British Review of Economic Issues*, III, 1981, pp. 63–75.

12 The struggle for recognition

1 For a fuller discussion, see E. A. Glader, *Amateurism and Athletics*, New York, 1978.

2 What follows is based on C. Brookes, *English Cricket*, Newton Abbot, 1978; and W. F. Mandle, 'The professional cricketer in England in the nineteenth century', *Labour History*, XXIII, 1972, pp. 1–16.

3 'Professionalism in English sports', *Saturday Review*, 14 April 1888.

4 The subordination was not absolute. Although they dressed separately, the amateurs and professionals of Yorkshire, Lancashire and Leicestershire entered the field of play by the same gate (Minutes of Lancashire C. C. C., 9 December 1910; Minutes of Leicestershire C. C. C., 4 March 1901). It should also be noted that the requirement for professionals to pay for their own travel and accommodation would have encouraged separation.

5 Minutes of Leicestershire C. C. C., 19 September 1906.

6 W. Vamplew, *The Turf*, London, 1976.

7 J. Runciman, 'The ethics of the turf', *Contemporary Review*, LV, 1889, p. 163; Earl of Suffolk, *Racing and Steeplechasing*, London, 1886, p. 245.

8 Quoted in J. Fairfax-Blakeborough, *The Analysis of the Turf*, London, 1927, p. 143.

9 Earl of Suffolk, 'Gentlemen riders', *Badminton Magazine*, II, 1896, p. 495. Detailed regulations can be found in Appendix 2a.

10 R. P. P. Rowe and C. M. Pitman, *Rowing*, London, 1898, pp. 3–4.

11 *Bell's Life*, 26 June 1831. See also T. A. Cook, 'Rowing', in *Victoria County History of Oxfordshire*, II, London, 1907, p. 369.

12 Rowe and Pitman, *Rowing*, p. 130.

13 Quoted in P. Lovesey, *The Official Centenary History of the Amateur Athletic Association*, London, 1979, p. 22.

14 Rowe and Pitman, *Rowing*, pp. 149–51.

15 N. Wigglesworth, 'A history of rowing in the north-west of England', *British Journal of Sports History*, III, 1986, p. 153.

16 R. C. Lehmann, *Rowing*, London, 1898, p. 327. Professional racing was practically restricted to sculling and occasional watermen's regattas.

17 For an extract from the A. R. A.'s constitution, see Appendix 2b.

18 Lehmann, *Rowing*, pp. 326–7.

19 W. Meisl, 'The importance of being amateur', in A. Natan (ed.), *Sport and Society*, London, 1958, p. 152. Ironically Kelly's son John became head of the United States Olympic Committee and his daughter, Grace, married Prince Rainier of Monaco, whose father was one of the most active members of the International Olympic Committee (A. Guttmann, 'The belated birth and threatened death of fair play', *Yale Review*, 1985, p. 532). The artisan ban had been lifted by 1939 but the A. R. A. maintained a prohibition on those

who worked 'in and about boats' until 1948 (N. Wigglesworth, 'A history of rowing', p. 153).

20 For a brief history, see Lovesey, *Centenary History*, pp. 6–14. More details can be found in J. R. Ross, 'Pedestrianism and Athletics in England and Australia in the Nineteenth Century: A Case Study in the Development of Sport', B. H. M. S. (Hons.), University of Queensland, 1985.

21 Quoted in M. Shearman, *Athletics and Football*, London, 1888, pp. 52–3.

22 Lovesey, *Centenary History*, p. 22.

23 Lovesey, *Centenary History*, pp. 24–5; Glader, *Amateurism*, p. 103.

24 Lovesey, *Centenary History*, p. 28; Shearman, *Athletics*, pp. 217–18.

25 Lovesey, *Centenary History*, pp. 29–32.

26 Shearman, *Athletics*, p. 222. An extract from the A. A. A. regulations can be found in Appendix 2c.

27 E. B. Mitchell, *Boxing*, London, 1889, p. 138; J. Ford, *Prizefighting*, Newton Abbot, 1971, pp. 35–64; A. J. Papalas, 'Professors and amateurs: aspects of pugilism in the Regency period', in *Proceedings of Thirteenth North American Society for Sport History Conference*, 1985, pp. 41–2.

28 Mitchell, *Boxing*, p. 146; J. Arlott, *The Oxford Companion to Sports and Games*, London, 1975, p. 116. For changes in the rules and in the legal status of boxing, see 'Boxing and sparring', *Saturday Review*, 26 January 1884.

29 A. F. Bettinson and B. Bennison, *The Home of Boxing*, London, 1919, pp. 14–15. See also A. Giddens, 'Sport and Society in Contemporary England', M. A., University of London, 1961, pp. 34–7.

30 There was no generally accepted authority until the British Boxing Board of Control was set up in 1929. An earlier version in 1919 failed to secure legitimisation because it was insufficiently independent of the National Sporting Club (M. Golesworthy (ed.), *The Encyclopaedia of Boxing*, London, 1965, p. 34).

31 In 1883 it was renamed the National Cyclists' Union in order to embrace tricyclists, who were, at that time, the majority of riders.

32 Earl of Albermarle and G. Lacy Hillier, *Cycling*, London, 1896, p. 234.

33 The interests of the vast majority of cyclists were in riding rather than in racing and they were catered for by the Cyclists' Touring Club, founded as the Bicycle Touring Club in 1878 (Shearman, *Athletics*, pp. 252–8).

34 Shearman, *Athletics*, p. 235.

35 Shearman, *Athletics*, p. 223.

36 Shearman, *Athletics*, p. 245; G. Lacy Hillier, 'Cycling', in Earl of Suffolk, H. Peek and F. G. Aflalo (eds.), *The Encyclopaedia of Sport*, London, 1900, I, p. 289.

37 Duncans, 'The cycle industry', *Contemporary Review*, LXXIII, 1898, p. 509; J. and E. R. Pennell, 'Cycling: past, present and future', *New Review*, IV, 1891, p. 176.

38 H. S. C. Everard, 'A haver with Tom Morris', *Badminton Magazine*, I, 1895, p. 338.

39 H. Hutchinson, 'Golf during thirty years', *Quarterly Review*, CCXII, 1906, p. 111.

40 Hutchinson, 'Golf', p. 113; T. E. Elias, 'Golf: an historic survey', in *British*

Sports and Sportsmen, London, 1935, p. 17; H. Seton-Kerr, *Golf*, London, 1907, p. 8.

41 Hutchinson, 'Golf', p. 113.

42 F. Kinloch, 'Golf of yesterday and today', *Chamber's Journal*, LXXXIII, 1906, p. 675.

43 Quoted in Elias, 'Golf', p. 27.

44 N. L. Jackson, 'Professionalism and sport', *Fortnightly Review*, LXVII, 1900, pp. 154–61.

45 J. A. H. Catton, *The Real Football*, London, 1900, p. 53.

46 G. Green, *The History of the Football Association*, London, 1953, pp. 98–9; C. E. Sutcliffe and F. Hargreaves, *History of the Lancashire Football Association, 1878–1928*, Blackburn, 1988, pp. 153–4).

47 *The Book of Football*, London, 1906, p. 114.

48 Minutes of Sheffield Wednesday F. C., 15 January, 26 November, 3 December 1883. The official reaction to Forest's initiative was to censure them for 'disgraceful [conduct] calculated to lower the game of football in public estimation' (Minutes of Sheffield Wednesday F. C., 15 January 1883).

49 Sheffield Wednesday Circular to Players, 3 November 1883.

50 Green, *Football Association*, p. 99.

51 Green, *Football Association*, pp. 99–100.

52 How would Sheffield Wednesday have explained the 5s. for 'wages' paid to those who played against Aston Villa and Bolton in September 1884? It is possible that these were broken-time payments, but normally these were shown as 'expenses' or in 'lieu of wages'. Even then 5s. to each player, irrespective of occupation, is suspicious.

53 Green, *Football Association*, pp. 101–2.

54 F. O'C. Slingo to president, Wednesday F. C., 30 August 1884, Minutes of Sheffield Wednesday F. C.

55 Green, *Football Association*, pp. 102–8, 134–5.

56 Catton, *Real Football*, p. 68.

57 A. Davis, 'England's international teams and how they are selected', in *The Book of Football*, p. 229.

58 Minutes of Football League, 15 October 1905; C. W. Alcock, *Association Football*, London, 1906, p. 76.

59 The old-boy sides had failed to dominate the Amateur Cup and eventually started this exclusive competition of their own (H. Hughes-Onslow, 'The association football crisis', *Badminton Magazine*, XXIV, 1907, pp. 43–4).

60 'Association football: a retrospect and a lament', *Saturday Review*, 3 March 1900.

61 Hughes-Onslow, 'Football crisis', p. 44; P. C. McIntosh, 'An historical view of sport and social control', *International Review of Sports Sociology*, VI, 1971, p. 7. See also the Report of the Football Association, 'The Football Association and the Amateur Football Association', April 1912.

62 W. Dick in *Scottish Football Annual 1874/75*, p. 10; and *1877/78*, p. 35.

63 Minutes of Scottish Football Association, 2 October 1873; *Scottish Football Annual 1882/83*, p. 59.

64 R. Livingstone, 'Existing evils', in *Scottish Football Annual 1881/82*, p. 38.

65 Annual Report of Scottish Football Association 1884/85.
66 Annual Report of Scottish Football Association 1883/84.
67 In 1885 Glasgow Rangers entered the F. A. Cup but refused to play Rawten-
   stall because their team included professionals. This cost Rangers a 10s. fine.
   Presumably Scottish thrift overcame amateur scruples, for next year Rangers
   reached the semi-final of the English tournament (J. Allen, *The Story of the
   Rangers*, Glasgow, 1924, p. 43).
68 Annual Report of Scottish Football Association 1885/86.
69 Annual Report of Scottish Football Association 1886/87.
70 For an extract from the S. F. A. rules governing professionalism, see Appendix
   2e.
71 Annual Report of Scottish Football Association 1887/88.
72 Annual Report of Scottish Football Association 1890/91. All the League clubs,
   with the exception of St Mirren and Abercorn, were alleged to have colluded
   in the deduction of money from gate-receipts to illegally pay players (*Scottish
   Sport*, 14 October 1892).
73 Annual Report of Scottish Football Association 1893/94, 1895/96.
74 This survey is based on K. Macklin, *The History of Rugby League Football*,
   London, 1962, pp. 16–36; E. Dunning and K. Sheard, *Barbarians, Gentlemen
   and Players*, Oxford, 1979, pp. 147, 166–74, 207–12; A. Budd, *Football
   (Rugby)*, London, 1899, pp. 20–1; T. Delaney, *The Roots of Rugby League*,
   Keighley, 1984; and U. A. Titley and R. McWhirter, *Centenary History of the
   Rugby Football Union*, London, 1970, pp. 111–16.
75 M. Shearman, W. J. Oakley, G. O. Smith and F. Mitchell, *Football*, London,
   1899, pp. 273–4. See also the letter from an 'old forward' in *Leeds Daily
   News*, 28 August 1895; and C. J. N. Fleming, 'Rugby football', *Badminton
   Magazine*, III, 1896, p. 559.
76 For an extract from the R. F. U.'s rules on professionalism, see Appendix 2f.
77 First Annual Report of Northern Rugby Football Union, quoted in *Bradford
   Observer*, 28 August 1896. Even F. S. Jackson, the England and Yorkshire
   amateur cricketer, whilst not in favour 'in the strictest sense of the words, of
   professionalism in rugby football', recognised that 'if working men in the
   North were to play, it was only just they should receive recompense for at least
   the time they were compelled to lose' (*Bradford Observer*, 4 November 1896).
78 Minutes of Northern Rugby Football Union Committee, *passim*.
79 Minutes of Northern Rugby Football Union Committee, 8 May 1902.
80 Macklin, *Rugby League*, pp. 34–6.
81 P. C. W. Trevor, 'Football', *Badminton Magazine*, XII, 1901, p. 212.
82 E. H. D. Sewell, 'Rugby football', *Fortnightly Review*, LXXXV, 1909,
   pp. 984–5; B. Dobbs, *Edwardians at Play*, London, 1973, p. 111.
83 N. L. Jackson, *Association Football*, London, 1899, p. 241; D. D. Molyneux,
   'The Development of Physical Recreation in the Birmingham District from
   1871 to 1892', M. A., University of Birmingham, 1957, p. 155. Nevertheless,
   Jackson was willing to organise the Corinthians soccer team, which frequently
   played against professional teams and which did very well out of the
   gate-money in terms of hospitality received.
84 See, for example, H. H. Almond, 'Football as a moral agent', *Nineteenth

Century, XXXIV, 1893, pp. 902–9; C. W. Alcock, *Association Football*, London, 1890, p. 61; Hughes-Onslow, 'Football crisis', p. 42; G. O. Smith, 'Football', *Pall Mall Magazine*, XIII, 1897, p. 570; and H. Graves, 'A philosophy of sport', *Contemporary Review*, LXXVIII, 1900, p. 883.

85 Fleming, 'Rugby football', p. 565.

86 Quoted in A. W. Myers, *C. B. Fry*, London, 1912, p. 113. See also G. O. Smith, *Football (Association)*, London, 1898, p. 33; Annual Reports of Scottish Football Association, *passim*; C. W. Alcock, 'An appreciation of the professional', in B. O. Corbett *et al.*, *Football*, London, 1907, p. 124; and An Old Player, 'Football: the game and the business', *World Today*, I, 1902, pp. 75–6.

87 'Boat-racing', *Gentleman's Magazine*, II, 1868, p. 174.

88 E. H. D. Sewell, 'The state of the game', *Fortnightly Review*, LXXXIX, 1911, p. 941. See also J. H. C. Fegan *et al.*, *Football, Hockey and Lacrosse*, London, 1900, p. 29.

89 H. Gordon, 'The test matches in England', *Badminton Magazine*, XIV, 1902, p. 533. See also D. Birley, *The Willow Wand*, London, 1979, pp. 29–37, for a discussion of Grace's cricketing ethics.

90 'Football accidents', *Saturday Review*, 10 December 1892; *British Almanac and Companion 1889*, p. 374.

91 W. D. Adams, 'The growth of English pastimes', *British Almanac and Companion 1886*, p. 78; Graves, 'Philosophy', p. 883; M. Shearman, 'Amateur', in Earl of Suffolk, H. Peek and F. G. Aflalo (eds.), *The Encyclopaedia of Sport*, London, 1900, p. 3.

92 Lovesey, *Centenary History*, pp. 41–4.

93 See chapter 17.

94 H. F. Abell, 'The football fever', *Macmillan's Magazine*, LXXXIX, 1904, pp. 279–80; R. J. Sturdee, 'The ethics of football', *Westminster Review*, LIX, 1903, p. 182; Shearman, 'Amateur', p. 3; 'Sport and decadence', *Quarterly Review*, CCXI, 1909, p. 495.

95 E. Ensor, 'The football madness', *Contemporary Review*, LXXIV, 1898, p. 760.

96 E. Needham, *Association Football*, London, 1900, pp. 3–4.

97 Sturdee, 'Ethics', p. 183; C. Edwardes, 'The new football mania', *Nineteenth Century*, XXXII, 1892, p. 623; Runciman, 'Ethics', p. 163.

98 Trevor, 'Football', p. 216.

99 Abell, 'Football fever', p. 278; C. S. Colman, 'The football season', *Badminton Magazine*, II, 1896, p. 542.

100 Budd, *Football*, p. 23.

101 S. S. Harris, 'The famous Corinthian F. C. 1883–1906', in *The Book of Football*, p. 207.

102 Trevor, 'Football', p. 215; Budd, *Football*, pp. 21–2; Smith, *Football (Association)*, pp. 30–1.

103 C. J. Apperley, 'The turf', *Quarterly Review*, XLIX, 1833, p. 437, lists several gentlemen riders with good records, but in fact they rode mainly at private meetings from which professionals were excluded. In 1887 George 'Mr Abington' Baird, millionaire son of a Scottish ironmaster, had a winning

percentage almost as good as that of the champion professional jockey, but he was a rarity, perhaps driven to prove himself on the racetrack because of the rebuffs which he received from English society ('The last surprise of the racing season', *Saturday Review*, 3 December 1887).

104 H. S. C. Everard, 'Golf: a retrospect', *Badminton Magazine*, XVIII, 1904, p. 35. A calculation based on the surveys of golf in the *Victoria County Histories* shows that the amateur course records averaged 3.7 strokes more than the professional ones.

105 *Cycling*, London, 1898, pp. 44, 63.

106 In the Lord's and Oval fixtures between 1891 and 1910, although the players won 23 of the 40 fixtures, the gentlemen managed 10 victories and 7 draws.

107 On the latter, see chapter 14. More research is needed on the comparative backgrounds of those who legislated for, those who were taught by, and those who employed, professionals.

108 'Professionalism in English sports', *Saturday Review*, 14 April 1888.

109 E. H. D. Sewell, 'Rugby football and the colonial tours', *Fortnightly Review*, LXXXII, 1907, p. 848; Harris, 'Corinthian F. C.', p. 209. A. N. Hornby, the Lancashire cricket captain – an amateur of course – did criticise the Corinthians, whom he alleged asked for larger guarantees than professional clubs, published no balance sheets, and distributed expenses surpassing the wages of professionals (P. M. Young, *Football in Sheffield*, London, 1962, p. 67).

110 Shearman, 'Amateur', p. 2. See also Creston, 'Football', *Fortnightly Review*, LV, 1894, p. 30.

111 *Bell's Life*, 2 November 1878.

112 Shearman, 'Amateur', p. 2.

113 Minutes of Warwickshire C. C. C., quoted in L. Duckworth, *The Story of Warwickshire Cricket*, London, 1974, pp. 85–6. Poideven eventually qualified for Lancashire but their minutes contain no details as to his remuneration.

114 P. Murphy, *Tiger Smith*, Newton Abbot, 1981, pp. 72–3.

115 H. Hutchinson, 'The parlous condition of cricket', *National Review*, XXXV, 1900, p. 791.

116 M. Cobbett, *The Man on the March*, London, 1896, p. 281.

117 Hutchinson, 'Parlous condition', p. 791; Minutes of Lancashire C. C. C., 7 March 1902.

118 Minutes of Leicestershire C. C. C., 28 September 1904. See also K. A. P. Sandiford, 'Amateurs and professionals in Victorian county cricket', *Albion*, XV, 1983, pp. 37–8.

119 H. Gordon, 'The past cricket season', *Badminton Magazine*, XVII, 1903, pp. 405–6.

120 *Wisden Cricketers' Almanack 1897*, p. lviii; H. Gordon and H. D. G. Leverson-Gower, 'The state of amateurs in cricket', *Badminton Magazine*, XIV, 1902, p. 327.

121 Sandiford, 'Amateurs and professionals', p. 38.

122 *Wisden Cricketers' Almanack 1897*, p. liv.

123 B. Darwin, *W. G. Grace*, London, 1978, pp. 34, 68, 113.

124 E. Midwinter, *W. G. Grace*, London, 1981, pp. 155–6.
125 *Wisden Cricketers' Almanack 1897*, p. lviii.
126 W. J. Lias, 'The future of rugby football', *Badminton Magazine*, XIII, 1901, pp. 607–8; G. Williams, 'How amateur was my valley: professional sport and national identity in Wales 1890–1914', *British Journal of Sports History*, II, 1985, pp. 252–3.
127 Titley and McWhirter, *Centenary History*, p. 116.
128 Dobbs, *Edwardians*, p. 96.
129 Shearman, 'Amateur', p. 2; Earl of Suffolk, 'Gentlemen riders', pp. 495–6.
130 *South Wales Daily News*, 30 September 1901, quoted in Williams, 'How amateur', p. 255; Trevor, 'Football', p. 219.
131 Shearman, 'Amateur', p. 2.
132 Shearman, *Athletics*, pp. 187–8; Cobbett, *The Man*, p. 277; Graves, 'Philosophy', p. 886; R. M. Conway, 'Cross country running', *Badminton Magazine*, VII, 1898, p. 571; Lovesey, *Centenary History*, pp. 44–6.
133 Shearman, *Athletics*, pp. 187, 221, 226, 236.
134 'Athletes of the year', *Strand Magazine*, VIII, 1894, p. 730.
135 Graves, 'Philosophy', pp. 882–3; Albermarle and Hillier, *Cycling*, pp. 43–4.

13 Earnings and opportunities

1 Although a few former public schoolboys turned professional, most paid cricketers appear to have come from the skilled working class (K. A. P. Sandiford, 'Amateurs and professionals in Victorian county cricket', *Albion*, XV, 1983, p. 39; W. F. Mandle, 'The professional cricketer in England in the nineteenth century', *Labour History*, XXIII, 1972, p. 4). In soccer Tischler and Mason agree that professionals were drawn from the working class, skilled and unskilled, though Mason argues that the skilled were dominant, especially before 1900 (A. Mason, *Association Football and English Society, 1863–1915*, Brighton, 1980, pp. 89–92; S. Tischler, *Footballers and Businessmen*, New York, 1981, pp. 92–3). Jockeys were most definitely working class in origin (W. Vamplew, *The Turf*, London, 1976, p. 151).
2 R. Onslow, *The Heath and the Turf*, London, 1971, p. 51; Q. Gilbey, *Champions All*, London, 1971, p. 156; Vamplew, *The Turf*, p. 152.
3 Mandle, 'Professional cricketer', pp. 5–6.
4 I am grateful to Professor John Osborne, Dickinson College, for pre-publication access to his material.
5 C. Edwardes, 'The new football mania', *Nineteenth Century*, XXXII, 1892, p. 624; Mason, *Association Football*, pp. 92–4.
6 Minutes of Sheffield Wednesday F. C., 28 February 1900.
7 W. I. Bassett, 'Big transfers and the transfer system', in *The Book of Football*, London, 1906, p. 160.
8 J. E. Handley, *The Celtic Story*, London, 1960, p. 65.
9 Minutes of Essex C. C. C., 23 February 1892; Minutes of Leicestershire C. C. C., 16 October 1895; *Yorkshire C. C. C. Year Book 1894*, p. 59. The term 'colt' did not necessarily imply a youngster. Those who played in Yorkshire's colts' matches ranged in age from 17 to 29, with the bulk being

over 20 (*Yorkshire C. C. C. Year Books*). Lancashire set an upper limit of 25 (Minutes of Lancashire C. C. C., 6 April 1910).

10   Minutes of Lancashire C. C. C., 20 January 1902; L. Duckworth, *The Story of Warwickshire Cricket*, London, 1974, pp. 59, 66.

11   Minutes of Leicestershire C. C. C., 6 July 1910; Minutes of Lancashire C. C. C., 10 December 1909.

12   Barnes opted out of first-class county cricket to play in the leagues, where he had a remarkable career, heading the bowling averages of whatever league he played in for 25 consecutive years. He was still playing for Staffordshire in the minor counties championship in 1934 when aged 61, and only gave up club cricket in 1940 (S. A. H. Burne, 'Cricket', in *Victoria County History of Staffordshire*, II, 1967, p. 370). Rhodes played 33 years for Yorkshire, did the double 16 times, and was first or second in the national batting averages on 11 occasions. In his first-class career he took 4,184 wickets at 16.7, scored 39,772 runs at 30.8, and took 708 catches (P. Thomas, *Yorkshire Cricketers, 1839–1939*, Manchester, 1973, pp. 154–9).

13   Annual Report of Surrey C. C. C. 1892, p. 122; Minutes of Leicestershire C. C. C., 25 March 1899. H. Gordon, 'The past cricket season', *Badminton Magazine*, XXXI, 1910, p. 442.

14   'Professional cricket', *Saturday Review*, 14 July 1883; H. Perkins, 'Lords and the M. C. C.', in Earl of Suffolk, H. Peck and F. G. Aflalo (eds.), *The Encyclopaedia of Sport*, London, 1911, p. 387. In 1889 the M. C. C. employed 42 professional bowlers and 53 in 1912 (*Wisden Cricketers' Almanack 1889*, p. 142; *1912*, p. 350).

15   *Yorkshire C. C. C. Year Book 1904*, p. 11; Minutes of Lancashire C. C. C., 29 January 1889; Annual Report of Kent C. C. C., 1900.

16   Annual Report of Essex C. C. C. 1910, 1911.

17   Minutes of Lancashire C. C. C., 9 December 1910.

18   Mason, *Association Football*, pp. 107–9.

19   J. Porter, *Kingsclere*, London, 1896, p. 223; M. Cobbett, *Racing Life and Racing Characteristics*, London, 1903, p. 232.

20   Calculated from data in *Yorkshire C. C. C. Year Books*.

21   Minutes of Lancashire C. C. C., 1898, *passim*.

22   Calculated from data in Football League Registration Books.

23   Minutes of Football League, 19 May 1899.

24   Calculated from data in the *Racing Calendar*.

25   Lord Hawke, 'On captaincy', *Badminton Magazine*, XIV, 1902, p. 474; Annual Reports of Kent C. C. C.

26   Minutes of Lancashire C. C. C., 2 June 1900.

27   Minutes of Lancashire C. C. C., 6 April 1898; Hawke, 'Captaincy', p. 474.

28   S. Wagg, *The Football World*, Brighton, 1984, p. 9. See also Minutes of Heart of Midlothian F. C.; and Minutes of Sheffield Wednesday F. C.

29   In 1921 the F. A. Council 'felt impelled to express their strong opinion that the game of football is quite unsuitable for females' (G. Green, *The History of the Football Association*, London, 1953, p. 533); C. Ramsden, *Ladies in Racing*, London, 1973.

30   R. Heyhoe Flint and N. Rheinberg, *Fair Play*, London, 1976, pp. 25–6.

31 H. S. C. Everard, 'Golf in 1899', *Badminton Magazine*, x, 1900, p. 204.

32 A. R. Haig-Brown, 'The lesson from New Zealand', *Badminton Magazine*, XXII, 1906, p. 45.

33 Minutes of Lancashire C. C. C., 8 January 1909.

34 Calculated from data in *Wisden Cricketers' Almanack 1906*. See also the comment of G. L. Jessop, 'Some hints to young bowlers', *National Review*, XXXIII, 1899, p. 242.

35 Calculated from data in *Wisden Cricketers' Almanack 1913*.

36 Calculated from data in *Wisden Cricketers' Almanack 1894; 1913*. See also H. Gordon, 'Youth in cricket', *Fortnightly Review*, LXXXVII, 1910, p. 986; and R. Bowen, *Cricket*, London, 1970, 143–4.

37 On the American invasion, see Vamplew, *The Turf*, pp. 49–61.

38 T. Sloan, *Tod Sloan*, London, 1915, p. 97.

39 A. E. T. Watson, 'The American jockey invasion', *Badminton Magazine*, XXIV, 1907, pp. 424–5.

40 Admittedly a Jockey Club regulation, designed to protect valuable horse-flesh from misuse by immature riders, had served to reduce the number of jockeys seeking mounts. This was the setting, in 1860, of a minimum weight to be carried of 5½ st. (raised to 6 st. in 1891), which cut down the opportunities for young riders, often mere children, who would have to carry too much deadweight for the liking of most trainers. However, following complaints from some trainers and owners, a weight allowance for apprentices was instituted and racecourse executives were encouraged to hold some races solely for apprentices. Although critics felt that the allowance system ruined some races by nullifying the work of the handicapper, it undoubtedly gave many youngsters rides and experience which otherwise would not have come their way (A. E. T. Watson, 'The racing season', *Badminton Magazine*, XXII, 1906, p. 427; 'Sport in 1886', *British Almanac and Companion 1887*).

41 Annual Reports of Scottish Football Association 1894, 1913.

42 *Athletic Journal*, 17 September 1889; Green, *Football Association*, pp. 190, 289.

43 P. C. W. Trevor, 'The season's football', *Badminton Magazine*, VIII, 1899, p. 429; Green, *Football Association*, p. 413; E. Needham, *Association Football*, London, 1900, p. 83.

44 Mandle, 'Professional cricketer', p. 3.

45 D. P. Blaine, *Encyclopaedia of Rural Sports*, London, 1870, p. 375.

46 Minutes of Leicestershire C. C. C., 24 June 1891; Minutes of Lancashire C. C. C., 8 August 1887.

47 Calculated from data in Thomas, *Yorkshire Cricketers*; and A. B. de Lugo, 'Surrey county players 1844–1901', in Lord Alverstone and C. W. Alcock (eds.), *Surrey Cricket*, London, 1902, pp. 473–81; Minutes of Leicestershire C. C. C., 30 September 1896; 13 July 1898.

48 'Sport and decadence', *Quarterly Review*, CCXI, 1909, p. 499. See also the comments of Lord Hawke, 'The unwritten laws of cricket', *Badminton Magazine*, XXI, 1905, p. 136.

49 Minutes of Football League, 24 June 1904.

50 Football League Circular to Clubs, 3 April 1911.

51 Minutes of Football League, 20 May 1895; 13 August 1897.

52 Bassett, 'Big transfers', p. 160; Minutes of Sheffield Wednesday F. C., 1908–10, *passim*.

53 Calculated from data in Annual Reports of Scottish Football Association; and Minutes of Football League Management Committee (assumes as many players were registered with second-division as with first-division clubs).

54 Minutes of Lancashire C. C. C., 23 April 1895; 8 January 1909; Minutes of Leicestershire C. C. C., 10 September 1902; Duckworth, *Warwickshire Cricket*, p. 112.

55 Minutes of Essex C. C. C., 7 July 1891; Duckworth, *Warwickshire Cricket*, p. 53.

56 The Druid, *Post and Paddock*, London, 1895, p. 36.

57 E. Spencer, *The Great Game*, London, 1900, p. 128.

58 C. E. Sutcliffe, J. A. Brierley and F. Howarth, *The Story of the Football League, 1888–1938*, Preston, 1939, p. 126.

59 J. J. Bentley, 'Is football a business?', *World's Work*, 1912, p. 393.

60 W. I. Bassett, 'The day's work', in *The Book of Football*, pp. 110–13.

61 Minutes of Sheffield Wednesday F. C., 21 January 1889.

62 E. Needham, 'How to become an international', in B. O. Corbett *et al.*, *Football*, London, 1907, p. 37; Minutes of Heart of Midlothian F. C., 13 December 1905.

63 Bassett, 'Day's work', p. 110. The chairman of Bury F. C. also maintained that 'if we induced our players to work more and ask less it would be for the good of the game and the good of the players themselves'. Quoted in P. M. Young, *Football on Merseyside*, London, 1964, p. 71.

64 T. A. Cook, *A History of the English Turf*, London, 1905, p. 544; J. Welcome, *Fred Archer*, London, 1967, p. 88; C. Richardson, *The English Turf*, London, 1901, p. 276.

65 S. G. Galtrey, *Memoirs of a Racing Journalist*, London, 1934, p. 184.

66 Vamplew, *The Turf*, pp. 146–7.

67 Cook, *English Turf*, p. 521.

68 'The turf: its frauds and chicaneries', *Contemporary Review*, XXII, 1873, p. 32; The Druid, *Scott and Sebright*, London, 1895, p. 61.

69 Earl of Suffolk, *Racing and Steeplechasing*, London, 1886, p. 245; 'Race-course and covert side', *Saturday Review*, 5 January 1884.

70 L. H. Curzon, *A Mirror of the Turf*, London, 1892, p. 346.

71 *Ruffs Guide to the Turf 1906*.

72 *Bloodstock Breeders Review*, II, 1913, p. 346.

73 L. H. Curzon, 'The horse as an instrument of gambling', *Contemporary Review*, XXX, 1877, p. 39; E. M. Humphris, *The Life of Fred Archer*, London, 1923, pp. 48–9; 'In and about Newmarket', *Strand Magazine*, II, 1891, p. 167.

74 Porter, *Kingsclere*, p. 233.

75 Cobbett, *Racing Life*, p. 232.

76 'Jockeys and jockeyship', *Badminton Magazine*, XVIII, 1904, p. 148.

77 Minutes of Leicestershire C. C. C., 23 July 1894; 8 December 1900.

78 H. Gordon, 'Cricket twenty years ago and now', *Badminton Magazine*, XIV,

1902, p. 613; C. Booth, *Life and Labour of the People of London*, London, 1896, VIII, p. 146.

79 *Wisden Cricketers' Almanack 1897*, p. lviii.
80 Minutes of Lancashire C. C. C., 6 August 1897.
81 Duckworth, *Warwickshire Cricket*, p. 92; Minutes of Essex C. C. C. and Leicestershire C. C. C., *passim*.
82 Lancashire players received £10 each in 1904 (Minutes of Lancashire C. C. C., 27 September 1904); each member of Yorkshire's winning team obtained £20 in 1901 and £15 in 1909 (*Yorkshire C. C. C. Year Book 1902; 1910*).
83 Minutes of Lancashire C. C. C., 5 January 1912; Minutes of Leicestershire C. C. C., 16 December 1908; 8 September 1909.
84 Hawke, 'Captaincy', p. 476. George Hirst once earned £52 10s. in a season (Thomas, *Yorkshire Cricketers*, p. 77).
85 Sandiford, 'Amateurs and professionals', pp. 40–1.
86 Duckworth, *Warwickshire Cricket*, pp. 62, 105.
87 Duckworth, *Warwickshire Cricket*, p. 121.
88 Quoted in Duckworth, *Warwickshire Cricket*, p. 43. Lilley was not alone. See Sandiford, 'Amateurs and professionals', p. 45.
89 A. G. Steel, 'Bowling', in A. G. Steel and R. H. Lyttelton, *Cricket*, London, 1893, p. 103.
90 Minutes of Lancashire C. C. C., 9 August 1887; *Wisden Cricketers' Almanack 1897*, p. lviii; Bowen, *Cricket*, p. 139.
91 Annual Report of Kent C. C. C. 1897.
92 Minutes of Lancashire C. C. C., 21 February 1899.
93 Minutes of Lancashire C. C. C., 1906, *passim*.
94 Minutes of Lancashire C. C. C., 6 August 1914.
95 Mandle, 'Professional cricketer', p. 6.
96 Minutes of Lancashire C. C. C., 20 February 1904; 6 September 1907.
97 'Notes', *Badminton Magazine*, VIII, 1899, p. 472.
98 Mandle, 'Professional cricketer', p. 9.
99 Calculated from data in *Wisden Cricketers' Almanack*. The early overseas figures are affected by the all-professional tours of 1876/77, 1881/82, 1884/85, 1886/87 and 1887/88.
100 The hope of William Ansell, chairman of Warwickshire C. C. C., quoted in Duckworth, *Warwickshire Cricket*, p. 51.
101 Minutes of Leicestershire C. C. C., 30 December 1891; 19 October 1892. For other unfortunate examples, see Sandiford, 'Amateurs and professionals', pp. 41–2.
102 *Yorkshire C. C. C. Year Book 1907*.
103 *Cricket*, VI, 1887, p. 426.
104 Minutes of Lancashire C. C. C., 27 September 1892; 27 February 1894.
105 Calculated from data in Thomas, *Yorkshire Cricketers*; and *Yorkshire C. C. C. Year Books*.
106 For surveys, see Mason, *Association Football*, pp. 95–102; and club histories in *The Book of Football*.
107 W. McGregor, 'Birmingham (late Small Heath) F. C.', in *The Book of*

Football, p. 119; W. McGregor, 'The League and the League system', in *The Book of Football*, p. 173.

108 Football Association Circular on Financial Arrangements between Clubs and Players, 10 January 1910.

109 Wage Books of Heart of Midlothian F. C.

110 R. Crampsey, *The Scottish Footballer*, Edinburgh, 1978, p. 26.

111 Crampsey, *Scottish Footballer*, p. 7.

112 Minutes of Professional Footballers' Association, 15 January 1912.

113 Minutes of Scottish Football Association, 23 November 1910.

114 Minutes of Professional Footballers' Association, 15 December 1908.

115 W. McGregor, 'The £ s. d. of football', in *The Book of Football*, p. 62.

116 Green, *Football Association*, p. 408.

117 Minutes of Sheffield Wednesday F. C., *passim*; Bentley, 'Football', p. 391; Minutes of Football League, 1910–14, *passim*.

118 Annual Report of Plymouth Argyle F. C. 1912.

119 Green, *Football Association*, p. 415.

120 Minutes of Football League, 20 April 1891; 19 February 1894; 10 March 1899; 3 November 1902.

121 Mason, *Association Football*, pp. 97–8; Wagg, *Football World*, p. 14.

122 Sutcliffe *et al.*, *Football League*, pp. 119–20.

123 A. Mason, 'The blues and the reds', *Transactions of the Lancashire and Cheshire Archaeological Society*, 1984, p. 115.

124 Minutes of Football League Management Committee, 9 August 1912.

125 K. Macklin, *The History of Rugby League Football*, London, 1962, pp. 7, 21.

126 Macklin, *Rugby League*, p. 58. This may have been the formalisation of accepted practice (J. A. H. Catton, *The Real Football*, London, 1900, p. 186).

127 Minutes of Northern Rugby Football Union, 22 February 1910.

14 Close of play

1 Minutes of Football League, 18 December 1891.

2 Minutes of Sheffield Wednesday F. C., 9 April 1913; 22 April 1914.

3 L. Duckworth, *The Story of Warwickshire Cricket*, London, 1974, pp. 68–72.

4 Minutes of Leicestershire C. C. C., 27 October 1897; 1 October 1902.

5 See the comments of C. S. Colman, 'The football season', *Badminton Magazine*, II, 1896, p. 540; W. J. Oakley, 'The defence', in M. Shearman *et al.*, *Football*, London, 1899, p. 146; A. G. Guillemard, 'The season of 1875–76 – the rugby union', in *The Football Annual*, London, 1876, p. 84; E. Needham, *Association Football*, London, 1900, p. 54. S. Tischler, *Footballers and Businessmen*, New York, 1981, p. 97, states that owing to 'injury and illness' only 61 of the 1,701 starting line-up players in the season 1913/14 played in every match. This, however, ignores scapegoating and loss of form.

6 Minutes of Football League, 4 May 1891.

7 J. Hutchinson, *The Football Industry*, Glasgow, 1982, p. 46.

8 Minutes of Scottish Football Association, 11 February 1913. However, in the

late 1920s he was earning £1,500 p.a. as a manager of Middlesbrough (S. Wagg, *The Football World*, Brighton, 1984, p. 56).

9 Minutes of Sheffield Wednesday F. C., 18 April 1900. Poor Fred went on to coach in Germany, where he was interned at the outbreak of war in 1914 (Wagg, *Football World*, p. 229).

10 Minutes of Sheffield Wednesday F. C., 18 September 1901.

11 In his study of modern American horse-racing Marvin Scott has hypothesised that increasing weight generally *follows* rather than precedes the closing of career opportunities. He suggests that it becomes a face-saving device for those who see little future for themselves in racing (M. B. Scott, 'The man on the horse', in J. W. Loy and G. S. Kenyon (eds.), *Sport, Culture and Society*, London, 1969, p. 427). There may be something in this as regards those jockeys who never made the breakthrough into regular employment, but historically those who made the grade virtually starved themselves during the racing season in order to keep earning the money to which they had become accustomed.

12 W. Vamplew, *The Turf*, London, 1976, pp. 164–5.

13 W. F. Mandle, 'The professional cricketer in England in the nineteenth century', *Labour History*, XXIII, 1972, p. 14.

14 Minutes of Lancashire C. C. C., 19 July 1912. Bolton Wanderers pared their playing strength in 1898 with the aim of saving £1,200 (P. M. Young, *Bolton Wanderers*, London, 1961, p. 71).

15 Minutes of Lancashire C. C. C., 30 November 1833; 7 July, 5 August 1884; 26 June 1885; P. Wynne Thomas and P. Arnold, *Cricket in Conflict*, London, 1984, p. 49.

16 H. Gordon, 'The past cricket season', *Badminton Magazine*, XIII, 1901, p. 413.

17 Minutes of Lancashire C. C. C., 31 January 1902.

18 Minutes of Leicestershire C. C. C., 8 January 1901; D. Frith, *The Slow Men*, London, 1985, p. 56.

19 See chapter 17.

20 'Professional cricket', *Cricket*, VI, 1887, p. 425.

21 Minutes of Football League, 31 August 1908.

22 Duckworth, *Warwickshire Cricket*, p. 121.

23 H. Gordon, 'The coming cricket season', *Badminton Magazine*, XVI, 1903, p. 148.

24 Minutes of Lancashire C. C. C., 22 August 1902; 2 October 1903; 26 February 1904.

25 J. Porter and E. Moorehouse, *John Porter of Kingsclere*, London, 1919, p. 63; L. H. Curzon, *The Blue Riband of the Turf*, London, 1890, p. 359.

26 D. Batchelor, *The Turf of Old*, London, 1951, p. 181; J. Fairfax-Blakeborough, *The Analysis of the Turf*, London, 1927, p. 123; E. Moorehouse, *The Romance of The Derby*, London, 1908, p. 65.

27 Duckworth, *Warwickshire Cricket*, p. 49. See also Minutes of Lancashire C. C. C., 31 January 1890; and Minutes of Leicestershire C. C. C., 11 June 1894.

28 *Cricket*, IX, 1890, p. 93.

29 Mandle, 'Professional cricketer', pp. 13–14.
30 Minutes of Heart of Midlothian F. C., 28 November 1902; 21 October 1895; 19 November 1910.
31 Minutes of Sheffield Wednesday F. C., 5 February, 2 April 1902.
32 Two lines of research still need to be pursued. Different base years would show if careers lengthened or shortened over time, and positional career differences merit examination.
33 This may partly be a function of the expansion of the Football League, an expansion which enabled inter-team movements to be traced more easily.
34 For modern studies, see P. Hill and B. Lowe, 'The inevitable metathesis of the retiring athlete', International Review of Sport Sociology, IX, 1974, pp. 5–32; and D. R. Houlston, 'The occupational mobility of professional athletes', International Review of Sport Sociology, XVII, 1982, pp. 15–24. For an individual sportsman's view of the decision to retire, see J. Kramer, 'Getting out: the football player', in J. T. Talamini and C. H. Page (eds.), Sport and Society, Boston, 1973, pp. 355–60.
35 Creston, 'Football', Fortnightly Review, LV, 1894, p. 34. In Scotland the S. F. A. Annual Reports show an average of 105 reinstatements to the amateur ranks between 1894 and 1906.
36 W. I. Bassett, 'The day's work', in The Book of Football, London, 1906, p. 113. See also A. Mason, Association Football and English Society, 1863–1915, Brighton, 1980, pp. 118–20.
37 See chapter 15.
38 H. J. Spenser, 'The athletic master in public schools', Contemporary Review, LXXVIII, 1900, p. 113. Exceptions include John Jones (Tottenham), who coached at the Abbey School, Beckenham; J. Ross, who went to Ampleforth College for a few days in 1887; and T. D. Bradshaw, who became assistant coach at Harrow in 1907 (Minutes of Football Association, 15 November 1897; Mason, Association Football, p. 120).
39 Calculated from data in Wisden Cricketers' Almanack; and Minutes of Leicestershire C. C. C., 15 May 1895.
40 Minutes of Lancashire C. C. C., 2 April 1895.
41 Calculated from data in the Racing Calendar.
42 Bloodstock Breeders Review, VI, 1917, p. 373; Fairfax-Blakeborough, Analysis, p. 124.
43 One student of modern American racing found it very difficult to get jockeys to discuss accidents (Scott, 'Man on the horse', p. 429).
44 J. Ford, Prizefighting, Newton Abbot, 1971, pp. 35–64; S. K. Weinberg and H. Arond, 'The occupational culture of the boxer', American Journal of Sociology, LVII, 1952, pp. 460–9.
45 On cricket, see Mandle, 'Professional cricketer', pp. 14–15.
46 See, for example, J. Klein, Samples from English Culture, London, 1965, pp. 196–7. J. H. Goldthorpe et al., The Affluent Worker in the Class Structure, Cambridge, 1969, p. 37, found that even the more highly paid manual workers demonstrated a markedly different financial strategy to white-collar workers, with only 13% of the former planning to save with a time scale of over three to four months compared to 42% of the latter. The

rural working class have the poorest savings record of all, a finding which may have implications for jockeys; an English survey of 1953 found that one-third of rural income units were without any savings. Cited in W. Runciman, *Relative Deprivation and Social Justice*, London, 1968, p. 88.

47 P. Thomas, *Yorkshire Cricketers, 1839–1939*, Manchester, 1973, pp. 195–8.
48 G. Fordham to C. Wood, 1 October 1887, York Racing Museum.

15 Not playing the game: unionism and strikes

1 C. Richardson, *The English Turf*, London, 1901, p. 226.
2 Minutes of Sheffield Wednesday F. C., 28 June 1914; Minutes of Leicestershire C. C. C., 18 January, 14 June 1911; Minutes of Lancashire C. C. C., 2 September 1890.
3 Minutes of Lancashire C. C. C., 10 October 1899; *Yorkshire C. C. C. Year Book 1905*, p. 11; W. F. Mandle, 'The professional cricketer in England in the nineteenth century', *Labour History*, XXIII, 1972, p. 15.
4 D. Kynaston, *Bobby Abel*, London, 1982, p. 147.
5 C. P. Korr, 'West Ham United Football Club and the beginnings of professional football in east London, 1895–1914', *Journal of Contemporary History*, XIII, 1978, p. 230.
6 Minutes of Heart of Midlothian F. C., 29 November 1897.
7 Minutes of Heart of Midlothian F. C., 13 October 1902.
8 Minutes of Sheffield Wednesday F. C., 1 February, 28 April, 11–12 June, 20 August 1911; 29 June 1914.
9 C. E. Sutcliffe, J. A. Brierley and F. Howarth, *The Story of the Football League, 1888–1938*, Preston, 1939, p. 119.
10 Lord Hawke, 'On captaincy', *Badminton Magazine*, XIV, 1902, p. 475.
11 Minutes of Leicestershire C. C. C., 24 July, 14 August 1895; Duckworth, *The Story of Warwickshire Cricket*, London, 1974, p. 121.
12 See chapter 14.
13 Annual general meeting of Lancashire C. C. C., 29 January 1892.
14 Minutes of Lancashire C. C. C., 21 June 1892.
15 Korr, 'West Ham', p. 230.
16 *The Book of Football*, London, 1906, pp. 28, 113, 234; Minutes of Sheffield Wednesday F. C., 5 February, 2 April 1902.
17 A. Mason, *Association Football and English Society, 1863–1915*, Brighton, 1980, p. 178.
18 Minutes of Sheffield Wednesday F. C., 22 June, 7 September 1898; 16 October 1907; 19 February 1908. Wolves adopted a similar policy (P. M. Young, *The Wolves*, London, 1959, p. 65).
19 P. Murphy, *Tiger Smith*, Newton Abbot, 1981, p. 9.
20 Minutes of Leicestershire C. C. C., 12 September 1906.
21 See chapter 12.
22 See especially chapter 9.
23 See chapter 17.
24 See chapter 13.
25 Minutes of Football League, 19 May 1899.

26 Annual Report of Scottish Football Association 1895/96; Minutes of Scottish Football Association, 31 March 1910.

27 Minutes of Northern Rugby Football Union, 15 March 1910.

28 W. Vamplew, *The Turf*, London, 1976, pp. 167–8.

29 B. Dabscheck, '"Defensive Manchester": a history of the Professional Footballers' Association', in R. Cashman and M. McKernan (eds.), *Sport in History*, St Lucia, 1979, p. 237.

30 Duckworth, *Warwickshire Cricket*, pp. 45–6.

31 F. J. Wall, *Fifty Years in Football*, London, 1935, p. 120. In 1903 the F. A. relented to the extent that the rule banning professionals from all administrative posts in soccer could, if the Council thought fit, be rescinded for players who had announced their retirement from the game (Green, *The History of the Football Association*, London, 1953, p. 417).

32 Mandle, 'Professional cricketer', p. 10; D. Frith, *The Slow Men*, London, 1985, p. 46; J. R. Mackay, *The Hibees*, Edinburgh, 1985, p. 22; J. A. H. Catton, *The Real Football*, London, 1900, p. 125.

33 Vamplew, *The Turf*, p. 106.

34 A. Maley, *The Story of Celtic*, Glasgow, 1939, pp. 28, 44.

35 Mandle, 'Professional cricketer', pp. 11–12; W. G. Grace, *Cricket*, Bristol, 1891, p. 164.

36 C. W. Alcock, 'The Australians at the Oval', in Lord Alverstone and C. W. Alcock (eds.), *Surrey Cricket*, London, 1902, pp. 272–4; Kynaston, *Bobby Abel*, pp. 140–5.

37 M. P. Jackson, *Industrial Relations*, London, 1984, p. 50. On strikes in this period, see M. H. Haynes, 'Strikes', in J. Benson, *The Working Class in England, 1875–1914*, London, 1985, pp. 89–132.

38 Quoted in M. Golesworthy (ed.), *The Encyclopaedia of Association Football*, Newton Abbot, 1977, p. 165.

39 Catton, *Real Football*, pp. 186–7; Minutes of the Football League, 14 October, 11 November 1898; 28 April 1899.

40 In 1919 the name was changed to the Association Football Players' and Trainers' Union and in 1958 to the Professional Footballers' Association. For histories of the Union, see Dabscheck, 'Defensive Manchester', pp. 227–57; S. Tischler, *Footballers and Businessmen*, New York, 1981, pp. 105–20; A. Mason, *Association Football*, pp. 110–17.

41 Dabscheck, 'Defensive Manchester', p. 233.

42 Quoted in Dabscheck, 'Defensive Manchester', p. 234.

43 Dabscheck, 'Defensive Manchester', p. 234.

44 Minutes of Association Football Players' Union, 16 December 1907.

45 Minutes of Association Football Players' Union, 23 December 1907.

46 Minutes of Football League, 5 September 1910; Football League Management Committee, Circular to Clubs, 14 April 1915.

47 For more details, see Dabscheck, 'Defensive Manchester', pp. 237–41; and Sutcliffe *et al.*, *Football League*, pp. 118–19.

48 Quoted in Dabscheck, 'Defensive Manchester', p. 238.

49 Football Association Circular, 3 May 1909.

50 Minutes of Association Football Players' Union, 7 May 1909.

51 Minutes of Sheffield Wednesday F. C., 25 August 1909; Minutes of Football League, 27 August 1909.

52 Minutes of Association Football Players' Union, 21 October 1909.

53 Minutes of Association Football Players' Union, 2 November 1909.

54 Dabscheck, 'Defensive Manchester', p. 241.

55 Minutes of Association Football Players' Union, 1 April 1908.

56 See chapter 9.

57 Minutes of Association Football Players' Union, 2 February 1910.

58 Sutcliffe *et al.*, *Football League*, pp. 119–20; Minutes of Football League, 7 March 1910.

59 Minutes of Association Football Players' Union, 15 December 1908.

60 The maximum allowed was 10% after one year, 15% after two years, 25% after three years, 35% after four years, and 50% after five years (Sutcliffe *et al.*, *Football League*, p. 119).

61 Green, *Football Association*, p. 419; Sutcliffe *et al.*, *Football League*, pp. 120–2.

62 Minutes of Association Football Players' Union, 3 June 1912.

63 Minutes of Football League, 26 May 1913; 23 September 1912; Minutes of Association Football Players' Union, 14 October, 28 October 1912.

64 Minutes of Football League, 15 November 1912.

65 Minutes of Association Football Players' Union, 10 February 1913; Minutes of Football League, 18 April 1913.

66 *Athletic News*, 21 December 1908, cited in both Mason, *Association Football*, p. 132; and B. Dobbs, *Edwardians at Play*, London, 1973, p. 254. The latter figure, in particular, seems suspect as it required an average of over 18 players from each club. Unfortunately the pre-war subscription registers are extant only from September 1910 to April 1913.

67 Subscription Registers of Association Football Players' Union.

68 Minutes of Association Football Players' Union, 9 October 1911; 8 January, 18 November 1912; Minutes of Scottish Football Association, 27 February, 17 December 1912; 18 February 1913.

69 Golesworthy (ed.), *Encyclopaedia of Football*, p. 166. Unfortunately the records of this union are missing.

70 Minutes of Association Football Players' Union, 13 October 1913.

71 Minutes of Association Football Players' Union, 1 December 1913.

72 Tischler, *Footballers and Businessmen*, p. 109.

73 Minutes of Football League, 30 September 1914; Minutes of Association Football Players' Union, 9 October 1914.

74 Only one instance of a threatened strike is detailed in the pre-1915 records of the Rugby League. Several Castleford players refused to play in a cup tie against Bramley unless they obtained extra money. All were suspended *sine die* and, although this punishment was later rescinded, only one had his contract renewed (Minutes of Northern Rugby Football Union, 10 June 1902; 3 September 1903). T. Delaney, *The Roots of Rugby League*, Keighley, 1984, pp. 100–2, documents several other disputes, none of which appear to have spread beyond the individual club.

75 It is still difficult to persuade high earners to take concerted action with other

players on some issues (R. C. Berry, W. B. Gould and P. B. Staudohar, *Labour Relations in Professional Sports*, Dover, 1986, pp. 15–17).

76 Earl of Suffolk, *Racing and Steeplechasing*, London, 1886, p. 106; J. Welcome, *Fred Archer*, London, 1967, pp. 142–9.

77 *Wisden Cricketers' Almanack 1897*, p. lviii.

78 *Lillywhite's Companion 1882*, quoted in Mandle, 'Professional cricketer', p. 12.

79 Quoted in C. Brookes, *English Cricket*, Newton Abbot, 1978, p. 109.

80 There is some confusion as to when this began. *Wisden Cricketers' Almanack 1880*, p. 15, says it was 1857 though reorganisation took place in 1864, whereas Mandle, 'Professional cricketer', p. 15, citing M. C. C., *Marylebone Cricket Club Scores and Biographies*, xv, says it was 1862.

81 Mandle, 'Professional cricketer', p. 15.

82 *The Times*, 2 May 1867.

83 *Wisden Cricketers' Almanack 1887*, p. xix.

84 *Cricket*, 27 March 1890.

85 Lord Harris, *The History of Kent County Cricket*, London, 1907, pp. 47–8, 493; *Yorkshire C. C. C. Year Book 1899*.

86 J. Kent, *The Racing Life of Lord George Cavendish Bentinck*, London, 1892, p. 152.

87 D. J. Hanes, *The First British Workmen's Compensation Act 1897*, London, 1968, p. 103.

88 Minutes of Football League, 3 November 1902; Minutes of Football Mutual Insurance Federation, 14 August 1908.

89 The Rugby League also found insurance at reasonable rates difficult to obtain and it proposed a national insurance scheme to be operated by member clubs, but nothing appears to have developed (Minutes of Northern Rugby Football Union, 6 July 1910).

90 Minutes of Football League, 9 September 1912. A similar view was held by the Scottish Health Commission (Minutes of the Scottish Football Association, 13 August 1912).

91 Jack Hobbs did claim that most professionals were still able to look on cricket as a sport (J. B. Hobbs, 'The compensation of cricket from a professional's point of view', *Badminton Magazine*, xxxvi, 1913, p. 693).

16 Labour aristocrats or wage slaves?

1 For a survey of workers' wage rates, see A. Mason, *Association Football and English Society, 1863–1915*, Brighton, 1980, pp. 103–5.

2 E. J. Hobsbawm, *Labouring Men*, London, 1965, p. 272.

3 This is a gross simplification of a very complex matter. For further discussion, see E. J. Hobsbawm, 'The aristocracy of labour reconsidered', in *Problems of Work and the Labour Force in Enterprise in the 19th and 20th Centuries*, Theme B9, Seventh International Economic History Congress, Edinburgh, 1978; and R. Gray, *The Aristocracy of Labour in Nineteenth-Century Britain, c. 1850–1900*, London, 1981.

4 Quoted in G. Green, *The History of The Football Association*, London, 1953, p. 419.
5 Member of Football League Management Committee, quoted in S. Tischler, *Footballers and Businessmen*, New York, 1981, p. 91.
6 See, for example, J. W. Hunt and K. A. Lewis, 'Dominance, recontracting, and the reserve clause: major league baseball', *American Economic Review*, LXVI, 1976, p. 936; and H. G. Demmert, *The Economics of Professional Team Sports*, Lexington, 1973, p. 22.

17 Ungentlemanly conduct

1 'Professional cricket', *Saturday Review*, 14 July 1883.
2 M. Shearman, *Athletics and Football*, London, 1888, p. 227.
3 H. H. Almond, 'Football as a moral agent', *Nineteenth Century*, XXXIV, 1893, p. 907.
4 J. Ford, *Prizefighting*, Newton Abbot, 1971, pp. 188–90; K. Chesney, *The Victorian Underworld*, London, 1972, p. 328.
5 See chapter 12.
6 Initially referees in soccer had acted on appeal from the umpires appointed by each team, but, by 1891, the latter had become linesmen. Their duty was to assist the referee, who had full authority to make decisions without waiting for an appeal (C. W. Alcock, *Association Football*, London, 1890, pp. 61–4; G. O. Smith, 'Referees', in M. Shearman *et al.*, *Football*, London, 1899, p. 157). In Scotland, in 1887, referees had been given the power, 'without consulting the umpires', to deal with players for violent play because rough play had reached such 'serious dimensions' (Annual Report of Scottish Football Association 1886/87).
7 C. W. Alcock, *Association Football*, London, 1906, pp. 7–8.
8 Minutes of Football League, 21 January 1892; 6 November 1903; 5 September 1904; 28 September 1909; 12 August 1910; 6 January 1911; 9 September 1912.
9 Minutes of Scottish Football Association, 8 December 1909.
10 Minutes of Football League, 11 October 1893; 11 September 1894; 16 October 1894.
11 Minutes of Football League, 5 December 1897.
12 Minutes of Football League, 3 February 1908.
13 Calculated from Minutes of Football League.
14 C. E. Sutcliffe and F. Hargreaves, *History of the Lancashire Football Association, 1878–1928*, Blackburn, 1928, p. 131.
15 'Notes', *Badminton Magazine*, VI, 1898, p. 471.
16 H. Gordon, 'The coming cricket season', *Badminton Magazine*, XXIV, 1907, p. 428.
17 Earl of Suffolk, *Racing and Steeplechasing*, London, 1886, p. 73; 'The state of the turf', *Badminton Magazine*, XIV, 1902, p. 332.
18 See articles entitled 'The state of the turf', *Badminton Magazine*, XIX, 1904, p. 551; and XX, 1905, p. 187.

19 A. E. T. Watson, 'Sportsmen of mark – Lord Hamilton of Dalzell', *Badminton Magazine*, XXI, 1905, pp. 246–7.

20 C. Richardson, *The English Turf*, London, 1901, pp. 225–6.

21 T. Weston, *My Racing Life*, London, 1952, pp. 26–8, is explicit on this for a long period.

22 'Backing and pulling', *Saturday Review*, 6 July 1889; G. Chetwynd, *Racing Reminiscences*, London, 1891, II, appendix.

23 J. Rice, *The History of the British Turf*, London, 1879, p. 273; L. H. Curzon, *A Mirror of the Turf*, London, 1892, p. 359.

24 R. Black, *The Jockey Club and its Founders*, London, 1891, p. 319; Earl of Ellesmere, 'Concerning stewards', *Badminton Magazine*, XII, 1901, p. 394.

25 Lord Beaufort to Mr Greenfield, 9 February 1893; and Lord Durham to C. Wood, 27 January 1897, York Racing Museum Archives.

26 Rapier, 'Notes,' *Badminton Magazine*, II, 1896, p. 425.

27 See W. Vamplew, *The Turf*, London, 1976, pp. 50–1, 103–4.

28 *Bloodstock Breeders Review*, III, 1914, p. 337; 'Notes', *Badminton Magazine*, XIII, 1901, pp. 589–90.

29 T. Sloan, *Tod Sloan*, London, 1915, pp. 101, 187.

30 'The state of the turf', *Saturday Review*, 8 December 1900.

31 G. Lambton, *Men and Horses I Have Known*, London, 1924, p. 256; 'Doping', *Badminton Magazine*, XLII, 1913, p. 88.

32 A. E. T. Watson, 'Racing in 1896', *Badminton Magazine*, III, 1896, p. 686.

33 Curzon, *Mirror*, pp. 270, 276.

34 C. E. Sutcliffe, J. A. Brierley and F. Howarth, *The Story of the Football League, 1888–1938*, Preston, 1939, p. 113.

35 Whether these men adopted similar attitudes in their business activities has not been adequately examined. Indeed business ethics as a whole need to be put on the research agenda of business and economic historians.

36 Only Sunderland lost points, two in 1890/91 for fielding an ineligible player (Sutcliffe *et al.*, *Football League*, p. 226). North of the Border penalties were more severe. In the same season a similar offence to that of Sunderland cost Celtic, Cowlairs and Third Lanark four points each and Renton were actually expelled from the Scottish League in 1890 for playing against a team which was under an S. F. A. ban (J. E. Handley, *The Celtic Story*, London, 1960, p. 29). Unfortunately non-access to the Scottish League records meant that the deterrent effect of this could not be assessed.

37 J. Harding, *Football Wizard*, Derby, 1985, p. 104.

38 Football Association, Report of the Commission into Complaint against Middlesbrough F. C., 16 January 1911.

39 Lord Harris, 'Cricket', *Contemporary Review*, XLVIII, 1885, p. 125.

40 *Wisden Cricketers' Almanack 1895*, p. lxvii.

41 As a comment on unfair play within cricket the phrase was established by the 1860s (R. Bowen, *Cricket*, London, 1970, p. 112). It became accepted in its wider context by the early 1900s (E. H. Partridge, *A Dictionary of Catch Phrases*, London, 1981, p. 326).

18 The madding crowd

1 D. Richter, 'The role of mob riot in Victorian elections 1865–1885', *Victorian Studies*, XV, 1971, p. 25. For examples, see R. Price, *An Imperial War and the British Working Class*, London, 1972, pp. 175–6; H. Cunningham, 'Jingoism in 1877–78', *Victorian Studies*, XIV, 1971, pp. 429–53; V. Bailey, 'Salvation army riots, the "skeleton army" and legal authority in the provincial town', in A. P. Donajgrodzki (ed.), *Social Control in Nineteenth-Century Britain*, London, 1977, pp. 231–53.

2 'Modern horse racing', *Edinburgh Review*, CLI, 1880, p. 412; 'Turf ethics in 1868', *Broadway*, 1868, pp. 379–80; E. Spencer, *The Great Game*, London, 1900, pp. 223–6.

3 *Hansard*, 3rd Series, CCXXXVII, 29 January 1878; CCXL, 13 June 1878; CCXLIII, 14 February 1879.

4 L. H. Curzon, *A Mirror of the Turf*, London, 1892, p. 328; J. Fairfax-Blakeborough, *The Analysis of the Turf*, London, 1927, p. 271; R. Black, *Horse-Racing in England*, London, 1893, p. 185.

5 Letter to John Bowes, 7 June 1870, Racing and Personal Correspondence of John Bowes, D/Sc. Box 162, Durham County Record Office.

6 E. Dunning, P. Murphy, J. Williams and J. Maguire, 'Football hooliganism in Britain before the First World War', *International Review of Sport Sociology*, XIX, 1984, p. 217.

7 K. A. P. Sandiford, 'English cricket crowds during the Victorian age', *Journal of Sport History*, IX, 1982, pp. 17–18.

8 *Scottish Athletic Journal*, 23 August 1887.

9 Minutes of Football League Management Committee, 3 February 1892; 7 October 1895; Minutes of Football Association Emergency Committee, 23 February to 8 March 1911; *Bradford Observer*, 28 March 1896.

10 For some recent analyses, see R. Ingham, *Football Hooliganism*, London, 1978; P. Marsh, E. Rosser and R. Harre, *The Rules of Disorder*, London, 1978; Sports Council, *Public Disorder and Sporting Events*, London, 1978; R. Carroll, 'Football hooliganism in England', *International Review of Sport Sociology*, XV, 1980, pp. 77–92; E. Dunning, J. Maguire, P. Murphy and J. Williams, 'The social roots of football hooligan violence', *Leisure Studies*, I, 1982, pp. 139–56; J. Pratt and M. Salter, 'A fresh look at football hooliganism', *Leisure Studies*, III, 1984, pp. 201–19; S. Wagg, *The Football World*, Brighton, 1984, pp. 194–219.

11 He, of course, was the type of sports spectator often criticised for being too active at sports events. Others, however, were castigated in many quarters for being too passive, for watching from the terraces rather than playing the game themselves. Such criticism never seems to have been levied against opera-goers for their failure to sing along with the cast or against art-gallery visitors for not daubing their own canvases. For an interesting discussion, see A. Guttmann, 'On the alleged dehumanisation of the sports spectator', *Journal of Popular Culture*, XIV, 1980–1, pp. 275–82. For speculation as to why the working man became emotionally attached to a team, see R. Holt, 'Working-class

football and the city: the problem of continuity', *British Journal of Sports History*, III, 1986, pp. 10–12.

12 G. Guthrie, 'What's the good of football?' in *Scottish Football Annual 1889/90*, p. 34. For other examples of this recognition, see J. H. Gettins, 'Football and national life', in B. O. Corbett *et al.*, *Football*, London, 1907, p. 54; E. Ensor, 'The football madness', *Contemporary Review*, LXXIV, 1898, p. 752; J. H. Muir, *Glasgow in 1901*, Glasgow, 1901, pp. 196–7; and C. J. N. Fleming, 'Rugby football', *Badminton Magazine*, III, 1896, p. 564.

13 C. F. G. Masterman, *The Condition of England*, London, 1911, p. 116.

14 L. Mann and P. Pearce, 'Social psychology of the sports spectator', in D. Glencross (ed.), *Psychology and Sport*, Sydney, 1978.

15 *Glasgow Herald*, 19 April 1909; Minutes of Scottish Football Association, 19 April, 7 June 1909.

16 T. Keates, *History of the Everton Football Club 1878/79–1928/29*, Liverpool, 1929, p. 147.

17 Scores of Lancashire Cricket Club, 22–24 July 1907; H. Gordon, 'Cricket and crowds', *Badminton Magazine*, XXIX, 1909, p. 200.

18 'International cricket', *Saturday Review*, 6 September 1884.

19 P. F. Warner, *Lord's 1787–1945*, London, 1946, p. 113; W. J. Ford, 'Thoughts on spectators', *Badminton Magazine*, XIII, 1899, p. 529; *Spectator*, 11 July 1896.

20 'Football notes', *Tinsley's Magazine*, XLVI, 1889–90, p. 65. See also the similar view taken by C. B. Fry, 'Football', *Badminton Magazine*, I, 1895, p. 485.

21 C. Francis, *History of the Blackburn Rovers Football Club, 1875–1925*, Blackburn, 1925, p. 27.

22 G. Green, *The Official History of the F. A. Cup*, London, 1960, p. 33.

23 B. Dobbs, *Edwardians at Play*, London, 1973, p. 178; W. Vamplew, *The Turf*, London, 1976, p. 128; Minutes of Lancashire C. C. C., 23 May 1913.

24 'Rioting at Lillie Bridge', *Saturday Review*, 24 September 1887.

25 'Turf ethics in 1868', *Broadway*, 1868, pp. 379–80. See also P. H. L. Wynter, 'Racing', in *Victoria County History of Oxford*, II, 1907, p. 367.

26 C. Edwardes, 'The new football mania', *Nineteenth Century*, XXXII, 1892, p. 622.

27 Football League Management Committee Circular, 13 January 1910.

28 Vamplew, *The Turf*, pp. 117–18.

29 Minutes of Football League, 14 October 1892.

30 Minutes of Football League, 26 November 1898.

31 H. G. Hutchinson, 'The parlous condition of cricket', *National Review*, XXXV, 1900, p. 790; 'Test match cricket of 1912', *Blackwood's Magazine*, CXCII, 1912, p. 857.

32 Francis, *Blackburn Rovers*, pp. 150–1.

33 Minutes of Football League, *passim*.

34 L. B. Tebbutt to T. J. Matthews, 24 May 1913, Lancashire C. C. C. Archives.

35 'Lord Cadogan on the turf', *Saturday Review*, 17 January 1885. On one occasion at least, rationing by price was used specifically as a crowd control mechanism. In 1874 the M. C. C. raised the charge for the Eton v. Harrow

match from 1s. to 2s. 6d. in order to exclude the poorer cricket watchers, whom it blamed for unruly behaviour the previous year (Sandiford, 'Cricket crowds', pp. 11–12).

36 M. D. Smith, 'Sport and collective violence', in D. W. Ball and J. W. Loy (eds.), *Sport and Social Order: Contributions to the Sociology of Sport*, Reading, Mass., 1975, p. 313.

37 Minutes of Football League Management Committee, 15 February 1895; 14 April 1898.

38 Gordon, 'Cricket and crowds', p. 100.

39 H. Gordon, 'Cricket now – and then', *Badminton Magazine*, XXV, 1907, p. 291; G. O. Smith, 'Football', *Pall Mall Magazine*, XIII, 1897, pp. 570–1.

40 Minutes of Football Association, 9 May 1892; 6 February 1897.

41 G. Green, *The History of the Football Association*, London, 1953, p. 149; J. J. Bentley, 'Is football a business?', *World's Work*, 1912, p. 393; Select Committee on Betting, *British Parliamentary Papers 1901*, V, q. 376, 2906; E. Needham, *Association Football*, London, 1900, p. 7.

42 Green, *Football Association*, pp. 535–6; Minutes of Football League, 24 February 1913.

43 Francis, *Blackburn Rovers*, p. 164; Minutes of Football Association Emergency Committee, 9 March to 12 April 1911.

44 Vamplew, *The Turf*, p. 140; M. Huggins, '"Mingled pleasures and speculation": the survival of enclosed racecourses on Teesside, 1855–1902', *British Journal of Sports History*, III, 1986, p. 161.

45 Minutes of Football Association, 16 December 1895; 5 February 1896; Minutes of Football League, 15 February 1906; Minutes of Scottish Football Association, 27 February 1912.

46 Minutes of Sheffield Wednesday F. C., 21 February 1906. The Football Association then closed the ground for two weeks so that 'spectators might be taught that misbehaviour at the conclusion of a match could not be tolerated'.

47 Quantified historical data on sports crowd misbehaviour is seriously deficient. For the period under study reliance has currently to be placed on the pioneering work of Dunning *et al.*, 'Football hooliganism in Britain', pp. 215–40, despite its admitted deficiencies.

48 R. Ord, 'Horseracing in the north of England', *Badminton Magazine*, XIV, 1903, p. 174; F. G. Aflalo, 'The sportsman's library: a note on some books of 1901', *Fortnightly Review*, LXX, 1901, p. 1041; J. Lewis, 'The much-abused referee', in *The Book of Football*, London, 1906, p. 263. See also J. H. Gettins, 'Football and national life', in Corbett *et al.*, *Football*, pp. 54–5.

49 Calculated from data in Dunning *et al.*, 'Football hooliganism in Britain', p. 222. On the basis of a detailed study of the *Leicester Daily Mercury*, Dunning *et al.* have argued that football crowd behaviour generally did not improve between 1895 and 1915. It can be suggested that their conclusion, based on the absolute number of incidents reported, might be vitiated by considering the number of incidents in relation to the number of matches played or to the total attendance. Nor did their research adequately distinguish League and non-League football. The situation in Scottish soccer is indeterminate. The Hampden riot may have been a one-off frustration

disorder triggered off by poor organisation. Nevertheless, figures of clubs being cautioned by the Scottish Football Association for crowd misbehaviour increased from an average of 5 or 6 in the seasons 1903/04–1908/09 to an average of 19 in the three pre-war seasons (calculated from Annual Reports of Scottish Football Association). No earlier aggregated figures are available. However, this increase may be partially a statistical illusion in that it reflects a firmer line being taken by the Association, and the latter years also include cautions issued by the Scottish Junior Football Association which cannot be isolated from the aggregate figures. In addition it would seem that clubs were not being penalised solely for invasions and assaults but for 'objectionable practices by spectators [such as] the blowing of whistles, the prevalence of obscene language, and the use of ratchets and bells' (Minutes of Scottish Football Association, 26 October 1910). It may be that spectators north of the Border had a different relationship with their clubs. See H. F. Moorhouse, 'Professional football and working-class culture: English theories and Scottish evidence', *Sociological Review*, XXXII, 1984, pp. 285–315.

50 Ensor, 'Football madness', p. 757; Ford, 'Thoughts on spectators', p. 527.
51 Minutes of Leicestershire C. C. C., 15 July 1903.
52 H. Gordon, 'The past cricket season', *Badminton Magazine*, XXI, 1905, p. 437; Gordon, 'Cricket and crowds', p. 198.
53 P. C. W. Trevor, 'The future of cricket', *Fortnightly Review*, XC, 1911, pp. 532–3; H. Gordon, 'The coming cricket season', *Badminton Magazine*, XXX, 1910, p. 390; 'Cricket prospects', *Saturday Review*, 12 May 1900.
54 On this, see 'Test match cricket of 1912', p. 854.
55 The Football Association Committee which visited the Stockport County ground in 1911, following its closure for crowd violence in 1910, found nothing to censure in the fact that 'there was shouting and strong remarks and improper language used by some of the spectators towards visiting players' (Minutes of Football Association Emergency Committee, 25 September to 15 November 1911).
56 Warner, *Lord's*, p. 396.
57 Warner, *Lord's*, p. 397.
58 Fry, 'Football', p. 485; H. Gordon, 'Cricket characteristics', *Badminton Magazine*, XII, 1901, p. 25. Sandiford, 'Cricket crowds', p. 19, has argued that Victorians who watched the game at club and village levels were less well-to-do than those at Lord's or the Oval, but reported misbehaviour was not greater. If true, and more research is needed on the lower reaches of cricket, it may be a function of crowd size. Most serious crowd trouble at first-class cricket was, as Sandiford himself points out (p. 18), the result of unexpectedly large attendances.
59 F. C. Mather, *Public Order in the Age of the Chartists*, Manchester 1959, p. v; V. A. C. Gatrell, 'The decline of theft and violence in Victorian and Edwardian England', in V. A. C. Gatrell, B. Lenman and G. Parker (eds.), *Crime and the Law: The Social History of Crime in Western Europe Since 1500*, London, 1980, pp. 286–9. See also D. Woods, 'Community violence', in J. Benson (ed.), *The Working Class in England, 1875–1914*, London, 1985, pp. 165–205.

60 Richter, 'Role of mob riot', p. 29. It has been shown in a sporting context, though with a wider social relevance, how difficult it was to change the working-class code of manliness which emphasised physical toughness without the 'self-restraint' and 'decency' of the middle-class version (J. Maguire, 'Images of manliness and competing ways of living in late Victorian and Edwardian Britain', *British Journal of Sports History*, III, 1986, pp. 265–87).

61 Bailey, 'Salvation army riots', p. 232.

62 The structural strains thesis could also explain the remonstrance disorders of the suffragettes. They were not sports fans, but they saw demonstrations at, and against, sports events as a means of publicising women's poor social, political and economic status. It is difficult, however, to see the University cricket match disorder as emanating from structural strains. The participants in that disturbance were hardly deprived of power or esteem in wider society. Possibly some form of group identification stemming from socialisation at their University helped produce conflict. Certainly 'local patriotism [was] interested' in the result of the University game ('Cricket fifty years ago', *Saturday Review*, 29 April 1882). Nevertheless, this incident is reputed to have divided 'Cantab against Cantab', so perhaps it was simply a frustration riot with spectators angry that the unwritten laws of cricket had been broken (Warner, *Lord's*, p. 113).

63 These conclusions are based on E. H. Hunt, *British Labour History, 1815– 1914*, London, 1981; S. Meacham, 'The sense of an impending clash: English working-class unrest before the First World War', *American Historical Review*, LXXVII, 1972, pp. 1343–64; J. Lowell, *British Trade Unions, 1875– 1933*, London, 1977; G. Dangerfield, *The Strange Death of Liberal England*, New York, 1963; and D. Kynaston, *King Labour*, London, 1976.

64 Minutes of Football Association Council and Emergency Committee, *passim*; Minutes of Scottish Football Association, *passim*; H. Graves, 'A philosophy of sport', *Contemporary Review*, LXXVIII, 1900, p. 888.

Bibliography

Anonymous works appear at the end of the appropriate section.

MANUSCRIPT AND ARCHIVAL SOURCES

Annual Reports and/or Financial Statements of Birmingham F. C., Blackburn Rovers F. C., Blackpool F. C., Bolton Wanderers F. C., Bradford City F. C., Bristol City F. C., Bristol Rovers F. C., Burnley F. C., Bury F. C., Celtic F. C., Clyde F. C., Derby F. C., Derbyshire C. C. C., East Stirlingshire F. C., Essex C. C. C., Falkirk F. C., Football League, Fulham F. C., Hamilton Academicals F. C., Hampshire County Cricket Ground Co., Heart of Midlothian F. C., Hibernian F. C., Kent C. C. C., Lancashire C. C. C., Leicestershire C. C. C., Liverpool F. C., Manchester City F. C., Middlesbrough F. C., Motherwell F. C., Newcastle United F. C., Northern Rugby Football League, Oldham Athletic F. C., Partick Thistle F. C., Plymouth Argyle F. C., Preston North End F. C., Queen's Park Rangers F. C., Rangers F. C., St Johnstone F. C., St Mirren F. C., Scottish Football Association, Southampton F. C., Stoke City F. C., Surrey C. C. C., Tottenham Hotspur F. C., Warwickshire C. C. C., Warwickshire County Cricket Ground Co., West Bromwich Albion F. C., Yorkshire C. C. C.

Bowes Papers, Racing and Personal Letters of John Bowes, Durham County Record Office

Minutes of Association Football Players' Union, Essex C. C. C., Football Association, Football Association Emergency Committee, Football League, Football League Management Committee, Heart of Midlothian F. C., Lancashire C. C. C., Leicestershire C. C. C., Northern Rugby Football League, Northern Rugby Football Union, Professional Footballers' Association, Scottish Football Association, Sheffield Wednesday F. C.

Prospectus of Aberdeen F. C., Ayr F. C., Bradford City F. C., Dumbarton F. C., East Stirlingshire F. C., Falkirk F. C., Fulham Football and Athletic Club, Hamilton F. C., Heart of Midlothian F. C., Leicester City F. C., Motherwell F. C., Newbury Racecourse Company, Partick Thistle F. C., St Johnstone F. C., St Mirren F. C., Small Heath F. C.

Registration Books of Football League

Shareholders' Registers of Aberdeen Cycling and Athletic Association, Aberdeen F. C., Aberdeen Skating, Cycling and Yachting Co., Airdrieonians F. C., Aston Villa F. C., Ayr Racecourse Syndicate, Ayr United F. C., Blackburn Rovers F. C., Blackpool F. C., Bolton Wanderers F. C., Bradford City F. C., Bristol City F. C., Burnley F. C., Bury F. C., Celtic F. C., Clyde F. C., Cowdenbeath F. C., Derby F. C., Dumbarton F. C., Dundee Athletic Grounds, Dundee Football and Athletic Club, Dundee F. C., Dundee Hibernian F. C., East Fife F. C., East Stirlingshire F. C., Eastville Rovers F. C., Edinburgh Cycling Academy, Edinburgh Ice Rink, Edinburgh Lawn Tennis Co., Everton F. C., Falkirk F. C., Fulham F. C., Glasgow Indoor Bowling and Recreation Co., Glasgow Real Ice-Skating Palace, Glasgow Swimming Baths, Grimsby Town F. C., Hamilton Academicals F. C., Hamilton Park Racecourse, Hampshire County Cricket Ground Co., Haydock Park Racecourse Company, Heart of Midlothian F. C., Hibernian F. C., Huddersfield Town F. C., Kilmarnock F. C., Lanark Racecourse, Leeds Cricket, Football and Athletic F. C., Partick Thistle F. C., Plymouth Argyle F. C., Portsmouth F. C., Preston North End F. C., Queen's Park Rangers F. C., Rangers F. C., Reading F. C., Rochdale Hornets R. L. F. C., St Bernard's F. C., St Johnstone F. C., St Mirren F. C., Sheffield United F. C., Small Heath F. C., Southampton F. C., Stoke City F. C., Tottenham Hotspur F. C., Warwickshire County Cricket Ground Co., Wednesday F. C., West Bromwich Albion F. C., West Ham United F. C., Woolwich Arsenal F. C.

Subscription Registers of Association Football Players' Union

Wage Books of Heart of Midlothian F. C.

York Racing Committee Records

York Racing Museum

PARLIAMENTARY PAPERS

Hansard's Parliamentary Debates
Select Committee on Betting, *British Parliamentary Papers 1901*, V
Select Committee on Betting, *British Parliamentary Papers 1902*, V
Select Committee on Horses, *British Parliamentary Papers 1873*, XIV

CONTEMPORARY PUBLICATIONS

Newspapers and periodicals

Athletic Journal
Athletic News
Bell's Life
Bloodstock Breeders Review
Bradford Observer
British Almanac and Companion
Cricket
Cricket Field

Evening Times Football Annual
Glasgow Herald
Leeds Daily News
Leicester Daily Mercury
Racing Calendar
Ruffs Guide to the Turf
Scottish Athletic Journal
Scottish Football Annual
Scottish Sport
Spectator
Sporting Repository
Wisden Cricketers' Almanack
Yorkshire C. C. C. Year Book
Yorkshire Post

Articles and contributions to books

Abell, H. F. 'The football fever', *Macmillan's Magazine*, LXXXIX, 1904
Adams, W. D. 'The growth of English pastimes', *British Almanac and Companion 1886*
Aflalo, F. G. 'The sportsman's library: a note on some books of 1901', *Fortnightly Review*, LXX, 1901
Alcock, C. W. 'The Australians at the Oval', in Lord Alverstone and C. W. Alcock, *Surrey Cricket*, London, 1902
   'An appreciation of the professional', in B. O. Corbett *et al.*, *Football*, London, 1907
Almond, H. H. 'Football as a moral agent', *Nineteenth Century*, XXXIV, 1893
An Old Player. 'Football: the game and the business', *World Today*, I, 1902
Apperley, C. J. 'The turf', *Quarterly Review*, XLIX, 1833
Baille-Grohman, W. A. 'The shortcomings of our sporting literature', *Fortnightly Review*, LXII, 1902
Bassett, W. I. 'Big transfers and the transfer system', in *The Book of Football*, London, 1906
   'The day's work', in *The Book of Football*, London, 1906
Bentley, J. J. 'Is football a business?' *World's Work*, 1912
Bessant, W. 'The amusements of the people', *Contemporary Review*, XLV, 1884
Bonnett, F. 'Old-time sports', in *Victoria County History of Nottinghamshire*, II, London, 1910
   'Racing', in *Victoria County History of Nottinghamshire*, II, London, 1910
Bryden, H. A. and Cuming, E. D. 'Racing', in *Victoria County History of Sussex*, II, London, 1907
Budd, A. 'The Northern Union', in A. Budd, C. B. Fry, B. F. Robinson and T. A. Cook, *Football*, London, 1897
Cadogan, Lord. 'The state of the turf', *Fortnightly Review*, XXXVII, 1885
Catton, J. A. H. 'Competitive county cricket', *Badminton Magazine*, XXXIV, 1912
Charrington, C. 'Communal recreation', *Contemporary Review*, LXXIX, 1901
Colman, C. S. 'The football season', *Badminton Magazine*, II, 1896

Connell, R. M. 'The association game in Scotland', in *The Book of Football*, London, 1906
  'The Scottish Football League and its history', in *The Book of Football*, London, 1906
Conway, R. M. 'Cross country running', *Badminton Magazine*, VII, 1898
Cook, T. A. 'Rowing', in *Victoria County History of Oxfordshire*, II, London, 1907
Creston, 'Football', *Fortnightly Review*, LV, 1894
Curzon, L. H. 'The horse as an instrument of gambling', *Contemporary Review*, XXX, 1877
Davis, A. 'England's international teams and how they are selected', in *The Book of Football*, London, 1906
  'The Southern League: its rise and progress', in *The Book of Football*, London, 1906
Day, W. 'Our national pastime', *Fortnightly Review*, XLVI, 1888
De Lugo, A. B. 'Surrey county players 1844–1901', in Lord Alverstone and C. W. Alcock (eds.), *Surrey Cricket*, London, 1902
Ditchfield, P. H. 'Sport ancient and modern', in *Victoria County History of Berkshire*, II, London, 1907
Duncans. 'The cycle industry', *Contemporary Review*, LXXIII, 1898
Durham, Lord. 'Turf reform', *New Review*, II, 1890
Dutt, W. A. 'The last camping match', *Badminton Magazine*, IX, 1899
Edwardes, C. 'The new football mania', *Nineteenth Century*, 1892
Ellesmere, Earl of. 'Concerning stewards', *Badminton Magazine*, XII, 1901
Ensor, E. 'The football madness', *Contemporary Review*, LXXIV, 1898
Everard, H. S. C. 'A haver with Tom Morris', *Badminton Magazine*, I, 1895
  'Golf in 1899', *Badminton Magazine*, X, 1900
  'Golf: a retrospect', *Badminton Magazine*, XVIII, 1904
Fleming, C. J. N. 'Rugby football', *Badminton Magazine*, III, 1896
Ford, W. J. 'Thoughts on spectators', *Badminton Magazine*, XIII, 1899
Fry, C. B. 'Football', *Badminton Magazine*, I, 1895
Gettins, J. H. 'Football and national life', in B. O. Corbett *et al.*, *Football*, London, 1907
Gordon, H. 'Cricket characteristics', *Badminton Magazine*, XII, 1901
  'The past cricket season', *Badminton Magazine*, XIII, 1901; XV, 1902; XVII, 1903; XXI, 1905; XXXI, 1910
  'Cricket twenty years ago and now', *Badminton Magazine*, XIV, 1902
  'The test matches in England', *Badminton Magazine*, XIV, 1902
  'County cricket', *Badminton Magazine*, XVI, 1903
  'The coming cricket season', *Badminton Magazine*, XVI, 1903; XXIV, 1907; XXX, 1910
  'Cricket problems of today', *Badminton Magazine*, XIX, 1904
  'From colts match to test match', *Badminton Magazine*, XVIII, 1904
  'Is first class cricket losing its popularity?', *Badminton Magazine*, XXI, 1905
  'A cricket problem', *Badminton Magazine*, XXII, 1906
  'Cricket', in *Victoria County History of Sussex*, II, London, 1907
  'Cricket now – and then', *Badminton Magazine*, XXV, 1907

'Cricket and crowds', *Badminton Magazine*, XXIX, 1909

'Youth in cricket', *Fortnightly Review*, LXXXVII, 1910

'The real meaning of this cricket season', *Fortnightly Review*, XCI, 1912

Gordon, H. and Leverson-Gower, H. D. G. 'The state of amateurs in cricket', *Badminton Magazine*, XIV, 1902

Graves, H. 'A philosophy of sport', *Contemporary Review*, LXXVIII, 1900

Guillemard, A. G. 'The season of 1875–76 – the rugby union', in *The Football Annual*, London, 1876

Guthrie, G. 'What's the good of football?', in *Scottish Football Annual 1889/90*.

Haig-Brown, A. R. 'The lesson from New Zealand', *Badminton Magazine*, XXII, 1906

Hamilton, Lord. 'The financial aspects of racing', *Badminton Magazine*, XXIII, 1906

Harris, Lord. 'Cricket', *Contemporary Review*, XLVIII, 1885

Harris, S. S. 'The famous Corinthian F. C. 1833–1906', in *The Book of Football*, London, 1906

Hawke, Lord. 'On captaincy', *Badminton Magazine*, XIV, 1902

'The unwritten laws of cricket', *Badminton Magazine*, XXI, 1905

Hobbs, J. B. 'The compensation of cricket from a professional's point of view', *Badminton Magazine*, XXXVI, 1913

Hodgson, W. E. 'The degradation of British sport', *National Review*, XVII, 1891

Hughes-Onslow, H. 'The association football crisis', *Badminton Magazine*, XXIV, 1907

Hutchinson, H. 'The parlous condition of cricket', *National Review*, XXXV, 1900

'Golf during thirty years', *Quarterly Review*, CCXII, 1906

Jackson, N. L. 'Professionalism and sport', *Fortnightly Review*, LXVII, 1900

Jessop, G. L. 'Some hints to young bowlers', *National Review*, XXXIII, 1899

Kinloch, F. 'Golf of yesterday and today', *Chamber's Journal*, LXXXIII, 1906

Lewis, J. 'The much-abused referee', in *The Book of Football*, London, 1906

Lias, W. J. 'The future of rugby football', *Badminton Magazine*, XIII, 1901

Livingstone, R. 'Existing evils', in *Scottish Football Annual 1881/82*

Longueville, T. 'Racing and its fascination', *New Review*, VI, 1892

Lyttelton, F. 'More about the cricket problem', *Badminton Magazine*, XI, 1900

Lyttelton, R. H. 'Cricket', *Badminton Magazine*, III, 1896

M. C. C., *Marylebone Cricket Club Scores and Biographies*, XV, n.d.

MacFarlane, H. 'Football of yesterday and today: a comparison', *Monthly Review*, XXV, 1906

McGregor, W. 'Birmingham (late Small Heath) F. C.', in *The Book of Football*, London, 1906

'The League and the League System', in *The Book of Football*, London, 1906

'The £ s. d. of football', in *The Book of Football*, London, 1906

'Characteristics of the crowd', in B. O. Corbett *et al.*, *Football*, London, 1907

McKenzie, M. 'Training: its bearing on health', *New Review*, V, 1891

Mersey Thompson, R. F. 'Ethics of horse-racing', *National Review*, XXXIII, 1899

Morrison, J. H. 'The rise of Newcastle United', in *The Book of Football*, London, 1906

Needham, E. 'How to become an international', in B. O. Corbett *et al.*, *Football*, London, 1907

Oakley, W. J. 'The defence', in M. Shearman *et al.*, *Football*, London, 1899

Ord, R. 'Horseracing in the north of England', *Badminton Magazine*, XIV, 1903

Pennell, J. and Pennell, E. R. 'Cycling: past, present and future', *New Review*, IV, 1891

Perkins, H. 'Lords and the M. C. C.', in Earl of Suffolk, H. Peck and F. G. Aflalo (eds.), *The Encyclopaedia of Sport*, London, 1900

Robertson, J. B. 'The figure system', *Badminton Magazine*, XXXVI, 1913

Runciman, J. 'The ethics of the turf', *Contemporary Review*, LV, 1889

Sachs, E. T. 'Modern racing and the Derby', in F. G. Aflalo, *The Sports of the World*, London, II, n.d.

Sewell, E. H. D. 'Rugby football and the colonial tours', *Fortnightly Review*, LXXXII, 1907
  'The past cricket season', *Fortnightly Review*, LXXXVIII, 1910
  'The state of the game', *Fortnightly Review*, LXXXIX, 1911
  'Rugby football', *Fortnightly Review*, LXXXV, 1909; XCII, 1912
  'Has public interest in first class cricket declined', *Badminton Magazine*, XXXVII, 1913

Shearman, M. 'Amateur', in Earl of Suffolk, H. Peck and F. G. Aflalo (eds.), *The Encyclopaedia of Sport*, London, 1900

Shillcock, W. 'The ball and the boot – how they are made', in *The Book of Football*, London, 1906

Sirius. 'Football', *Gentleman's Magazine*, X, 1873

Smart, H. 'The present state of the turf', *Fortnightly Review*, XXXVIII, 1885

Smith, G. O. 'Football', *Pall Mall Magazine*, XIII, 1897
  'Referees', in M. Shearman *et al.*, *Football*, London, 1899

Smith, J. H. 'The history of the Northern Union', in *The Book of Football*, London, 1906

Spenser, H. J. 'The athletic master in public schools', *Contemporary Review*, LXXVIII, 1900

Steel, A. G. 'Bowling', in A. G. Steel and R. H. Lyttelton, *Cricket*, London, 1893

Strutfield, G. H. 'Racing in 1890', *Nineteenth Century*, XXVII, 1890

Sturdee, R. J. 'The ethics of football', *Westminster Review*, LIX, 1903

Suffolk, Earl of. 'Gentlemen riders', *Badminton Magazine*, II, 1896

Trevor, P. C. W. 'The season's football', *Badminton Magazine*, VIII, 1899
  'Football', *Badminton Magazine*, XII, 1901
  'The future of cricket', *Fortnightly Review*, XC, 1911
  'Then and now – cricket', *Badminton Magazine*, XXXVI, 1913

Verrall, G. H. 'The financial aspect of racing from another point of view', *Badminton Magazine*, XXIII, 1906

Vigilant. 'Recollections of Epsom and the Derby', *English Illustrated Magazine*, 1891–2

Walker, R. D. 'Lord's up to date', *Badminton Magazine*, X, 1900

Warner, P. F. 'The end of the cricket season', *Badminton Magazine*, XXXV, 1912
  'The coming cricket season', *Badminton Magazine*, XXXVI, 1913

Watson, A. E. T. 'Racing in 1896', *Badminton Magazine*, III, 1896
  'Racing', in Earl of Suffolk, H. Peck and F. G. Aflalo (eds.), *The Encyclopaedia of Sport*, London, 1900
  'Sportsmen of mark – Lord Hamilton of Dalzell', *Badminton Magazine*, XXI, 1905
  'The racing season', *Badminton Magazine*, London, XXII, 1906
  'The American jockey invasion', *Badminton Magazine*, XXIV, 1907
Whiz. 'Newmarket', *Gentleman's Magazine*, VII, 1871
Wynter, P. H. L. 'Racing', in *Victoria County History of Oxfordshire*, III, London, 1907

'Association football: a retrospect and lament', *Saturday Review*, 3 March 1900
'Athletes of the year', *Strand Magazine*, VIII, 1894
'Backing and pulling', *Saturday Review*, 6 July 1889
'Boat-racing', *Gentleman's Magazine*, II, 1868
'Boxing and sparring', *Saturday Review*, 26 January 1884
'Cricket fifty years ago', *Saturday Review*, 29 April 1882
'Cricket prospects', *Saturday Review*, 12 May 1900
'Cycling for health and pleasure', *Chamber's Journal*, LXXII, 1895
'Doping', *Badminton Magazine*, XLII, 1913
'English field sports', *Bentley's Quarterly Review*, III, 1859
'Football accidents', *Saturday Review*, 10 December 1892
'Football notes', *Tinsley's Magazine*, XLVI, 1889–90
'In and about Newmarket', *Strand Magazine*, II, 1891
'International cricket', *Saturday Review*, 6 September 1884
'Jockeys and jockeyship', *Badminton Magazine*, XVIII, 1904
'Lord Cadogan on the turf', *Saturday Review*, 17 January 1885
'Modern horse-racing', *Edinburgh Review*, CLI, 1880
'Owners and owning', *Badminton Magazine*, XVII, 1903
'Professional cricket', *Saturday Review*, 14 July 1883
'Professional cricket', *Cricket*, VI, 1887
'Professionalism in English sports', *Saturday Review*, 14 April 1888
'Racecourse and covert side', *Saturday Review*, 5 January 1884
'Racing', *Saturday Review*, 20 July 1888
'Rioting at Lillie Bridge', *Saturday Review*, 24 September 1887
'Sport and decadence', *Quarterly Review*, CCXI, 1909
'Sport in 1886', *British Almanac and Companion 1887*
'Test match cricket of 1912', *Blackwood's Magazine*, CXCII, 1912
'The cycle and the trade of the Midlands', *Chamber's Journal*, LXXIV, 1897
'The last surprise of the racing season', *Saturday Review*, 3 December 1887
'The racing season', *Saturday Review*, 5 April 1884
'The state of the turf', *Badminton Magazine*, XIV, 1902; XIX, 1904; XX, 1905
'The state of the turf', *Saturday Review*, 8 December 1900
'The turf: its frauds and chicaneries', *Contemporary Review*, XXII, 1873
'Turf ethics in 1868', *Broadway*, 1868

Books

Albermarle, Earl of and Lacy Hillier, G. *Cycling*, London, 1896
Alcock, C. W. *Association Football*, London, 1890
   Association Football, London, 1906
Bettinson, A. F. and Bennison, B. *The Home of Boxing*, London, 1919
Black, R. *Horse-Racing in England*, London, 1893
   The Jockey Club and its Founders, London, 1891
Blaine, D. P. *Encyclopaedia of Rural Sports*, London, 1870
Booth, C. *Life and Labour of the People of London*, London, 1896
Budd, A. *Football (Rugby)*, London, 1899
Budd, A. *et al.*, *Football*, London, 1900
Catton, J. A. H. *The Real Football*, London, 1900
Cawthorne, C. J. and Herod, R. S. *Royal Ascot*, London, 1900
Chetwynd, G. *Racing Reminiscences*, London, 1891
Cobbett, M. *The Man on the March*, London, 1896
   Racing Life and Racing Characteristics, London, 1903
Cook, T. A. *A History of the English Turf*, London, 1905
Curzon, L. H. *The Blue Riband of the Turf*, London, 1890
   A Mirror of the Turf, London, 1892
Day, W. *The Racehorse in Training*, London, 1880
The Druid, *Post and Paddock*, London, 1895
   Scott and Sebright, London, 1895
Egan, P. *Book of Sports*, London, 1832
Fegan, J. H. C. *et al.*, *Football, Hockey and Lacrosse*, London, 1900
Grace, W. G. *Cricket*, Bristol, 1891
Harris, Lord. *The History of Kent County Cricket*, London, 1907
Hone, W. *The Everyday Book*, London, 1830
Jackson, N. L. *Association Football*, London, 1899
Kent, J. *The Racing Life of George Cavendish Bentinck*, London, 1892
Lehmann, R. C. *Rowing*, London, 1898
Masterman, C. F. G. *The Condition of England*, London, 1911
Mitchell, E. B. *Boxing*, London, 1889
Moorehouse, E. *The Romance of the Derby*, London, 1908
Muir, J. H. *Glasgow in 1901*, Glasgow, 1901
Myers, A. W. *C. B. Fry*, London, 1912
Needham, E. *Association Football*, London, 1900
Porter, J. *Kingsclere*, London, 1896
Porter, J. and Moorehouse, E. *John Porter of Kingsclere*, London, 1919
Rice, J. *The History of the British Turf*, London, 1879
Richardson, C. *The English Turf*, London, 1901
Rowe, R. P. P. and Pitman, C. M. *Rowing*, London, 1898
Rowntree, B. S. *Poverty*, London, 1901
Seton-Kerr, H. *Golf*, London, 1907
Shearman, M. *Athletics and Football*, London, 1888
Shearman, M., Oakley, W. J., Smith, G. O. and Mitchell, F. *Football*, London, 1899
Sloan, T. *Tod Sloan*, London, 1915

Smith, G. O. *Football (Association)*, London, 1898
Spencer, E. *The Great Game*, London, 1900
Strutt, J. *The Sports and Pastimes of the People of England*, London, 1834
Suffolk, Earl of. *Racing and Steeplechasing*, London, 1886
Suffolk, Earl of, Peck, H. and Aflalo, F. G. (eds.), *The Encyclopaedia of Sport*, London, 1900
Watson, A. E. T. *The Turf*, London, 1898
Whyte, J. C. *History of the British Turf*, London, 1840

The Book of Football, London, 1906
Cycling, London, 1898

PUBLICATIONS SINCE 1920

Articles, papers and contributions to books

Adelman, M. L. 'Academicians and American athletics: a decade of progress', *Journal of Sport History*, X, 1983
Appleby, A. B. 'Grain prices and subsistence crises in England and France, 1590–1740', *Journal of Economic History*, XXXIX, 1979
Armstrong, W. A. 'The use of information about occupation', in E. A. Wrigley (ed.), *Nineteenth-Century Society*, Cambridge, 1972
Ashplant, T. G. 'London working men's clubs, 1875–1914', in E. and S. Yeo (eds.), *Popular Culture and Class Conflict, 1590–1914*, Brighton, 1981
Bailey, P. 'Custom, capital and culture in the Victorian music hall', in R. D. Storch (ed.), *Popular Culture and Custom in Nineteenth-Century England*, London, 1982
Bailey, V. 'Salvation army riots, the "skeleton army" and legal authority in the provincial town', in A. P. Donajgrodzki (ed.), *Social Control in Nineteenth-Century Britain*, London, 1977
Baker, W. J. 'The leisure revolution in Victorian England: a review of the recent literature', *Journal of Sport History*, VI, 1979
'The state of British sport history', *Journal of Sport History*, X, 1983
Blanchard, I. 'Labour productivity and work psychology in the English mining industry, 1400–1600', *Economic History Review*, XXXI, 1978
Bradley, I. 'The English Sunday', *History Today*, XXII, 1972
Brailsford, D. 'Puritanism and sport in seventeenth-century England', *Stadion*, I, 1975
'Sporting days in eighteenth-century England', *Journal of Sport History*, IX, 1982
'The locations of eighteenth-century spectator sport', in J. Bale and C. Jenkins (eds.), *Geographical Perspectives on Sport*, Birmingham, 1983
'Religion and sport in eighteenth-century England: "for the encouragement of piety and virtue, and for the preventing or punishing of vice, profanement and immorality"', *British Journal of Sport History*, I, 1984
Burne, S. A. H. 'Cricket', in *Victoria County History of Staffordshire*, II, 1967
Cairns, J. 'Economic analysis of league sports: a critical review of the literature',

Department of Political Economy Discussion Paper 83–01, University of
Aberdeen, 1983

Cairns, J., Jennett, N. and Sloane, P. J. 'The economics of professional team
sports: a survey of theory and evidence', *Department of Political Economy
Discussion Paper 84–06*, University of Aberdeen, 1984

Carr, R. 'Country sports', in G. E. Mingay (ed.), *The Victorian Countryside*, II,
London, 1981

Carroll, R. 'Football hooliganism in England', *International Review of Sport
Sociology*, XV, 1980

Clapham, J. H. 'Economic history as a discipline', in E. R. A. Seligman (ed.),
Encyclopaedia of the Social Sciences, New York, 1963

Coats, A. W. 'The classical economists and the labourer', in A. W. Coats (ed.), *The
Classical Economists and Economic Policy*, London, 1971

Cohen, J. S. 'The achievements of economic history: the Marxist school', *Journal
of Economic History*, XXXVIII, 1978

Cole, A. H. 'Perspectives on leisure time business', *Explorations in Entrepreneurial History*, I, 1963–4, Supplement

Cole, W. A. 'Factors in demand 1700–80', in R. Floud and D. McCloskey (eds.),
The Economic History of Britain since 1700, I, Cambridge, 1981

Coleman, D. C. 'Labour in the English economy of the seventeenth century',
Economic History Review, VIII, 1955–6

'Gentlemen and players', *Economic History Review*, XXVI, 1973

Covick, O. 'Sporting equality in professional team sports leagues and labour
market controls: what is the relationship?', *Sporting Traditions*, II, 1985–6

Crump, J. '"The great carnival of the year": the Leicester races in the 19th
century', *Transactions of the Leicestershire Historical and Archaeological
Society*, LVIII, 1982–3

Cunningham, H. 'Jingoism in 1877–78', *Victorian Studies*, XIV, 1971

'The metropolitan fairs: a case study in the social control of leisure', in A. P.
Donajgrodzki (ed.), *Social Control in Nineteenth-Century Britain*, London,
1977

'Leisure', in J. Benson (ed.), *The Working Class in England, 1875–1914*,
London, 1985

Dabscheck, B. 'The wage determination process for sportsmen', *Economic
Record*, LI, 1975

'"Defensive Manchester": a history of the Professional Footballers' Association', in R. Cashman and M. McKernan (eds.), *Sport in History*, St Lucia,
1979

Daly, G. and Moore, W. J. 'Externalities, property rights and the allocation of
resources in major league baseball', *Economic Inquiry*, XIX, 1981

Davenport, D. S. 'Collusive competition in major league baseball: its theory and
institutional development', *American Economist*, XIII, 1969

Davis, L. E. 'Self-regulation in baseball, 1909–71', in R. G. Noll, *Government and
the Sports Business*, Washington, 1974

Davis, R. 'English foreign trade, 1660–1700', *Economic History Review*, VII,
1954

Delves, A. 'Popular recreation and social conflict in Derby, 1800–1850', in E. and

S. Yeo (eds.), *Popular Culture and Class Conflict, 1590–1914*, Brighton, 1981

Dingle, A. E. 'Drink and working-class living standards in Britain, 1870–1914', *Economic History Review*, XXV, 1972

Dixon, D. '"Class law": the Street Betting Act of 1906', *International Journal of the Sociology of Law*, VIII, 1980

Doyle, P. J. 'Some problems for the regional historian of rugby league', *Journal of Local Studies*, I, 1980

Dunning, E., Maguire, J., Murphy, P. and Williams, J. 'The social roots of football hooligan violence', *Leisure Studies*, I, 1982

Dunning, E., Murphy, P., Williams, J. and Maguire, J. 'Football hooliganism in Britain before the First World War', *International Review of Sport Sociology*, XIX, 1984

El Hodiri, M. and Quirk, J. 'An economic model of a professional sports league', *Journal of Political Economy*, LXXIX, 1971

Elias, T. E. 'Golf: an historic survey', in *British Sports and Sportsmen*, London, 1935

Eversley, D. E. C. 'The home market and economic growth in England, 1750–1780', in E. L. Jones and G. E. Mingay (eds.), *Land, Labour and Population in the Industrial Revolution*, London, 1967

Feinstein, C. H. 'Capital formation in Great Britain', in P. Mathias and M. M. Postan (eds.), *Cambridge Economic History of Europe*, VII, Cambridge, 1978

Field, A. J. 'Occupational structure, dissent and educational commitment: Lancashire, 1841', *Research in Economic History*, IV, 1979

Floud, R. and Wachter, K. W. 'Poverty and physical stature: evidence on the standard of living of London boys 1770–1870', *Social Science History*, VI, 1982

Fogel, R. W. *et al.*, 'The economics of mortality in North America, 1650–1910: a description of a research project', *Historical Methods*, XI, 1978

Freudenberger, H. and Cummins, G. 'Health, work and leisure before the Industrial Revolution', *Explorations in Economic History*, XIII, 1976

Gatrell, V. A. C. 'The decline of theft and violence in Victorian and Edwardian England', in V. A. C. Gatrell, B. Lenman and G. Parker (eds.), *Crime and the Law: The Social History of Crime in Western Europe since 1500*, London, 1980

Gourvish, T. 'The standard of living, 1890–1914', in A. O'Day (ed.), *The Edwardian Age*, London, 1979

Gratton, C. and Lisewski, B. 'The economics of sport in Britain: a case of market failure', *British Review of Economic Issues*, III, 1981

Guttmann, A. 'On the alleged dehumanisation of the sports spectator', *Journal of Popular Culture*, XIV, 1980–1

'Recent work in European sport history', *Journal of Sport History*, X, 1983

'The belated birth and threatened death of fair play', *Yale Review*, 1985

Halladay, E. 'Of pride and prejudice: the amateur question in English nineteenth-century rowing', *International Journal of the History of Sport*, IV, 1987

Hardy, S. 'Entrepreneurs, organisations, and the sport marketplace: subjects in search of historians', *Journal of Sport History*, XIII, 1986

Harley, C. K. 'British industrialisation before 1841: evidence of slower growth during the Industrial Revolution', *Journal of Economic History*, XLII, 1982

Harrison, A. E. 'The competitiveness of the British cycle industry, 1890–1914', *Economic History Review*, XXII, 1969

Harrison, B. 'Religion and recreation in nineteenth-century England', *Past and Present*, XXXVIII, 1967

'Animals and the state in nineteenth-century England', *English Historical Review*, LXXXVIII, 1973

Hay, D. 'Poaching and the game laws on Cannock Chase', in D. Hay, P. Linebaugh and E. P. Thompson, *Albion's Fatal Tree*, London, 1975

Hay, J. R. 'Employers and social policy in Britain: the evolution of welfare legislation, 1905–14', *Social History*, IV, 1977

Haynes, M. J. 'Strikes', in J. Benson (ed.), *The Working Class in England, 1875–1914*, London, 1985

Henricks, T. S. 'Sport and social hierarchy in medieval England', *Journal of Sport History*, IX, 1982

Hill, P. and Lowe, B. 'The inevitable metathesis of the retiring athlete', *International Review of Sport Sociology*, IX, 1974

Hobsbawm, E. J. 'The aristocracy of labour reconsidered', in *Problems of Work and the Labour Force in Enterprise in the 19th and 20th Centuries*, Theme B9, Seventh International Economic History Congress, Edinburgh, 1978

Hopkins, E. 'Working hours and conditions during the Industrial Revolution: a re-appraisal', *Economic History Review*, XXXV, 1982

Holt, R. 'Working-class football and the city: the problem of continuity', *British Journal of Sports History*, III, 1986

Hoskins, W. H. 'Harvest fluctuations in English economic history 1480–1619', *Agricultural History Review*, XI, 1964

'Harvest fluctuations in English economic history 1620–1759', *Agricultural History Review*, XVI, 1968

Houston, D. R. 'The occupational mobility of professional athletes', *International Review of Sport Sociology*, XVII, 1982

Howkins, A. *Whitsun in Nineteenth-Century Oxfordshire*, History Workshop Pamphlet No. 8, Oxford, 1973

'The taming of Whitsun: the changing face of a nineteenth-century rural holiday', in E. and S. Yeo (eds.), *Popular Culture and Class Conflict, 1590–1914*, Brighton, 1981

Hueckel, G. 'Agriculture during industrialisation', in R. Floud and D. McCloskey (eds.), *The Economic History of Britain since 1700*, I, Cambridge, 1981

Huggins, M. '"Mingled pleasure and speculation": the survival of the enclosed racecourses on Teesside, 1855–1902', *British Journal of Sports History*, III, 1986

Hunt, J. W. and Lewis, K. A. 'Dominance, recontracting, and the reserve clause: major league baseball', *American Economic Review*, LXVI, 1976

Hutchinson, J. 'Some aspects of football crowds before 1914', in *Society for Study of Labour History Conference*, University of Sussex, 1975

Jable, J. T. 'The English Puritans: suppressors of sport and amusement?', *Canadian Journal of History of Sport and Physical Education*, VII, 1978

Jones, E. L. 'Agriculture, 1700–80', in R. Floud and D. McCloskey (eds.), *The Economic History of Britain since 1700*, I, Cambridge, 1981

Jones, J. C. H. 'The economics of the national hockey league', *Canadian Journal of Economics*, II, 1969

Korr, C. P. 'West Ham United Football Club and the beginnings of professional football in east London, 1895–1914', *Journal of Contemporary History*, XIII, 1978

'The men at the top: the board of directors of the West Ham United Football Club', in W. Vamplew (ed.), *The Economic History of Leisure: Papers presented at the Eighth International Economic History Congress*, Budapest, 1982

Kramer, J. 'Getting out: the football player', in J. T. Talamini and C. H. Page (eds.), *Sport and Society*, Boston, 1973

Lindhert, P. H. and Williamson, J. G. 'English workers' living standards during the Industrial Revolution: a new look', *Economic History Review*, XXXVI, 1983

Lowerson, J. R. 'English middle-class sport, 1880–1914' in J. R. Cox (ed.), *Aspects of the Social History of Nineteenth-Century Sport*, Liverpool, 1982

'Joint stock companies, capital formation and suburban leisure in England 1880–1914', in W. Vamplew (ed.), *The Economic History of Leisure: Papers presented at the Eighth International Economic History Congress*, Budapest, 1982

'Sport and the Victorian Sunday: the beginnings of middle-class apostasy', *British Journal of Sports History*, I, 1984

Lyons, J. S. 'The Lancashire cotton industry and the introduction of the power-loom, 1815–1850', *Journal of Economic History*, XXXVIII, 1978

McCann, P. 'Popular education, socialization and social control: Spitalfields 1812–1824', in P. McCann (ed.), *Popular Education and Socialization in the Nineteenth Century*, London, 1977

McIntosh, P. C. 'An historical view of sport and social control', *International Review of Sports Sociology*, VI, 1971

McKendrick, N. 'Home demand and economic growth', in N. McKendrick (ed.), *Historical Perspectives*, London, 1974

McKibben, R. 'Working-class gambling in Britain 1880–1939', *Past and Present*, LXXXII, 1979

Magoun, F. P. 'Football in medieval England and in middle-English literature', *American Historical Review*, XXXV, 1929

'Scottish popular football, 1424–1815', *American Historical Review*, XXXVII, 1931

Maguire, J. 'Images of manliness and competing ways of living in late Victorian and Edwardian Britain', *British Journal of Sports History*, III, 1986

Malcolmson, R. W. 'Leisure', in G. E. Mingay (ed.), *The Victorian Countryside*, London, 1981

Mallea, J. R. 'The Victorian sporting legacy', *McGill Journal*, X, 1975

Mandle, W. F. 'The professional cricketer in England in the nineteenth century', *Labour History*, XXIII, 1972

'Games people played: cricket and football in England and Victoria in the late nineteenth century', *Historical Studies*, XV, 1973

Mangan, J. A. 'Athletics: a case study of the evolution of an educational ideology', in B. Simon and I. Bradley (eds.), *The Victorian Public School*, Dublin, 1975

Mann, L. and Pearce, P. 'Social psychology of the sports spectator', in D. Glencross (ed.), *Psychology and Sport*, Sydney, 1978

Mason, A. 'The blues and the reds', *Transactions of the Lancashire and Cheshire Archaeological Society*, 1984

Matthews, G. R. 'The controversial Olympic Games of 1908 as viewed by the New York Times and the Times of London', *Journal of Sport History*, VII, 1980

Meacham, S. 'The sense of an impending clash: English working-class unrest before the First World War', *American Historical Review*, LXXVII, 1972

Meisl, W. 'The importance of being amateur', in A. Nathan (ed.), *Sport and Society*, London, 1958

Metcalfe, A. 'Organized sport in the mining communities of south Northumberland, 1800–1889', *Victorian Studies*, XXV, 1981–2

Mokyr, J. 'Demand versus supply in the Industrial Revolution', *Journal of Economic History*, XXXVI, 1977

Moorhouse, H. F. 'Professional football and working-class culture: English theories and Scottish evidence', *Sociological Review*, XXXII, 1984

Myerscough, J. 'The recent history of the use of leisure time', in I. Appleton (ed.), *Leisure Research and Policy*, Edinburgh, 1974

Neale, W. C. 'The peculiar economics of professional sport', *Quarterly Journal of Economics*, LXXVIII, 1964

Noll, R. G. 'Alternatives in sports policy', in R. G. Noll (ed.), *Government and the Sports Business*, Washington, 1974

'Attendance and price setting', in R. G. Noll (ed.), *Government and the Sports Business*, Washington, 1974

Oddy, D. J. 'Working-class diets in late nineteenth-century Britain', *Economic History Review*, XXIII, 1970

Ó Gráda, C. 'Agricultural decline', in R. Floud and D. McCloskey (eds.), *The Economic History of Britain since 1700*, II, Cambridge, 1981

Outhwaite, R. B. 'Food crises in early modern England: patterns of public response', in *Economic Fluctuations and Policy Responses in Pre-Industrial Europe*, Theme B7, Seventh International Economic History Congress, Edinburgh, 1978

P. E. P. 'English professional football', *Planning*, XXII, 1966

Papalas, A. J. 'Professors and amateurs: aspects of pugilism in the Regency period', in *Proceedings of Thirteenth North American Society for Sport History Conference*, 1985

Payne, P. L. 'The emergence of the large-scale company in Great Britain, 1870–1914', *Economic History Review*, XX, 1967

Perkins, H. J. 'The "social tone" of Victorian seaside resorts in the north-west', *Northern History*, II, 1975

Phillips, S. K. 'Primitive Methodist confrontation with popular sports: case study of early nineteenth-century Staffordshire', in R. Cashman and M. McKernan (eds.), *Sport: Money, Morality and the Media*, Sydney, 1981

Pollard, S. 'Factory discipline in the Industrial Revolution', *Economic History Review*, XV, 1963–4

'Labour in Great Britain', in P. Mathias and M. M. Postan, *Cambridge Economic History of Europe*, VII, Cambridge, 1978

Pratt, J. and Salter, M. 'A fresh look at football hooliganism', *Leisure Studies*, III, 1984

Reid, D. A. 'The decline of St Monday 1766–1876', *Past and Present*, LXXI, 1976

'Interpreting the festival calendar: wakes and fairs as carnivals', in R. D. Storch (ed.), *Popular Culture and Custom in Nineteenth-Century England*, London, 1982

'"To boldly go where no worker had gone before": railway excursions from Birmingham 1846–1876'. Paper presented at the Eighth International Economic History Congress, Budapest, 1982

Richter, D. 'The role of mob riot in Victorian elections 1865–1885', *Victorian Studies*, XV, 1971

Roberts, E. 'Working-class standards of living in Barrow and Lancaster, 1890–1914', *Economic History Review*, XXX, 1977

Robertson, J. B. 'The principles of heredity applied to the racehorse', in Earl of Harewood (ed.), *Flat Racing*, London, 1940

Rottenberg, S. 'The baseball players' labour market', *Journal of Political Economy*, LXIV, 1956

Rühl, J. K. 'Religion and amusements in sixteenth- and seventeenth-century England', *British Journal of Sports History*, I, 1984

Rule, J. G. 'Some social aspects of the Industrial Revolution in Cornwall', in R. Burt, *Industry and Society in the South West*, Exeter, 1970

'Methodism, popular beliefs and village culture in Cornwall, 1800–50', in R. D. Storch (ed.), *Popular Culture and Custom in Nineteenth-Century England*, London, 1982

Sanderson, M. 'Education and the factory in industrial Lancashire 1780–1840', *Economic History Review*, XX, 1967

Sandiford, K. A. P. 'Cricket and the Victorians: a historiographical essay', *Historical Reflections*, IX, 1982

'English cricket crowds during the Victorian age', *Journal of Sport History*, IX, 1982

'Amateurs and professionals in Victorian county cricket', *Albion*, XV, 1983

'Cricket and the Victorian society', *Journal of Social History*, XVII, 1983

Schofield, J. A. 'The development of first-class cricket in England: an economic analysis', *Journal of Industrial Economics*, XXX, 1982

Schwarz, L. D. 'The standard of living in the long run: London 1700–1860', *Economic History Review*, XXVIII, 1985

Scott, M. B. 'The man on the horse', in J. W. Loy and G. S. Kenyon (eds.), *Sport, Culture and Society*, London, 1969

Scott, P. 'Cricket and the religious world in the Victorian period', *Church Quarterly*, III, 1970

Skully, G. W. 'Pay and performance in major league baseball', *American Economic Review*, LXIV, 1974

Sloane, P. J. 'The economics of professional football: the football club as a utility maximiser', *Scottish Journal of Political Economy*, XVIII, 1971

'Restriction of competition in professional team sports', *Bulletin of Economic Research*, XXVIII, 1976

Sport in the Market, Hobart Paper No. 85, London, 1980

Smith, M. 'Victorian music hall entertainment in the Lancashire cotton towns', *Local Historian*, 1968–71

Smith, M. D. 'Sport and collective violence', in D. W. Ball and J. W. Loy (eds.), *Sport and Social Order: Contributions to the Sociology of Sport*, Reading, Mass., 1975

Stedman Jones, G. 'Working-class culture and working-class politics in London 1870–1900: notes on the remaking of a working class', *Journal of Social History*, VIII, 1975

Storch, R. D. 'The plague of the blue locusts: police reform and popular resistance in northern England, 1840–1857', *International Review of Social History*, XX, 1975

'The policeman as domestic missionary: urban discipline and popular culture in northern England, 1850–1880', *Journal of Social History*, IX, 1976

'The problem of working-class leisure: some roots of middle-class moral reform in the industrial north', in A. P. Donajgrodzki (ed.), *Social Control in Nineteenth-Century Britain*, London, 1977

'Introduction: persistence and change in nineteenth-century popular culture', in R. D. Storch (ed.), *Popular Culture and Custom in Nineteenth-Century England*, London, 1982

'"Please to remember the fifth of November": conflict, solidarity and public order in southern England, 1815–1900', in R. D. Storch (ed.), *Popular Culture and Custom in Nineteenth-Century England*, London, 1982

Struna, N. L. 'The declaration of sports reconsidered', *Canadian Journal of History of Sport*, XIV, 1983

Taylor, J. *From Self-Help to Glamour: The Working Man's Club, 1860–1972*, History Workshop Pamphlet No. 7, Oxford, 1972

Taylor, W. T. 'History of Derbyshire cricket', in *Wisden Cricketers' Almanack 1953*

Thompson, E. P. 'Time, work-discipline and industrial capitalism', *Past and Present*, XXXVIII, 1967

'Patrician society, plebeian culture, *Journal of Social History*, V, 1972

Tranter, N. L. 'The labour supply 1780–1860', in R. Floud and D. McCloskey (eds.), *The Economic History of Britain since 1700*, I, Cambridge, 1981

'Popular sports and the Industrial Revolution in Scotland: the evidence of the Statistical Accounts', *International Journal of the History of Sport*, IV, 1987

Turner, M. 'Agricultural productivity in England in the eighteenth century: evidence from crop yields', *Economic History Review*, XXXV, 1982

Vamplew, W. 'Unsporting behaviour: the control of football and horse-racing crowds in England, 1875–1914', in J. H. Goldstein (ed.), *Sports Violence*, New York, 1983

Walton, J. K. 'Residential amenity, respectable morality and the rise of the entertainment industry: the case of Blackpool 1860–1914', *Literature and History*, I, 1975

'The demand for working-class seaside holidays in Victorian England', *Economic History Review*, XXXIV, 1981

Walton, J. K. and Poole, R. 'The Lancashire wakes in the nineteenth century', in R. D. Storch (ed.), *Popular Culture and Custom in Nineteenth-Century England*, London, 1982

Weinberg, S. K. and Arond, H. 'The occupational culture of the boxer', *American Journal of Sociology*, LVII, 1952

Wigglesworth, N. 'A history of rowing in the north-west of England', *British Journal of Sports History*, III, 1986

Williams, G. 'How amateur was my valley: professional sport and national identity in Wales 1890–1914', *British Journal of Sports History*, II, 1985

Williamson, J. G. 'Why was British growth so slow during the Industrial Revolution?', *Journal of Economic History*, XLIV, 1984

Winter, J. M. 'Britain's "lost generation" of the First World War', *Population Studies*, XXXI, 1977

Wiseman, N. C. 'The economics of football', *Lloyds Bank Review* 1977

Woods, D. 'Community violence', in J. Benson (ed.), *The Working Class in England, 1875–1914*, London, 1985

Wrightson, K. 'Alehouses, order and reformation in rural England, 1590–1660', in E. and S. Yeo (eds.), *Popular Culture and Class Conflict, 1590–1914*, Brighton, 1981

Wrigley, E. A. 'A simple model of London's importance in changing English society and economy, 1650–1750', *Past and Present*, XXXVII, 1967

'Memorable Olympic boilovers', *Sport Magazine*, November 1956

Books

Allen, J. *The Story of the Rangers*, Glasgow, 1924

Altham, H. S. *Hampshire County Cricket*, London, 1958

Appleby, A. B. *Famine in Tudor and Stuart England*, Stanford, 1978

Arlott, J. *The Oxford Companion to Sports and Games*, London, 1975

Ashton, T. S. *An Economic History of England*, London, 1959
   Economic Fluctuations in England, 1700–1800, Oxford, 1959

Barker, T. C. *The Glassmakers*, London, 1977

Batchelor, D. *The Turf of Old*, London, 1951

Benson, J. *The Penny Capitalists*, Dublin, 1983

Berry, R. C., Gould, W. B. and Staudohar, P. B. *Labour Relations in Professional Sports*, Dover, 1986

Bienefeld, M. A. *Working Hours in British Industry*, London, 1972

Birley, D. *The Willow Wand*, London, 1979

Bowen, R. *Cricket*, London, 1970

Brailsford, D. *Sport and Society*, London, 1967

Brookes, C. *English Cricket*, Newton Abbot, 1978

Browne, T. H. *A History of the English Turf, 1904–1930*, London, 1931

Cecil, R. *Life in Edwardian England*, London, 1972

Chesney, K. *The Victorian Underworld*, London, 1972

Church, R. A. *Economic and Social Change in a Midland Town*, London, 1966

Coldham, J. D. *Northamptonshire Cricket*, London, 1959

Coleman, D. C. *The Economy of England, 1450–1750*, Oxford, 1977

Court, W. H. B. *British Economic History, 1870–1914*, Cambridge, 1965

Crafts, N. F. R. *British Economic Growth during the Industrial Revolution*, Oxford, 1985

Craig, D. *Horse-Racing*, London, 1982

Crampsey, R. *The Scottish Footballer*, Edinburgh, 1978

Cunningham, H. *The Volunteer Force*, London, 1975
  Leisure in the Industrial Revolution, London, 1980

Dangerfield, G. *The Strange Death of Liberal England*, New York, 1963

Darwin, B. *W. G. Grace*, London, 1978

Delaney, T. *The Roots of Rugby League*, Keighley, 1984

Demmert, H. G. *The Economics of Professional Team Sports*, Lexington, 1973

Denhardt, R. M. *Foundation Dams of the American Quarterhorse*, Norman, 1982

Dobbs, B. *Edwardians at Play*, London, 1973

Duckworth, L. *The Story of Warwickshire Cricket*, London, 1974

Dunning, E. and Sheard, K. *Barbarians, Gentlemen and Players*, Oxford, 1979

Elmsley, C. *British Society and the French Wars, 1793–1815*, London, 1980

Fairfax-Blakeborough, J. *The Analysis of the Turf*, London, 1927

Fairgrieve, J. *Away wi' the Goalie*, London, 1977

Fletcher, R. and Howes, D. *Rothmans Rugby League 1982–83 Yearbook*, Aylesbury, 1982

Ford, J. *Prizefighting*, Newton Abbot, 1971

Francis, C. *History of the Blackburn Rovers Football Club, 1875–1925*, Blackburn, 1925

Fraser, W. H. *The Coming of the Mass Market, 1850–1914*, London, 1981

Frith, D. *The Slow Men*, London, 1985

Galtrey, S. G. *Memoirs of a Racing Journalist*, London, 1934

Genders, R. *League Cricket in England*, London, 1952
  Worcestershire County Cricket, London, 1952

Gilbey, Q. *Champions All*, London, 1971

Glader, E. A. *Amateurism and Athletics*, New York, 1978

Goldthorpe, J. H., Lockwood, D., Bechhofer, F. and Platt, J. *The Affluent Worker in the Class Structure*, Cambridge, 1969

Golesworthy, M. (ed.), *The Encyclopaedia of Cricket*, London, 1964
  The Encyclopaedia of Boxing, London, 1965
  The Encyclopaedia of Association Football, Newton Abbot, 1977

Gratton, C. and Taylor, P. *Sport and Recreation: An Economic Analysis*, London, 1985

Gray, R. *The Aristocracy of Labour in Nineteenth-Century Britain, c. 1850–1900*, London, 1981

Green, G. *The History of the Football Association*, London, 1953
  The Official History of the F. A. Cup, London, 1960

Handley, J. E. *The Celtic Story*, London, 1960

Hanes, D. J. *The First British Workmen's Compensation Act 1897*, London, 1968

Harding, J. *Football Wizard*, Derby, 1985
Harrison, B. *Drink and the Victorians*, Pittsburgh, 1971
Heyhoe Flint, R. and Rheinberg, N. *Fair Play*, London, 1976
Hill, C. *Society and Puritanism in Pre-Revolutionary England*, London, 1964
Hobsbawm, E. J. *Labouring Men*, London, 1965
   Industry and Empire, London, 1968
Hodgson, D. *The Manchester United Story*, London, 1977
   The Liverpool Story, London, 1978
Holderness, B. A. *Pre-Industrial England*, London, 1976
Hole, C. *English Sports and Pastimes*, London, 1949
Humphris, E. M. *The Life of Fred Archer*, London, 1923
Hunt, E. H. *Regional Wage Variation in Britain, 1850–1914*, Oxford, 1973
   British Labour History, 1815–1914, London, 1981
Hutchinson, J. *The Football Industry*, Glasgow, 1982
Ingham, R. *Football Hooliganism*, London, 1978
Jackson, M. P. *Industrial Relations*, London, 1984
Kay, J. *Cricket in the Leagues*, London, 1972
Keates, T. *History of the Everton Football Club, 1978/79–1928/29*, Liverpool, 1929
Klein, J. *Samples from English Culture*, London, 1965
Kynaston, D. *King Labour*, London, 1976
   Bobby Abel, London, 1982
Lambton, G. *Men and Horses I Have Known*, London, 1924
Laslett, P. *The World We Have Lost*, London, 1973
Lee, A. J. *The Origins of the Popular Press in England, 1855–1914*, Towata, 1976
Lee, C. H. *British Regional Employment Statistics, 1841–1971*, Cambridge, 1979
Leicester, C. *Bloodstock Breeding*, London, 1959
Lemmon, D. *The Wisden Book of Cricket Quotations*, London, 1982
Lloyd, A. *The Great Prize Fight*, London, 1977
Lovesey, P. *The Official Centenary History of the Amateur Athletic Association*, London, 1979
Lowell, J. *British Trade Unions, 1875–1933*, London, 1977
Lowerson, J. and Myerscough, J. *Time to Spare in Victorian England*, Hassocks, 1977
McCann, P. *Popular Education and Socialization in the Nineteenth Century*, London, 1977
Mackay, J. R. *The Hibees*, Edinburgh, 1985
Macklin, K. *The History of Rugby League Football*, London, 1962
McLeod, H. *Religion and the Working Class in Nineteenth-Century Britain*, London, 1984
McNee, G. *The Story of Celtic*, London, 1978
Malcolmson, R. W. *Popular Recreations in English Society, 1700–1850*, Cambridge, 1973
Maley, A. *The Story of Celtic*, Glasgow, 1939
Mangan, J. A. *Athleticism in the Victorian and Edwardian Public School*, Cambridge, 1981
Marsh, P., Rosser, E. and Harre, R. *The Rules of Disorder*, London, 1978

Mason, A. *Association Football and English Society, 1863–1915*, Brighton, 1980

Mather, F. C. *Public Order in the Age of the Chartists*, Manchester, 1959

Mathias, P. *The Transformation of England*, London, 1979

Meacham, S. *A Life Apart*, London, 1977

Midwinter, E. *W. G. Grace*, London, 1981

Mitchell, B. R. and Deane, P. *Abstract of British Historical Statistics*, Cambridge, 1962

Mitchell, B. R. and Jones, H. G. *Second Abstract of British Historical Statistics*, Cambridge, 1971

Mortimer, R. *The Jockey Club*, London, 1958

Moynihan, J. *The Chelsea Story*, London, 1982

Munsche, P. B. *The English Game Laws 1671–1831*, Cambridge, 1981

Murphy, P. *Tiger Smith*, Newton Abbot, 1981

Murray, W. L. *The Old Firm*, Edinburgh, 1984

Nicholson, W. *Micro-Economic Theory*, Hinsdale, 1978

O. E. C. D. *Historical Statistics, 1960–1981*, Paris, 1983

   Economic Surveys: United Kingdom, Paris, 1986

Onslow, R. *The Heath and the Turf*, London, 1971

Partridge, E. H. *A Dictionary of Catch Phrases*, London, 1981

Pelling, H. *A History of British Trade Unionism*, London, 1977

Perkins, H. *The Origins of Modern English Society, 1780–1880*, London, 1972

Phelps-Brown, E. H. and Browne, M. *A Century of Pay*, London, 1968

Plumb, J. H. *The Commercialisation of Leisure in Eighteenth-Century England*, Reading, 1974

Plumptre, G. *The Fast Set*, London, 1985

Price, R. *An Imperial War and the British Working Class*, London, 1972

Ramsden, C. *Ladies in Racing*, London, 1973

Richardson, C. *Racing at Home and Abroad*, London, 1923

Rickman, J. *Homes of Sport: Racing*, London, 1952

Routh, G. *Occupations and Pay in Great Britain, 1906–60*, London, 1965

Runciman, W. *Relative Deprivation and Social Justice*, London, 1968

Sanderson, M. *Education, Economic Changes and Society in England, 1780–1870*, London, 1983

Saville, J. *Rural Depopulation in England and Wales, 1851–1951*, London, 1957

Sports Council. *Public Disorder and Sporting Events*, London, 1978

The Sportsman. *British Sports and Pastimes: Racing*, London, 1920

Spufford, M. *The Great Reclothing of Rural England*, London, 1984

Sutcliffe, C. E. and Hargreaves, F. *History of the Lancashire Football Association, 1878–1928*, Blackburn, 1928

Sutcliffe, C. E., Brierley, J. A. and Howarth, F. *The Story of the Football League, 1888–1938*, Preston, 1939

Thirsk, J. *Economic Policy and Projects*, Oxford, 1978

Thomas, P. *Yorkshire Cricketers, 1839–1939*, Manchester, 1973

Thompson, E. P. *The Making of the English Working Class*, London, 1963

Tischler, S. *Footballers and Businessmen*, New York, 1981

Titley, U. A. and McWhirter, R. *Centenary History of the Rugby Football Union*, London, 1970

Turner, M. E. *Enclosures in Britain, 1750–1830*, London, 1984
Vamplew, W. *The Turf*, London, 1976
　The Economic History of Leisure: Papers Presented at the Eighth International Economic History Congress, Budapest, 1982
Vance, N. *The Sinews of the Spirit*, Cambridge, 1981
Vernon, L. and Rollin, J. *Rothmans Football Year Book 1977–78*, London, 1978
Wagg, S. *The Football World*, Brighton, 1984
Wall, F. J. *Fifty Years in Football*, London, 1935
Walton, J. K. *The English Seaside Resort*, Leicester, 1983
Walvin, J. *Leisure and Society, 1830–1950*, London, 1978
Warner, P. F. *Lord's, 1787–1945*, London, 1946
Webber, R. *The Phoenix History of Cricket*, London, 1960
Welcome, J. *Fred Archer*, London, 1967
Weston, T. *My Racing Life*, London, 1952
Wilson, G. B. *Alcohol and the Nation*, London, 1940
Wynne Thomas, P. and Arnold, P. *Cricket in Conflict*, London, 1984
Young, P. M. *The Wolves*, London, 1959
　Manchester United, London, 1960
　Bolton Wanderers, London, 1961
　Football in Sheffield, London, 1962
　Football on Merseyside, London, 1964
　A History of British Football, London, 1969

Theses

Bilsborough, P. 'The Development of Sport in Glasgow, 1850–1914', M. Litt., University of Stirling, 1983
Giddens, A. 'Sport and Society in Contemporary England', M. A., University of London, 1961
Macken, S. 'Economic Aspects of Bloodstock Investment in Britain', Ph. D., University of Cambridge, 1986
Molyneux, D. D. 'The Development of Physical Recreation in the Birmingham District from 1871 to 1892', M. A., University of Birmingham, 1957
Rees, R. 'The Development of Physical Recreation in Liverpool during the Nineteenth Century', M. A., University of Liverpool, 1968
Roberts, E. H. 'A Study of Growth of the Provision of Public Facilities for Leisure Time Occupations by Local Authorities of Merseyside', M. A., University of Liverpool, 1933
Ross, J. R. 'Pedestrianism and Athletics in England and Australia in the Nineteenth Century: A Case Study in the Development of Sport', B. H. M. S. (Hons.), University of Queensland, 1985
Smith, M. B. 'The Growth and Development of Popular Entertainment and Pastimes in the Lancashire Cotton Towns, 1830–1870', M. Litt., University of Lancaster, 1970

Index

Printed in the United Kingdom by
Lightning Source UK Ltd., Milton Keynes
138927UK00001B/164/A